Into the Dark

Hannah Arendt and Totalitarianism

INTO THE
DARK

HANNAH ARENDT
AND TOTALITARIANISM

Stephen J. Whitfield

TEMPLE UNIVERSITY PRESS
Philadelphia

Library of Congress Cataloging in Publication Data

Whitfield, Stephen J 1942–
    Into the dark.

    Bibliography: p.
    Includes index.
    1. Totalitarianism. 2. Arendt, Hannah. I. Title.
JC481.W47   321.9   80-17236
ISBN 0-87722-188-X

Temple University Press, Philadelphia 19122
© 1980 by Temple University. All rights reserved
Published 1980
Printed in the United States of America

In memory of

H A N S   W E I S S F E L D

(b. Berlin 1923,

d. Auschwitz 1944)

CONTENTS

PREFACE AND ACKNOWLEDGMENTS

THIS is a book about the most sorrowful subject I can imagine. The pages that follow can be deemed a memento mori, a reminder of the cruelty and death that have been the unmistakable signs of political absolutism in our century.

The forbidding nature of this theme has led me to adopt a somewhat oblique approach. This is not a history of totalitarianism but an analysis of the theory that has been devised to account for it. And the focus here is not upon the several versions of that theory but upon the one interpretation of modern tyranny that, with qualification and modification, can draw the fullest implication from this political catastrophe. It is my argument that Hannah Arendt's *The Origins of Totalitarianism*, along with its extension and amendment in *Eichmann in Jerusalem*, adds up to the most convincing single effort to grasp the meaning of the German and Russian regimes of the 1930s and 1940s. I have therefore sought to explicate Arendt's work in the light of its internal consistency and its force of suggestion. That work has also been evaluated in the light of historical evidence, some of which was inaccessible at the time she wrote.

Close reading of any author is likely to reveal unresolved tensions and peculiar omissions. Such flaws are not, I hope, neglected in the pages that follow. But the criticisms that are presented are not intended to be corrosive. They indicate an intellectual engagement which cannot easily be separated from admiration, and they represent a struggle to wrest from the insights of one thinker not merely what is verifiable but what increases wisdom. I feel no need to disguise the fact that my deepest purpose in writing this book is moral, to fulfill the obligation of remembrance. But the impulses behind it have, I trust, produced not moralism but exegesis. I have tried to interpret a theory in terms of its cohesiveness and its compatibility with relevant facts.

Some limitations of this study should be noted here. Although episodes in Arendt's career are mentioned, this book is in no way a biography. It is an example of intellectual history. And though I have attempted to place her interpretation of totalitarianism within the context of her thought, the scope of Arendt's interests and opinions could not be accommodated and analyzed. Philosophy, politics, history and literature piqued her curiosity, to put it mildly. A systematic examination would, if it followed chronology, have to begin with Arendt's praise of the Athenian *polis* and conclude with her Bicentennial reckoning with Watergate. And while this book subjects her theory to the most detailed evaluation it has yet received, the focus is on the third part of *The Origins of Totalitarianism*, which does not in fact deal with its origins at all. That section is, as Dwight Macdonald noted, "an integrated essay in political theory rather than a collection of historical studies."[1] My own fascination with such intersections of politics and ideas was undoubtedly ignited when I read Arendt's book as an undergraduate; but I am now an historian of American political culture, not of modern Germany or of the Soviet Union. This study does however draw upon— as conscientiously as I can—pertinent scholarly literature in English about both societies. It also utilizes *samizdat* and other memoirs of the Stalinist period published in the West.

Arendt's work has been an adornment of American intellectual life, and its impact has already registered in several
areas of inquiry.[2] But I have generally abstained from mea-
suring her influence so soon after her own death.

This exposition of part of Arendt's thought is intended to
testify to the continued saliency and urgency of her concerns.
Yet I have inserted no original explanations of Nazism and
Stalinism, nor have I offered any new definitions of totalitarianism. By using the term, Arendt meant something historically specific; but she herself never provided a succinct
definition, a crisp summation. Other scholars of despotism are
not of course obliged to take her word for it; but, in an exegetical study such as this one, confusion might be minimized
if the meaning of "totalitarianism" was kept constant throughout the book. Such consistency might help clarify the issues
Arendt's work raises; but even after relevant historical data
are introduced and alternative interpretations weighed, there
is no way to *prove* a theory such as hers. It can, however, be
vindicated. That, at any rate, is the intention of this book,
whose motto might well be William Blake's: "Whenever I
tell any truth, it is not for the sake of convincing those who do
not know it, but for the sake of defending those that do."

This effort has elicited the kind of support that makes me
almost pathetically grateful, and it is a pleasure to record my
appreciation here. Colleagues in the Department of American
Studies at Brandeis University have established a congenial
and stimulating atmosphere; and among them I would especially like to thank Lawrence Fuchs and Jacob Cohen for
their unwavering loyalty and friendship, manifested, in part,
in severely critical readings of an earlier draft of this book.
The intelligence and judgment of my wife, Donna Arzt, are
implicated in virtually all phases of this project, though my
greater debts to her are owed elsewhere. Richard King has

been an unusually perceptive reader, as well as one of my favorite writers and a cherished friend. For their advice, sustenance and skepticism, I am also much obliged to Henry Feingold, Hayim Goldgraber, Shael Herman, Robert Meyerson, Jerry Muller, Sharon Muller, Joshua Rothenberg and especially Richard Tedlow. They have saved me from some errors and embarrassments, even as they have justified my faith in the vitality of the ideals of scholarship and friendship.

Leonard W. Levy first planted the suggestion that my general interest in the history of totalitarianism might be concentrated in a study of Arendt, and John P. Diggins accelerated its publication through his own enthusiasm and keenness. I have never made a secret of the inspiration their own writings have given me. Although Hans A. Schmitt and Wolfgang Leonhard had nothing directly to do with the writing of this book, they taught me much about modern Europe (though I fear they may think it was not enough). A grant from Jack S. Goldstein, the Dean of Faculty at Brandeis, facilitated research; and in this respect I am also most thankful for the support of certain creditors, such as my mother and my in-laws. The counsel and skills of Gerard F. McCauley have also been necessary to the realization of this project. Ina Moses and Grace Short brought not only inimitable efficiency but also infectious cheerfulness to the typing responsibilities they assumed. I also thank the university's librarians, including Hedy Haas and especially Richard Boleman. And Francis and Bette Cole know, I hope, how much I owe them. All of these persons have enlarged my awareness that, though writing is an individual, isolated and even austere enterprise, it is cushioned by the indulgence and kindness of others.

Into the Dark

Hannah Arendt and Totalitarianism

Chapter 1

🚩

INTRODUCTION

I N the dying years of the Weimar Republic, Karl Jaspers predicted that "those among our young people who, thirty years hence, will do the things that matter are . . . now quietly biding their time; and yet, unseen by others, they are already establishing their existence by means of an unrestricted spiritual discipline." It would be tempting to wonder whether the philosopher might have had one of his students in particular in mind. In any event, three decades after publishing a doctoral dissertation that Jaspers supervised, Hannah Arendt herself drew political hope from the sheer fact of youth: "Human action . . . is bound up with human plurality, which is one of the fundamental conditions of human life insofar as it rests on the fact of natality, through which the human world is constantly invaded by strangers, newcomers whose actions and reactions cannot be foreseen by those who are already there."[1] Against fatality she counterposed natality, against futility the wondrous possibility of spontaneity, against despair the chance of vital endeavor and original thought.

Of course neither Jaspers nor his student could have foreseen that Arendt's thought was to take shape in response to the major political and moral catastrophe to emerge within Western civilization in the twentieth century. In 1931 neither could have realized that totalitarianism would expel Arendt from her homeland and endanger her life. Arriving safely in America, she learned a new language and reoriented her work from philosophy and classics to political history and theory. Her dissertation had been on the idea of love in St. Augustine, who, in assigning his pupil Orosius the task of producing a "world history" to be included in *The City of God*, assumed that only one section of the book was required to present a "true compilation of the evils of the world."[2] It was to be the fate of Hannah Arendt to extend the work of Orosius.

She was not without credentials for the task of synthesis and speculation. Born into a middle-class family in Hanover in 1906, Arendt grew up in the hometown of Kant, Königsberg (now Kaliningrad) in East Prussia. She studied under the most formidable figures in twentieth-century German philosophy—not only Jaspers but also Martin Heidegger and Edmund Husserl—before receiving a doctorate from the University of Heidelberg. When the Nazis came to power, she was imprisoned but managed to flee to Paris, where she lived until 1940, when the Vichy regime put her in a concentration camp for five weeks. It was an experience about which she wrote only once, briefly. In the following year she came to the United States, having been granted a visa through the intervention of President Roosevelt.[3]

Already during the disintegration of the Weimar Republic, Arendt had begun to study Nazi anti-Semitic doctrines and propaganda. Upon the suggestion of Salo W. Baron, professor of Jewish history at Columbia University, she contributed, as early as 1942, a paper on French anti-Semitism to the journal he edited, *Jewish Social Studies*. Later articles that appeared in *Partisan Review, Jewish Frontier* and other journals were incorporated (though rather imperfectly) into *The Origins of Totalitarianism*. She disliked this title, for the third, final and most important section of the book does not treat "origins" at all.[4] Its British title was more accurate, if also more nebulous: *The Burden of Our Times.*

Published shortly before Arendt became an American citizen, her analysis of anti-Semitism, imperialism and totalitarian movements and regimes was greeted with extraordinary acclaim upon its appearance in the spring of 1951. A representative reviewer, H. Stuart Hughes, called Arendt's book "remarkable," "a salutary mental shock," "deeply thought-out and conscientiously documented," "the product of a rigorously trained and scrupulously honest mind." Dwight Macdonald went even further, hailing her as "the most original and profound—therefore most valuable—political theoretician of our times." Her capacity for drawing conclusions that were simultaneously shocking and persuasive was deemed comparable only to Marx's.[5] Mary McCarthy echoed these sentiments, recalling that *"The Origins of Totalitarianism* was a piece of scholarship so novel and so unexpected in its findings that it was read like a detective story by those who first laid hands on it. . . . The combination of tremendous intellectual power with great common sense makes Miss Arendt's insights into history and politics seem both amazing and obvious." Alfred Kazin later paid tribute to her explication of totalitarianism as the most outstanding book written in thirty years. (Coincidentally his praise came exactly thirty years after Jaspers' speculations on youth.) Kazin observed that Arendt's "thinking has a moral grandeur suitable to the terror of her subject."[6]

Macdonald, McCarthy and Kazin also were or became her friends. McCarthy, W. H. Auden and two groups of political theorists dedicated books to her;[7] and Anthony Hecht's Holocaust poem, "More Light! More Light!," was dedicated to her and her husband, Heinrich Blücher. Arendt became the first woman appointed full professor at Princeton and the only

American to receive Denmark's Sonning Prize for "contributions to European civilization." Other winners had included Winston Churchill, Albert Schweitzer, Bertrand Russell and Niels Bohr. The West Germans awarded her the Lessing Prize and the Freud Prize, and she received numerous honorary degrees as well as the Emerson-Thoreau Medal of the American Academy of Arts and Sciences. For the young editor of *Commentary*, an invitation to Arendt's New Year's Eve party was proof of "making it" among New York intellectuals in the 1950s. In the following decade the caricaturist David Levine was permitted to draw and quarter for the *New York Review of Books* anyone but Hannah Arendt.[8] After her death late in 1975 at the age of sixty-nine, further assessments only seemed to amplify the high respect accorded her in her lifetime. Political theorist Judith Shklar wrote that Arendt's flair for weaving "speculative philosophy, the history of ideas and common experience . . . into a single web" was reminiscent "only of one predecessor, Hegel." The British political scientist Bernard Crick considered her books the expression of a unified body of thought "just as comprehensive as those of Hobbes, Hegel, Mill and Marx."[9]

Arendt's thought has already been the subject, in English, of three books, five doctoral dissertations and an entire issue of the quarterly *Social Research*, plus a growing number of articles.[10] This book proposes to examine, more fully than has hitherto been attempted, the theory that made her "an intellectual celebrity."[11] For in the aftermath of the Second World War, as the shock of Nazi brutality reverberated, summoning little besides numbed incredulity, and as the Cold War against the Soviet empire intensified, *The Origins of Totalitarianism* offered the coherence—however disconsolate—of explanation. Her book insisted that totalitarianism was unprecedented—though its roots were entangled in the Europe of the nineteenth century. Her work showed the similarity of the Nazi and Soviet systems, yet eschewed any of the standard schools of interpretation—Marxist, liberal, psychoanalytic, religious—whose explanatory inadequacy she demonstrated through the example of her own magisterial insight. A little over a decade later, she supplemented her theory with a controversial "report" on Nazi genocide, *Eichmann in Jerusalem,* which helped redefine the ancient problem of evil.

Blessed with independence of judgment and singularity of vision, Arendt rarely told American intellectuals what they were used to hearing, but instead what many apparently felt they needed to know. She had an uncommonly large audience for a philosopher, though in her studies of totalitarianism, she wrote primarily as an historian, exposing the foundations of modern political extremism. In her books she included few dates or facts, of which American readers are so characteristically fond. She seemed to take for granted an erudition she had at her fingertips—and those fingertips were as sensitive as a safecracker's. Nor could readers have been attracted by her prose style, which was rarely elegant and which offered few concessions or compensations. Her writing, especially on the subject of totalitarianism, tended to be uncompromising in its bleakness, almost un-American in the integrity of its pessimism. She was the dark lady of American intellectuals. For Arendt had—in the lapidary phrase of Henry James—"the imagination of disaster."[12]

The Origins of Totalitarianism was her first book in English, but it patently testified to concerns that were European in spirit. The manuscript had been completed in 1949, except for its preface, which was not written until shortly after the outbreak of the Korean War. In tracing the most fearsome political experience of our epoch, Arendt was in a sense responding to a call issued by another contributor to *Partisan Review,* George Orwell. In 1948 the British journalist had read David Rousset's memoir of Buchenwald and three other camps, *Les Jours de Notre Mort* (later translated as *The Other Kingdom*). Orwell had concluded that the "horrible phenomenon" of the S.S. state was "part of the pattern of our time" that needed a comprehensive analysis. What was required, he wrote, was "for someone to write a scholarly work on concentration and forced-labour camps, drawing on Rousset and all the others."[13]

Arendt's study was to fulfill Orwell's requirement more successfully than any other analysis, yet her work marked the most sophisticated—not the first—stage in the elucidation of totalitarianism. Scholarship in the comparative study of the Communist, Nazi and Fascist dictatorships was at least a decade old when her book was published, and polemical literature and journalistic reflections on totalitarianism were even older. The word itself was intended to be honorific when Italian Fascists coined it in the years immediately following the march on Rome. The philosopher Giovanni Gentile incorporated it into the official exposition of Fascist doctrine, and in 1932 Mussolini called himself a totalitarian in an article he wrote for the *Enciclopedia Italiana*. Paradoxically the term was far more applicable to the more ruthless and more complete dictatorships of Hitler and Stalin, but they themselves rarely used the label. The attempts of some Nazi theoreticians to translate Mussolini's *lo stato totalitario* were unsuccessful because of the primacy of race over state in the lexicon of the Germanic ideology. "Totalitarianism" became pejorative in the Russian language, and was applied only to so-called Fascist regimes, and not to Stalin's government or to the Bolshevik party.[14]

The word was not listed in the first edition of the *Encyclopedia of the Social Sciences*, published in 1930. Hans Kohn, an emigré historian who had attended the same Prague *Gymnasium* as Franz Kafka, published an essay in 1935 on "Communist and Fascist Dictatorship: A Comparative Study." In it he asserted that "the two types of dictatorship are entirely opposite as regards their aims and their philosophy of life. They are similar (and different from all other forms of dictatorship) in claiming absoluteness for their philosophy and in their effort to indoctrinate the masses."[15] Though Kohn's essay was perhaps the first in English to stress the distinctiveness of tyrannies whose brutal methods blurred their apparent ideological antagonisms, he did not employ the word "totalitarian" to characterize such regimes.

The earliest significant contribution to political thought to do so was Walter Lippmann's *The Good Society*. Published in 1937, Lippmann's defense of classical liberalism against the encroachments of collectivism has sometimes been taken for a top-heavy tract against the New Deal. *The Good Society* was far more than that, for it placed the constitutional conflicts that emerged during the Great Depression within the context of the political crisis of Western society. "Though despotism is no novelty in human affairs," Lippmann wrote, "it is probably true that at no time in twenty-five hundred years has any western government claimed for itself a jurisdiction over men's lives comparable with that which is officially attempted in the totalitarian states." Perhaps other despotisms, he added, have been as cruel. "There has been none which was more inclusive." In Russia, Germany and Italy, "these ancient centers of civilization, several hundred millions of persons live under what is theoretically the absolute dominion of the dogma that public officials are their masters and that only under official orders may they live, work, and seek their salvation."[16]

Even after the German and Italian dictatorships had been reduced to rubble and the full-scale terror of Soviet Communism had receded, Lippmann continued to write under the pressure of the totalitarian threat. In 1947 he called it "the supreme political heresy of our time," for it was a perversion

of democracy itself. Such tyranny seemed to spring "directly
from the people" and constituted a deranged extension of the
doctrine of popular sovereignty. Lippmann was, in international affairs, still capable of thinking in conventional
terms of *Realpolitik*. For it was also in 1947 that he articulated his view that the Soviet Union was dangerous not primarily because of its ideological dynamism but because it inherited the expansionist tendencies of Czarism. Nevertheless,
his own elitism and desire to check majoritarianism revealed
how responsive the most exemplary—if not most influential—
of American journalists had been to totalitarianism.[17]

Lippmann was hardly alone in formulating the case for
democratic humanism against the ideological fanaticism and
terror that were stalking Europe. In the year that *The Good
Society* was published, the young editors Philip Rahv and
William Phillips were withdrawing *Partisan Review* from
Communist sponsorship and launching an independent, radical assault on Stalinism. That their magazine was anti-Fascist
and anti-Nazi could be taken for granted. In the framework of
intellectual life in the 1930s, what made *Partisan Review* distinctive was certainly not that it found the Third Reich repel-
lent. Its achievement was rather to inaugurate the revision—
and soon the virtual rejection—of Marxism. The devastation
that Stalinism had wreaked not only on the Russian population but on the socialist dream had called into question the
rational and ethical premises that had animated a generation
of American intellectuals. The editors and contributors to
Partisan Review continued to disagree among themselves
about many domestic and foreign issues, but they were united
in the fervor with which they condemned totalitarianism of
the left. Reflecting on that period, Edmund Wilson later took
pride in noting how he, Max Eastman, Bertram Wolfe, Sidney
Hook and others "extricated ourselves from the various official versions" of Marxism. "We in this country did our share

in bringing out into the open" the fallacies of Marxist doctrine and the moral squalor that was its corollary.[18] Here these American intellectuals went far beyond Trotsky, whose influence on *Partisan Review* has been somewhat exaggerated. For Trotsky, despite his prescience in calling for the defense of Weimar democracy against Nazism and despite the eloquence of his pamphlets against Stalinism, did not criticize the Bolshevik bureaucracy on democratic principles; and he supported the Soviet invasions of Poland and Finland.[19] It might be added that when in the 1970s France's *Nouveaux Philosophes* attacked the barbarian essence of Marxism, their arguments not only echoed Albert Camus' writings of the 1950s, but also the earlier work of ex-Marxist American intellectuals.

Another editor of *Partisan Review*, Dwight Macdonald, did much to shape the American definition of totalitarianism in the decade prior to publication of Arendt's volume. When Rahv and Phillips supported American intervention in the Second World War, Macdonald resigned from the journal and established *Politics*, which ran from 1944 until 1949. A pacifist who also switched from Marxism to anarchism, Macdonald wrote with remarkable sensitivity about the impact of total war and totalitarian cruelty upon the human personality. His pacifism did not prevent him from exposing and analyzing the horrible debasement of Nazism, and also kept him from any disillusionment about our ally, the Soviet Union. *Politics* kept alive the fragile hope of international solidarity against authoritarianism and violence. The three most famous articles it published were all by Europeans—Camus, Bruno Bettelheim and Simone Weil. As early as 1945 the magazine drew attention to the writing of Hannah Arendt, who later praised Macdonald's "astounding relevance" and "his extraordinary flair for significant fact and significant thought" in delineating the contours of contemporary tyranny.[20]

In the 1940s the nature and threat of totalitarianism had become an important ingredient in the thought of influential American intellectuals. But no historian can fail to notice the role of emigré scholars, themselves—like Arendt—refugees from Fascism and Nazism. Perhaps the most famous was an Austrian economist who had become a British subject in 1938. Before joining the faculty of the University of Chicago, Friedrich A. Hayek published *The Road to Serfdom*, arguing that central planning was intrinsically totalitarian. In a treatise dedicated "to the Socialists of all parties," Hayek attempted to demonstrate that "economic control is not merely control of a sector of human life which can be separated from the rest; it is the control of the means for all our ends." To avoid the coercive regimentation of Germany, Italy and Russia, Hayek argued, a competitive economy based upon the security of private property was not simply appealing; it was logically and politically necessary. *The Road to Serfdom* became the publishing sensation of 1944, and its impact went well beyond business constituencies. That Hayek had established a common ground of liberalism against its totalitarian adversaries is indicated by the letter he received from John Maynard Keynes: "We all have the greatest reason to be grateful to you for saying so well what needs so much to be said. You will not expect me to accept quite all the economic dicta in . . . [the book]. But morally and philosophically I find myself in agreement with virtually the whole of it, and . . . deeply moved."[21]

Some of "the Socialists of all parties" were unpersuaded, and developed their own lines of analysis of the origins of totalitarianism. Most of the leading scholars of Frankfurt's Institute for Social Research escaped to the United States, where they published several influential studies of the Nazism they had fled. In *Behemoth*, published in 1942 and revised two years later, Franz Neumann described the Third Reich as "totalitarian monopoly capitalism." That meant that Germany exhibited "a monopolistic economy—*and* a command economy. It is a private capitalistic economy, regimented by the totalitarian state."[22] Such a categorization seemed to exempt Neumann, the former legal adviser to Weimar's Social Democrats, from the need to compare German totalitarianism with that of the Soviet Union. Other representatives of the Frankfurt School, such as Erich Fromm and Theodor W. Adorno, did likewise, though they brought a psychological curiosity and depth missing in Neumann's *Behemoth*. In *The Authoritarian Personality*, published in 1950, Adorno and his associates devised an F Scale to measure totalitarian psychological potential on the right, but not on the left—despite the plausibility of similar patterns of submissiveness and domination, rigidity and paranoia.[23] The psychoanalyst Erik Erikson, who was not associated with the Frankfurt School, offered a more inclusive construct in his notion of "totalism," by which the young in particular forsake wholeness and diversity for "total immersion in a synthetic identity (extreme nationalism, racism or class consciousness)." That potential, which Erikson feared was universal, could be activated by special historical circumstances. Only an historical perspective could fully penetrate the many types found in a totalitarian state—"fanatic apostles and the shrewd revolutionaries; lonely leaders and oligarchic cliques; obedient bureaucrats and efficient managers, soldiers, engineers; sincere believers and sadistic exploiters; willing followers, apathetic toilers, and paralyzed opponents; unnerved victims and bewildered would-be and could-be victims."[24]

When Arendt provided that kind of historical comprehension, the concept of totalitarianism had already become a staple of American intellectual and political discourse. It had become firmly entrenched in the vocabulary of polemic and of scholarship. The term evoked the disturbingly modern efficiency of violence and coercion, combined with the mass virulence that the more stable and casual despotisms of the past had not aroused. Although totalitarian tendencies were suspected in many countries, the theory itself was generally applied to Nazi Germany and the Soviet Union, and to Fascist Italy and the Communist governments of Eastern and Central Europe and of China. The dictatorships of Franco's Spain, Peron's Argentina and similar regimes were sometimes incorporated into the theory as well. As with the rest of the inventory of the social sciences, the meaning of totalitarianism did not go undisputed; and the scope of its applicability was subject to controversy. Nor did the widespread use of the term mean that it was without detractors who deplored its imprecision and its susceptibilty to exploitation and propaganda. But by the early 1950s, few American intellectuals were willing to deny the actuality of totalitarianism or that the term connoted a genuine and distinctive political phenomenon.

Within a decade after *The Origins of Totalitarianism* was greeted with such praise, this consensus began to show signs of decomposition. In the 1960s the theory that Arendt's book helped to clarify no longer seemed to provide an accurate description of certain aspects of modern reality. The influence of the theory eroded most noticeably among students of Communist regimes and among specialists in comparative politics. Yet oddly enough the term did not disappear from the general vocabulary of politics. Instead it was appropriated and extended—often indiscriminately—far outside the sphere of analysis where it had once commanded such assent. In the past two decades the idea of totalitarianism has undergone a metamorphosis.[25] No estimation of the pertinence of Arendt's work can therefore be attempted without tracing the fate of the concept in the 1960s and 1970s. For as the term was transmuted in American scholarly and intellectual life, the historical value of her understanding of modern tyranny became all the more necessary to assert and to vindicate.

The first sign of change was not drastic. Having emerged from the matrix of Fascism, the idea was closely connected in the United States with the democratic opposition to Italian and German aggression. But with the military triumph of the Grand Alliance, and with the lengthening shadow that the Cold War cast thereafter, it became apparent that only one country still harbored the potential for the dynamic expansion that so recently had provoked world war. The meaning of totalitarianism therefore underwent no more than a shift in emphasis. From a phenomenon with several dangerous centers, it came to be defined primarily as having only one manifestation. Some intellectuals and publicists therefore argued that the same reasoning and morality that had required American warfare against the Axis states compelled a stance of vigilance and bellicosity against the dominant military power on the continent of Europe. On this point Hook, for example, was explicit: "Whoever believed that Nazi expansionism constituted a threat to the survival of democratic institutions must conclude by the same logic and the same type of evidence that Soviet Communism represents today an even greater threat to our survival, because the potential opposition to totalitarianism is now much weaker in consequence of World War II."[20]

Eastman had on occasion found himself Hook's philosophical adversary; but, if anything, he demanded an even stronger challenge to Russian foreign policy. Scorning anything that smacked of appeasement while Stalin was alive, Eastman asserted that "war is inevitable if . . . we let Stalin drive us back and back until we have to fight a war of national survival. We saw that happen in the case of Hitler and we paid the cost." Like Hook, Eastman stressed the contrast between democracy and totalitarianism; but he added that the Soviet Union had realized the potential of total control more fully than the Third Reich had managed to achieve. "Stalin's . . . police state is not an approximation to, or something like, or in some respects comparable with Hitler's," the ex-radical insisted. "It is the same thing, only *more* ruthless, *more* cold-blooded, *more* astute, *more* extreme in its economic policies, *more* explicitly committed to world conquest, and *more* dangerous to democracy and civilized morals." Bertram Wolfe also advocated a more vigorous foreign policy to combat a regime that exemplified, more than any other, the meaning of totalitarianism. "The Soviet state," Wolfe wrote in 1957, "has existed longer, is more total, the power of Stalin and his successors more absolute, the purges bloodier and more sweeping and continuous, the concentration camps larger . . . than anything Mussolini dreamed of or Hitler introduced. Only in his crematoria did Hitler's imagination exceed the deeds of Stalin." Wolfe's study of *Communist Totalitarianism* made only five passing references to Nazism and denied that much could be deduced by a systematic comparison of Russia with other totalitarian states.[27] The shift in the paradigm from, say, Neumann's *Behemoth* and its preoccupation with Nazism was therefore quite apparent.

Hook and Wolfe went on to describe post-Stalinist Russia primarily in terms of continuity and only slightly relaxed control. But most other analysts contended that, while Russia remained authoritarian and repressive, it could no longer be aptly considered totalitarian. Fissures in the system seemed to be widening. The revolts in Poland and Hungary in 1956, though effectively crushed, would have been unimaginable earlier. The stunning denunciations of Stalin's brutality at the Twentieth Party Congress, the "thaw" in Soviet culture and the later break in diplomatic relations with China all seemed to require an adaptation of the theory of totalitarianism severe enough to suggest its abandonment. Soviet foreign policy was still highly antagonistic toward the West, but some of the xenophobia associated with the late dictator had waned; and many American liberals and radicals—if not, generally, conservatives—hoped to make the most of it.

Already in Eisenhower's second term, a less frosty relationship between Russia and the United States had begun to develop; and the assumption of inevitable conflict began to recede. The summons to battle, the note of urgency no longer sounded so clearly. Totalitarianism had ceased to become an exigent contemporary problem. Several instances of this declension can be cited.

On the eve of the Second World War, for example, the American Philosophical Society had sponsored a conference devoted exclusively to the subject of totalitarianism. The scholars, gathered in Philadelphia, concluded that contemporary tyranny seemed to cut across the earlier divisions of left and right, transcended older categories of political analysis. A manifest sense of crisis animated the proceedings, for the regimes of Germany, Italy and Russia were calling into question civilized order itself. A little over a decade later, the American Academy of Arts and Sciences organized a second conference on the problem of totalitarianism. The essential similarity of Nazi Germany and the Soviet Union was taken for granted. In his keynote address George F. Kennan called totalitarianism "a source of sorrow and suffering to the human race . . . [that] has overshadowed every source of human woe in our times . . . It has demeaned humanity in its own sight, attacked man's confidence in himself, made him realize that he can be his own most terrible and dangerous enemy." The diplomat-historian added, "Although we Americans have not been directly affected by it, to many of our countrymen it has come to appear as the greatest of all our American problems— to some of them, I fear, as the only one."[28]

Yet in the following decade this sense of significance disappeared, and no further conferences devoted to the phenomenon were organized. Instead, at the 1967 meeting of the American Political Science Association, one session was presented on the topic of totalitarianism. One of the three participants concluded that the concept was too archaic, inexact and confusing to be useful in comparative analysis; and another scholar argued that the world, including its Communist part, had changed so much since the term had become popular that "it does not serve the cause of comparative political analysis or of political understanding to cling to the concept of totalitarianism."[29] In the following year, Herbert Spiro in the authoritative *International Encyclopedia of the Social Sciences* dismissed the concept as a relic of earlier conflict with the Soviet Union, as an icicle of the Cold War. Ignoring evidence that comparisons of Fascist and Communist regimes had been made as early as 1929 (long before the Cold War), Spiro asserted that the contemporary use of the theory "for propaganda purposes has tended to obscure whatever utility it may have had for systematic analysis and comparison of political entities." The assumption that both leftist and rightist regimes could be classified and understood within such a conceptual scheme came to be widely discarded.[30]

The eclipse of the theory was shown perhaps even more dramatically in the writings of those who had adhered to it. In the 1950s Daniel Bell wrote a set of essays, dedicated to Hook, that called for an end to ideology, because the consequences of "chiliastic hopes" had been disastrous. The insertion of the apocalyptic into politics had produced "the rise of fascism and racial imperialism in a country that had stood at an advanced stage of human culture; the tragic self-immolation of a revolutionary generation that had proclaimed the finer ideals of man; destructive war of a breadth and scale hitherto unknown; [and] the bureaucratized murder of millions in concentration camps and death chambers." What the political liberal had appealed for seemed to coincide, in the 1970s, with what the sociologist believed was occurring. In *The Coming of Post-Industrial Society*, published in 1973, Bell did not mention totalitarianism in his identification of present trends and future possibilities within the Soviet system.[31]

Zbigniew K. Brzezinski had applied the model of totalitarianism in his own early studies of the Russian polity, especially in *The Permanent Purge* (1956), which stressed the ingredient of terror in the circulation of Soviet elites. His collaborative venture with Carl J. Friedrich, *Totalitarian Dictatorship and Autocracy*, published the same year, established itself as the most influential version of the concept of totalitarianism, apart from Arendt's. Yet by the end of the decade, Brzezinski minimized its usefulness in the apprehension of contemporary Russia. In *Political Power: USA/USSR* (1964), totalitarianism was not even listed in the index. On the contrary he and his co-author, Samuel P. Huntington, discussed the function of specific interest groups within the Soviet political system. Fnally there is the case of the most respected American textbook on that system, Merle Fainsod's *How Russia is Ruled*. Its first edition concluded in 1953 with the prediction that "the totalitarian regime does not shed its police-state characteristics; it dies when power is wrenched from its hands." The absolute power Stalin had wielded was reduced far less dramatically than that, and Fainsod did not repeat his generalization in a new edition a decade later. In 1979 Jerry F. Hough revised his mentor's text, not only softening its title to *How the Soviet Union is Governed* but also presenting a succinct criticism of the limitations of the theory of totalitarianism itself. Moreover Hough substituted for Fainsod's figures on the devastation of Old Bolsheviks during the Great Terror a milder statistic on the decline in party

membership during the 1930s. Fainsod's historical discussion
of the forced-labor camps of the Gulag archipelago was also
omitted, as was any mention of Felix Dzerzhinsky, the creator
of Lenin's secret police, the Cheka.[32]

For such scholars totalitarianism had become a nightmare
from which Europe, and especially the Soviet Union, had
awakened. Yet even as the idea was subsiding in scholarly discourse, it was given new life in the political language of the
1960s and 1970s. Those who championed a militant foreign
policy, for example, often claimed that this was the lesson of
the 1930s, when the Western powers had tragically failed to
resist totalitarianism. Even after the pressures of the Cold War
seemed to be reduced, the memories of Munich were invoked
to justify resistance to another manifestation of totalitarian
expansionism. During the Cuban missile crisis, President Kennedy announced that "the 1930s taught us a clear lesson: aggressive conduct, if allowed to go unchecked and unchal-
lenged, ultimately leads to war." This judgment was hardly
unique to the author of *Why England Slept*; his successor
defended American military intervention in South Vietnam
on similar grounds. "The central lesson of our time is that the
appetite of aggression is never satisfied," President Johnson
insisted. "To withdraw from one battlefield means only to
prepare for the next."[33] Although many scholars, including
Arendt, ridiculed this historical analogy, it could not be
stopped from surfacing, and was often directed against those
who protested American involvement in Vietnam. During the
1972 campaign Vice President Agnew warned that Senator
McGovern would be worse than Chamberlain at Munich.
Hook, a Nixon supporter that year, asked in an open letter to
the Democratic party nominee: "Is there any wonder . . . that
to many liberals and democrats your foreign policy smells of
'the spirit of Munich'?"[34]

The memories of the earlier confrontation with totalitarianism were not only useful in garnishing the defense of hard-line foreign policies. The 1930s also provided the rhetorical arsenal with which many radicals assaulted American society, charging it with genocidal tendencies, even though some of the young had only the vaguest understanding of the historical experience of totalitarianism. Thus, when Diana Trilling returned to her alma mater in 1971, she discovered that almost none of the Radcliffe students she met had ever heard of the Spanish Civil War. One of them, after admitting her ignorance, nevertheless added: "I do know enough to know it was our fault!" Generational change was never more plausible as an explanation for the alteration of political attitudes, for when Orwell had mentioned to Arthur Koestler that "history stopped in 1936," Koestler immediately understood and agreed. Both had in mind the Spanish Civil War, in which Orwell had been wounded and Koestler nearly executed, and the rise of totalitarianism in general. Such an emphasis was shared by Herbert Marcuse, who claimed that "the end of a historical period and the horror of the one to come were announced in the simultaneity of the civil war in Spain and the trials in Moscow."[35] It was an era that symbolically had begun when a Spanish Fascist general shouted, "Long live death!"; it ended, perhaps, with the extermination camps.

Yet Marcuse's own writings lent dignity to the notion, which many young radicals espoused, that totalitarianism suffused all of contemporary Western society. The phenomenon could not be confined to a certain historical period or to especially demonic regimes. This transfiguration of the concept was accomplished by underscoring the technological and bureaucratic facets of advanced industrial societies and by dismissing the liberating possibilities of dissidence in thought and conduct. An oxymoronic "totalitarian democracy" had managed, by preserving "the illusion of popular sovereignty," to establish "the most efficient system of domination."

Though Marcuse denied that such totalitarianism depended upon violence to achieve the aim of complete control, his description of modern America bore a striking resemblance to Lippmann's description in *The Good Society* of Nazi Germany and Stalinist Russia. For the United States, the emigré intellectual charged, displayed an "innate need of expansion and aggression" and was loathsome for "the brutality of its fight against all liberation movements."[36] Another inescapable presence in the counterculture discernible by the middle of the 1960s was Norman Mailer, who likewise stretched the definition of totalitarianism far beyond its original purview in American thought. The novelist stigmatized modern architecture, for instance, as "the perfect expression of the totalitarian *geist,* enormous power without detail, commitment, curiosity, mystery, or variety." Mailer conceded that other Americans were proud of such buildings, and of jet planes and superhighways. His rejoinder was "that what characterizes all totalitarian movements is that they're swollen with pride, and empty pride. . . . One of the essences of totalitarianism is that it enjoys precisely destroying the particular. . . . I think that at the very heart of totalitarianism is the desire to cheat life."[37] Such recklessness and imprecision in exploiting the charged emotions of anti-totalitarianism contributed to the often thoughtless formulation of radical criticism in the 1960s.

One consequence was the distortion of historical understanding. When Theodore Roszak, who coined the term "counterculture," defined totalitarianism as technocratic control, he was obscuring the distinctive agony that the Nazi and Soviet regimes had inflicted upon countless millions. When Arthur Koestler, whose own interests had shifted from politics to science, mentioned in passing the crimes of Stalin, Leslie Fiedler complained that Koestler's reminder was irrelevant to the actuality of the 1960s, which the reviewer defined primarily in terms of popular culture and drugs.[38] That such a reminder of human cruelty *ought* to have been relevant, that the young ought to have been better educated about the antecedents of their own world, did not occur to Fiedler. In such a cultural climate, the record of the recent past could be rather easily fudged. Garry Wills, for example, cited John F. Kennedy's Inaugural appeal for *civitas* as an expression of totalitarianism, but managed to write an historical essay on the Cold War and domestic anti-Communism without so much as mentioning Stalin.[39]

It was therefore not surprising that scholars more directly affiliated with the New Left attempted to cast doubt on whether the Soviet Union had ever been totalitarian. Here a distinction must be emphasized. It was one thing for political scientists to conclude that Russia in the era of Khrushchev and Brezhnev was no longer totalitarian; such a view is persuasive. It was another thing to deny the validity of the concept for the era of Stalin. Lillian Hellman's memoir, *Scoundrel Time* (1976), which Wills' essay introduced, dismissed Stalin's "sins" in a couple of very short, cryptic passages.[40] It was left to younger writers to excuse Stalinism altogether. In introducing an edition of the dictator's writings, Bruce Franklin performed this remarkable feat of cosmetics. The literature professor assured readers that "the workers and peasants of the Soviet Union, who knew Stalin best," regarded him as "one of the great heroes of modern history, a man who personally helped win their liberation." Michael Parenti added that Stalin could not have been a tyrant because his death did not bring "joyful dancing in the streets." (Nor, for that matter, did the assassination of Czar Alexander II. One wonders whether the political scientist would have accepted the converse as a criterion of goodness. According to one observer, "a shock wave of sorrow swept over Moscow with the news of the death of President Roosevelt" in 1945.) Parenti even doubted that Stalin's labor camp victims could have reached several millions, since the inmates who returned after his death only "numbered in the thousands."[41] Even if that statistic were remotely true, the possibility seemed excluded that more did not return because they were dead of exhaustion, starvation, disease and execution. Such efforts to efface the bloodstained legacy of totalitarianism were not entirely representative of revisionist history, but they were symptomatic of a milieu in which the response to the suffering inflicted only two or three decades earlier was strangely muffled.

Even with the translation and publication of Aleksandr Solzhenitsyn's works, it may be too much to expect that the historical consensus that *The Origins of Totalitarianism* helped to crystallize can be regained. The theory that Arendt's writings articulated is not widely accepted, and the idea of totalitarianism has—it should be apparent—been misused. But that is not an argument that the theory cannot be applied with precision and sensitivity to penetrate the darkness. That Hannah Arendt did so, that she embodied the struggle of the civilized intelligence to comprehend an historical disaster, is the case that is presented in the following chapters.

Chapter 2

FEARFUL SYMMETRY

INTELLECTUALS are supposed to see questions where others have answers, to draw intricate distinctions and minute shadings where others see monochromatic patterns. Yet Arendt's most famous book simplified the contemporary world, presenting a startling dichotomy in which all political manifestations and forces were either for or against totalitarianism. The earlier distinctions between left and right ought to be dissolved, she argued, when confronted with the single phenomenon of Nazi Germany and Stalinist Russia. For only these two societies have been totalitarian, and they resemble no other nations—yet. They constitute an unprecedented and unique threat to the nontotalitarian world. Together the Third Reich and the U.S.S.R. represent "the burden of our times."

This stark proposition was not original to Arendt, though she claimed to have considered Nazism and Bolshevism as part of the same phenomenon as early as 1933. The first published indication of her central thesis appeared however in 1947, in a review of a Polish survivor's book on the Soviet labor camps.[1] The chief contribution of *The Origins of Totalitarianism* was not to introduce a novel conception of the similarity of the two political systems but to sustain that argument with the most imaginative interpretation of historical evidence and to insist on that similarity with unqualified vigor. By confronting the consequences of totalitarianism—the death camps and labor camps that Orwell had considered "part of the pattern of our time"—Arendt broke decisively with the approach to intellectual history that, given her training, she might have been expected to find congenial. In the realm of political ideas and values there seemed little justification for coupling the history of Nazism with that of Stalinism. That is why, in standard studies such as George Sabine's *History of Political Theory* (1937, 1950) and Ernst Nolte's *Three Faces of Fascism* (1966), Nazism has been compared to Mussolini's Italy in particular. Only when the emphasis shifts to political method and effect did Arendt's parallel make sense, though her refusal to qualify her argument or to admit complications into the parallel invited skepticism and rejection. She never indicated in which ways Nazi Germany and the Soviet Union differed, thus making her book vulnerable to charges of imbalance and exaggeration. Even Alfred Kazin, whose friendship and advice were important to the publication of her book, had some second thoughts about the parallel, which he considered the most dubious part of a generally brilliant book. Later, in the third volume of his autobiography, Kazin remembered only Marxist criticism of her parallel, which, if indeed dubious, would cripple *The Origins of Totalitarianism*. Two historians of the Cold War complained that Arendt should have distinguished "between one system proclaiming a humanistic ideology and failing to live up to its ideal and the other living up to its antihumanistic and destructive ideology only too well."[2] Even Orwell's language, in calling for a work of scholarship on totalitarianism based on the testimony of Rousset and other survivors, suggested such a distinction, for the Soviet forced-labor camps were presumably directed, however perverted in implementation, toward the achievement of rational industrial development. The

Nazi concentration camps by contrast were often deliberately without utilitarian purpose; they were irrational and nihilistic. Arendt herself acknowledged that the deaths of Soviet inmates were generally due to deprivation and neglect, unlike the deliberate mass murder that the Nazis inflicted upon European Jewry.[3]

If the distinction between left and right is to retain any validity, other differences between Germany and Russia should be noted—and have been by other historians. Nazism made its greatest electoral appeal to the lower middle class, Communism to those below. Within the National Socialist German Workers Party (N.S.D.A.P.) itself, the largest group originated in the lower middle class, with former industrial workers constituting little more than a fourth of the party's membership. Relative to the general German population, workers and farmers were underrepresented in Nazi ranks, while white-collar employees and the economically independent were overrepresented.[4] The situation of the Russian Communists was not quite comparable, given the absence of a multi-party system within which the Bolsheviks had to compete for votes, as the Nazis did in the period of the Weimar Republic. There is little information on the social composition of the party under Lenin and Stalin, and—given doctrinal necessities not operating in Germany—Soviet members had incentive to conceal bourgeois origins. At least through the early phase of the first Five Year Plan, working-class recruits to the party were preferred. But the requirements of industrialization made it difficult to exclude the rising class of technicians and managers; and at the Eighteenth Party Congress of 1939, preferential categories were abandoned for the sake of throwing party membership open to all "conscious and active workers, peasants, and intellectuals, loyal to the cause of communism." In the Stalinist leadership itself, however, almost no one was of middle class origin.[5]

The Nazis did much to besmirch and weaken the German civil service, the universities, the churches. Independent trade unions were eliminated, and the Junkers lost most of their influence in state affairs. Hitler imposed his will on the army more than did Bismarck—but not more so than Stalin, who dominated all aspects of Soviet institutional life, including the military. For Nazism in Germany never made as serious an effort to demolish previous elites and bureaucracies as did Bolshevism in Russia, which did much more than supplant the Czarist and aristocratic enclaves. Far less radical in its economic and social programs, Nazism left intact far more of the traditional orders of Germany than Communism did in Russia.[6] The Nazis hoped in important respects to turn back the clock of modernization and to dwell in an imagined Teutonic past; the Bolsheviks wanted to make the clock jump ahead, to hasten economic progress. The Nazis appealed to the irrational and the unconscious in the racial soul, whereas Bolshevik psychological theory assumed the rationality and consciousness of the toiling masses—admittedly requiring the direction of a vanguard infallibly responding to the signals of history. Though the ideologies of both movements depicted a world of constant strife and protracted struggle, the ultimate aim of Marxism—after the defeat of capitalism and imperialism—was irenic. But warfare and aggression were inextricably part of the Nazi world view; and *Mein Kampf* (*My Battle*), unlike the *Communist Manifesto*, envisioned no end to struggle.[7] In the Soviet Union the character ideal, however cruelly distorted under Stalin, was the class-conscious and patriotic worker. In the Third Reich the character ideal, though promulgated by the National Socialist German Workers Party, was the racially conscious and patriotic warrior.[8] An ethic of productivity and harmony could thus be contrasted with an ethic of incessant conflict.

Nor was there any equivalent in Soviet ideology to the role

of Hitler, which was explained by the head of the Nazi Association of Lawyers as follows: "The Fuehrer and Reich Chancellor is the constituent delegate of the German people. . . .
The Fuehrer is supreme judge of the nation. . . . There is no
position in the area of constitutional law in the Third Reich
independent of this elemental will of the Fuehrer." The
executive committee of the Nazi party never met after Hitler
became its First Chairman in 1921. When one member of the
Reich cabinet, which also never met, suggested that at least
the cabinet officers should get together informally over beer,
the Fuehrer rejected the idea. In the Soviet Union the awesome power of Stalin derived primarily from his position as
general secretary of the Communist Party, which in turn enjoyed its political and ideological legitimacy as the vanguard
of the working class. In theory it was not the will of a Leader
but the wisdom of the Party that was the source of authority
in the Soviet Union, and Stalin was careful to depict himself
as the faithful disciple of Marx and Lenin.[9]

Such differences between the two movements should not be
exaggerated, however. Arendt should have admitted qualifi-
cations into her thesis, but she was right not to regard the dis-
similarities as decisive. Nazi policy was not entirely without
utilitarian purpose, for example. Within the eighteen square
miles at Auschwitz, the capital of the Holocaust kingdom,
were industrial facilities so important that the Allies bombed
them—but not the gas chambers or railway lines—four times
in 1944. Life expectancy of the workers in these factories was
three to four months, of the workers in the nearby coal mines
one month. Despite the nihilism permeating the Nazi camps,
their economic functions increased as the war continued, two
million slave laborers helping prolong it.[10] The administrator
of this program of exploitation, Fritz Sauckel, was hanged at
Nuremberg after the chief American prosecutor called him
"the greatest and cruelest slaver since the Pharaohs."[11] Nazi

slave labor was on far less vast a scale, however, than that in
the Gulag archipelago; and *Arbeit macht frei* had its equivalent in the inscription over the gates of all the camps in the
Kolyma region: "Labor is a matter of honor, valor, and heroism." Death in the Soviet camps was quite as pervasive and
almost as predictable as in the S.S. state. Anyone whom the
Soviet regime sentenced to terms of ten years probably had
little chance to survive except as a trusty, and Solzhenitsyn has
recalled the warning of an older prisoner: "The only ones
who survive in camps are those who try at any price not to be
put on general-assignment work. From the first day." "At any
price?" "At any price!"[12] An American-born *zek* who was released from the Gulag archipelago recalled his ordeal in what
was termed "an extermination camp—not to the extent that
they [the authorities] were going out of their way to kill you,
but in that they didn't expect any of the *zeks* interned . . . to
survive—all were considered expendable."[13]

The Bolsheviks had more time and commitment to transform the economy than the Nazis did, and that difference cannot be minimized. Nevertheless, beginning in 1936 the Third
Reich also had an economic plan, at least nominally directed
by Goering. In Hitler's entourage were not only crackpots like
Streicher and Rosenberg but also a talented technocrat like
Speer. If German industry was less geared for war than the
Soviet Union, the reason was not only Hitler's indifference to
economic considerations but also his early conviction that the
strategy of lightning war would alone achieve victory.[14] The
rationalist penumbra of Russia's Five Year Plans disguised
the extraordinary chaos produced by the massive purges,
which demolished major segments of the managerial class
nurtured since the 1917 revolution. The Great Purge began
after collectivization had been forced upon—and accepted by
—the peasantry, and the later terror mounting before Stalin's
death occurred in an already fairly industrialized and ur-

banized nation.[15] The wastefulness and inefficiency of the Soviet economy under Stalin were, by utilitarian standards alone, a nightmare. In a nation supposedly laying the foundations of socialism, the regime hired more guards and watchmen—not even counting N.K.V.D. militia—than miners and railwaymen combined; it is a commonplace to contrast the efficiency of free labor with the inefficiency of slavery. During the Second World War itself, while the regime and the nation were threatened with destruction, large numbers of camp inmates able and willing to defend Holy Mother Russia against the German invaders were being guarded by Internal Guard Service and N.K.V.D. divisions that were also desperately needed at the front.[16] The construction of the White Sea–Baltic Canal cost the lives of an estimated one hundred thousand slave laborers; but when Solzhenitsyn visited the canal in 1966, it was virtually deserted, too shallow to be used. Because of the devastation of rural life, the Soviet Union was producing only as much grain when Stalin died as pre-Revolutionary Russia had been.[17]

Moreover, the adulation of Stalin—later denounced as "the cult of the personality"—reached proportions not exceeded in the Third Reich. Hitler's portrait was everywhere, even on postage stamps; but poets and artists were not required to celebrate his life, career and intellectual achievements. The Soviet regime claimed for Stalin a versatility and omniscience—in fields such as linguistics—rarely pretended for Hitler, whose "expertise" in many fields was usually confined to table talk, and only occasionally translated into German policy. The major exception was military, and this was fatal. Aryan newlyweds got the Fuehrer's autobiography, and he was hailed as "the greatest German of all times" and "the highest synthesis of his race." But it is doubtful whether, for nauseating obsequiousness and pervasiveness, anything exceeded the public praise heaped on Stalin for his seventieth birthday in 1949.[18]

And whatever the ideological differences, Stalin's actual power over the Communist Party by the mid-1930s was quite as complete as Hitler's dominance of the Nazi movement. An authoritative history of Bolshevism has concluded that Stalin governed "either through the party or without it, as he thought fit. . . . He summoned no Congress for over thirteen years, allowed meetings of the Central Committee but rarely, and even apparently avoided summoning the full Politburo."[19]

Arendt herself added another parallel that distinguished her own theory of totalitarianism. Her research into the subject began with an analysis of anti-Semitism, and this constituted part 1 of the book itself. The significance of Jew-hatred to the history of totalitarianism never left her, but only in retrospect did the relevance of anti-Semitism to the Soviet Union become apparent. In the third and final edition of *The Origins of Totalitarianism* (1966), she subscribed to the view that the specter of an international Jewish conspiracy, raised shortly before Stalin's death was to be the prelude to another onslaught of terror. The momentary concretization in the Doctors' Plot of the conspiracy projected by the "Protocols of the Elders of Zion" showed "how deep an impression this mainstay of Nazi ideology must have made on Stalin." The sinister and subterranean image of internationally organized Jewry "provided an ideologically . . . suitable background for totalitarian claims to world rule . . . [—] the last compliment Stalin paid to his late colleague."[20] Stalin may never have finished *Das Kapital*, but he apparently read *Mein Kampf*;[21] and the grisly fate probably awaiting Jews and others was halted only by his death.[22] History in the subjunctive is risky, but speculation may indicate the peculiar burden of the twentieth century. Despite Karl Marx's utter estrangement from both the Jewish religion and the Jewish people, his origins alone would have made him a victim not only of the totalitarianism that erupted in the land of his birth but perhaps also of the totalitarianism that professed to embody his ideas.

Anti-Semitism was central to Arendt's thesis. She defined totalitarianism as a challenge to common sense; to locate danger in a secret and pervasive conspiracy of Jews is to burst the boundaries of sanity. This mentality Richard Hofstadter labeled "the paranoid style," according to which history is more than a repository for conspiracies; instead "history *is* a conspiracy."[23] Such irrational fear of the Jews was therefore, in Arendt's estimation, integral to the totalitarian mind. It is noteworthy that Arendt regarded the Nazis—and, in the 1966 edition, Stalin—not as racists, but as anti-Semites—a distinction best formulated by a Holocaust survivor, theologian Emil Fackenheim: "The Nazis were not anti-Semites because they were 'racists' but rather racists because they were anti-Semites." The doom of the Gypsies was not quite comparable. They were mentioned neither in the 1920 party program nor in the 1935 Nuremberg Laws, and the repression of the Gypsies did not begin until 1938. Their gassing at Auschwitz began two years after that of the Jews, and the killing of Gypsy children was sporadic rather than systematic.[24] The full fury of racism was concentrated upon the Jews (though other lesser races would follow them to extinction). To gratify such hatred, the Nazis sought to destroy all traces of Jewish life in Europe—not only among the populations under German domination, but also in the countries allied with Germany—and to kill every Jewish child as well as adult.

The comparison nevertheless indicates the weakness of Arendt's claim for the centrality of Jew-hatred to totalitarianism. For however insidious and persistent anti-Semitism has been in Soviet history, it simply did not command the importance that it had in the Third Reich. The earliest extant document of Hitler's public career (September 16, 1919) objected to purely emotional anti-Semitism, which could not advance beyond sporadic outbursts of pogroms. Instead he favored a "rational anti-Semitism" whose "ultimate goal . . . must unalterably be the elimination of the Jews altogether." Such intentions were openly proclaimed, especially in the three years prior to the installation of systematic gassing in the death camps. The Fuehrer was willing to temper other racial policies, even yield to military demands that Slavic units (especially Ukrainians) be permitted to fight alongside the *Wehrmacht* against the Red Army. But with the Jews he was remorseless, no matter the outcome of the conventional war. The final words of Hitler's final recorded conversation (April 2, 1945) were as follows: "The world will be eternally grateful to National Socialism that I have extinguished the Jews in Germany and Central Europe."[25] While Allied bombers and the advancing Red Army were making a shambles of Berlin, he also offered as his last testament to the German people the adjuration to "scrupulous observance of the laws of race and to merciless opposition to the universal poisoner of all peoples, International Jewry." This particular obsession was not part of Stalin's mentality; and his anti-Semitism did not assume the systematic desire for destruction that characterized Nazi policy.[26]

A common response to Arendt's parallel was to disparage it, to dismiss it as a paradigm with only one example, as though she had extrapolated with insufficient evidence from her authentic knowledge of Nazism to the singular and more resistant case of the Soviet Union. Her insights into the German version of totalitarianism were often considered more impressive than her comments on Stalinism.[27] It is true that, because of the capture of Nazi archives after the Second World War, much was learned about the internal workings of the Third Reich that is still unknown about the Soviet system. But that does not in itself negate the applicability of the concept of totalitarianism. In fact, what is known about Soviet political

history has tended to confirm the accuracy of Arendt's speculations, which were offered without hesitancy or tentativeness
or a knowledge of the Russian language. In terms of unchal-
lenged control over the various institutions of state and society, the Stalinist apparatus came closer to achieving the aims
of totalitarian domination than did Hitler and his associates.
Some of the differences between the two regimes have the
effect of showing the Soviet Union to be a more fully-realized
demonstration of totalitarian aims than Nazi Germany.

For example, there was constant tension between the Nazi
regime and the *Wehrmacht*. The man who during four years
of fighting in the First World War had not risen above the
rank of corporal was often infuriated by the General Staff's
lack of enthusiasm for his military strategy, a carefulness
which he considered defeatism. Hitler did not gain complete
control over the high command until well into the war.[28] Even
then, military opposition to him developed, especially with
the prospect of German defeat; in the July 1944 assassination
attempt, a figure of the stature of Marshal Rommel was implicated. Even if, beyond the fabrications of German intelligence, some sort of plot involving Marshal Tukhashevsky had
been hatching, Stalin's control over the Red Army—whose
nature was avowedly political—was much more thorough than
Hitler's over the German Army.[29] Heroes of the Red Army,
like Tukhashevsky, were creatures of the Revolution, whereas
the *Wehrmacht* remained beguiled by "the conservative-
aristocratic dream of an autonomous army," free of totalitarian penetration.[30] In the Soviet Union, the influence of the
Russian Orthodox Church was permitted to expand during
the war to promote patriotic unification; but it was less independent than the Roman Catholic Church, with which Hitler
felt obliged to make a concordat. A *Kulturkampf* against
ecclesiastical power was scheduled had the Nazis been vic-
torious, but that never happened. Through his secretariat and

Into the Dark

egregiously loyal apparatus, Stalin exercised direct control over a party whose power was unrivaled. By contrast the Nazi party did not incorporate many state officials until the war.[31]

The fate of the elites also differed. If unrestricted violence is a mark of despotic power, Stalin was more lethal toward his closest associates and comrades. Hitler, who had Ernst Roehm and other S.A. leaders killed, along with some other erstwhile allies, otherwise generally had trouble ever firing those who fell out of favor. Disagreement with the Fuehrer or failure in the execution of his policies usually did not lead to show trials, exile or death but to private life, or—as in the cases of Goering or Rosenberg—further honors.[32] This twinge of loyalty was not shared by Stalin, though both had in common the hideous cruelty that made them supreme totalitarian rulers.

Even during the era of "total war," the Third Reich did not fully utilize its economic resources. The mystique of female domesticity ensured that women were never mobilized, as they were in the United States and Britain. (Speer was disturbed to see photographs in *Life* Magazine of American women streaming out of factories.) There were also as many German domestic servants in 1945 as there had been in 1939; and nearly all workers were allowed to work the first shift, since German factories shut down at night. No wonder then that, a year after Operation Barbarossa was launched against Russia, German armaments production was only a quarter of its 1918 level. Foreseeing Nazi defeat, some industrialists hastened it through hoarding of precious war material in order to ensure their own postwar corporate recovery. Outside the economy totalitarian rule was not identical with the "leadership principle." There was apparently no equivalent in the Stalinist bureaucracy of Himmler's secret defiance in closing down the killing facilities in the late fall of 1944, despite the incomparable importance to Hitler of the extinction of the

Jews. The Fuehrer's orders for a complete "scorched earth" policy as his armies retreated was likewise disobeyed.[33]

Even within the texture of society itself, there may have been greater obliteration of privacy and personal autonomy in the Soviet Union than in Germany. Exact figures are not known of those killed under Lenin and Stalin (the sixty-six million that Solzhenitsyn gingerly accepts is certainly far too high), but it can be generalized that the common people were more endangered under Soviet than under Nazi government. In Russia the risks were greater of random and even whimsical classification as *sozialno opassniye elemyenti* (socially dangerous elements). Apart from political opponents and Jews, the ordinary citizens of East Berlin may have been a little less "coordinated" under the N.S.D.A.P. in 1944 than under the K.P.D. in 1946.[34] It is therefore not surprising that, despite their ideological differences, Hitler privately considered Stalin a "genius" and "one of the greatest people alive."[35]

Though Arendt did not discuss which of the two regimes more successfully achieved the political objective of total domination, she deliberately excluded from her classification the Fascist orders that emerged in Europe in the interwar period. Her insistence on this point did not dispel confusion however. Hans Morgenthau, for instance, praised *The Origins of Totalitarianism* for defining Fascism as "a new form of government," although the term "Fascism" does not even appear in Arendt's index. H. Stuart Hughes, as though ignoring Arendt's stress on the similarity between Germany and the Soviet Union, also discussed her book as an example of "The Critique of Fascism." Karl Dietrich Bracher identified a school of interpretation that analyzed totalitarianism historically from 1922 until 1953, "from Mussolini's advent to Stalin's death." He cited the importance of *The Origins of Totalitarianism* without acknowledging that Arendt's book fit uneasily in such a scheme.[36] Though her book has been praised as among "the remarkable histories of fascism" and criticized for elevating "fascism into political philosophy,"[37] she asserted that totalitarianism could never be fully understood, its novelty and its distinctiveness could not be clarified, except by *contrast* to regimes such as Mussolini's.

Some leading Nazis themselves distinguished between their movement and Fascism. Goebbels considered Fascism superficial compared with National Socialism and dismissed Mussolini because he was "not a revolutionary like the Fuehrer or Stalin." Himmler called the two movements "fundamentally different," since Fascism lacked the "spiritual [and] ideological" qualities of Nazism. In the upper reaches of the Third Reich, "Fascism" was a pejorative term—Hitler was by no means proud of his Italian ally. In 1943 he also remarked that it had been fairly easy to inflict military defeat on the nations of Western Europe because "countries with an ideology have an edge on bourgeois states." In the East, on the other hand, "we met an opponent who also sponsors an ideology, even though a wrong one."[38] What gives *anti*-Fascist views their thread of consistency is their exaltation of ideological pretentiousness, and their cognate scorn for practical considerations and indeed for the value of human life.

For what separated totalitarian regimes from Fascist Italy, according to Arendt, was an ideological militancy that led to unparalleled ruthlessness, as well as a conspiratorial view of the rest of the world that led them to act with so much destructive terror that the rest of the world was indeed forced to unite against them.[39] Rather than maximize its ruin through *Götterdämmerung*, the Italian dictatorship simply collapsed, after having practiced gangsterism and crushed its political opponents for two decades. The Fascist regime left behind no cremated bodies of inferior races, no mass graves of slave laborers. Anti-Semitism was common to National Socialism, to the Hungarian Arrow Cross, to the Rumanian Iron Guard, to the French Action Française—but not to the Italian movement. This exception *The Origins of Totalitarianism* did not attempt to explain, and only later did Arendt single out the factor of national tradition—"the almost automatic general humanity of an old and civilized people." For Mussolini had not made massive terror a general policy, and in that sense his regime resembled the tyrannies of the past.[40]

By contrast the totalitarian regimes showed contempt for the lives of their own German and Russian citizens, who were treated as superfluous. The Nazi leadership not only brought upon humanity the conflagration of the Second World War but also prolonged it despite the heavy bombardment of German cities. Many thousands of German soldiers perished so that their leaders, especially Hitler, could survive in their bunkers a little longer. But while the Final Solution was in some respects unprecedented in the annals of cruelty and massacre, the massive destruction of human life in the Soviet Union preceded the German invasion. According to Robert Conquest's estimate, the purges in the U.S.S.R. cost twenty million lives.[41] With Stalin's war against the peasantry in the Ukraine (the cost was perhaps five million dead of starvation), his deportation of five nationalities during the Great Patriotic War and the Katyn massacre of the Polish officer corps, it was due to victory—not virtue—that the Soviet leadership was not in the dock at Nuremberg for crimes against humanity.[42] Such crimes put the totalitarian regimes in a new category of tyranny.

For the difference between Fascism and totalitarianism might be summed up in one word: genocide. The word itself—rooted in the Greek *genos* (race, tribe)—was invented in 1944 by Raphael Lemkin, a Polish Jewish attorney whose en-

tire family (except for a brother) was wiped out after the
German invasion of 1939. In exile in the United States, he
wrote that "new conceptions require new terms. By 'genocide'
we mean the destruction of a nation or of an ethnic group. . . .
It is intended . . . to signify a co-ordinated plan of different
actions aiming at the destruction of essential foundations of
the life of national groups, with the aim of annihilating the
groups themselves." Lemkin cited examples among the ancients and in the Middle Ages of such attempts at extermination, but claimed that the modern "techniques of genocide
represent an elaborate, almost scientific system developed to
an extent never before achieved by any nation." This system
should therefore be outlawed. Lemkin himself had fought for
such a prohibition in international law and in the criminal
codes as early as 1933. It became the essence of Count 3
(Crimes against Humanity) in the indictment of the twenty-
seven top German leaders at Nuremberg; and Lemkin lob-
bied successfully thereafter at the United Nations, which in
1948 adopted the Convention on the Prevention and Punishment of the Crime of Genocide. One analogue of Arendt's
theory was Lemkin's 1953 request that the United Nations
investigate the violation of the convention by the Soviet
Union and its satellites. Lemkin argued that the severity of
the Communist persecution of Jews and other minorities, by
his definition, constituted genocide.[43] That definition was
perhaps too broad to distinguish between oppression, however horrible, and the strategy of physical annihilation; and
in any event the claims of national sovereignty have immu-
nized from interference even conventional despotisms that
have threatened minority populations.

Ordinary dictatorships have been primarily interested in
the suppression of actual political opponents, in contrast to
the totalitarian desire for mass murder. When the *Einsatz-*

gruppen followed the German army into the Soviet Union, their assignment was to kill all Jews as well as all Communist functionaries (though not all Party members). In an address to S.S. generals in 1943, Himmler spoke freely of the extermination of the Jews. In discussing the fate of the Communists and their leaders in Greater Germany, however, the Reichsfuehrer S.S. observed that, "like most of the criminals," the Communist leaders had been locked up in concentration camps—but presumably not systematically murdered as a matter of policy. "Race" was therefore more threatening to Nazism than was political opposition, for no directive, whether published or secret, called for the extinction of non-Soviet Communists as a group. Another illustration of the difference between totalitarianism and Fascism can be found in Arthur Koestler's autobiography. His brother-in-law, a German Communist, had been arrested in the Soviet Union in about the same year (1937) the novelist was jailed by Franco's forces in Spain. "Public opinion and diplomatic pressure" secured Koestler's escape from a firing squad: "I would be saved though I was an enemy of Franco's rule and guilty according to its laws; whereas Ernie, who was innocent and a loyal supporter of the Soviet Union, was shot."[44]

Arendt may have been the first scholar to emphasize such grisly paradoxes and to theorize from the peculiar nature of totalitarian terror, which differed from other despotisms in extending imprisonment, torture and execution far beyond those who by thought or action rejected the policies or leaders of the regime. Nazi terror increased after the opposition movement and dissidents were already in exile or in concentration camps. In the Soviet Union the purges were intensified after the foes of Stalin and even of Bolshevism had already been exiled or eliminated.[45] In both societies human beings were killed for who they were rather than for what they had done.

In the Soviet Union many victims of the purges were selected on the basis of quotas for particular classifications of "class enemies."[46] One prominent Soviet prosecutor regarded guilt as an outmoded bourgeois concept, which accounts for the N.K.V.D. slogan: "Just give us a person—and we'll create the case." The abandonment of the bourgeois notion of guilt also explains the use of torture, which in Roy Medvedev's formulation "yields not truth but a distortion of the truth. . . . Torture is aimed not so much at finding the guilty person as at making the innocent one guilty."[47]

If the actions of the accused are irrelevant, if it is identity (or accident) that determines who shall live or die, then the eminent director V. E. Meyerhold could be executed after the concoction of a crime labeled "Meyerholdism" in the theatre. (The American Communist party developed a comic version; one of the charges leading to the removal of Earl Browder as general secretary in 1945 was "incurable Browderism.") Such "crimes" were neither conspiracies nor tendencies—just the fabrications of agencies of fear. One of the many harrowing incidents recounted in Solzhenitsyn's *The Gulag Archipelago* involved a transport guard's query to one of the prisoners as to why a twenty-five-year sentence had been meted out. When the prisoner answered that he had done nothing, the guard replied: "You're lying. The sentence for nothing at all is ten years." Over two decades before Solzhenitsyn's book appeared in the West, Arendt had observed that, for the totalitarian regimes, "the innocent and the guilty are equally undesirable."[48] Both categories depend upon the factual standards of the nontotalitarian world.

Arendt therefore attached great significance to the role of the police, those who—in Auden's famous revision of Shelley —were "the secret legislators of the world." She predicted that the police would replace the party as the key institution of any

totalitarian regime. But for Arendt to claim that Himmler—
whose submissiveness toward Hitler was pathological—was
"the most powerful man in Germany after 1936" was baffling.
The Reichsfuehrer S.S. never directly challenged the authority of Hitler himself and, in the final moments of the Third
Reich, was simply expelled from the party and stripped of his
offices. Arendt did not claim that the power of any of the
Soviet police chiefs exceeded that of Stalin, who apparently
had no difficulty dispatching the lives of Yagoda and Yezhov.
Arendt's stress on the power of the police, Carl J. Friedrich
therefore concluded, was an exaggeration.[49]

Her views were generally more complicated and subtle than
criticism of them might imply, and Friedrich's comment did
not do justice to her insights. She in fact argued that the establishment of a totalitarian regime means a real loss in police
power, which is a paradox. At its peak the central staff of the
Czarist Third Department, according to Solzhenitsyn, numbered forty-five persons—"a ridiculously small number for
even the remotest Cheka provincial headquarters in the country." Yet the Okhrana actively ferreted out opponents of the
Czarist regime, discovered plots, even infiltrated the Bolshevik
party, and so forth. The purpose of a totalitarian police force,
on the other hand, "is not to discover crimes," Arendt argued,
"but to be on hand when the government decides to arrest a
certain category of the population." The police are privy to
many secrets, but they are ignorant of their actual victims
until the Leader has defined them—and condemned them—
as a class or race or category of socially dangerous elements.[50]
Friedrich's claim that Arendt overestimated the role of the
police may be affected by his own inclusion of the milder
tyranny of Fascist Italy in his theory of totalitarianism. Moreover, it is surely relevant that, shortly after Stalin's death, his
heirs signaled an end to the full force of totalitarian rule by

having Beria shot. Totalitarian regimes are therefore not police states in the literal sense; and Arendt's theory indicated
both the limits of the power of the police and the significance
of pervasive terror in Germany and the Soviet Union.

🖋

Shortly before Nazism and Stalinism were established,
Julien Benda referred to the twentieth century as "the age of
the *intellectual organization of political hatreds*. It will be
one of its chief claims to notice in the moral history of humanity." For what distinguishes totalitarianism from all other
regimes is not only the scale of terror and the aim of total
domination of public and private life but ideology, which
Arendt meant in a special sense—as unthinking and expedi-
ent dedication to "the logic of an idea." Arendt's definition
owed little to the one that originated in Marxism, by which
an ideology constitutes a cluster of beliefs which function to
rationalize class interests competing with other class interests.
The responsibility of Marxists was to "unmask" ideologies, to
reveal the naked struggle of class interests; Arendt saw little
point to such unmasking. She did not think that ideologies
could be effectively criticized and analyzed; their adherents
could only be checked by superior force.[51] Ideological belief
consists exclusively of what the Leader or the party authorizes.
Conversation, which Jacques Barzun once defined as "the
sifting of opinion," is excluded from the discourse of the
ideologist, who is not interested in weighing views but in "announcing reality. . . . He's not leading a search party in the
style of the ruminating Cambridge philosophers," according
to one Sovietologist. "He's handing out the truth." The authoritarian definition of truth has been elaborated by Vladimir Bukovsky, who spent eleven years of his life in Soviet
labor camps and psychiatric hospitals: "Theories and conclusions" in Russia do not "develop out of the raw material of

life, but, on the contrary, the raw material of everyday life is created to fit in with the ruling theory." Instead of emerging "freely," experience is " 'interpreted' by the party." [52]

Though Arendt defined ideology etymologically as "the logic of an idea," her analysis owed nothing to the rationalist notion of "false consciousness" and was closer to Pareto's irrationalist separation of ideology from class interests. According to Arendt, to assent to totalitarian dogma is to be in the grip of an illusion—but that is not what she considered most relevant. For that illusion can be so compelling that it seeks to revise reality itself, to make itself true through action, as in Sorel's notion of "myth." Arendt's definition may be illumined by a distinction explained by Joseph Berger, perhaps the highest-ranking Comintern official to have survived the Gulag archipelago and to have emigrated to the West. In the camps Berger, a Polish Jew, learned the following distinction between two Russian words for "truth": *istina* "denotes the correspondence between the notion and the objective reality," while *pravda* was "the higher concept of truth, a truth elevated to the rank of an idea . . . that truth which needs to be attained, truth in action." [53] It is *pravda*, the desire to make something true through action, that encapsulates Arendt's understanding of the meaning of ideology for the totalitarian mind.

For this definition is not only authoritarian but activist. To the totalitarians, Arendt wrote, "the only relevant thing on earth is to be right, and the only relevant motive for actions is the determination to destroy and exterminate every fact and every person that may prove them wrong." It was therefore futile to argue with ideologues in power, that is, with representatives of a totalitarian regime. Such an argument would resemble a "debate with a potential murderer as to whether his future victim were dead or alive . . . forgetting . . . that the murderer, by killing the person in question, could promptly

provide proof of the correctness of this statement."[54] Thus the
Nazis could describe the Jews as subhuman, prior to making
the inmates of "the other kingdom" unrecognizable, discon-
nected from their former identities. Immediately upon ar-
rival in Auschwitz, Elie Wiesel was told by an older inmate
to resume his Talmudic studies somehow; for "otherwise in a
month you will no longer know what having a soul could
possibly mean." The deprivation of qualities assumed to be
human demonstrated the validity of the Nazis' image of their
victims. The futility of argument with ideologues in power
was revealed when Menachem Begin was prosecuted for his
Zionist activities in Poland under Article 58 of the *Soviet*
Constitution. When Begin asked his interrogator how legal-
ized conduct could be declared retroactively treasonable, he
was told: "Section 58 applies to everyone in the whole world.
. . . *In the whole world.* It is only a question of when he will
get to us, or we to him." Armed with ideological confidence
in the expansion of Soviet power, the judge sentenced Begin
to the Gulag archipelago.[55]

By permitting the destruction of one-third of German
homes and factories, Arendt added, the Nazi regime demonstrated that "the German people was fighting for its very
existence, which was, at the outset, a pure lie." To prove that
Nazism had arisen as a response to the immediate threat of
Bolshevism, the war was prolonged until the Red Army was
at the Elbe.[56] Here too the parallel with the Soviet Union can
be sustained, for the official description of the party deviation-
ists as representatives of "dying classes" was the prelude to
their extermination. In "announcing reality," the Soviet regime was also expounding a prophecy that would be made
true. The disappearance of Trotsky's name from the annals of
Soviet history, as though he had never existed, was the prelude
to physical disappearance. "When Trotsky learned that he
had never played a role in the Russian Revolution," Arendt

speculated, "he must have known that his death warrant had been signed."[57]

The blood from the ice axe in Coyoacan spattered on the uncompleted pages of Trotsky's biography of Stalin (which was unpublished even in the United States so long as the Soviet Union was a military ally). Ideology served not only as an instrument to form the future but also as a bludgeon to alter or obliterate the past. In the 1930s possession of a copy of John Reed's *Ten Days that Shook the World* became a ✳ felonious crime, because Stalin was unmentioned in this eye-witness report of the Revolution, and some of its heroes were currently being unmasked as "spies."[58] Among those arrested after the Second World War were certain comrades who had been Komsomols—teenage members of the Young Communist League—in the 1920s. Their crime was that they had voted for the Opposition—that is, they remembered the period when there indeed had been an Opposition. When Solzhenitsyn was arrested in 1945, one of the pieces of incriminating evidence was a photograph he possessed of Trotsky.[59] The Nazis were unable to obliterate the "Lorelei" from German memory, but they ascribed the poem to an unknown author and had Heine's grave destroyed when they occupied Paris.[60] Wielding the terrifying instruments of violence, the totalitarian regimes sought to ordain the future and expunge the past in accordance with the imperatives of ideology, to efface the continuity that marks civilized life.

According to the logic of totalitarianism, the leaders of the regimes did not exercise such power because they were infallible. Their followers believed instead that anyone who could implement terror and affect reality "with the superior methods of totalitarian organization can become infallible." Arendt therefore considered an "extreme contempt for facts" to be characteristic of the totalitarian mentality. In 1943 the Luftwaffe commander responsible for fighters reported to Goering that American fighters had penetrated German territory. They were shot down over Aachen, and the wreckage could be inspected there. But Goering refused to accept the facts: "I officially assert that the American fighter planes did not reach Aachen." When the commander persisted, the Reichsmarschall fumed: "I herewith give you an official order [*sic*] that they weren't there! Do you understand? The American fighters were not there! Get that! I intend to report that to the Fuehrer."[61] Such remarks went beyond the neglect or disparagement of inconvenient information, but suggested the presumption that reality could be reordered to correspond to ideological imperatives.

Arendt's definition of "the logic of an idea," her description of the unprecedented willingness to act upon that idea, was not in any way a description of intellectual rigor. Joachim Fest has written of the leaders of the Third Reich that "the indifference with which they accepted the most contradictory propositions of National Socialist ideology was due less to lack of intellectual ability than to the cynicism of practitioners of power who did not believe in ideologies but simply used them." Arendt was likewise struck by the refusal of the rulers to be shackled by their own ideologies, by their "superiority to their own avowed dogmas."[62] Beginning in the late 1920s, Stalin waged a brutal war in the countryside to achieve the collectivization of agriculture, promising the "liquidization of the *kulaks* as a class"; yet the term *kulak* was deliberately left undefined. During the Fourteenth and Fifteenth Party Congresses, the term was commonly used euphemistically to describe all the peasants.[63] Similarly, having selected from photographs the racial elite as members of the S.S., Himmler prohibited in the Third Reich any definition of the word "Jew"—though the Reich's legal experts had to do so in order to single out from the general population the group most obviously destined for annihilation. A vague or erroneous genealogical table could have lethal consequences, yet Hitler himself could not have passed such a test, since the identity of one of his grandfathers was unknown.[64] Having identified Jewry with Bolshevism and located its capital in Moscow, Hitler could nevertheless admire Stalin in private for "forging a state out of this Slavic rabbit breed."[65] The leaders' disregard of their own ideologies was bound to catch the foes of totalitarian rulers off balance. Influential strata in the Western democracies believed Stalin when he lied (for example, about the plots by enemies of the state) and refused to believe Hitler when he told the truth (for example, about the planned destruction of the Jews).

Since the totalitarian rulers regarded ideological slogans as "mere devices to organize the masses," the "scientific" character of Marxian socialism or of race theory mattered less than the command of the instruments of power, which could be turned in any direction. Thus Nazi Germany could rise above dogma to conclude an alliance with the embodiment of the Yellow Peril, the Japanese. Friendship was offered to Semites like the Palestinian Haj Amin el-Husseini, the Grand Mufti of Jerusalem (who considered Eichmann "the best friend of the Arab people"). Similarly, Stalin could interrupt the class struggle to campaign for a Popular Front with the Western capitalist powers and could form an alliance with Chiang Kai-Shek.[66] The supreme example of this flexibility was of course the Nazi-Soviet Pact, which the British cartoonist David Low illustrated by showing Hitler and Stalin bowing graciously toward each other: "The scum of the earth, I believe," Hitler coos to Stalin, who replies, "The bloody assassin of the workers, I presume." After the pact was signed, Foreign Minister Molotov criticized "some short-sighted people . . . who [were] carried away by oversimplified anti-Fascist agitation." He told the Supreme Soviet that "an ideology cannot be destroyed by force," and that it was "not only

senseless but criminal" to try to destroy Hitlerism through
war. For almost two years thereafter, the N.K.V.D. guards in
the Gulag archipelago were prohibited from calling their
prisoners "fascists," and the term vanished from the press.[67]
Adherence to a totalitarian movement therefore did not depend upon an ideological consensus, upon rigid devotion to
racial or class credos. The aim of totalitarianism, Arendt argued, was not to compel belief but rather to galvanize the
masses: "Totalitarian leaders are actually free to do whatever
they please and can count on the loyalty of their entourage
even if they choose to murder them."[68]

Arendt shrewdly noticed the extravagance of this loyalty.
Intrigue and rivalry were rampant at the top of the Nazi and
Bolshevik hierarchies but, in contrast to conventional autocracies, leading members of the movement never attempted a
coup d'etat. Not even the police chiefs—Müller, Heydrich,
Himmler and Yagoda, Yezhov, Beria—made any serious efforts to depose the Leader.[69] Yet Arendt may have overstressed
this combination of fanaticism and flexibility. The more fully
Arendt showed the totalitarian rulers to be exempt from
ideological commitments, the more closely they begin to resemble traditional dictators. To that extent the political dex-
terity of the German and Russian leaders made them, against
Arendt's intentions, seem to inhabit the common-sense world
of practical necessity. And indeed the picture is complicated
in ways that do not quite fit Arendt's interpretation of totalitarian motivation. If the Nazis were as cynical about the con-
tent of their own ideology as Arendt contended, the extermination of the Jews at the cost of military and economic
considerations remains inexplicable, and cannot be accounted
for by other ideological priorities. The Axis pact with the
Japanese had to be justified by labeling them the "Aryans of
the East," though all of the examples of alliances with class or
racial enemies can be more plausibly explained as recognition

of temporary political and military necessities than as cynicism toward dogmas as such. Expediency could, even in the mad universe of totalitarianism, transcend the compulsions of ideology.

Even the astonishing devotion of the followers could be exaggerated. In his testament Hitler expelled Himmler and Goering, not only for their interest in a negotiated peace, but for "their disloyalty to my person." Readers of Koestler's *Darkness at Noon* were likely to be impressed with Rubashov's submission to the logic of the purges, since his acceptance of death seemed the inexorable result of the premise of *parti-inost* (party spirit). Yet the novelist himself had to remind readers that, of the other two prisoners depicted in the book, "Harelip confesses because he is kept under torture; [and] the illiterate peasant confesses without even understanding the charge, for he will agree to anything that Authority orders him to do."[70] Arendt extended beyond its proper bounds a strategic insight into the systematic insult to common sense totalitarianism represented. Her failure to perceive the inhibitions upon even the ideological pursuit of unlimited terror, to locate the boundaries that the rest of the world imposed on the Nazi and Soviet regimes, especially in foreign policy, showed a tendency in her thought to develop the most far-fetched and implausible explanations of totalitarian behavior.[71] The very imagination that enabled her to penetrate the sinister madness of the logic of an idea and to track the meaning of unprecedented militancy and terror may have betrayed her into neglecting the signs of expediency, the evidences of familiar political conduct and psychological motivation, that could be found even in the regimes of Hitler and Stalin. Her terrifying series of illuminations of the fantastic was not always rectified by an awareness of the obvious. Observations that are unoriginal, she failed to realize, may nevertheless be true.

So long as it is granted that no two societies are exactly alike, and that to detect a parallel is not to assert an identity, Arendt's definition of totalitarianism as confined to Nazi Germany and Stalinist Russia is a convincing and well-supported position. Other regimes—past and present—have been headed by bloodthirsty tyrants, have systematically violated human rights, have monopolized the instruments of political expression, have threatened vulnerable minorities or attacked harmless neighbors. Such governments, for all their repugnant cruelty, ought to be analytically distinguished, however, from the legacy of Hitler and Stalin. No other modern dictatorship, left or right, demonstrated an equivalent willingness to use terror so indiscriminately, to disregard utilitarian considerations for the sake of ideological militancy, and to extinguish human life as did the Nazi and Bolshevik regimes. No other modern regime posed so direct a threat to the continuation of human culture, or inflicted suffering on so vast a scale.

Chapter 3

⚑

A THEORY AS HISTORY

ARENDT'S conceptual scheme obliged her to limn the most basic aspects of political life—the state, the nation, leadership, law—in the light of a tyranny she considered novel and unprecedented. By anchoring that scheme within an historical argument, she revealed the assumptions, biases, blind spots, ambiguities and emphases that this chapter seeks to highlight. The case for Arendt's description of totalitarianism is a forceful one, but it depends upon chronological and historical parameters that she by no means made clear. The most nominalist work of a trained philosopher, *The Origins of Totalitarianism* was also the most susceptible to empirical tests and evidentiary challenges. While generally respecting the power of her mind, George Lichtheim once dared to suggest that Arendt was, "to put it mildly, no historian."[1] Her indifference to professional standards was most apparent in her attempts to establish periodization for the emergence and decline of totalitarianism.

The military defeat of the Third Reich in 1945 was a convenient and unambiguous date for marking the end of German totalitarianism; but at different times she offered different dates to mark its origins. In the first and second editions of *The Origins of Totalitarianism*, Arendt asserted that the Nazis had established "authentic . . . totalitarian domination" after 1938, a judgment repeated in an essay in 1959: "The Third Reich was not by any means totalitarian during its early years. By 'early years' I mean . . . from 1933 to 1938."[2] Yet the text of her book also presented a conflicting date: "At the outbreak of the war, Germany was not yet completely totalitarianized, and . . . until roughly 1942 her economy was allowed to function more or less rationally." (In her view, it hardly needs to be repeated, totalitarianism meant the absence of utilitarianism, the triumph of illogic over common sense and self-interest. Yet centralized economic coordination was elsewhere rarely integral to her definition of totalitarianism, and does not in itself distinguish such a regime from a democratic polity.) Only in 1942, the year of the battle of Stalingrad and of the Wannsee conference to implement the Final Solution, did "the rules of totalitarian domination begin to outweigh all other considerations."[3] As though oblivious to these already muddled reckonings, the final edition of her book placed "the seemingly firm establishment" of totalitarianism back in 1933, the year of the Nazi accession to power. In her last statement on the subject of periodization, she offered still another date, observing that Germany was not "openly totalitarian" until the outbreak of the war in September, 1939.[4] Qualifying terms like "authentic" and "openly" and "completely" might of course smooth away these inconsistencies, but Arendt nowhere explained what she meant by such terms. Such mystification is no way to earn sympathy for the considerable problems involved in rooting the totalitarian model in a specific historical epoch.

Periodization was even less exact in her analysis of the Soviet Union. Arendt's definition of totalitarianism excluded the period of Lenin's dictatorship, yet she was quite sketchy in contrasting Leninism and Stalinism. In any event, by Arendt's interpretation, Stalin did not inherit a totalitarian movement; he created one, and, unlike Hitler, forged it while already in power. The year 1929 was the first of "clear-cut totalitarian dictatorship in Russia," since the introduction of the first Five Year Plan marked the repudiation of rational economic development and the pulverization of whatever autonomous institutions were still extant.[5] She also wrote, however, that the Soviet Union achieved "an authentic form of totalitarian domination" a year later, that is, "since 1930." And in the same edition of *The Origins of Totalitarianism*, Arendt felt compelled to offer yet another date; utter subservience to the will of the party secretary was not completed until 1938, when Stalin "rid himself of the whole administrative and military aristocracy" and through the labor book— the managers' required records of workers' conduct and attitudes—transformed the proletariat "into a gigantic forced-labor force."[6] Again Arendt preferred not to explain possible distinctions between "clear-cut" and "authentic" forms of totalitarian rule and other, lesser examples. Nor did she offer any justification for calling an uncompleted process—presumably before 1938—a case of totalitarian domination, as though there were such a thing as quasi-totalitarianism.

The issue here is less a matter of chronology than of interpretation. If the Soviet Union had a totalitarian regime before it had a totalitarian movement, then the social conditions for the ripening of unprecedented power had "to be organized afterward." Thus the regime itself had to uproot individuals and demolish autonomous social units "in order to make total loyalty—the psychological basis for total domination—at all possible." By first controlling the apparatus of the Bolshevik party, Stalin could bring the full force of the state to the task of atomizing society itself. This explanation of the origins of Soviet totalitarianism was, one of Arendt's critics admitted, quite clever.[7] But if it were wrong, a key link in the chain of her argument is broken, since the validity of the parallel so forthrightly asserted in her book would also be affected. For

she had to prove that the Soviet regime, like the Nazi movement, drew upon the vulnerability of the "structureless mass"
of "isolated individuals."[8]

Arendt therefore had to infer from Stalin and his closest
collaborators a degree of foresight and deliberation scarcely
demonstrated by the evidence offered in *The Origins of
Totalitarianism*. In citing estimates of the liquidation of the
bureaucracy in the 1930s, Arendt acknowledged that she had
"nothing but questionable sources to resort to. . . . It is precisely the official material that is nothing but propaganda."
The point was sound enough—but such disclaimers cannot
inspire confidence in the incontrovertibility of her argument.
Certainly she could not have recourse to any primary sources
emanating from the Kremlin, nor could Stalin's self-consciousness and deliberateness be conclusively demonstrated. Isaac
Deutscher had to subtitle his 1949 book on Stalin "a political
biography . . . since only one private letter of his has yet come
to light."[9] And even when motives can be far more fully
documented, it is one of the most persuasive of all historiographical conceits to disclose the gap between a leader's intentions and the unanticipated, often opposite consequences.
Arendt's grasp of the purposes and policies inherent in the
"modernization" of Russia may have exceeded Stalin's.

Nevertheless, there may be a way of salvaging Arendt's
delineation of the actual origins of totalitarianism. In 1926
Stalin had announced how the typical revolutions of the past,
such as the French in 1789, could be differentiated from the
Bolshevik revolution: "The bourgeois revolution is usually
consummated with the seizure of power, whereas in the prole-
tarian revolution the seizure of power is only the *beginning*.
The power is used as a lever for transforming the old economy
and organizing the new one."[10] This passage suggested, according to Richard Lowenthal, that "the achievement of the

classical democratic revolutions was to set free a social order that *already existed*, by removing political and legal obstacles to its functioning; while the totalitarian revolution uses its unheard-of concentration of power in an attempt to *create* a new social order." The party secretary was thus employing the vocabulary of Marxism to offer a program of dynamism from above that was quite un-Marxist in its origin. In announcing that the superstructure of the state (that is, a single party animated by ideology) would inaugurate social change, Stalin was outlining a policy which would result in the utter transformation of the material basis of society (that is, the social conditions of totalitarianism).[11]

Stalin thus displayed his own superiority to Marxist dogmas about the role of the state and the source of revolution; and in turning a revolutionary party into a totalitarian movement, he utilized the weapons of the state to terrorize citizens and pulverize social institutions. The isolation and anxiety that resulted were conveyed in a poem Osip Mandelstam wrote in 1934—which probably sent him to the labor camp where he died: ". . . Ten steps away no one hears our conversation/But where there's so much as half a conversation/We remember the Kremlin's mountaineer. . . ./His cockroach whiskers leer." A similar atmosphere of anxiety and fright, of suspicion and helplessness, of utter conformity and utter aloneness, was depicted in Brecht's *The Private Life of the Master Race* (1938), for only one other society created the kind of fear and trembling engendered in the Soviet Union as Stalin consolidated his rule. The parallel is reinforced if German totalitarianism is also seen as creating the social conditions that were earlier insufficient to impel mass escape from freedom. Arendt may have paid insufficient attention to the social meaning of the *Machtergreifung*, the seizure of power of 1933, for what William Sheridan Allen called the "atomization of the com-

munity at large" may have been, as his own monograph revealed, more the product than the precondition of total
rule.[12]

The first edition of Arendt's book appeared while Stalin
was very much alive and apparently planning a new set of
political purges and economic dislocations. It was only with
the second revised edition that she stressed the significance of
his death, which "was not merely followed by a successor
crisis and a temporary 'thaw' . . . but by an authentic, though
never unequivocal, process of detotalitarianization."[13] This
clumsy term was not linked to a specific date. For 1956 was
not only the year of Khrushchev's secret speech to the Twentieth Party Congress, but also of the defeat of the Hungarian
Revolution, which she considered a triumph of "totalitarian
imperialism." But certainly, by the end of the decade the
Soviet Union had stripped itself of enough of the vestiges of
Stalin's rule for Arendt to describe the regime as an attempt
at "enlightened despotism."[14] Confusingly enough, however,
this was considered the *second* "suspension of total domination"; the first, she mentioned in passing, had occurred during
the Great Patriotic War.[15] Stalin had indeed permitted a
limited relaxation in *partiinost* and ideological militancy
(whereas the terror had intensified in Nazi Germany during
the Second World War). But it is doubtful that such loosening
of controls, which was granted and then withdrawn at the
whim of the autocrat, ever went so far as to be characterized
as detotalitarianization. Arendt did not mention, for example,
the further brutalization and enslavement of the camp inmates during the war, though many of them felt a surge of
patriotic feeling and blindly hoped that greater exertions
might even win them their freedom.[16]

Her effort to establish the temporal boundaries of totalitarianism involved her in inconsistencies she was not inclined
to resolve. But Arendt should be credited with a capacity to

change her mind under the impact of historical change and
new evidence, especially the consequences of the death of
Stalin. In this respect her approach was superior to others.
She at least avoided Adam Ulam's 1960 description of the
post-Stalin era as "enlightened totalitarianism,"[17] which is
oxymoronic. Nor did Arendt draw a mistaken inference from
the contrast that George Steiner proposed in 1973: "The extraordinary thing is the amount of opposition in Russia and
the Russian passion for getting the news out. This did not
happen in Nazi Germany. Germany had no Alexander Solzhenitsyn, no [Mstislav] Rostropovich, no [Sviatoslav] Richter,
no [Yevgeny] Yevtushenko . . . smuggling out the manu-
scripts. . . . This is the extraordinary difference."[18] Quite apart
from the oddity of Steiner's examples (Rostropovich and Richter are musicians, and Yevtushenko has not resorted to *samizdat*), his distinction would not account for the virtually complete atrophy of this "Russian passion for getting the news
out" in the 1930s. If the willingness to bear witness is indeed
an attribute of the Russian character, it was effectively stifled
for three decades—the years that corresponded to Stalin's
totalitarian rule. Even for prisoners willing to scream out, the
opportunity was missing; in the vast Siberian emptiness, such
cries could not resonate. If German voices were largely silent,
that may be due to the Nazi policy of driving intellectuals and
artists into exile in the early years of the Reich and also, at
least until the war, of cynically dumping "the Jewish problem" on other nations, forcing them to reveal their own inhospitality toward refugees. Political dissidents and racial undesirables who were shrewd enough or lucky enough to
survive generally did not want to get the news out; they
wanted to get themselves out.

The emendation of Arendt's theory to take into account
Stalin's death did not go far enough, however, because its
periodization suggested a neglected dimension in the text it-

self. *The Origins of Totalitarianism* was completed four years
after the death of Hitler and, as it turned out, four years before the death of Stalin. The fact that both political systems
ceased to be totalitarian with the passing of the dictators
should have indicated how essential their personalities were
to the maintenance of totalitarian domination. Both leaders,
Robert C. Tucker argued, belonged "somewhere on the con-
tinuum of psychiatric conditions designated as paranoid"; and
their needs "were a powerful motivating factor in the dictatorial decision making."[19] The infliction of massive terror was
such a need; and though Arendt made such terror essential to
her theory of totalitarianism, she did not thereby make the
personality of the dictator an equally integral component of
the definition of total rule. Had she done so, the significance
of ideology would have been diminished, not only because
Hitler could violate or minimize the dogmas of National
Socialism without loss of power, but also because—in Arendt's
own terms—the rulers of post-Stalinist Russia could dismantle
the totalitarian system without jettisoning their Communist
ideology. Detotalitarianization in the Soviet Union coincided
with the propaganda assault on the "cult of the personality."
In Germany the process was even more rapid, if truncated; as
the Third Reich collapsed militarily, Hitler designated as his
successor not Party stalwarts like Goering or Himmler or
Bormann but Admiral Doenitz. While the establishment of
full-fledged despotism may be imaginable without having to
posit the necessity of a despot, such a distinction cannot be
historically validated.

Arendt did not sufficiently link the span of total rule with
the maturity and morality of two particular individuals, and
it is not difficult to guess why. For "if totalitarianism were the
systematic whole that she suggests," Margaret Canovan wrote,
"and were as she claims the outcome of the most general of
our century's trends, it would surely take more than the death

of one particular leader to stop it." In attaching such importance to the role of the dictator, Canovan was also arguing that totalitarianism bore a closer resemblance to older forms of despotism than Arendt had suspected.[20] But Canovan's argument only made sense if fuller recognition of the personalities of Hitler and Stalin were related to "the most general of our century's trends"; their personalities have no explanatory power as a substitute for analysis of general historical forces. The life and death of the dictator, far from constituting a severe challenge to the model of totalitarianism, is in fact necessary to salvage it. Ignoring the impact of Lenin's successor led Friedrich and Brzezinski to speculate in 1956 that, based on "the past course of evolution, it seems most likely that the totalitarian dictatorships will continue to become more total, even though the rate of intensification may slow down." This prediction was wrong. Scholars such as Tucker, Karl Dietrich Bracher and Leonard Schapiro therefore drew special attention to the careers and characters of Stalin and Hitler without surrendering the theory of totalitarianism as the best insight into the peculiarities of Nazi and Soviet history.[21] Since Arendt did not ignore the function of the leader in these movements and regimes, such emphasis would not have been inconsistent with other facets of her version of the theory, and in fact flows logically from her delineation of German and Russian political development.[22]

Despite ambiguities of periodization that still linger in her work, Arendt had an historian's deeper interest in change, in the transmutations of experience. Her realization that Nazism and Stalinism could not be properly understood as extensions of traditional tyranny illumined many of the local insights in *The Origins of Totalitarianism* and, later, in her portrait of Eichmann at the *Beth Hamishpat* (House of Justice) in Jerusalem. In insisting that these regimes were without precedent, Arendt knew that "this conclusion seems inevitable, yet it is extremely daring. For throughout our history there have been few forms of government, all of them already known to and described by the ancients." But the combination of ideology and terror marked a caesura in the long history of tyranny. Karl Marx's 1844 observation—"Germans have thought in politics what other peoples have done"—needed to be reversed. For "the Germans have *done* in politics," Dwight Macdonald argued a century later, "what other peoples up to now dared only to *think*."[23] That was also true, up to a point, of the Soviets. Arendt too noted that "the originality of totalitarianism is horrible, not because some new 'idea' came into the world, but because its very actions constitute a break with all our traditions; they have clearly exploded our categories of political thought and our standards for moral judgment."[24]

The horrible novelty of the phenomenon was reflected in language. Even as late as 1933, the word itself had not appeared in the Oxford English Dictionary. After the Second World War, she argued, the vernacular made of the term the incarnation of "supreme political evil. . . . Yet while popular language thus recognized a new event by accepting a new word, it invariably uses such concepts as synonyms for others signifying old and familiar evils" such as "terror and lust for power." Soon thereafter, Arendt attempted to demonstrate that totalitarianism meant a new *form* of government, and this demonstration Hans Morgenthau called her "obviously outstanding contribution . . . to political philosophy."[25]

Yet it was rare for so ambitious a foray in political thought to be so absorbed in the density of detail and narrative energy that are associated with the writing of history. When she made her contribution, no systematic treatise on dictatorship was available, nor did she herself write one. *The Origins of Totalitarianism* was organized primarily on historical principles,

rather than according to a cohesive scheme of classification—
such as Friedrich's and Brzezinski's six basic components: "an
ideology, a single party typically led by one man, a terroristic
police, a communications monopoly, a weapons monopoly,
and a centrally directed economy." Arendt herself stressed
only the first three of these features, perhaps because the last
two are also to be found in democratic polities as well. But her
book did revive the tradition of Montesquieu, whom she considered the last serious political theorist of the forms that
government assumes. Montesquieu's *The Spirit of the Laws*
drew an especially sharp distinction between despotism and
all other varieties of government;[26] Arendt further insisted on
a wide separation between totalitarianism and all other forms
of despotism.

This particular thesis was not entirely without precedent.
The 1939 symposium on totalitarian rule sponsored by the
American Philosophical Society included a paper by Carlton
J. H. Hayes on "The Novelty of Totalitarianism in the History of Western Civilization." Anticipating Arendt's view that
totalitarianism exploded common moral standards, the Columbia University historian claimed that "the exalting of
force and terrorism does not signify merely the immoral doctrine that the end justifies the means. It signifies an utter denial of any moral law superior to the might of dictators," and
thus stands in flagrant hostility to Judeo-Christian traditions
and principles. Hayes, soon to serve as ambassador to Franco's
more conventional authoritarian regime in Spain, offered
other resonant remarks about this "brand-new event in the
history of Western civilization." Like many others, he was
struck by the monopolization of the instruments of power, the
one-party rule, the effective use of propaganda, and the domination of individual and group life. He, too, was struck by the
command of the dictators over the masses, "for the masses
count nowadays as never before, and this is the first and most

fundamental of the novelties" of totalitarianism. In adapting themselves to modern technology and to the presence of the masses, the ruling elites who had just plunged the world into war confirmed the wisdom of the Marquis de Custine: "Tyranny invents only the means of consolidating itself."[27]

Without acknowledging Hayes's paper, Arendt extended these insights, articulating some of them with bold simplicity to underscore her argument, spinning others out into webs that suggested fine distinctions and intricate ramifications. She emphasized that neither the National Socialists nor the Bolshevik party under Stalin could be understood within the same analytic framework reserved for political groups in Western parliamentary systems. Nor were they examples of revolutionary parties, which "have a long tradition of constituting themselves as secret societies and using conspiratorial methods," but do not pretend "that the government they want to overthrow is itself such a conspiracy." For the Nazis and Bolsheviks "establish themselves openly and pretend that their opponents are members of a conspiracy. . . . They establish themselves as a counter-conspiracy in broad daylight."[28] Arendt noticed the extent to which the Nazis envied and imitated what they believed was the surreptitious, ubiquitous exercise of power manifested by the Jews, from whom Himmler claimed to have learned "the art of government." Hitler likewise admitted to having "learned by heart" the forged "Protocols of the Elders of Zion"—a claim Arendt need not have accepted at face value. Nevertheless, this pamphlet, the *locus classicus* of the conspiratorial mind, did exert an incalculable influence on Hitler, who made the "Protocols" required reading in German schools two years after he became Chancellor.[29] How deeply a fevered suspiciousness was locked into the Bolshevik mentality can be illustrated by an incident after the Second World War, when two Ukrainian representatives to the United Nations got caught up in the

holdup of a small New York delicatessen and one of them
was shot in the leg. Though the police found no political motive to the robbery, Andrei Vishinsky, the Soviet delegate,
was incredulous. "How could it have been a holdup?" he
asked. "It was a *small* delicatessen"—and in a country as
wealthy as America, why would anyone bother to stick up a
small store?[30] In this mental universe, accidents rarely happen
and malignity is common.

The paranoid style was clearly characteristic of Nazism, and
Hitler maintained till the end that international Jewry had
instigated the Second World War in order to contaminate and
destroy the Volk.[31] Stalin's purge of the opposition was officially justified, not as an ordinary factional struggle, but as
obligatory warfare against conspirators, against "spies and
wreckers." The party secretary announced in 1936 that "the
inalienable quality of every Bolshevik under present conditions should be the ability to recognize an enemy of the
Party no matter how well he may be masked." One Sovietologist, therefore, commented that "the chief distinctive feature"
of Stalinism was a "quite un-Leninist emphasis upon *conspiracy* as the hallmark of the present epoch."[32] If that emphasis distinguishes a totalitarian movement from a revolutionary party, Arendt ought to have revised her remarks about
the totalitarians' pretense "that the government they want to
overthrow is itself . . . a conspiracy," since it was of course
Lenin who directed the overthrow of the Kerensky regime
and Stalin who always designated himself as the legitimate
heir of Lenin. So long as Arendt insisted that totalitarian
methods were essentially introduced not by Lenin but by
Stalin, the conspiracy parallel could not be strictly upheld as
historically valid. Hitler denounced the representatives of the
Weimar Republic as "the November criminals"; but Stalin
did not introduce total rule in Russia by referring to "October criminals," that is, by denouncing an existing regime.

Furthermore, Arendt's statement that totalitarian rulers "fail
to understand that their own conspiracy may eventually provoke the whole world into uniting against them"[33] could
have been applied to the pretotalitarian Leninist regime,
which faced the hostility of the Western powers, including
military invasion, long before the extension of Stalinist brutality.

Though Arendt's statements about conspiracy mania
needed partial correction, her general perception was a source
of illumination. The mental and moral universe that the
Nazis and Bolsheviks inhabited often overlapped. In the final
series of elections held under the auspices of the Weimar Republic, some members and voters switched between the
N.S.D.A.P. and the K.P.D. without breaking stride, especially
in Berlin. After the transfer of power, Communist cadres
readily entered the Storm Troops.[34] When Foreign Minister
Ribbentrop returned from Moscow after signing the non-
aggression pact, he told Hitler that he had "felt more or less
as if he were among old Party comrades."[35] Despite the differences between the two political parties,[36] both presented
themselves essentially as *movements*, unrestrained by norms
or limits or their own principles. They defined themselves as
expressions of the leader's will and of collective purpose in
perpetual motion. Contemptuous of the trimming of compromise, the totalitarian movements sought, through unhesi-
tating and unscrupulous dynamism, to replicate the alleged
movement of history itself.[37] Fritz Morstein Marx, another
participant in the 1939 conference on totalitarianism, noted
how intent this new tyranny was "upon securing the univer-
sality of its absolutes. Faced with tangible obstacles, it may for
a time acquiesce, but it is bound to resume the pursuit of
these absolutes whenever the resistance disintegrates. . . . It is
unable to respect the distinction between persuasion and
brutal force."[38] Though in her opinion these absolutes could

be cynically revised if Hitler or Stalin so demanded, Arendt
would otherwise have endorsed this judgment, for such regimes, she argued, were inherently insatiable and threatening
to all. Fantastic in their aims, they were as unrestrained in
their means as the techniques of violence then made possible.

These movements were so unbounded that even the authority and the rules of the state were dismissed as bourgeois
and restrictive. Unlike the Italian Fascists, the Nazis refused
to identify the interests of their movement with that of the
state. These ideologues avoided traditional classifications of
their regime, Arendt observed, "as though, in this one matter,
they had always known that they would be entirely original."[39]
The Fuehrer told the 1935 Nuremberg party rally that "whatever can be solved by the State will be solved through the
State, but any problem which the State through its essential
character is unable to solve will be solved by means of the
Movement." He added that "Party, State, Army, Economics,
Administration are all but means to the end, and that end is
the safeguarding of the nation. That is a fundamental principle of National Socialist theory."[40] According to that theory,
the state was to be subservient to the party in its struggle for
the "conservation of race"; and these imperatives led to the
effort to conquer and to depopulate the East.[41] The N.S.D.A.P.
was also completely immune from judicial control. It could
not, for example, be sued for the torts of its agents. Party
courts enjoyed identical powers with ordinary courts. Party
documents were official documents. Here the contrast could
not be sharper with the Italy of Mussolini, who proclaimed,
"Fascism conceives of the state as an absolute in comparison
with which all individuals or groups are relative."[42]

Though the Bolshevik movement also dominated the state,
the parallel with Nazism could not be exact, if only because
Marxist doctrine promised that, with the complete end of
class antagonism, there would be no further need for govern-

ment. Yet, like the Nazis, the Communists sought to avail themselves fully of the instruments of the state and its command of the means of violence. "We are in favor of the state dying out," Stalin announced, "and at the same time we stand for the strengthening of the dictatorship of the proletariat. . . . That is the Marxist formula."[43] That formula hardly resolved the question of sovereignty. Yet it would be wrong to cite the Great Purge, as Franz Neumann did, as proof of the supremacy of the party over the state bureaucracy. For the *Yezhovschina* (the time of Yezhov) decimated the party as well as official organs, and ensured that Stalinist loyalists retained control over both. Lenin had ruled through the Bolshevik party, while Stalin ruled over it so completely that the effect upon cadres approximated that of the oath that the S.S. took not to Germany, but to Hitler. The Italian Fascist exaltation of the state was thus foreign to totalitarian thinking.[44]

Such movements were also inventive in their organizational development, as in the separation of members from sympathizers. Especially in the anti-Fascist campaigns of the Paris-based impresario Willi Münzenberg, the Comintern displayed great resourcefulness in drawing into its orbit assorted radicals, liberals and pacifists; and the formation of "papier-mache front organizations" was perhaps the most successful note that Communism struck in the United States in the 1930s. In the Soviet Union itself, real power could be distinguished from shadow government, as party organs duplicated and in effect displaced state functions. Voltaire's quip about the Holy Roman Empire as being none of those three things might have found its twentieth century analogue in the U.S.S.R., as the actual authority—but not the formal existence—of the *soviets* disintegrated. In both Germany and the Soviet Union, government officials tended to be figureheads by comparison with party leaders and agents. In the Third Reich only Himmler, the Minister of the Interior, and Goebbels, the Minister of

Propaganda, did not actually lose authority by becoming state functionaries.[45] The contrast with Western parliamentary systems—and their doctrine of the legal supremacy of the state—is too obvious to require elaboration.

Politics has ordinarily involved the quest for order, the delegation of power, held in balance for the sake of the equilibrium of the system. But in the totalitarian polity whirl is king, and everyone is kept off-balance. In keeping with its compulsive dynamism and arbitrary activism, totalitarianism kept reconstituting its ideological guardians and agents of terror. The Cheka became the G.P.U., which became the N.K.V.D., which became the M.V.D., which became the K.G.B. And "the whole history of the Nazi party," Arendt claimed, could "be told in terms of new formations within the Nazi movement," as the S.A. split off into the S.S., which split off into the Shock Troops, from which came the militant cores of the Death's Head units and the Armed S.S. This spinning diversity of organizational forms expressed the belief that permanent and complete domination could be achieved only through the constant motion of the cadres, who had not a goal but a direction. "Any form of legal or governmental structure," Arendt therefore concluded, could "be only a handicap."[46] Thus the most uncomprehending and automatic forms of obedience could coexist with the most bewildering and impenetrable chains of command of any modern state. The most abject instances of submissiveness in recent times occurred in regimes honeycombed with officials operating in reckless disregard of promulgated rules and of apparent hierarchical authority. The leadership principle, which was supposed to lend all activities coherence, coincided instead with a chaos of conflicting jurisdictions and duplicated and divided power.

Because Nazi Germany was not monolithic, some scholars concluded that it therefore was not totalitarian. Those critical

of the term have had little trouble showing the discrepancy
between the rulers' pretensions of total coordination (and the
functionaries' professions of *Kadavergehorsam*—corpse-like
obedience) on the one hand, and on the other the evidence of
separate bureaucratic fiefdoms and sometimes lethal infight-
ing and intrigue. As a British intelligence officer investigating
the disintegration of the Third Reich, H. R. Trevor-Roper
concluded that "the Nazi state was not (in any significant use
of the word) totalitarian." Its leaders constituted themselves
as "a court—a court as negligible in its power of ruling, as
incalculable in its capacity for intrigue, as an oriental sul-
tanate." Other historians have followed suit, not always acknowledging the priority of Trevor-Roper's insight. "Hitler's
regime could project such an image of concerted action in its
heyday," Rudolph Binion has written, "that it took historians
long years to break through the illusion of a masterminded
totalitarian machine." The editors of an important collection
of Nazi documents have also insisted that "the conventional
view of the Third Reich as a monolithic totalitarian state"
had to be discounted as historically untrue. So widely did this
new view prevail that a recent article on Fascism in the
American Historical Review did not even document the claim
that the proof of internal conflict had discredited the concept
of totalitarianism.[47]

   This apparent consensus should not, however, be taken as
a serious challenge to the analytical value of the idea of totalitarianism, for these critiques are themselves not free of ambiguity. Trevor-Roper acknowledged, for example, that the
Nazis enjoyed "absolute power" and that Hitler "reigned undisputed over his followers." In denying that the Third Reich
was totalitarian, the British historian meant that "policy, not
administration, was effectively controlled at the center," that
the bureaucracy was itself characterized not by lines of authority but by "a confusion of private empires, private armies,

and private intelligence services"; in other words, by "irresponsibility." Binion too noted "the mess of overlapping and crossed competences" in the Third Reich, yet also recognized that Hitler exercised "a despot's power" that "was conceded to him on all sides." The editors of *Documents on Nazism* explained that, in contrast to the monolithic model the regime itself tried to project, "the Third Reich was characterized by a mixture of both monocratic and pluralist elements." Arguing against the thesis that it was totalitarian, the editors asserted that the regime's "most outstanding characteristic . . . was its lack of formal structure."[48]

One irony of this scholarly debate is that Arendt herself stressed this "lack of formal structure." She had already shown how in the Third Reich dictatorial exercise of the leadership principle was combined paradoxically with absence of an efficient hierarchy. Citing studies like Ernst Fraenkel's *The Dual State* (1941), Arendt was impressed by the "fantastic thoroughness" with which the Nazis duplicated governmental administrative functions by the activities of the party organs. It was not the "monolithic structure" of totalitarianism that struck "all serious students of the subject" but its tangled lines of dual authority, its remarkable "shapelessness."[49] Although her agreement with this literature seems not to have been effectively communicated to some historians,[50] recent analyses of totalitarianism by several West German scholars have tended to confirm Arendt's judgment. Hans Buchheim for example argued that "totalitarian rule is no uniformly rationalized apparatus, equally effective in all its parts. . . . The totalitarian claim to power is realized only in a diffused way." Denying that "the power structures of totalitarian systems are monolithically compact," Joachim Fest found them "for the most part structurally chaotic. Behind the facade of conspiratorial solidarity, they seethe with rivalries, hostilities, intrigues." In Karl Dietrich Bracher's encyclopedic assessment, many scholars now adhere to "a more differentiated view of totalitarian politics" that rejects "the fiction of a monolithic, conflict-free rule." Yet "much as we know today about the chaotic, improvised state of the Third Reich, its basic drive toward totalitarian organization and mobilization still presents the most appropriate point of departure for an analysis of National Socialism."[51] The shapeless, lawless nature of this political system—which the leader's personal and ideological authority was intended to resolve—was part of its terrible novelty.

Nowhere was the strangeness of this form of government more evident than in the juridical realm. Aquinas for example had defined law as typified by "an ordinance of reason for the common good made by the authority who has care of the community and [which is] promulgated."[52] It is one measure of the totalitarian break with Western tradition that not one component in St. Thomas' definition was incorporated in the legal process of the totalitarian regimes. In Nazi Germany, both the party and the S.S. proclaimed, "The will of the Leader is the supreme law." (When Martin Niemöller was not convicted in 1937 for his allegedly treasonable sermons, Hitler reportedly screamed: "This is the last time a German court is going to declare someone innocent whom I have declared guilty." The pastor was rearrested by the Gestapo.) The Weimar constitution was never abrogated—simply disregarded. The orders of the Fuehrer transcended whatever statutes existed, and many of the operating rules of the Third Reich were never promulgated but were kept secret. The document that instituted the Final Solution—the death warrant for, among others, over a million Jewish children—has never been found and may never have existed.[53] So thoroughly had the rule of law been perverted that, when Germany was militarily defeated, unprecedented international tribunals had to be formed to pass judgment on its leaders lest they, in the words of Rebecca West, "enjoy a monstrous immunity simply because they had included among their crimes the destruction of the criminal courts."[54]

Such flagrant lawlessness seemed to represent a dramatic contrast with Soviet proclamations of human justice and "Socialist legality," and for a while some Western observers were fooled. After meeting Vishinsky in 1935, Harold Laski described the then procurator-general with embarrassing fulsomeness as "a man whose passion was law reform. . . . He combined in himself not merely the efficiency of the able administrator, but the vision of the statesman. He was doing what an ideal Minister of Justice would do if we had such a person in Great Britain." The next year a new Soviet constitution was introduced, which—as Isaac Deutscher described it—cast "a liberal veil of phrases and promises over the guillotine in the background." Two years thereafter Bukharin and every other associate of Stalin's who had drafted the constitution had been killed—except for that ideal Minister of Justice, Vishinsky. Like the Weimar constitution, the 1936 Soviet constitution was ignored rather than expunged. The totalitarian contempt for law, Arendt observed, offered a constant "challenge to the non-totalitarian world and its standards whose helplessness and impotence could be demonstrated daily."[55]

☙

Arendt's own explanation for the instrumental view of the state that the totalitarian rulers adopted, for their remarkable indifference to its formalities, its legalities and its *sancta*, probed deep into the peculiarities of this political system. She identified another similarity in the totalitarian regimes. Far from being extreme patriots, the Nazis were not nationalists at all (except opportunistically, when wooing the German voters). The Nazis did not think in nationalist terms, like the

Fascists, who tied their party interests to that of the state. They thought instead in supranational terms, like the Bolsheviks, and regarded Germany as only the temporary headquarters of an international movement of the racial elite. There was the odd fact that Hitler, a champion of the greater *Deutsches Volk*, did not become a German citizen until he ran for the presidency of the Weimar Republic in 1932; but Arendt was less impressed by the place of his birth than by the reason for his death. Hitler apparently chose to commit suicide not when he realized that the shattered German army could no longer protect German civilians and cities, but when he found out that certain S.S. units—the racial elite—were no longer reliable.[56]

Nihilism, Arendt argued, could not alone account for Nazi self-destructiveness. For if the Nazis and Bolsheviks had aims that did not fundamentally coincide with the interests of the German and Russian peoples they ruled, then the cruelty of the regimes toward their own citizens becomes more explicable. The totalitarian rulers regarded their own nationals as superfluous, as deserving of concentration camps and labor camps as were foreigners. Indeed German and Russian citizens were treated by their own governments as though they were conquered and subjugated peoples.[57] Arendt's case for the internationalism of the totalitarian movements was drawn almost entirely from an interpretation of Nazi documents and actions; undoubtedly she assumed the persuasiveness of the parallel with Bolshevism, which proclaimed that the world's workers have no fatherland. To have noticed the contempt that some of the leading Nazis had for the German people, to have grasped their self-definition as racists rather than nationalists—these were excellent examples of Arendt's gift for fresh and piercing insights. Her interpretation also, of course, coincided with other parts of the argument—the novelty of such regimes, their refusal to recognize limitations upon their actions. Ideologies based on race or class could hardly claim to halt at border crossings, which were discredited as the demarcations of previous governments whose legitimacy totalitarianism sought to subvert.

It is also undeniable that much of the appeal of Communism has been its claim of human solidarity across national boundaries. Among American adherents, the legendary speech of Israel Amter that began with "Workers and peasants of Brooklyn!" suggested, in its silly fashion, the rejection of at least one sort of parochialism. Whittaker Chambers remembered an early Party meeting in which the mother of Benjamin Gitlow shouted, "Cumreds! What are we doing to help the starving workers and peasants of Ireland?" The impact on Chambers was undeniable: "That short, squat, belligerent woman, pleading in a thick Yiddish accent for food for hungry Irish peasants, personified the brotherhood of all the wretched of the earth." That ideal soon dissolved however into something quite different. Chambers himself was drawn into the underground as a courier in the Russian military espionage system. For by the end of the 1920s at the very latest, international Communism had become little more than an expression of the needs of the Soviet state; and the image of worldwide solidarity was replaced by the requirements of a single national interest, formulated with the utmost cynicism. While negotiating the French-Soviet pact of 1935, Prime Minister Pierre Laval wanted to ensure that the Communist deputies in the Third Republic's Chamber of Deputies would no longer vote against military credits. He asked Stalin what should be done if the French Communists did not change their stance on national defense (though they did, of course). The Soviet leader replied: "Hang them." To emphasize the point, Stalin drew his finger across his throat, continuing to smile.[58]

Arendt was therefore wrong to assume the internationalism

of Bolshevik policy; and she was forced to concede that, in contrast to Hitler's warmongering, Stalin's "ruthlessness in domestic policies was always matched by an extreme caution in foreign affairs." Whatever the truth of her generalization that totalitarianism requires expansion "for ideological reasons, to make the world consistent,"[59] the Soviet Union hardly pursued the aggressive and reckless foreign policy characteristic of Nazi Germany. Whereas Hitler, just before the 1939 attack on Poland, wanted no settlement that would permit a German triumph *without* war,[60] Stalinist Russia generally conducted its foreign policy without such bellicosity, without the fabrication of such crises. Of the five wars in which the Soviet Union engaged, two were clearly unprovoked (Poland in 1939 and Finland in 1939–40), one was precipitated by Chinese seizure of a strategic railroad (in 1929), one was completely defensive (Germany in 1941–45), and the fifth (Japan in 1945) was hardly a conflict that Russia could be blamed for entering.[61] Its expansionism, its intimidation of smaller states, its unprovoked incorporation of territory in Eastern Europe were undoubtedly manifestations of what the Chinese Communists later denounced as "great power chauvinism." But it is one thing to attack Finland and annex the Baltic states or Bessarabia, another to inaugurate Operation Barbarossa without waiting for England to sue for peace. Stalin never did anything as risky as Khrushchev's attempt to place offensive missiles in Cuba in 1962—nearly doubling the Soviet capacity to strike at American targets, this was a highly provocative act that occurred at a time when, according to Arendt's own scheme, the Soviet Union was no longer totalitarian. A year after he crushed the Hungarian Revolution, Khrushchev asserted, "We are always ready to render timely assistance to a fraternal socialist state." Nor did Arendt, beguiled by the hypothesis of the logic of totalitarian expansionism, consider the extent to which important phases of Hitler's foreign policy were repetitions of the war aims of Wilhelmine Germany.[62]

Since the postwar American policy of military containment undoubtedly encouraged Soviet caution, there is no infallible way to disprove Arendt's thesis ascribing to totalitarian foreign policy an inherently dynamic aim of world domination.[63] The Strategic Air Command made it impossible to test Arendt's theory. On the other hand, the claim that Stalin repudiated nationalism, that the Soviet Union merely had been assigned as the temporary headquarters of an unstable and insatiable movement, is undercut by overwhelming evidence to the contrary. Already by the early 1930s, explicit references in Soviet ideological literature to a world socialist order became increasingly rare, and eventually disappeared, for the workers of the world were seen as having a particular motherland. The strongest case for Communism as merely an appendage of one country's foreign policy could be found in the Soviet domination of Eastern Europe. Economic relations in COMECON have scarcely been marked by fraternal reciprocity. Nor did it show the irrelevance of nationality that the Defense Minister in the first postwar government in Poland was a Russian general. The historical record has supported Churchill's view that, while the U.S.S.R. has been "a riddle wrapped in a mystery inside an enigma," its aims can be unravelled far more easily in terms of "Russian national interest" than by seeing it as a regime trying to make the world ideologically consistent.[64]

By dismissing the idea of national interest in the foreign policy of Stalinism, Arendt was committing the larger error of disparaging the significance of nationalism. The first two parts of *The Origins of Totalitarianism* added up to a parable of "the decline of the nation-state," in which the international appeal of anti-Semitism spread across national frontiers and

the imperialist subjugation of lesser races was instigated by
those who had lost the sense of national community. The
states that had emerged in the era of the ascendent bourgeoisie could no longer attract the allegiance of men who felt
themselves disinherited and superfluous, who found solace
and inspiration in the ideological movements of Pan-Slavism
and Pan-Germanism—the precursors, according to Arendt, of
totalitarianism. For in the nineteenth century, she maintained, two ideologies—socialism and racism—triumphed
over all others by pretending "to possess the key to history, or
the solution for all the 'riddles of the universe.' " One of them
"interprets history as an economic struggle of classes," the
other "interprets history as a natural fight of races." In the
dramaturgy of conspiracy and expansion that such movements
envisaged, nationalism played little part. Shortly before the
end of the Second World War, Arendt concluded that "European peoples . . . no longer behaved like nations and could no
longer be aroused by national feelings. Most of them were
unwilling to wage a national war—not even for the sake of
their independence." The charge that their governments were
unrepresentative often managed to stick; and the totalitarian
movements capitalized upon civic uncertainty and despair by
claiming to wage ideological warfare against international
finance capital or international Jewry. In 1963 Arendt continued to minimize the pertinence of nationalism. She argued
that war and revolution were the most important factors in
contemporary politics; other forces—nationalism and even
Communism and capitalism—"have lost contact with the
major realities of our world." [65]

Her indifference to the importance of national sentiments
and distinctions reproduced with striking fidelity the views of
Rosa Luxemburg, one of the very few political figures whom
Arendt unequivocally admired. *The Origins of Totalitarianism* adopted Luxemburg's major theoretical contribution

to Marxism: the interpretation of imperialism as an incessant process of expropriation, from the incorporation of precapitalist strata within capitalist countries to the domination of precapitalist areas of the globe itself. ("I would annex the planets if I could," Cecil Rhodes proclaimed.) Consistently disparaging the dream of Polish independence among her compatriots, Luxemburg helped to ignite the revolutionary élan of three Marxist parties. In the cosmopolitanism of the culture she inhaled, and in the intensity and breadth of her sympathies, Luxemburg herself approximated the definition of "the good European" whose prime representatives, according to Nietzsche, were the Jews. Virtually immune to the allure of nationalism, Arendt was also blind to its persistence. Not feeling its force, she assumed that the fault-lines of the modern world had to be elsewhere—in totalitarian movements alienated from the concept of national interest, and in war and revolution. In defense of Luxemburg's disdain for chauvinism, Arendt asked: "What, after all, has contributed more to the catastrophic decline of Europe than the insane nationalism which accompanied the decline of the nation-state in the era of imperialism?"[66]

According to her own earlier analysis, the answer would appear to be the protototalitarian movements, Pan-Germanism and Pan-Slavism, not nationalism. Such inconsistency signaled other intellectual problems. For example, the charge of insanity leveled against nationalism is logically distinct from the case against its continuing importance. But the most obvious objection to Arendt's chronicle of the decline of the nation-state, is historical; she exaggerated the reports of its death.[67] Nationalism and its institutional expressions prevailed in the nineteenth century, amidst the imperialist scrambles for what was left of unconquered territory. The Pan-German and Pan-Slavic movements, she asserted, managed "to enlist state support and establish themselves as official national doctrines"—an observation that in itself should have suggested the residual force of national organization. Although nationalism did not exactly thrive in the era of totalitarianism, it did help inspire the resistance movements to Nazi occupation, and in the Soviet Union it enjoyed a new lease on life under the aegis of the Great Patriotic War. So of course did Pan-Slavism as totalitarian pressure was released to promote national unity;[68] if, indeed, patriotism and tribalism are antipodes, Arendt's theory could not easily account for this concurrence. Nationalism also survived the era of totalitarianism, and as the Soviet Union lurched toward enlightened despotism, Arendt failed to indicate what had replaced the dynamic of world domination. However prescient her 1963 insight into the importance of war and revolution, even the disastrous American failure in Vietnam cannot be understood without acknowledging the power of the movement for Vietnamese national independence.

Arendt's blind spot assumed even larger dimensions in conjunction with her discussion of the two nineteenth-century ideologies that defeated nationalism, that exalted the primacy of race and class. *The Origins of Totalitarianism* offered a penetrating analysis of anti-Semitism, especially interesting in the discrepancy shown between the actual position of the Jews in European society and the central role ascribed to them in racist ideology. But Arendt made contradictory claims about the ideological roots of Bolshevism. At one point she boldly asserted that "Nazism and Bolshevism owe more to Pan-Germanism and Pan-Slavism (respectively) than to any other ideology or political movement." Yet she also described the vision of "history as an economic struggle of classes" as the only serious competition to the racist movements. In identifying both Pan-Slavism and Marxism as the primary source of Russian Communism, Arendt neither recognized nor explained this contradiction. She recognized the importance of "the fanatical adoption by the Bolsheviks of the greatest anti-national doctrine, Marxism";[69] the grammatical construction of her sentence left the puzzling implication that they were Bolsheviks prior to or independent of being Marxists.

The issue here is not the accuracy of her portrayal of Pan-Slavism. At least Hans Kohn, the leading American authority on the topic, listed no major errors of fact or interpretation in his review of *The Origins of Totalitarianism*. It is interesting that Hitler told Mussolini in March 1940 that Stalin was drifting away from "Bolshevism of a Jewish international character" and toward "a kind of Slav-Muscovite nationalism." And the boundaries of the Pan-Slav union that Nicolai Danilevsky envisioned in the late nineteenth century were largely achieved in 1945. There were only two noteworthy exceptions: Stalin annexed Königsberg (where Arendt grew up) and excluded Istanbul and Greece (though, if his aim was incessant expansion, that was not for lack of trying). The problem with Arendt's treatment of Pan-Slavism was instead one of proportion and emphasis.[70] Arendt's analysis was far too sketchy, incomplete and therefore unconvincing to replace the far more plausible thesis that Bolshevism—in its vocabulary, its justifications, its methods—is a branch of Marxism.

To interpret Fascism itself as the invention of Russian reactionaries is one intriguing hypothesis that she did not consider, despite its congeniality to Arendt's delineation of the fearful symmetry of modern tyranny. For an historical work, *The Origins of Totalitarianism* reveals very little curiosity about the specifically Russian features of Stalinism. Nor did she speculate about possible parallels with the Russian Fascists' contempt for freedom and humanitarianism, their repudiation of objective law, and their effort to reconcile elitism with the revolt of the masses. But only recently have the Russian Fascists found their historian, and their political judg-

ment and insight hardly inspire confidence. It nevertheless
ought to be reported that, during the Great Patriotic War, the
exiled Manchurian leader of the Fascists, K. V. Rodzaevsky,
at first hailed the German victories of 1941, for he assumed
that Hitler would invite him to rule over a restored "national
Russia." After the German defeat, however, Rodzaevsky concluded that Stalin had all along been a crypto-Fascist who had
fulfilled the exiled extremist's own goals. Expecting Stalin to
make use of his "political talents," Rodzaevsky turned himself over to Soviet authorities, who quickly interrogated the
Manchurian candidate in Moscow and gave him a show trial
before shooting him.[71]

Whatever the omissions in Arendt's discussion of Pan-
Slavism, her comments on Marxism were even briefer. Even
if one discounts Paul Samuelson's eccentric judgment that
Marx was "a minor post-Ricardian,"[72] it was rather idiosyn-
cratic of her to ignore the socialist tradition, which the Bolsheviks themselves constantly acknowledged. A couple of
scholars have associated Arendt with the leftist position, and
some radical students in the 1960s admired her writings. But
her highly laudatory essays on Marxists like Luxemburg,
Bertolt Brecht and Walter Benjamin are misleading, since
Arendt lacked genuine sympathy for their ideological convictions. She had no affiliation with socialism (apart from an
early review of Mannheim's *Ideology and Utopia* in a left-
wing Weimar journal), and did not share the dreams of its
adherents.[73] "If I can be said to 'have come from anywhere,' "
she once explained, in a rare personal reference, "it is from
the tradition of German philosophy." It was from that tradition that Marx came as well, and even Lenin claimed that
Capital could not be adequately understood without also following Hegel's *Logic*. That radical implications have been
drawn from that tradition Arendt did not investigate. She was
aware of a lacuna in her treatment of the ideological origins

of Bolshevism; Stalin could not be properly understood without fuller reference to Lenin and Marx. Arendt admitted that
she came late to the study of Marxism and claimed that she
suppressed her unfavorable views in order not to risk lending
some dignity to the McCarthyist repression of the 1950s.[74] Her
judgment here was dubious. Not only was it most unlikely
that her mandarin exegesis of the *Marx-Engels Collected
Works* would have contributed to the inquisitorial excesses of
that decade, but it was quite incongruent with a sense of intellectual honor to curtail one's service to truth lest political
primitives accidentally find themselves in agreement. Such
dangers did not cause her to revise her bleak vision of the
sources of Stalinist conduct.

In any event, Arendt managed to correct her earlier neglect
of Marxism in 1958, only a year after the death of the Wis-
consin Senator. Having realized the extent to which the Soviet
ideology was indebted to the Western tradition of political
philosophy, Arendt intended to write a sequel to *The Origins
of Totalitarianism*. That work was never written, but the
fruits of her Guggenheim Foundation grant to study Marxism
included some essays in *Between Past and Future* and the
book that made her philosophical reputation. *The Human
Condition* was a disquisition not only on politics but on the
diminished possibilities of meaningful work and activity. Her
interpretation of the Marxian intellectual enterprise, which
defined man not as rational but as *animal laborans,* has been
subjected to severe and cogent criticism, though neither consensus nor silence seems likely ever to settle over the question
of what Marx *really* meant, or how faithful Lenin was to his
master's vision.[75] A later work, *On Revolution,* was less
couched in philosophical idiom and more relevant to the
question of tyranny. "Marx's place in the history of human
freedom will always remain equivocal," she argued, because
that "most ancient of all" political questions, he believed, was

less exigent an issue than abundance. In concluding from the failure of the French Revolution that freedom and affluence are incompatible, Marx taught his successors that the former ideal should be sacrificed. Edmund Wilson had labeled Marx both Prometheus and Lucifer, but Arendt saw only the danger posed to politics by the introduction of "the social question." For her, Marx's achievement meant the end of a valid tradition that had begun with ancient thought, which, in George Lichtheim's summation, "draws no distinction between society and the state, or between the individual and the citizen . . . Greco-Roman thinking is quite innocent of sociological notions about the interaction of economics and politics."[76] Arendt's thought was therefore something of a throwback to the ancients in her indifference to these "sociological notions."

Did Marxism thereby lead inexorably to totalitarian rule? Did it—as a unified body of doctrine, as a mode of social analysis, or as a form of political organization—possess inherent tendencies that made Stalinism not merely a perversion but a probability? It is perhaps the most haunting question in the history of socialism, and has evoked a variety of answers. The belief that Stalin was the genuine heir of Marx and Lenin was shared by the Soviet dictator himself and by J. Edgar Hoover, though many scholars have considered the line of descent far too sinuous, the conclusion too deterministic. American democratic socialists from Sidney Hook to Michael Harrington have denied that the origins of tyranny could be traced to Marx's thought, rooted as it was in post-Enlightenment dreams of redemption injected with phophetic urgency. Others, like Luxemburg and Solzhenitsyn, underscored the sinister qualities of Lenin's authoritarianism. Marxist historians like Deutscher and Roy Medvedev condemned Lenin's successor without supplying a satisfactory explanation—perhaps because it would have to be non-Marxist—for the transmogrification of Russian socialism into Stalinism.[77]

Arendt contributed little to this debate, which has swirled primarily within the left. Though *The Origins of Totalitarianism* found little pertinence in the Marxist tradition, she did write shortly after Stalin's death that "Marxism could be developed into a totalitarian ideology because of its . . . misunderstanding of political action as the making of history. . . . The decisive element is the belief in history which teaches certain procedures by which one can bring about the end— and of course never does." The danger of such an ideology was therefore that it had an eschatology which it converted into an agenda. A totalitarian movement sought to push the clock forward, without realizing that time itself would be unaffected. Human beings can act in politics, often disastrously; but they cannot do, according to Arendt, what the Marxist ideology promises, which is to "make history." This illusion helped explain the dreadful nature of a totalitarian regime. For its ideology demanded the effort—enhanced by the techniques of indoctrination and the instruments of torture and expansion—to "change reality to such an extent that the premise [i.e., the power to make history] could practically achieve the dignity of the self-evident."[78]

The problem with this explanation, however, was that Arendt did not elaborate her answer. Was the fatal confusion of political action with the making of history checked by other elements within Marxist doctrine or organization resistant to totalitarianism? If democratic socialism is a contradiction in terms, because of the inherent obstacles to the radical alteration of reality, why did totalitarianism emerge relatively late in the development of Marxism, and in only one country (and satellite countries and movements under its direct influence)? Why, in other words, did so integral a tendency dis-

close itself only through the rule of one man, only to dissolve
somewhat after his death? Nor did Arendt specify the relationship between the commitment to make history and the desire
to end it. The greatest brutality to have resulted from Marxist
political action was inflicted under a regime that offered little
doctrinal justification for its policies. Stalin and his apparat-
chiks were far less interested than their predecessors in claiming the sanction of Marxist texts for their deeds.

Arendt's account of the origins of Soviet totalitarianism involved a fundamental contradiction. If that phenomenon
owes more to Pan-Slavism than to any other ideology or movement, and if Pan-Slavism was characterized by utter indifference to economics, how then can Stalinism also have emerged
from Marxism, which Arendt stigmatized for having injected
economics into politics? The directness of this contradiction
only heightened the difficulty posed by her interpretation of
Pan-Slavism, which, if it inspired the Stalinists, could not explain how their regime converted Russia from backwardness
to the dominant industrial power on the continent. The philosopher Nicholas Berdyaev sought to resolve such a contradiction by claiming that "Communism was the inevitable fate
of Russia" because "Marxism, itself so un-Russian in origin
and character, assumed a Russian style . . . approaching Slavo-
philism." The evidence for this adaptation of Marxism to
Pan-Slavism is quite thin, however—the shift of the capital to
Moscow and the Kremlin, and the proclamation of *ex Oriente
lux*.[79] But Lenin also admired the achievements of Frederick
W. Taylor and Henry Ford. Happily Arendt had little use for
essentialist and mystical notions of causality, yet she herself
offered no deeper insight into the genesis of Soviet totalitarianism in Pan-Slavic thought, which—to be consistent—she
should have praised for its un-Marxist indifference to the
political causes of misery.

Yet in her hostility to the introduction of the social ques-

tion, she of all people disdained one of the impediments—
perhaps the major one—to the emergence of totalitarian
movements. The Pan-Germanic and Pan-Slavic ideologies had
indeed been strikingly indifferent to economics,[80] but the actual political appeal and writ of the totalitarian rulers drew
upon material needs and economic instability. Amidst the
deepening economic crisis of the Weimar Republic, as the
specter of unemployment replaced the devastations of inflation, the power of a demagogue who vaguely promised not
only guns but butter, not only Aryan racism but German
restoration, was magnified. Had the Weimar government
managed to confront the Depression intelligently and com-
passionately, Hitler might well have returned to—or even
remained in—obscurity. J. M. Keynes' letter to Franklin D.
Roosevelt, who took office a little over a month after Hitler
became Chancellor, has often been quoted: "You have made
yourself the trustee for those in every country who seek to
mend the evils of our condition by reasoned experiment within the framework of the existing social institutions."[81] Had
there been justification for writing such a letter to Heinrich
Brüning, humanity would have been spared immeasurable
suffering. Stalinism had an economic pretext, too. The party
secretary was able to introduce totalitarianism into the authoritarian system he inherited amidst a festering agricultural
crisis and ostensibly to honor the imperatives of rapid industrialization. Thus the legacy of Russian poverty and weakness
was supposed to be transcended. Yet economic factors alone
do not explain the emergence of totalitarianism. If the
strength of Nazism rose as the Depression in Germany deepened, there was no such "justification" in the Soviet Union,
which boasted of its immunity to the capitalist cycles of boom
and bust. Unprecedented tyranny was nevertheless introduced
there. But the economic context of the 1930s should not have
been as neglected as it was in *The Origins of Totalitarianism*.

Had the Weimar Republic found the resources to use effective, democratic means to stem unemployment and pauperiza-
tion, had the Marxist-Leninist party been more measured,
scrupulous and sensitive in its confrontation with the endur-
ing misery of the Russian masses, had there in other words
been different responses to the social question, totalitarianism
would have been more quickly and clearly understood as an
unappeasable craving for power, not as the promised end to
suffering.

It was somehow typical of Arendt to take an audacious and
independent stance, offering a historical analysis that did not
connect the rise of totalitarianism with the persistence and
intensification of want. She was less impassioned about the
violence and disruption of revolution, or its folly and futility,
or the breakdown of order, than about the break in the Western tradition it represented. She preferred to attack revolution, and the Marxist program with which it has for over a
century been associated, at its strongest point: the demand for
justice. But it reflected little credit upon the sublimity of her
conception of politics to dismiss the social significance of deprivation, to ignore the inescapable problem of economics, to
prefer that the collective efforts of humanity not encompass
solutions to the pressing needs of the impoverished. In a curi-
ous way, the ideal of politics that Arendt developed was an
instance of an ideology in the Marxist sense—a representation
of particular interests which in fact opposed the interests of
other strata of society. This vision of self-government was
therefore tempting to "unmask," as Hanna F. Pitkin did in a
Dissent essay on conservative political thought: "It is difficult
to believe in the great value that theorists like Aristotle,
Tocqueville and Arendt attach to political life, if, by definition, it is impotent to deal with real needs of most people."[82]
On one significant level at least, Arendt's political ideal would
most likely appeal to those who could afford to be indifferent

to economic pressures, or who would prefer that the cry for social justice be muted.

Because Arendt did not devise a good case for human government devoid of a benign purpose—like the alleviation of economic misery and social injustice—her political philosophy lacked a certain combat-readiness. In her general views of the meaning of the political life, she offered no systematic opposition to what she most abhorred and what she analyzed with such skill. But *The Origins of Totalitarianism* was primarily an historical interpretation, not an abstract treatise, much less a set of dire warnings and exhortations. Her account of the disintegration of European politics filled the conceptual frame of the book, and gave historical specificity to her despair. In tracing the drive toward total domination, which is the subject of the next chapter, Arendt recorded the legacy of a world barely fit for civilized habitation.

Chapter 4

🏵

FROM ANOMIE
TO ANNIHILATION

IN an imaginary letter, Saul Bellow's Professor Moses Herzog asked Heidegger when and where "the fall into the quotidian" took place.[1] Arendt, Heidegger's student, would have answered by referring to the displacement of politics by society. The theory of mass society has been called the most pervasive of all sociological constructs, except for Marxism; and Arendt has been regarded as one of its most incisive proponents.[2] Her own discussion of mass society was fragmentary and evocative rather than systematic, more like Nietzsche's or Burckhardt's than Ortega y Gasset's. She never formulated the differences and similarities between totalitarianism and mass society with the precision essential to sound political sociology. She may have blurred the differences in the kinds of experience available as a continent underwent industrialization and urbanization.[3] But her view of modern tyranny cannot be understood apart from her description of the texture of European social life.

The masses are those "not held together by a consciousness of common interest, and they lack that specific class articulateness which is expressed in determined, limited and obtainable goals." They "stand outside all social ramifications and nor-

[90]

mal political representation." They are the unorganized, those who—because of their sheer numbers coagulating in the great cities, or because of their indifference to their own fate—could not be integrated into the political units and class structure of European society. For amidst the ebbing fortunes of the nation-state, the masses emerged in the nineteenth century upon the ruins of the system of class stratification; the effects were devastating.[4] In obliterating the boundaries of groups, in corroding corporate loyalties, mass society weakened the sense of collectivity and thus dampened the possibility for action, which depends upon esprit de corps. Mass society engendered loneliness and a sense of alienation from authority and from government—making it easy to wish for its destruction. This kind of polity also encouraged a feeling of superfluousness, and—as surcease from the pain of loneliness—promoted the relief found in idcology, a rigid logic imposed upon the emptiness of social life.[5]

Thus, both public and private life were endangered by human beings who lived in moral isolation, in "self-centered bitterness." Feeling useless and expendable, bereft of common interest, they did not care about other human beings because they did not care about themselves. Noteworthy not so much for "brutality and backwardness" as for the condition of "isolation and lack of normal social relationships," the masses were indifferent to life.[6] Disorganization, desperation and mistrust had important political ramifications; out of mass society sprang the mob—"primarily a group in which the residue of all classes are represented," Arendt wrote. "The mob always will shout for the 'strong man,' the 'great leader.' For the mob hates [high] society from which it is excluded." The nineteenth-century European mob was "not only the refuse but also the by-product of bourgeois society." The Commandant in Kafka's "The Penal Colony" is perhaps the most disturbing literary embodiment of mass psychology as Arendt described it: "the radical loss of self-interest, the cynical or bored indifference in the face of death or other personal catastrophes, the passionate inclination toward the most abstract notions as guides for life, and the general contempt for even the most obvious rules of common sense." But while Kafka's Commandant commits suicide to verify the destructive efficiency of the machine, Arendt ascribed no peculiar danger or importance to technology as such. She certainly feared the doomsday possibilities inherent in postwar politics, but she tended to think in terms of perennial antinomies, such as freedom and authority, rather than to stress the precariousness that modern means of destruction have produced. Though Geoffrey Barraclough classified her theory in terms of the unprecedented terror made possible by the application of science, she was more interested in the totalitarian mind than in its instruments of coercion and control, which her book barely mentioned.[7]

Arendt drew most heavily perhaps from the romanticist and conservative-aristocratic recoil from the industrial order and in particular from Gustave LeBon's *The Crowd*. This dramatic little book anticipated much of Arendt's description of the social psychology of the mob—its incapacity to distinguish true from false, its immunity to "the notion of improbability," its fanaticism, its disdain for self-interest, its indifference. LeBon was especially struck by the leaders of the crowd, who were "especially recruited from the ranks of those morbidly nervous, excitable, half-deranged persons who are bordering on madness." The demagogues' "convictions are so strong that all reasoning is lost upon them. . . . They sacrifice their personal interest, their family—everything. The very instinct of self-preservation is entirely obliterated in them." Having risen directly from the masses, these leaders could at their boldest get away with anything. "Ill-treat men" at will, LeBon wrote in 1895, "massacre them by millions, be the cause of invasion upon invasion—all is permitted" the leader whom the mob has accepted as its master. No wonder, then, that Hitler was so impressed by LeBon's descriptions of demagogy and propaganda that passages of *Mein Kampf* bordered on plagiarism.[8]

LeBon's writings also prefigured Arendt's emphasis upon the irresponsibility and danger of bureaucratic rule, which she characterized as the style of modern imperialists, and one that permitted "administrative massacres." But while LeBon saw the greatest threat to liberty in the rule of functionaries of the state whose power exceeded that granted them by parliamentary assemblies, his main concern was the hegemony of the demagogues and the eclipse of rightful authority.[9] By contrast Arendt's analysis of mass society was less classifiable as conservative, for she argued that liberals fearful of the loss of freedom and conservatives anxious about the decline of authority were both right. "We are . . . confronted," she claimed, "with a simultaneous recession of both freedom and authority in the modern world."[10] This paradox, this interaction that is so crucial to the definition of politics, introduced a new construct that neither right nor left adequately recognized, though it is often enough perceived in ordinary life.

Freud's *Group Psychology and the Analysis of Ego* (1921) was also much indebted to LeBon's *The Crowd*; but Arendt herself chose not to pursue the psychological ramifications of the eruption of the masses into history, cues that Erich Fromm and other members of the Frankfurt School had picked up. Instead she preferred to "look at all the lonely people/Where do they all come from?"—lines from John Lennon and Paul McCartney's song "Eleanor Rigby" that suggest that the theory of mass society has seeped from sociological into popular idiom. Arendt's ideas were also paralleled in Oscar Lewis's anthropological definition of "the culture of poverty," whose constituents are the descendants of Marx's *lumpenproletariat*.

Neither the Puerto Ricans in *La Vida* nor the mob in
Arendt's work are to be confused with the industrial working
class, which is capable of organized life and collective action.
What is distinctive about Arendt's own use of the theory is
that she connected it to the origins of totalitarianism, though
even here she was hardly the first to do so. At the 1939 conference of the American Philosophical Society, Carlton Hayes
noted how the deracinated mass character was highly "susceptible to demagogic purveying of easy panaceas," and that
"extraordinary economic insecurity . . . is apt to produce an
extraordinary psychological maladjustment." [11] At the same
conference, Fritz Morstein Marx made a similar but more
elaborate point about "the dynamic character of totalitarianism, its boundlessness, its millenial aspirations, its fanatic self-
assertion: all these point up the tragic insecurities of 'mass
man,' insecurities magnified, in Italy as well as Germany and
Russia, by the material and ideational dislocations of the
World War and its aftermath." Seven years later sociologist
Gerard DeGré underscored the similarity between totalitarianism and mass society in that both "systematically destroyed
all independent groups and autonomous opinion." Yet they
differ from one another too; mass society engenders social isolation, while totalitarian regimes crush the atomized citizen
with "the full power of an omnipotent Leviathan state." [12]
Arendt amplified these insights by locating diachronically
the process of disintegrating class divisions and national authority that resulted in the growth of the mob and of the
totalitarian movements. There can be mass societies without
giving birth to such regimes; but such regimes, which assert
their legitimacy through plebiscites and phony elections, are
inconceivable without mass society. Nazi and Bolshevik authority thus constituted a grotesque caricature of popular
sovereignty.

    Kazin suspected that *The Origins of Totalitarianism* "left

its haunting and influential vibration on literary intellectuals"
because its subject was "the subversion of great men and great
thoughts by the social process. . . . Social attrition and despair
turned resentment into a raging flame." Nevertheless,
Arendt's analysis of nineteenth century European society has
been criticized as historically inaccurate and riddled with ambiguities. "Those who hold that mass society causes totalitarianism," Leon Bramson argued, "must deal with the obvious
fact that totalitarianism came to Russia, a backward and relatively underdeveloped nation, as well as to urbanized and
industrialized Germany. . . . It has not made its appearance in
. . . England and the United States." Bramson charged that
Arendt, like Marx, was oversimplifying the issue by "ignoring
existing divisions and loyalties within the classes and across
them, of a local, regional and national character."[18] Homoge-
nization is often the price that is paid for generalization,
though it is not fully defensible for Arendt to have minimized
the cataclysmic impact of the First World War on the civility
and stability which a century of statesmanship had made possible. That blood bath was a shock from which neither Eastern nor Western Europe recovered.

Arendt's view of nineteenth century European history was
indeed unduly schematic, for she sought to correct standard
interpretations of the period that focused exhaustively upon
nationalism and class differences. Unlike most professional
historians, she worked the night shift, disclosing the underside
of European society. Her subject was the ferocity that erupted
when the mobs screamed "death to the Jews!" in the Dreyfus
affair, the despair that led some of the mob to plunge overseas
into the African heart of darkness. She diagnosed the symp-
toms that had sometimes been too subtle to be detected by
conventional political historians, though the disease itself
would prove to be terminal. Surely the origins of totalitarianism are more likely to be found in deracination and des-

peration than in attributing pseudo-democratic tyranny to an
excess of patriotism or class consciousness. Arendt's interpretation of Stalinism as the artificial creation of the conditions
of totalitarian rule goes far to meet one of Bramson's specific
objections; even he, while unconvinced, conceded that this
effort to salvage the theory of mass society was "ingenious."[14]

In accounting for the origins of Nazi and Soviet totalitarianism, Arendt might well have been obliged to explain more
fully the absence of such dictatorship in much of the Western
world. Her theory would have been more comprehensive and
persuasive had Arendt dealt more fully with the United States
than her fleeting remarks permitted. Though she mentioned
several times in passing the erosions of liberty in the United
States, as well as certain similarities with totalitarian thinking,
she also realized that "America, the classical land of equality
of condition and of general education with all its shortcom-
ings, knows less of the modern psychology of masses than perhaps any other country in the world." Tocqueville, the French
student of prison reform who described equality of conditions
as the axial principle of American society, was somewhat less
sanguine, however. He feared that the specific demands of a
democratic society might generate a "species of oppression . . .
unlike anything that ever before existed in the world." He
groped unsuccessfully for a name that might denote such a
despotism, but it is safe to assert that such a system ought not
to be called totalitarian. Such a government, Tocqueville
speculated, would offer citizens an escape from freedom, a retreat into "perpetual childhood," and a compensating economic security. But this despotism would not be conducted
with terror. It would not be irrational in its ends or violent in
its instruments. In envisioning the possibility of a new serfdom that would be "minute, regular, provident and mild,"
Tocqueville sounded less like a prophet of twentieth century

tyranny than merely an inspiration for certain conservative critics of the welfare state.[15]

As for Great Britain, Arendt rather lamely explained that no totalitarian movement emerged there because the imperialist appeal could not compete with the two-party system, and moderation triumphed over the "insanity" of incessant expansionism. No British movement of any significance offered a program that combined conquest of lesser breeds with ideological animus against the Jews, and the generally democratic and pragmatic character of British society made it resistant to totalitarian impulses. Czarist Russia sponsored both Pan-Slavism and anti-Semitism and yet, however justified its reputation for cruelty and irrationality, did not produce a vigorous totalitarian movement either. Arendt clearly wished to distinguish the Bolshevism of Lenin from Stalin's. The former was neither a mass leader nor an anti-Semite; and, according to Arendt, the "Pan-Slavs . . . found out that the liquidation of Lenin's Russian Revolution had been thorough enough to make it possible for them to support Stalin wholeheartedly."[16]

Mass society, in chronological terms alone, preceded the eruption of totalitarianism, giving Arendt's theory its coherence; but it is not sufficient to explain the establishment of total rule in some societies but not in others, which is why Arendt's theory is incomplete and unsatisfying. Most of Western Europe and the United States fit the general definitions of mass society—they indeed provoked the theory. Yet in historical terms Germany was the aberration, the only large industrial order which ripened into a totalitarian state. According to Arendt's theory, an exception was apparently responsible for the rule. As elucidated so imprecisely in *The Origins of Totalitarianism*, the theory of mass society would have been better validated had the populations of France or Fascist Italy shown more overt totalitarian tendencies than they actually did. Yet tiny Austria, to which not enough attention is paid in the histories of Nazism, produced not only Hitler but Eichmann (they even had the same history teacher). Ernst Kaltenbrunner, the chief of the Gestapo, was also an Austrian, as were the commandants and officials who ruled over almost half the Jews exterminated in the Holocaust.[17] The fact that Austria resembled Germany more than any other country suggests the probability that Arendt erred in minimizing the force of national traditions.

Nevertheless, despite the specific deficiencies of Arendt's application of the image of mass society, there is at least something broadly compelling about the theory. Some evidence suggests that, especially after 1929, the Nazi party appealed strongly to those Germans who had previously been politically apathetic, who had ordinarily not voted in elections, who were especially isolated from communal and other social organizations, and who were likely to harbor authoritarian attitudes.[18] There is surely some link between modern dictatorship and (to appropriate David Riesman's very different use of the term) "the lonely crowd." To the anxiety already endemic in mass society, the tyranny of the modern state gave form to fear, further sundering the fragile bonds of human solidarity. Only under a totalitarian regime, with its rigidly enforced uniformity and radical isolation, with its demand for absolute loyalty and its absence of community, could the following incident have occurred. At a district conference of the Communist party, the new secretary called for a tribute to Stalin. Everyone rose and began applauding, and then no one wanted to be the first to stop applauding. N.K.V.D. men were in the hall, joining in the adulation, and observing the others. Desperation set in, until after eleven minutes, one man sat down and the others immediately stopped their manifest enthusiasm for Comrade Stalin. That night, according to Solzhenitsyn, the man was arrested, given a ten-year sentence and told:

"Don't ever be the first to stop applauding!"[19] Unlike earlier autocracies, even enthusiasm had to be extreme. Arrests for such crimes as inadequate adulation did not have to occur everywhere to achieve their purpose.

Montesquieu had earlier noted the extent to which tyranny depends upon isolation—"of the tyrant from his subjects and . . . of the subjects from each other through mutual fear and suspicion."[20] These dislocations were intensified under the conditions of a peculiarly modern form of despotism. In the pulverization of an independent spirit, in the distintegration of personality, in the loss of self-interest, in the abject submission to group domination, modern society permitted the triumph of the absurd. In the totalitarian state, the masses seem to lose themselves in selfless loyalty; many ordinary citizens seem to lose themselves in identification with the tyrant. Leaders and led seemed interchangeable in the fake tribute tyranny paid to egalitarian sentiments. Hitler's regimental adjutant from World War I remembered him as an especially "dutiful subordinate" who had never demonstrated any leadership capacities. That may be the significance of Charlie Chaplin's decision, in his 1940 political comedy, to play the roles of both *The Great Dictator* and the little barber, however radically separated from one another. But at the same time, it had ceased to be funny to see a little man become a big one.[21] Boundaries disappeared, structure collapsed. A situation in which "everything is permitted" was Nietzsche's definition of nihilism. As life became meaningless, so did death. Arendt observed that, amidst the eclipse of genuine authority and genuine autonomy, the members of totalitarian movement were willing to die the death of robots. But devoid of private conscience and conviction, they were unable to die the death of martyrs.[22]

The feeling of meaninglessness meant the "loss of common sense. . . . Totalitarian phenomena . . . are only the most spec-

tacular instances of the breakdown of common sense," that is,
a shared understanding of the world that presupposes something in common. In an atomized society, in the isolated universe that was enlarged in Nazi Germany and created in Soviet Russia, the thinness of social relationships did not permit
the threading of common experiences into common perceptions and common sense, though very many citizens undoubtedly shared vulnerability and anxiety. What was at stake in
the emergence of totalitarianism was the nature of reality itself, Arendt concluded, for with the "extreme contempt for
facts as such" came the coincident "stringent logicality" of
ideological thinking.[23] In translating her book into German,
she "rendered 'totalitarian' as '*total*' when dealing with facts
and as '*totalitär*' when the term had begun to acquire ideological connotations." But the distinction dissolved when common sense was abolished. Analytically, facts and ideology are
two sides of the same coin under regimes aiming at absolute
domination, in which "all facts can be changed and all lies can
be made true" under the pressure of ideological fanaticism.[24]

Thus anything was possible and everything was permitted
in a world in which *die Juden sind unser Unglück*—the
motto of *Der Stürmer* taken from Treitschke. It did not matter whether or not the "Protocols of the Elders of Zion" were
authentic or a forgery. According to the Nazi Ministry of
Propaganda and Public Enlightenment, the bigger the lie the
better, and truth was whatever might be believed. In the
Soviet Union, three secret police chiefs in a row—all appointed by the vigilant and omniscient Stalin—were executed as
longstanding spies and traitors. Yona Yakir, the highest-ranking Jew in the Red Army, and K. V. Pauker, the Jew who
headed the N.K.V.D.'s Operations Department, were executed for plotting with Nazi Germany. Another Jew, Mikhail
Moiseevich Kaganovich, the prewar Minister of Aviation Industry, was accused of conspiring to became vice-president of

a Nazi-dominated Russian government, had the Wehrmacht defeated the Red Army.[25] In such a world neither facts nor common sense could gain a hearing; both the Gestapo and the G.P.U. were more interested in torture than in the truth, in establishing themselves as ministries of fear. But here again the difference between the two secret police agencies made the Soviet regime more totalitarian than the Third Reich. For while the Gestapo also tried to ferret out information to warrant trial and punishment, G.P.U. interrogators were interested in "guilt" whether or not any evidence existed to support the suspicions of their superiors.[26]

If anything, Arendt did not sufficiently develop her definition of the totalitarian mentality as the abolition of "reality." In 1928, less than a decade before he himself was to be shot, Grigori Pyatakov signified the disruption of an intelligible and accessible world when he avowed that he could have no life outside the party. He "would be ready to believe that black was white, and white was black, if the party required it."[27] While Arendt labeled anti-Semitism, for example, as the violation of common sense, she did not characterize Stalinism in similar terms. Yet the purge trials cry out for such an interpretation. Even Khrushchev, assuredly without intending a special vocabulary, noted in his 1956 secret speech "how absurd, wild and contrary to common sense were the charges of counter-revolutionary crimes." One example, which Khrushchev undoubtedly forgot, was that in the Ukraine during the purge trials, he had referred to Commander Yakir as "riff-raff who wanted to let in the German Fascists."[28] Such charges, whether expressed out of ignorance, fear or conviction, were hallmarks of the madness of the era. Yet the loyalty and submissiveness of so many of the victims were also noteworthy, like that of the Commandant in "The Penal Colony." Arendt's own theory could easily have been made stronger and more symmetrical by analyzing not only anti-Semitism but also the *Yezhovschina* as an outrage against common sense. For to her totalitarianism was more than incomparable cruelty, terror and decimation of human life. It meant that the Western tradition had been broken, and would not recover. It signified "the ruin of our categories of thought and standards of judgment."[29]

At first glance this stress upon ruin might seem to owe something to Kant's definition of "radical evil" in his *Religion Within the Limits of Reason Alone*. But for the earlier philosopher from Königsberg, what "corrupts the very basis of all maxims" is the perversion that is innate to humanity, its unwillingness to subordinate its inclinations to the moral law, the confusion of morality and *amour-propre*, self-interest hidden in the folds of philanthropy.[30] For Arendt "radical evil" was literally the establishment of hell on earth, not because of the power of self-interest, but because of the loss of both self-interest and communal bonds. There can be no standards of judgment where there is no common sense, no shared grasp of reality, no congruence. Arendt managed to evoke the connection between social dislocation and psychological homelessness, between the loss of meaning and the logic of an idea, between feelings of emptiness and isolation and the willingness to make the world into a desert. For totalitarian regimes introduced something terrifyingly new in the world: "absolute evil." Though Arendt was criticized for using a "semimetaphysical" term "detached from any specific historical context," her description of it was quite precise. Arendt wrote of the radical evil of totalitarianism because of "nothing to fall back on in order to understand a phenomenon that nevertheless confronts us with its overpowering reality and breaks down all standards we know. . . . Radical evil has emerged in connection with a system in which all men have become equally superfluous."[31]

Little in social science was adequate to decipher the breakdown of common sense, of utilitarian motives, of the relationship between means and ends. Little in moral philosophy was of help in delineating codes of conduct in the Nazi and Soviet camps. Little in the Western religious tradition—apart from the fantasies of satanic punishment—constituted a warning signal for such crimes. Nothing in the legal tradition had envisaged so many "crimes which men can neither punish nor forgive." (The difficulty of judgment at Nuremberg was not diminished when one of the Soviet judges bitterly denounced the Nazi policy of arbitrary arrests and forced deportations to slave labor camps, where conditions were so brutal and no communication with the outside world was permitted.) Nothing in Western politics constituted a precedent for the astringent extremism of "all or nothing," for such unqualified consistency in implementing the logic of an idea.[32]

Totalitarian intentions and consequences were already foreshadowed in 1917. Alfred Rosenberg, the Baltic German who would soon help introduce Hitler to the "Protocols of the Elders of Zion," submitted a design in Moscow for a diploma in engineering. The future Reich Minister for the Occupied Eastern Territories drew a gigantic crematorium with an adjacent graveyard. The willingness to lay waste to much of the living world, the threat posed not only to tradition but to hope, can be ascertained not only from such plans but also in the ways that the shock registered in the nontotalitarian world. The break with normality, with sanity, with common sense, with the continuity of norms and aspirations foreclosed the possibilty of reconciliation with so terrible a reality. The process of healing was not entirely available to those who perceived—even from afar—the final implications of totalitarianism. One individual example can be cited here, as a small measure of how far the meaning of the inhumane has carried. In 1945, Susan Sontag, as a twelve-year-old, visited a Santa Monica bookstore where she noticed photographs of Bergen-

Belsen and Dachau. Nothing she had seen"—in photographs or in real life—ever cut me as sharply, deeply, instantaneously." They depicted something, Sontag wrote, "I had scarcely heard of and could do nothing to affect, . . . suffering I could hardly imagine and could do nothing to relieve. When I looked at those photographs, something broke. Some limit had been reached, and not only that of horror; I felt irrevocably grieved, wounded, but a part of my feeling started to tighten; something went dead, something is still crying." [33] These are among the reasons Arendt was justified in locating the intervention of "radical evil" in modern experience, and in dreading its residual influence.

⚎

This pervasive and unprecedented phenomenon was the consequence not only of the rise of mass society but of the specific failure of the nation-state to guarantee human rights. Only in this century has it become fully apparent that human status is dependent upon civic status. Contrary to the Declaration of Independence, equality is not a datum of birth; it is not "natural." Instead, Arendt believed, it is "the result of human organization insofar as it is guided by the principle of justice. . . . We become equal as members of a group on the strength of our decision to guarantee ourselves mutually equal rights." [34] Only through our association with others do we realize (in both senses) our own particularity and individuality, and thus do we define what it means to be human. The sense of community therefore clothed the nakedness of being merely human, ensuring not only all the cultural possibilities with which life can be adorned but the most basic rights which make human existence possible.

Jews like Arendt might be expected to have a special interest in understanding how society determines civic—and therefore human—status. Their history in the Diaspora is a test

case in toleration. Often they were protected, secure, successful in adapting and accommodating themselves to the envi-
ronment of Christendom. Nevertheless, in medieval Europe
they were confined to special quarters, economically restricted,
sometimes forced to forsake their religion, sometimes expelled
from entire principalities and kingdoms, on occasion slaughtered. The eighteenth-century *philosophes* had proclaimed
the rights of man, to be protected not by the Church, nor by
an international organization, but by the nation-state. Yet
even a relatively open nation like England showed, through
the refractions of some of its subtlest minds, how precarious
those rights could be. In the nineteenth century Thomas Arnold condemned "that low Jacobinical notion of citizenship,
that a man acquires a right to it by the accident of his being
littered *inter quattuour maria* [between four seas], or because
he pays taxes." The eminent father of Matthew Arnold insisted that religion was the cement of society, which is why
Jews could not really be Englishmen. In the far more calami-
tous twentieth century, T. S. Eliot ominously echoed these
sentiments, arguing that a truly Christian society could not
permit many "free-thinking Jews" to dwell in it.[35]

The particular vulnerability of the Jews of Europe was
demonstrated shortly after Eliot's remarks when rights once
proclaimed as inalienable turned out to be unenforceable.[36]
Neither England nor any continental nation offered a haven
for the persecuted, nor did they regard the universal rights of
man as binding. In this respect Trotsky's fate was not only
conspicuous but emblematic: banished from the Soviet Union
in 1929, he was forced to wander from Turkey to France to
Norway before his rendezvous with death in Mexico. In 1936,
when the Norwegian Ministry of Justice had moved to expel
him, Trotsky thundered: "You think yourselves secure and
free to deal with a political exile as you please. But the day is
near—remember this!—the day is near when the Nazis will

drive you from your country. . . ." That prophecy came true
four years later.[37] Arendt was fortunate to escape to France,
where the international rights of man had been declared almost a century and a half earlier. Yet seven years after her
flight to Paris, she was put in what she later described as the
"notorious" concentration camp of Gurs. She got out after five
weeks; the inmates who remained when the Final Solution was
extended to France were all deported to Auschwitz. After the
war, for Soviet citizens who otherwise showed reluctance to return to the motherland, the French government permitted the
N.K.V.D. to set up a concentration camp near Paris, at Beau-
regard.[38] Evidence of the fragility of the rights of man can
even be detected in the memoirs of so civilized an American
as George Kennan, himself an eloquent foe of totalitarianism.
After having been interned for five months in Germany after
its declaration of war on the United States, the diplomat arrived in Lisbon only to discover that half his staff would remain "in order to free space on the exchange vessel for Jewish
refugees." Kennan was more troubled by such favored treatment (after all, "the refugees were not citizens") than by the
fate of the stateless Jews had they not gotten passage.[39] Deprived of citizenship, some did manage to be admitted, in sufficient numbers for the Dutch minister in Ottawa to observe
that the United States "has been swamped with Jews and
other undesirable elements. It is a fact that Jews, having once
obtained permission for their families to join them, if only
temporarily, are exceedingly difficult to get rid of again." The
diplomat's fears were excessive, since on that same day, the
Nazis carried out their most savage raid on Amsterdam's Jewish community.

   Arendt's own experience helps account for the special brilliance of chapter 9 of *The Origins of Totalitarianism*, in
which she articulated the agony of the homeless and stateless.
Flight and exile; the loss of home, family, friendship, lan-

guage; incarceration and another narrow escape—these shocks surely deepened her meditations on the deprivation of community and on the meaning of humanity. In a very rare use of the first person in her book, Arendt wrote, "We became aware of the existence of a right to have rights."[40]

She was unable to suggest, however, how those rights might be acknowledged and the members of the human community genuinely protected. Arendt was far too realistic to discuss as viable the alternative of world government. Indeed, given the dynamism she attributed to totalitarianism, she feared that any global form of domination might well be based on the perversion of the appeal for solidarity in the Volk and in the "proletariat." She did not see any hope in more limited kinds of declared rights, like "the rights of Englishmen"; Arnold and Eliot had hinted how those limits might be defined. The problem was precisely that neither Englishmen nor anyone else saw any alternative to the nation-state; and Arendt herself, at least in *The Origins of Totalitarianism*, did not propose any substitute for national guarantees of international human rights.

A lesser flaw in Arendt's chapter was that she did not sufficiently distinguish the policies of the two totalitarian regimes. Before the night of Stalinism fell, Russians who fled the Revolution and the civil war were perhaps the most enviable of all political refugees. Under Stalin and thereafter, however, the problem was not one of refugees at all. Far from creating large categories of homeless persons, the Soviet regime sought to keep its nationals within its borders; high proportions of those who served their government abroad were killed upon their return—or killed themselves rather than be repatriated.[41] For the approximately twenty million Soviet citizens who died as a result of the Purges, statelessness was not the beginning of their ordeal nor a precondition of their radical vulnerability. Arendt's description of the plight of the homeless therefore is almost entirely applicable to Nazi Germany, which initially did not seek the extermination of German Jews and other undesirables but rather the traditional aim of political anti-Semitism, which was their expulsion. (Arendt's own maternal grandparents fled to Königsberg to escape Czarist anti-Semitism.) A more complete analysis of the totalitarian extirpation of human rights might therefore have stressed the unusual aspects of each regime. The Soviet Union broke precedent with previous tyrannies by preventing nearly all its citizens from leaving or from living freely abroad. Nazi Germany abided by all the medieval precedents in the treatment of Jews, such as expulsion. Only with the war came the qualitative leap to systematic and thorough deprivation of all rights, finally of life itself, which was not the official policy of Church or state even in the Dark Ages.[42]

The singular case of one family helps mark the decline of human rights. Prior to the Bolshevik revolution, the liberal jurist V. D. Nabokov had been a courageous opponent of Czarist anti-Semitism. His son Sergei died in a Nazi concentration camp. His other son, Vladimir, married to a Jew, got out of France in 1940 in part because the director of a Jewish refugee agency in Paris remembered the novelist's father's struggle in behalf of Russian Jews. Luckily, before Bolshevism, the public defense of rights was still possible. Indeed Arendt regarded the most consequential deprivation of human rights as the loss "of a place in the world which makes opinions significant and actions effective."[43] To be stateless was to be weightless, to be diminished not only by the loss of freedom but by the feeling of personal insignificance. The Germans and Austrians whose sense of superfluousness and isolation was translated into totalitarianism inaugurated policies that reduced others to pariahs. Those whom modern industrialism had uprooted and dislocated made others homeless and disinherited. Yet Arendt noted that what contributed immeasurably to the violation of human rights was the acceptance throughout the civilized world of the totalitarian definition of undesirable persons. What was without precedent, what not even the Jews of medieval Europe had to face, was the denial of membership in any community whatsoever, the abrogation of asylum—since the alternative of religious conversion was also forbidden. What had never happened to refugees before was "not the loss of a home but the impossibility of finding a new one." In March 1938 the Polish government declared that its citizens living outside the country would require a special passport stamp to be permitted to return. The 70,000 Polish Jews living in Germany and Austria soon discovered that Polish consulates were refusing to stamp their passports, thus revoking their citizenship. The Gestapo rounded up the stateless Polish Jews in an attempt to dump them on Polish territory anyway. This action provoked not only an international crisis but led the distraught son of one such family to shoot a German diplomat in Paris. The assassination was the excuse for *Kristallnacht*. The critic Walter Benjamin, like Arendt a German Jew interred in Vichy France, committed suicide in 1940 when Spain closed its border and he learned that an emergency American visa made out in Marseilles would not be honored. "The world is divided into two groups of nations," Chaim Weizmann once bitterly observed, "those that want to expel the Jews and those that do not want to receive them." Even a slave, Arendt noted, "had a distinctive character, a place in society"; not even the Jews were enslaved in the Middle Ages. But those who were stripped of citizenship in the 1930s and 1940s were refused the possibility of equality, of association with the human family. They were anonymous, isolated, doomed on a continent in which "belonging to the community into which one is born is no longer a matter of course and not belonging no longer a matter of choice."[44] The likely fate of such persons—"administrative massacres"—was conveyed concisely in the opening line of Jakov Lind's short story, "Soul of Wood": "Those who had no papers entitling them to live lined up to die."[45]

Such extreme situations, which Arendt barely escaped, heightened her comprehension of the erosion of social defenses against barbarism. Though she was indifferent to the appeal of both internationalism and nationalism, she insisted that the human status is the creation of the community. Rights are not "natural" but social; and what was terrifying about the totalitarian era was the deprivation of the right from which all others in society flow: "the right to have rights." That phrase originated with Arendt, who regarded it as more basic than the strategic liberties embodied in the Bill of Rights, more necessary than economic security and freedom from want and fear. She insisted that the manmade belief in the possibility of equality, the sense of human dignity, made all other rights possible and, it might be hoped, "inalienable."

Arendt's illuminating treatment of the fractured rights of man helped also to expand the contours of American law. Her influence here is worth tracing. Stephen J. Pollak's law review article on "The Expatriation Act of 1954" relied in key parts of its argument upon her discussion of statelessness. "No description of expatriation as the loss of particular rights is adequate," Pollak wrote. "For expatriation represents a loss of the right to have rights—loss of membership in an organized community capable of guaranteeing any rights at all. The individual becomes a stateless person, with no right to stay anywhere on the face of the earth." The author not only cited *The Origins of Totalitarianism* but later acknowledged Arendt as "a major source of original thinking concerning the problems of stateless persons." In condemning the Expatriation Act, Pollak opposed such "punitive denationalization causing an increase in statelessness, a practice . . . notoriously identified with the totalitarian states."[46]

Three years later, however, the Supreme Court upheld the constitutionality of the Expatriation Act in a case involving a native-born American about to be deprived of citizenship for having voted in a Mexican election. Nevertheless Chief Justice Warren dissented (with Justices Black and Douglas concurring with him) and cited Pollak's article as one source of support for the view that "citizenship is man's basic right. . . . It is nothing less than the right to have rights." In this spirit the Chief Justice continued: "Remove this priceless possession and there remains a stateless person, disgraced and degraded in the eyes of his countrymen. He has no lawful claim to protection from any nation, and no nation may assert rights on his behalf."[47] Thus only the incorporation of the individual within the political community would ensure the enforcement of imprescriptible rights.

Warren's view did not become law of the land until *Trop* v. *Dulles* in 1958, when for the majority the Chief Justice proclaimed that the Eighth Amendment prohibits denationalization as a form of punishment. In declaring part of the 1940 Nationality Act unconstitutional, Warren observed that "the expatriate has lost the right to have rights." The conclusion therefore followed that citizenship could not be lightly abrogated, for it is neither "a license that expires upon misbehavior" nor could be "lost every time a duty of citizenship is shirked." (By contrast both the 1936 and 1977 Soviet constitutions provide that, if duties are shirked, rights are surrendered.) Five years later Arendt's influence became even more apparent in the majority opinion in *Kennedy* v. *Mendoza-Martinez*. Justice Goldberg quoted directly from *The Origins of Totalitarianism* in a case involving deportation for avoidance of military service in wartime, for which Pollak filed an *amicus curiae* brief for the ACLU. In invalidating two pro-

visions of Congressional acts of 1940 and 1952, Goldberg
acknowledged the force of Arendt's observations on the calam-
itous loss of community implicit in the deprivation of citizenship.[48] This advance in the recognition of human rights, to
which Arendt's book contributed, gave democrats some cause
for satisfaction.

Beginning with the anomie of modern society, a process can
be charted that would extend to the anonymity of civil status
and culminate in the darkness of the annihilation camps.
With the murder of the juridical person and the denial of his
legal personality, an abyss opened up. After the destruction of
the right to have rights came the descent into hell.

The depth of that final descent was unbelievable, and remains so. With terrible urgency, Arthur Koestler tried to tell
American readers early in 1944 what it had meant for the
"escaped victims or eyewitnesses . . . haunted by our memories, [to] go on screaming on the wireless, yelling at you in
newspapers and in public meetings, theatres and cinemas."
Yet of course very few ever bothered to listen to Koestler and
the others, who "started on the night when the epileptic van
der Lubbe set fire to the German Parliament: we said that if
you don't quench those flames at once, they will spread all
over the world; you thought we were maniacs." Then, with
the World War, came the extermination of European Jewry.
"So far," Koestler reported, "three million have died. It is the
greatest mass-killing in recorded history; and it goes on daily,
hourly, as regularly as the ticking of your watch." In corrupt-
ing all standards of judgment and shattering previous maxims
of morality, this radical evil enforced upon humanity a new
definition of reality. Those who disbelieved atrocities no
longer had the right to tell the screamers they were insane;
those who disbelieved were no longer connected with his-

torical actuality. "Were it not so," Koestler concluded, "this war would have been avoided, and those murdered within sight of your day-dreaming eyes would still be alive."[49]

In *Darkness at Noon* Koestler himself got terrifyingly close to the totalitarian mind, rubbing against its grotesque demands of guilt and confession and humiliation, tracing how the logic of an idea compelled its adherents to sign their own death warrants. As a Communist Koestler had visited the Soviet Union early in the 1930s; as a German journalist he witnessed and combated the rise of Nazism; like Arendt, he had been imprisoned in a Vichy internment camp and had been released upon the application of outside pressure. Perhaps only two other novelists, Orwell and Kafka, were comparable in their capacity to unlock the totalitarian mind.

Though Orwell lacked direct experience of the societies of Nazi Germany and Soviet Russia, he managed in *1984* to project the character of total domination and fear, including torture, enervating terror, and the utter corruption of language and therefore of thought. In a dystopia based closely on the contemporary tyrannies of the 1940s, Orwell made the texture of "Ingsoc"—desolate, isolate, completely mendacious—as frightening as the precise instruments of sadism.

Though Kafka died in 1924, so uncannily did he convey the atmosphere of nihilism and unreason, of emptiness and menace, of authoritarian indifference to individual fate and life, that his writings became a "component element of the living world" that embraced the concentration camps. The Commandant's machine in the penal colony tatoos on the arms of its victims their capital crimes, like the numbers on the forearms of the Reich's inmates whose crime was that they existed. Joseph K. had already been conceived when, George Steiner noted, "the night knock has come on innumerable doors, and the name of those dragged off to die 'like a dog!' is legion." Gregor Samsa had already been imagined when the

Nazis designated those to be gassed as vermin,[50] and Stalin himself, in a 1937 speech signaling an extension of the Purges, urged that the enemies of Marxism-Leninism "be squashed like disgusting vermin." A survivor of Buchenwald recalled the offices there, "cluttered with impeccable and bustling prisoner-clerks, grey-faced and serious, straight out of the world of Kafka, who . . . write everything down meticulously."[51] Pure fiction had turned into a nightmarish reality.

Among social scientists and historians of totalitarianism, only Arendt can be spoken of in the same breath as these imaginative writers. Perhaps only certain novelists, rather than other scholars, displayed an equally specific and intense power to evoke and express such horrible crimes against human life and dignity. In a sense *The Trial, Darkness at Noon,* and *1984* were the most significant precedents for *The Origins of Totalitarianism,* for all four works exhibited an eerie authority in tracking the subterranean passions, paranoic obsessions and grisly extremism of the totalitarian mentality. More exactly than any other philosopher or political analyst, Arendt had, as Henry James once wrote of Hawthorne, a "cat-like facility of seeing in the dark."[52] Especially in the third part of *The Origins of Totalitarianism,* virtually every page revealed an awesome capacity to stare into the abyss without flinching and without falling. Indeed the author showed remarkable moral and intellectual poise trying to communicate such knowledge to a readership accustomed to common sense or rationality or economic explanations. Her subject was the historical process that began with the social problem of whether the Jews were fit to enter the salons and ended with the political conclusion that the Jews were unfit to inhabit the earth. Yet Arendt exposed the maniacal without yielding to it and described the chaos without imitating it. Addressing a normal world that had failed to understand or to oppose totalitarianism until too late, Arendt did not quite become one of the screamers, even while delineating the contours of extreme evil. It was her unusual combination of sobriety and passion, her flair for finding historical phenomena that were morally significant, that lifted her book above its errors of fact and emphasis and lodged it on that shelf of works that comment most forcefully and seriously about the human predicament.

Arendt herself apparently understood that the impact of her analysis did not depend only upon her soundness as a scholar, and her claims for the validity of her interpretations were not fully or incontrovertibly supported by the scaffolding of archival material and published sources. In part that was due to her subject, for the Soviet regime was not inclined to make its government records accessible to scholars. (When the Chinese Communists entered the Korean War in late 1950, Senator Joe McCarthy demanded that the United States march to Moscow and Peking, if need be, to find out the reason, leading two contemporary observers to call the proposed move "the costliest quest for primary sources ever undertaken.")[53]

Nevertheless it is possible to exaggerate the impediments to the study of Soviet totalitarianism. In writing about the Soviet camps, for example, Arendt relied upon David Dallin and Boris Nicolaevsky's *Forced Labor in Soviet Russia*, in which the authors remarked that camp "literature . . . is more abundant than is commonly assumed." They listed 125 camps. Max Eastman told the American Federation of Labor in 1948 that "the worst fact in modern history, strangely enough, is the least talked of: the reintroduction into the civilized world of human slavery in its most cruel and brutal form."[54] Yet that was a fact the trade union movement hardly sought to suppress; in completing research for *The Gulag Archipelago*, Solzhenitsyn was astonished to learn that the A.F. of L. had already published a map of the network of forced-labor camps a year before Eastman's address.[55] Historians of the Third Reich have had ample access to the archival materials not destroyed at the time of its military disintegration. Here the historiographical problem has been more one of interpretation than of documentation; for example, much of the implementation of Hitler's perhaps nonexistent order for the Final Solution was couched in esoteric and ambiguous language.[56] Both dictatorships sought to make themselves as unfathomable and impenetrable as possible; the analyst of totalitarianism, therefore, needs speculative powers as well as diligence and soundness, a talent not only for collating but for decoding.

That is why Arendt doubted that sedulous competence would ever suffice to grasp the meaning of the totalitarian experiment. Social scientists needed to understand that "limitations which usually are thought to be inherent in the human condition could be transcended, that behavior patterns and motives which usually are identified . . . with human psychology in general are abolished or play a quite secondary role." Under totalitarian regimes, she added, "objective necessities conceived as the ingredients of reality itself, adjustment to which seems a mere question of elementary sanity, could be neglected." Social scientists and other normal men and women are bound to recoil with baffled incomprehension before "complete senselessness . . . insane consistency . . . [and] unprecedented crimes for the sake of . . . ideology."[57] Such acts and motives not only sicken; they overwhelm the imagination and maddeningly frustrate the effort to comprehend them.

When Bruno Bettelheim tried to explain to his American professional colleagues what he had observed at Buchenwald and Dachau, he confronted the failure of the normal world to pay heed even when the screamer was a peer writing with some authority. His article, "Individual and Mass Behavior in Extreme Situations," was finished in 1942, but was rejected for over a year by psychiatric and psychoanalytic journals.

Editors assumed Bettelheim was exaggerating. They wondered why he had not kept written records while he was an
inmate. They regretted that his data were unverifiable. They
noted that his observations could not have been replicated.
They informed him that their readers would find his article
too baffling to be acceptable, even if he were not inflating the
horror of what he had undergone and witnessed.[58]

Moreover, social science was not designed to accommodate
the dreadful reality of the death camps, where there was no
surcease from suffering, where the worst nightmares were
preferable to the daily actuality of the inmates, where there
was no warrant for the hope of redemption. "The totalitarian
hell proves only that the power of man is greater than . . .
[anyone] ever dared to think," Arendt asserted, "and that man
can realize hellish fantasies without making the sky fall or the
earth open." In Rolf Hochhuth's historical tragedy and Christian drama, *The Deputy*, this horror is embodied in the character of The Doctor, based on the mephitic Joseph Mengele
of Auschwitz, who accepts responsibility for completely un-
pardonable crimes and defies God to respond to the slaughter
of the innocents: "I've ventured what no man/has ever ventured since the beginning of the world./I took the vow to
challenge the Old Gent,/to provoke Him so limitlessly/that
He would have to give an answer. . . . Well, hear the answer:
not a peep. . . ." From the heavens was only silence and no
promise of divine judgment. No wonder then that the poet
Paul Celan, who was saved as a child from a labor camp even
as his parents were being murdered in a death camp, wrote
that the victims didn't pray to God but for God ("nicht *an*
Gott aber *für* Gott"). For those who dared to imagine surviving, no retribution would have seemed possible, no act of
revenge adequate. Therefore, Arendt paraphrased Yeats, "the
worst have lost their fear and the best have lost their hope."[59]

In seeking to conjure up the images of this utter desolation, those who have written about the camps—Soviet as well as Nazi—have made hell the most recurrent motif. However overused in common speech, no other component of our vocabulary can begin to suggest the terror. Both Arendt and George Kennan located the Soviet labor camps as a region between earth and hell, while the Nazi camps were hell "in the most literal sense . . . in which the whole of life was thoroughly and systematically organized with a view to the greatest possible torment."[60] Only in the most frenzied and ghastly efforts of imagination—the medieval paintings of hell—was there anything comparable to what the inmates endured.[61] Hell was no longer a religious doctrine, a folk superstition, a sadomasochistic fantasy. It was actuality. For in the camps, Terrence Des Pres concluded, "the whole of life's demonic undertow has found, at last, its specific image."[62]

A friend of Albert Speer's warned him "never to accept an invitation to inspect a concentration camp in Upper Silesia. Never, under any circumstances." Not only was it impermissible to describe, Speer was told; it was impossible to describe. The camp was Auschwitz. Those who somehow managed to survive had difficulty crediting the reality of what they had barely lived through. Even those who had suffered in purgatory could not believe the testimony from hell. In 1942, after having spent five years in the Soviet camp in Karaganda and in the Nazi concentration camp at Ravensbrueck, Margarete Buber-Neumann simply could not believe the first report she heard of what was happening in Auschwitz. It was natural and common for the survivor, returning to the outside world, to be "assailed by doubts with regard to his own truthfulness, as though he had mistaken a nightmare for reality." No wonder then that the survivor was ordinarily defeated by the effort to understand and communicate the actuality of the camps. Describing the Gulag archipelago, Solzhenitsyn realized that

"Europe, of course, won't believe it. Not until Europe itself *serves time* will she believe it."[63]

Arendt explained the difficulty of understanding the "other kingdom," which "can never be fully embraced by the imagination," because "it stands outside of life and death." It was, in Rousset's description, "a universe apart, totally cut off, the weird kingdom of an unlikely fatality," another planet, a "phantom world" of the living dead, of dead souls. In the German camps they were known as *Muselmänner*, or Moslems, in the Russian camps as *dokhodyagi* (goners). Those who died generally did so without rage or caring; those who lived were marked by "complete extinction of feeling." Death, though painful, was robbed of its sting, just as life was devoid of purpose and value. In this "atmosphere of madness and unreality," both life and death seemed equally impersonal and meaningless, equally anonymous and irrelevant. Arendt added: "The status of the inmates in the world of the living, where nobody is supposed to know if they are alive or dead, is such that it is as though they had never been born."[64] This observation was reinforced by Jakov Lind, who escaped the Final Solution by passing as an Aryan: "We all exist by miracle or coincidence. . . . The human condition is to let others die and go on *as if* nothing had happened, the *as if* that accepts such a condition is the human part of it." Nadezhda Mandelstam could not pretend that nothing had happened when her husband was sent away, and recalled what the totalitarian system demanded: "A person can be considered dead from the moment he was sent to a camp. . . . This meant he vanished so completely that it was regarded as tantamount to physical death. Nobody bothered to tell a man's relatives when he died in camp or prison: you regarded yourself as a widow or orphan from the moment of his arrest." In a sense Nadezhda Mandelstam was lucky; when a package she had mailed her husband was returned, she surmised that he was dead.[65]

Arendt concluded that the real point of the camps was not suffering, however intense and pervasive, but oblivion. She argued that when the S.S. replaced the S.A. as the rulers of hell, the rabid sadistic brutality that had decimated the population in the early years was replaced by "an absolutely cold and systematic destruction of human bodies, calculated to destroy human dignity; death was avoided or postponed indefinitely."[66] In fact sheer delight in gratuitous and wanton cruelty, which typified the vindictively deranged S.A., was quite common in the camps till the end, as the evidence even in Rousset's memoir showed. Both the dead and the dying, however, were swallowed up in a universe of nihilism and superfluousness that was shrouded in secrecy and mystery, under "night and fog." But the inmates were not only cut off from the outside world of the living; they were also severed from one another. Pain, Arendt wrote elsewhere, is "the most private and least communicable" of all human experiences, the most difficult for other persons to assimilate. The purpose of all that pain, Solzhenitsyn wrote, was to crush the *zek*'s body and spirit "once and for all and to cut him off from all others once and for all." Having survived Nazi camps, Rousset memorialized "the hundreds of thousands of us . . . living in absolute solitude." In this world of extreme isolation and universal pain, bereft of human solidarity, where "murder is as impersonal as the squashing of a gnat," martyrdom was impossible.[67]

This futility comprised one of the major themes of Arendt's writings on the subject of totalitarianism. Her first attempt to define the similarity of the Nazi and Stalinist systems had insisted on their abolition of martyrdom—which in the Greek meant to bear witness. "One of the discoveries of totalitarian governments," she wrote half a year before her death, "was the method of digging giant holes in which to bury unwelcome facts and events, a gigantic enterprise which could be achieved only by killing millions of people who had been the actors or the witnesses of the past. For the past was condemned to be forgotten as though it had never been."[68] Sometimes the "holes of oblivion" were the actual graves of the victims, like the ravine at Babi Yar or in the forest at Katyn. More often the victims simply disappeared into the Arctic night, or left no traces other than ashes, or the mountain of shoes that Edward R. Murrow, after the liberation of Buchenwald, had tried to describe to radio listeners. Totalitarian murder was nothing if not complete. Prior to his own suicide, Goebbels had his wife and six children killed. Stalin had Kirov assassinated (possibly), then had Kirov's murderer and bodyguard shot, then had those who had killed the bodyguard also killed. But Arendt noted that the conventional murderer, whether criminal or political, "leaves behind him a corpse; and although he tries to efface the traces of his own identity, he has no power to erase the identity of his victim from the memory of the surviving world."[69] But that was the accomplishment of totalitarianism. After Auschwitz, Majdanek and Treblinka, the most lethal of Nazi death camps was Belzec, where about 600,000 persons were massacred. There was only one known survivor.

As always, Arendt struck off revealing distinctions and discriminations, but much evidence could also controvert her judgments. The Nazi intention to kill the Jews had priority over shrouding them in oblivion, which is why over a million Jews died of starvation and disease before deportation to the camps and about a million more were murdered in the open by *Einsatzgruppen*. Those sent to the camps were often gassed immediately, without any records being kept; it was simply false to generalize that under the S.S. "death was avoided or postponed indefinitely." Nor did it make much sense to stress the oblivion of the camps as more horrible than the suffering within, since these purposes were not inconsistent. For both the Nazi and Soviet systems deliberately and indiscriminately mixed "political" and "racial" prisoners with ordinary criminals and sadists, thus ensuring the prevalence of the worst elements of humanity and the triumph of the most primitive antisocial impulses. In the Stalinist camps, it was common for the gangs of degraded criminals to play cards for the prize of a political inmate's limb, or organ, or life. The Gulag was indeed, as Karl Jaspers said of the Third Reich, a *Verbrecher-staat* (criminal state).[70] The ineffable cruelty that was essential to the Nazi system should not obscure the fact that torture and torment were integral to the Soviet labor camps as well, where the living conditions may have been more desperate than those the Nazis granted their victims.[71] In the Gulag archipelago, suffering was no less conscious a program than oblivion. Arendt was right to underscore the destruction of human and communal feeling, but a more balanced judgment would have to incorporate evidence of social bonds that remained, the threads of friendship and family that remained intact even under the most unspeakable circumstances. Though not accounted for in Arendt's analysis, the ties of community, however fragile, however tenuous, did not entirely disappear.[72]

The issue of martyrdom is more complicated. Looking at that mountain of shoes, Edward R. Murrow thought it possible to imagine a person, a few persons, who once wore those shoes; but he could not imagine beyond that, and suspected that his listeners would be utterly unable to grasp the sheer enormity of such crimes ("I pray you to believe what I have said").[73] But on such a scale, the very meaning and importance of death had dissolved, the capacity of mourners to weep for the deceased strained past the breaking point. Neither consciousness nor conscience could absorb the shock that, as Eliot wrote in the aftermath of World War I, "death had undone so many." In what was known as the civilized world, more outrage was registered when forty-five Jews were killed in Kishinev in 1903, or when the nurse Edith Cavell was executed in Belgium in 1914, than when eleven million Jews and non-Jews were killed by the Nazis in the camps, ghettos and ravines of Europe. Koestler screamed in vain because there were too many to be saved. After the war there were too many to be remembered.

But the problem of understanding victimhood was more than that of scale. Surely only a minority, however significant, of the Jews whom the Nazis murdered died in their own eyes *al kiddush ha-shem* (for the sanctification of the name of God); and in any event they would have been exterminated even had they renounced their faith. Since the Jews were given no choice whether or not to die for the sake of religion or conviction, it is rather difficult to see them as direct descendants of those who died because of what they believed. The victims of Nazi racism, Bettelheim has argued, were therefore not martyrs; they were just killed.[74] The contrary view was expressed by the State of Israel, which granted posthumous citizenship to the six million and which established Yad Vashem as a Martyrs' and Heroes' Remembrance Authority. Maurice Samuel asserted that the six million "too have testified, even if reluctantly or uncomprehendingly, with their lives. They were at least the witnesses to the fidelity of their fathers, who imposed their Jewish identity on them." However consoling the latter view, it flies in the face of the historical data. In some cases the actual fathers of the victims wished through conversion to impose the opposite of Jewish identity upon their children. They were killed anyway. In the second century, as he was being tortured by the Romans, Rabbi Akiba knew why and for what principles he was dying. Could the same be said for the Christian grandsons of Bismarck's banker

Bleichröder, pleading with an unrelenting Eichmann to be spared deportation to the East?[75] That made the Holocaust historically distinct. Even the Armenians could have escaped slaughter at the hands of the Turks by conversion to Islam.

Since totalitarianism made martyrdom virtually impossible, Arendt provided an explanation that differed from Bettelheim's. She claimed that those holes of oblivion simply swallowed up all traces of the living. Here too she was wrong, for even in the massive anonymity of the Nazi brutality, some names have survived beyond the circle of family mourners: Hannah Senesh, Edith Stein, Marc Bloch, Jean Moulin, Dietrich Bonhoeffer, Theodor Lessing, Hans and Sophie Scholl of the White Rose. Perhaps these names are not widely known, and in any event even a longer list would be pitifully short. But special notice should be taken of Anne Frank, whose diary has been translated into forty languages and dialects. It has been estimated that sixty million people have either read the diary, or attended the play or have seen the film based on the book. "Her voice was preserved out of the millions that were silenced, this voice no louder than a child's whisper," Anne Frank's biographer wrote. "It has outlasted the shouts of the murderers and has soared above the voice of time."[76] Written so soon after the Holocaust, *The Origins of Totalitarianism* could not have taken into account the discovery of the diaries of Chaim Kaplan, Emanuel Ringelblum and others. Even at Auschwitz the *Sonderkommando* who delivered the corpses from the gas chambers to the crematoria miraculously managed to write down and hide reports of what they had witnessed. Survivors of Bergen-Belsen formed an organization to commemorate those who perished; and in Israel *Yizkor* books have been published about many of the communities—and their members—from the vanished world of East European Jewry.[77] Many thousands of names have in fact been preserved.

After the Eichmann trial Arendt wisely changed her mind, commenting that the Nazis' "efforts to let their opponents 'disappear in silent anonymity' were in vain. The holes of oblivion do not exist. Nothing human is that perfect, and there are simply too many people in the world to make oblivion possible." Someone, she insisted, "will always be alive to tell the story." That is scant comfort, but Arendt's reassurance gave precise and fresh meaning to Walter Benjamin's statement that "it is only for the sake of the hopeless that hope has been given to us."[78] After the final revised edition of *The Origins of Totalitarianism* was published in 1966, the horror of Stalinism was often recorded in dissident literature, usually in the form of *samizdat*. *The Gulag Archipelago* is the most spectacular, the most ferocious and the most comprehensive of the efforts to fill the holes of oblivion and ensure that the victims of totalitarianism did not die in vain. Other very piercing works were written by survivors of the camps and prisons (Evgenia Ginzburg, Joseph Berger, Lev Kopelev, Pyotr Yakir) or their relatives (Nadezhda Mandelstam, Roy Medvedev). Only a portion of this vast literature has been translated into English. Nor was getting the news out confined to Russia. Rudolf Margolius survived Dachau to become a high official in the Czech Communist government, and was executed after the anti-Semitic purge trials in 1952. His wife, a survivor of Auschwitz, received a death certificate three years later, with the place of burial left blank.[79] But she fled Czechoslovakia in 1968; and, like the survivors of the purge trials Artur London and Eugen Loebl, Heda Kovály lived long enough to tell the story. Such books generally require prodigious feats of memory and reconstruction, thus fulfilling what Lao Tse regarded as the first task of politics: "the rectification of names."

What was utterly dreadful about totalitarianism, what it sought to accomplish in its central institution—the annihilation camp—was to alter the human condition itself. After ravaging the bonds of community, after isolating the victim, after destroying his juridical and moral personality, the physical destruction of the individual was not difficult to achieve. In implicating the inmates of the camps in the organization and goals of the Nazi regime, in blurring the line between murderers and victims by making so many inmates into accomplices, these "ghastly marionettes with human faces" could be forced as readily to kill others (at least indirectly) as to be marched off passively to their own deaths.[80] The Nazi commandment was thereby obeyed: Thou shalt kill. The Stalinist commandment was: Thou shalt bear false witness—which, in the context of the Soviet penal system, amounted to the same thing as murder. Realizing the infinite possibilities of torture and bestiality, the Nazis reduced their victims to *Untermenschen*, creatures who could no longer be recognized as human. In the Soviet system, citizens were required to inform; and through false confession, many of the victims were forced to put the seal on their own deaths. Forced to denounce his superior as well as himself, the economist I. I. Rubin "understood perfectly well," his sister recalled, "that by his 'confession' he had put an end to his life as an honorable, uncorrupted worker. . . . But that was not the main thing: the main thing was that he was destroyed as a man."[81]

What totalitarianism sought to crush was more than body and spirit, more even than the lives of multitudes. It tried to extirpate the possibility of creating something new in the world, which was the obverse of the terrible novelty of totalitarianism. At the end of the revised edition of her book, Arendt quoted St. Augustine: *Initium ut esset homo creatus est* ("that a beginning be made man was created"). For one of the recurrent themes of her political thought was this sense that "beginning, before it becomes a historical event, is the supreme capacity of man; politically, it is identical with man's freedom." Action, she proclaimed, is possible only through the establishment of community, upon the confirmation of one's own identity through others. To be isolated is to be incapable of action and therefore deprived of freedom. The S.S. had bound the thighs of pregnant women, for totalitarianism intended to make of the earth a wasteland "before a new beginning . . . had time to assert itself," before the faith that Arendt had in natality could be realized. That is why tyrants, according to Montesquieu, sought to isolate their subjects, and why the totalitarian regimes, according to Arendt, sought to annihilate the spontaneity which is "man's power to begin something new out of his own resources."[82]

Had totalitarianism extended itself across the globe, the danger to humanity would have been even more frightening than might have been suspected. Arendt was quite specific about what she meant: "Human nature as such is at stake." Totalitarianism aimed not only to snuff out the lives of so many with such maximum pain, but also to transform human nature. Just as the adherents of totalitarian movements were willing to die the deaths of automatons, to show a corpse-like and mindless obedience, so too the victims were to die the deaths of zombies, inanimate creatures who were no longer psychologically comprehensible. Because neither masters nor their most burned-out slaves seemed to care if they themselves lived or died, as if it had not mattered whether or not they had been born, totalitarianism had to be "the concern of all men." Its manifest intention, Arendt warned, was "to destroy the essence of man."[83]

The actuality of the totalitarian nightmare was indeed appalling; but the bleakness of her book was not entirely justified and her pessimism noticeably exceeded the historical evidence. Human nature was never so directly endangered. Only in the most fragmentary fashion did Nazi ideology project such a goal. Alfred Rosenberg's *Myth of the Twentieth Cen-*

tury had defined the chief racial task of the movement as the
will "to create out of a new myth of life a new type of man."
But though Rosenberg was hanged at Nuremberg, none of the
other defendants admitted having read his book; and Hitler
himself could not finish it.[84] The most intense commitment of
the Bolsheviks toward the creation of "new Soviet man" occurred in the period prior to the heightening of Stalinist
power, before the full weight of totalitarianism could be felt.
It was the first Minister of Education, Lunacharsky, who envisaged a "new man with a new psychology," conscious and
purposive and feeling collective responsibility for the building of socialism. Trotsky proclaimed that "the average human
type" under socialism would "rise to the heights of an Aristotle, a Goethe, or a Marx." This belief that man would "become immeasurably stronger, wiser and subtler"[85] may have
been silly but it was not sinister. In any event, Trotsky became the heresiarch of the movement, and under Stalinism
utopian standards were hardly encouraged. Because post-
Stalinist Russia has not articulated the dogma of the infinite
plasticity of human nature, Arendt's definition of totalitarianism cannot be considered applicable to the current period.
And her theory was further undermined by her own explicit
denial that behaviorism—in its Pavlovian version, the official
psychology of the Soviet state, even under Stalin—sought "to
transform the nature of man." Even though the death camp
has been referred to as the "perfect Skinner box," Arendt herself felt unable to judge the effectiveness of the Nazi experiment in revising human character.[86] However horrifying their
acts of mutilation and destruction, the Nazis may not have
inflicted permanent damage to "the essence of man," which
may have proved more resilient than some had dared to believe. Some impressionistic evidence at least suggests the extent to which many survivors managed to summon up the

resources to find their way back to autonomy and meaning, to construct new lives from the ashes of the Holocaust.

This was a topic on which Arendt herself adopted inconsistent positions. She celebrated the Hungarian rebellion of 1956 because it "sounded like an ultimate affirmation that human nature is unchangeable, that nihilism will be futile." [87] On the other hand Arendt was inclined to drop the entire issue of human nature, however indispensable it was to her definition of totalitarianism. The problem struck her as "unanswerable in both its individual psychological sense and its general philosophical sense," for to analyze it "would be like jumping over our own shadows." Moreover, she commented, "nothing entitles us to assume that man has a nature or essence in the same sense as other things." For even if human nature could be conceived, "only a god could know and define it. . . . This is why attempts to define human nature almost invariably end with some construction of a deity, that is, with a god of the philosophers." [88]

Unfortunately Arendt did not explain why the need to construct a deity is an argument *against* the belief in a human essence, since she herself believed in a deity. In *The Origins of Totalitarianism*, Arendt acknowledged the merit of Plato's view that, in order to deal with depravity, "not man, but a god, must be the measure of all things." [89] She later conjectured that the erosion of religious faith had indeed helped make totalitarianism possible. Even though she did not reassert her claim that there is a human essence, Arendt did suggest that it could be defined for individuals: "Who somebody essentially *is*, we know only after he is dead." [90] But if there is posthumous knowledge, then surely it could be inferred that the individual, while alive, is endowed with an essence, however impenetrable. And if there is an individual essence, then a deity could be hypothesized that would know humanity as a species, even though individual knowers cannot. The believer in the god of the philosophers did not herself reconcile or clarify these views on the problem of human nature, however.

Its solution could have practical consequences, as Arendt's analysis of the decline of the rights of man suggested. In that chapter she did not explain whether the rights enunciated at the end of the eighteenth cenutry were insufficiently applied by the nation-states of the twentieth century, or whether the very concept of universal rights was pointless because they could not be philosophically justified. Arendt, in other words, did not propose or indicate how the decline could best be arrested. For if there is no human nature, as she explicitly argued, upon what basis can anyone—especially if deprived of citizenship—appeal to the principle of "the right to have rights"? How can human dignity and security be guaranteed if common humanity is not recognized and respected? If that guarantee has collapsed under the weight of mass society and the shock of totalitarianism, how else can rights be restored except through the idea of an inviolable human essence?

It was hardly sound to have suggested that particular communities defend particular principles ("the rights of Englishmen") merely because particular historical communities were no longer willing to assert universal rights. Such a solution offered no safety to the persecuted, especially when several communities agreed about the pariahs and denied them refuge. Moreover the refusal to assert the standard of a shared humanity could encourage a dictatorship to commit genocide with impunity—so long as such a regime did not engage in aggressive warfare against its neighbors. At Nuremberg the chief American prosecutor conceded that what the Third Reich had done to German Jews was, however abhorrent, not punishable—except insofar as such persecution was connected to the Second World War itself. No state, Justice Jackson averred, had the right to sit in judgment on how another state treated its minorities. The implication here is that it would have been worse for, say, the British and French armies to have intervened in Germany's internal affairs than for the Nazi regime, having sealed its borders, to have slaughtered those Germans who had been citizens in 1933. Jackson's position tolerated the intolerable in the Soviet Union as well, where the victims of the Purges were generally not even killed for being members of minorities. Stalin's cautious foreign policy in the 1930s, which did not arouse the interference of Western powers within Soviet borders, helped sanction the murder of more millions than the S.S. could accomplish. Even after the Holocaust and the Nuremberg trials, Richard Rubenstein concluded, "the right of a state to define the conditions under which capital punishment will be inflicted has not been impaired."[91]

The "idea of humanity" as "the sole regulating idea of international law" therefore ought to remain a claim worth preserving—as Arendt herself realized, in criticizing Hobbes' tribalism, by appealing to a sense of solidarity with the human species.[92] If too many human beings can no longer accept god as the measure of all things, if the option of religious belief in an ultimate judgment is no longer open, then at least humanity—a commonly understood idea of human status— ought to be the measure against the demands of Volk and Fuehrer, class and party. That measure can be vindicated only through some essential idea of what it means to be human, and is not subject to empirical tests. In implicitly abandoning one of the criteria by which she defined the threat of totalitarianism, Arendt corroded the philosophical defense against the very tyranny her book helped make comprehensible.

Chapter 5

Chapter 5

🖋

A TEXT IN CONTEXT

THE problems of the human status Arendt tackled were so fundamental and suggestive that her view of totalitarianism naturally invites discussion of its place in her wider philosophical framework. Her writings certainly encourage the impression of breadth of philosophic concern. Since her vocation as a political thinker was based upon as intellectually rigorous a classical education as Germany could offer, it was possible for her to develop the reputation of a builder of systems comparable in comprehensiveness to those of Hobbes, Hegel, Mill and Marx. "Dr. Arendt's mind," one influential interpreter of existentialism wrote, "is something of an eighth wonder." And she herself managed to suggest, even in her journalism, that enormous erudition and thoughtfulness lay behind even the occasional pieces. The material at her command ranged from the pre-Socratics to the modern poets; and one British explicator of contemporary literature conceded that "in comparison with her mind, most of the literary minds on current exhibition seemed thin, slack, frivolous."[1] Arendt contrived to convey so eerie an authority that doubt and disagreement seemed a bit impertinent. She was also largely indifferent to criticism and polemics—the star wars of the New York intellectuals—and quite reticent about acknowledging her own changes of mind. Such an intellectual career certainly enhanced the view that each of her books and articles complemented the others.

Only rarely did students of her work suggest variation or tension in her thought, such as the oscillation between activist and contemplative themes. Development has also on occasion been noticed; the books after *The Human Condition* stressed a "politics of compromise much more than a politics of individual excellence." Only after publishing *The Political Thought of Hannah Arendt* did Margaret Canovan, faced with students' questions, come to realize how deeply that thought was marred by a "serious inconsistency." For Arendt was an elitist, a critic of mass society and of the popular demand that politics satisfy economic needs. Yet she had also been astonished by the Hungarian Revolution in 1956; the possibility of popular resistance to totalitarianism was a brief but inspiring refutation of her own theory of the reduction of humanity to automatons. In this singular example of the direct democracy of ordinary people, Arendt for once saw hope for a world without the totalitarian regimes whose origins were in mass society. This tension between elitism and egalitarianism was never reconciled, and Canovan therefore found it "baffling that a thinker of such intellectual power should be so inconsistent."[2] Canovan's later perspective was virtually unique, however, for almost all commentators have shared the view of the Cologne philosopher Ernst Vollrath, who asserted that "every attempt to show some discontinuities in her work is inherently doomed."[3]

The aim of this chapter, however, is to do precisely that. For there are more inconsistencies and discontinuities in her writings than have been discerned, and the claim for the "essential unity of thought and purpose in her major works"[4] deserves closer scrutiny than it has received. In particular this chapter is addressed to the relation of her view of totalitarianism to the rest of her writings, which are incorporated here only insofar as they shed light on Arendt' theory of modern tyranny. For *The Origins of Totalitarianism* made her reputation, and upon it she based her claim that this particular "burden of our times" was the most significant and urgent problem of the twentieth century. A thinker as alert and prolific as was Arendt might well have been inclined to move on to other subjects—though, in a sense, even the greatest writers usually have only one theme, which a lifetime is not sufficient to elucidate. The issue here is not her "right" to enlarge the scope of her speculative powers, nor the propriety of her doing so, but whether indeed the books she left behind constitute a consistent *oeuvre*. It is argued here that her work after *The Origins of Totalitarianism*, except for *Eichmann in Jerusalem*, ought not be categorized as supplementing the earlier vision, nor as variations on a theme; it indicated a loss of interest in modern tyranny so decisive that genuine disjunctions emerged, contradictions that could not easily be reconciled.

After Arendt's study of Nazism and Stalinism was published, she engaged herself more directly in philosophical speculation; and it became clearer that authentic politics was for her "essentially dramaturgic," as Sheldon Wolin argued. Historical assertions of a special sort were crucial to her political thinking, and her historical model was Athenian. "It consisted of public performances staged in a clearly defined public realm and witnessed by an audience of equals engrossed in what was taking place and indifferent to calculations of material benefits or consequences. Political men," he added, "were . . . engaged in a contest, an *agon*, a striving for excellence defined in terms of praiseworthy acts which exceeded normal standards and evoked awe and admiration from the spectators." The central institution of the private sphere of the Greeks was the household, which was the realm of necessity and inequality. There tasks had to be divided hierarchically, and the authoritarianism of the Athenian household made allowance for slavery. The central institution of the public sphere was the *polis*, the realm of freedom where destiny could be seized and life reshaped. The head of the household was free to enter it and there hoped to find honor and glory among those who were his peers. This public realm, Arendt wrote, "was permeated by a fierce *agonal* spirit, where everybody had constantly to distinguish himself from all others . . . through unique deeds or achievements."[5]

Freedom and equality were inseparable in the *agora*, the arena in which the possibilities of action were multiplied. Action was defined in terms of both speaking and doing, both individual and collective enterprise. She regarded politics as the supreme form of the active life because it was the vehicle by which freedom was realized, by which identity was understood and recognized, by which the threat of oblivion and the sense of futility could be successfully challenged. As the public realm was isonomic, with no man ruling or being ruled by another, equality did not conflict with freedom, which she considered "the *raison d'etre* of politics," even as "its field of experience is action."[6] The *polis* was the platform for launching individual acts of heroism, and it ensured that the community would remember such deeds. There human achievements would be endowed with significance, and the spontaneous and free would be assured of permanence. There human beings need not submit to the laws of necessity and of nature but could create their own laws. This combustible mixture of competition and cooperation inspired Arendt to passages of eloquence on the sublimity of the political life. She wrote with evident passion of "the joy and the gratification that arise out of being in company with our peers, out of acting together and appearing in public, out of inserting ourselves into the world by word and deed, thus acquiring and sustaining our personal identity and beginning something entirely new."[7] Birth and death circumscribe the human condition, but from its third irreducible fact—plurality—Arendt drew an antidote to despair.

So sharp a dichotomy between the private and public realms, such rapturous praise of Athenian politics, so uncomplicated a presentation of the blending of freedom and equality, thought and deed, individuality and community, suggested that Arendt's vision of politics was not to be subjected to historical and empirical tests. Its validity depended upon classifying it as an historical fiction, like the state of nature or the primal horde or the laissez-faire state.[8] Arendt was probably influenced here by Walter Benjamin, who entrusted her with the manuscript of his "Theses on the Philosophy of History" shortly before he took his own life. At least in writing of antiquity, Arendt certainly shared Benjamin's belief that "to articulate the past historically does not mean to recognize it 'the way it really was' (Ranke)." Instead the writing of history "meant to seize hold of a memory as it flashes up at a moment of danger"—for Arendt this meant the danger of obliterating the memory of what genuine political life requires.[9] In refusing to see the classical period as 'it really was," Arendt did not pause to consider the conclusions drawn by students of the history of Athens, which even in the fifth century B.C. permitted considerable mixing of politics and economics, of the public and private spheres.[10] Even a superficial reading of the *Iliad* reveals that the Greeks engaged in the Trojan War "for Helen and all her wealth" (Book 3, line 285), though admittedly that episode occurred seven centuries before the efflorescence of Periclean Athens. In dismissing the political value of economics, Arendt's thought revealed, but did not defend, an idealist, if not conservative stance. For the free men of this ideal *polis*, one critic has observed, "helped themselves to what they needed economically outside of politics, by forcibly excluding from the political realm those who needed to raise economic questions. What is so noble about that picture?" The chiaroscuro of that picture would hardly have eluded Walter Benjamin who, as a Marxist, was well aware of the "anonymous toil" of our ancestors. For that reason, he insisted, "there is no document of civilization which is not at the same time a document of barbarism."[11] But that was a complication that Arendt ignored.

Only one mass society had given birth to a totalitarian movement that seized power, yet from that exception Arendt constructed her general account of the dangers implicit in the *Gesellschaften* that European countries had become. Her picture of political authenticity was likewise drawn primarily from the Athenian experience. Nor did Arendt wonder why so appealing an institution as the *polis* turned out to be so fragile and so temporary. It is no historian's obligation to trace the fate of an institution that did not quite exist, at least as she described it. But she should have dealt with the presumption that the infrequent appearance of the idealized *polis* in the past might offer scant hope for resurrection in the future. What the Athenians themselves failed to sustain was not likely to be a viable goal for their posterity; and even though Arendt's "classic theme" was "decline and corruption," she did not indicate how her vision of the *polis*—with Achilles as the paradigmatic political actor—might arrest that declension.[12] Surely in her invocation of antiquity, she did not wish to make history into a mortuary science; and yet it is hard to resist the conclusion that a unrealizable hope is in fact an illusion. In using as the epigraph for *The Origins of Totalitarianism* Jaspers' "*Weder dem Vergangenen anheimfallen noch dem Zukünftigen. Es kommt darauf an, ganz gegenwärtig zu sein,*" she was announcing a refusal to yield to nostalgia and a dedication to the needs of the present that her ideal of politics belied.

Very rarely did Arendt attempt to bring her normative sense of politics to bear on contemporary issues, and her most direct foray cannot be counted a success. In 1959, a year after *The Human Condition* formulated the distinction between the public and private realms, Arendt confronted the issue of the desegregation of American public education. "The color problem in world politics," she began, "grew out of the colonialism and imperialism of European nations—that is, the one great crime in which America was never involved." This opening was not auspicious; even if the active American participation in the slave trade were ignored, she apparently forgot about totalitarianism, a crime from which she had earlier exempted the United States! Her major argument was even more striking; for after Federal troops desegregated Central High School in Little Rock in defiance of a demagogic governor and racist mobs, Arendt came out against desegregation. She saw "no basic political right . . . at stake" in the enforcement of *Brown* v. *Board of Education*, for education was part of the social sphere, in which parents enjoyed "the private right over their children and the social right to free association." The social sphere, Arendt continued, is naturally one of inequality and discrimination, in contrast to the public sphere with its principle of equality. In Little Rock those spheres clashed. Arendt therefore advised the government that, in implementing the Fourteenth Amendment's promise, made almost a century earlier, of "equal protection of the laws," it should "be guided by caution and moderation."[13]

It can be argued that Arendt's political conclusion flowed inexorably from her philosophical premise requiring separation of public and private spheres. But even here her logic was faulty. She expressed no comparable opposition to Southern laws that prevented black parents and children from social association with whites. Such segregationist laws and practices themselves invaded the private sphere, and could only be effectively opposed by superior Federal force. Moreover she advised blacks to concentrate on a different priority: the abolition of anti-miscegenation laws. This proposal, based as it was on her belief that the government was unduly interfering in private affairs, should have suggested to her—if nothing else—how inextricable the two realms are in the modern polity. Nor did she explain how the Constitution, which she was soon to praise as the "greatest achievement of the American people,"[14] was unable, by her own reading, to guarantee the rights of black children against racism. Criticism of Arendt's article was severe, with one reputable political scientist dismissing it as "a horrible joke."[15] Perhaps this first attempt within the arena of American politics *ganz gegenwärtig zu sein* should be treated with charity and its significance played down, especially since Arendt herself had privately repudiated her "Reflections on Little Rock" by 1964.[16]

A more ambiguous application of her theory of politics was her eulogy for John Fitzgerald Kennedy, who she felt "had the highest possible opinion of what he was doing. . . . And he really gave this whole realm a kind of dignity and intellectual splendor—whatever you may call it—which it never had before, even under Roosevelt." She added: "This was somebody whose whole life was determined by a sense for action. And that is so extremely rare—that is, on a high level—so extremely rare in our century, that when it comes nobody knows what to do with it."[17] What was peculiar about this assessment of the late President was that Arendt did not say whether Kennedy's high opinion of his performance was justified, or whether the various actions in which he was engaged were good or bad, once the atmosphere of intellectual splendor had been pierced. She did not explain what the political consequences were of the cultural grandeur Kennedy bestowed upon the Presidency. Though Arendt was evasive on these matters, it seemed to be enough for her that Kennedy exuded the aura of Greek eloquence and taste for action. However admirable these attributes are in the abstract, the nuclear era rendered this political ideal, with its risk of bellicosity and the prestige it attached to bravado, problematic.

Arendt rarely addressed herself to immediate political issues or to questions of policy, which may suggest how dubious was the applicability of her classical ideal to the realm between past and future in which she claimed to dwell. She was unable to demonstrate how the vision of the *polis* offered a constructive critique of modern institutional life. It points to a discontinuity in Arendt's thought that she could not bring Athens to America. In a 1972 symposium, the author of *Crises of the Republic* was in fact confronted with the practical ramifications of her speculative insights; and the inadequacy and even, perhaps, the naivete of her responses—at least on the printed page—are apparent. When asked what, apart from the planning and making of war, might transpire in the public space, Arendt could think of only one other topic of discourse. Citing the medieval cathedrals as public spaces, she mentioned "the question of God." The authority on *The City of God* could contribute little to urban studies. When asked about living conditions in contemporary societies, Arendt failed to indicate how political wisdom could illuminate what she dismissed as "the administration of things." Indeed since everyone should enjoy decent living standards, and since minimal conditions of food, shelter and welfare could presumably be calculated and agreed upon, "that they should then be subject to debate seems to me phony and a plague. . . . There shouldn't be any debate about the question that everybody should have decent housing."[18] Such a response did not answer any questions; it begged them—and seemed to deflate the nature and purpose of government in the very act of glorifying politics.

Indifference to the claims of activism was not entirely a fault, however. At least Arendt did not announce that her writings were of immediate relevance, nor did she exhort her audience that, armed with them, they would have a world to win. Her modesty was a fine way of implying that the buyer should beware also in the marketplace of ideas. As a scholar and thinker, she did not exalt *praxis* which, in the hands of the Frankfurt School, so rarely meant doing anything practical. Arendt generally understood the limited role philosophers might expect to play in the modern world, and how risky it was to be drawn into policy debates. Her abstractness prevented her work from being enlisted in causes by crusaders who would only have misconstrued it. Even during the Cold War, she offered no advice to American strategists, and thus avoided the error of, say, Bertrand Russell, who between 1945 and 1950 recommended a preventive war against the Soviet Union unless Stalin accepted the authority of a world government. "The argument I have been developing," he wrote, "is as simple and as inescapable as a mathematical demonstration." When Russell later veered to the opposite extreme of advocating unilateral Western nuclear disarmament, his advice was equally disparaged for its unsoundness and widely disregarded, providing an object lesson in the perils of an unduly schematic application of philosophy to politics.[19] Arendt paid a certain penalty for her disinclination to harmonize her ideal of the past with the needs of the present. But in avoiding rigorous consistency, Arendt was also endorsing the canny good sense of Benjamin Franklin that "the most exquisite folly is made of wisdom spun too fine."

Also interesting was Arendt's failure to draw a contrast between the Athenian ideal and the totalitarian regimes, though at least one student of Arendt's intellectual legacy found this juxtaposition a compelling one: "Totalitarian governments destroy the individual and his freedom by destroying his ability to act and speak. History and language cease to be meaningful in totalitarian regimes. The totalitarian state is therefore the antithesis of the *polis*," because Arendt defined freedom not in terms of individual will or spirit but through its appearance in the public realm, where it is realized through action with others. By contrast with the public realm, the social realm is "both historically and conceptually related to totalitarianism" through imperialism and expansionism, which represented "the invasion of the political by household concerns."[20]

This last statement involved an obvious misreading of Arendt's section on imperialism, for neither the mobs nor masses, the Pan-Slavic or Pan-Germanic movements had any interest in the economic concerns of the household. But the general contrast offered a valid interpretation of Arendt's views. Totalitarianism did stifle the capacity to speak, which is politically inseparable from the possibility to act. An early and influential admirer of her writings, Dwight Macdonald, observed that from "Stalin's barbarous oratorical style alone, one could deduce the bureaucratic inhumanity and the primitiveness of modern society."[21] Orwell of course made barbarism of language integral to the despotism of Big Brother; for in the obfuscation of words, the stupid reversals of meaning, the senselessness of the official and demotic discourse of *1984* were refracted the violations of common sense and human caring, and the denial of freedom itself. The Final Solution would have been no less dreadful had it been less euphemistically called mass murder, but the drab jargon of bureaucracy may have facilitated the divorce of language from thought and conscience. At least there was a correlation between the decomposition of the word and the destruction of men. Pericles' funeral oration, which Arendt was not alone in identifying as the most resonant expression of the heroic style in politics, could of course be easily contrasted with the public culture of Western democracies, with their cant and mumbling.

But both the maddening loquacity and insipidity of much

modern speech and the inspired oratory of the Greeks could even more convincingly be contrasted with totalitarianism. In Koestler's autobiography there is a revealing incident, which took place after he returned to Vienna in 1933 from the Socialist Motherland. While talking in a cafe on a nonpolitical topic, Koestler was interrupted by a friend from Berlin who inquired, "Why do you talk in a whisper?" "Do I?," Koestler replied. "I thought I was talking normally." "In Berlin you used to yell, and now you whisper," the friend observed. "That is all I want to know about Russia." No wonder then that the following year, at the First Writers' Congress in the Soviet Union, Isaac Babel, who was to perish in the camps six years later, referred to himself as "the master of the genre of silence." In the year the Nazis seized power in Germany, the Viennese Karl Kraus devoted one page of his four-page journal, *Die Fackel*, to a simple statement: "I shall say nothing." For "the word expired as this world awakened."[22]

Silence ultimately meant oblivion—one aim of totalitarian regimes. The *polis*, Arendt argued, was saved by the poets, by those who memorialized the valor of free men and through the gift of tongues perpetuated their legacy. The public realm guaranteed that the hallowed activity of politics would not be forgotten, for "the organization of the *polis* . . . is a kind of organized remembrance." Without Homer, a main character announces in Tom Stoppard's play *Travesties*, the Trojan War would be "dust. A forgotten expedition prompted by Greek merchants looking for new markets. A minor redistribution of broken pots. But it is we who stand enriched, by a tale of heroes, of a golden apple, a wooden horse, a face that launched a thousand ships—and . . . Ulysses. . . ." Arendt too cherished the contributions of the storyteller, the poet, the commemorators of the actions in the public space. Thus the grandeur of the human enterprise can be salvaged from the futility of a merely animal or natural existence, and can be distinguished from the secrecy of totalitarian regimes and the falsity of their language. "Ancient thought draws no distinction between society and the state, or between the individual and the citizen," George Lichtheim once noted. "In current parlance classical political theory is totalitarian, though it permits free discussion among citizens on ways of governing the *polis.*"[23] To Arendt that permission of free discussion is the guarantee of free action and therefore precisely why ancient thought must be understood as the antithesis of totalitarianism. Free political expression makes everything else—the hope of something new in the world—possible.

Arendt hoped for the restoration of speech in the modern era in the popular councils that spontaneously emerged in many revolutions. In France they appeared as Revolutionary sections of the Paris Commune and as *sociétés populaires*; they reappeared in 1871. In Russia they emerged as *soviets* in 1905 and in 1917; in Germany after the Great War, they were known as *Räte*. They are mentioned in the form of wards in the private letters of Jefferson. And as the novelist Ignazio Silone pointed out, when Red Army tanks rumbled into Budapest in 1956, they crushed the world's only free and functioning *soviets*, the Hungarian Revolutionary and Workers' Councils. Those who hurled stones at tanks did not have specific economic grievances. Instead, Arendt observed, their sole demand was for "freedom and truth"—the ancient disinterest of the *polis.* She was therefore unstinting in her praise for this "entirely new form of government, with a new public space for freedom"—that is, for the collective action that can render life significant.[24]

Arendt's vindication of the councils, which preceded the New Left's early appeal for "participatory democracy,"[25] fudged some of the historical evidence and identified a tradition that in fact was far more disparate than she recognized.[26] But her defense of the councils implied more than opposition to the totalitarian stifling of free expression and spontaneous action. That opposition was, alas, a losing cause, and could not be cited as an example of political efficacy. For the superior force of the Bolsheviks had no difficulty overpowering the *soviets*, just as the Hungarian rebels were defeated in 1956. What especially intrigued her about these organizations was that they promised to be "the best instruments . . . for breaking up the modern mass society, with its dangerous tendency toward the formation of pseudo-political mass movements." Representation on these revolutionary bodies was not based upon ideology or on programmatic appeal but on personal trust, and the councils therefore intruded themselves into modern history as "the only democratic alternative we know to the party system." [27]

Here was a clue to the distinctive, perhaps even eccentric position Arendt occupied in recent political thought. Her own profound hostility to totalitarianism did not reconcile her, as it did so many other thinkers, to the parliamentary system. She did not spurn Lenin's cynically relativist definition of politics—who/whom (*k'to kovo*)—merely to endorse Harold Lasswell's streetwise description of it as "who gets what." Arendt was not yet thirteen when the abdication of the Kaiser made a new government and constitution possible, but she never adopted genuinely progressive sentiments and never became a liberal. The birth of her own political consciousness coincided with the half-life of German democracy in the Weimar period, and she remembered the contempt she felt for the republic: "George Grosz's cartoons seemed to us not satires but realistic reportage. . . . Should we mount the barricades for *that*?" [28] She never lost her distaste for ordinary Western politics in the modern era, never ceased being a *Vernunftrepublikaner*. In this respect it is tempting to define her attitudes as marked by the political heritage of Germany, a nation in which the fragility of liberal democratic institutions

has long been recognized. The essence of her thought, therefore, did not directly vindicate the liberal democratic state,
which she supported much as an outsider, like a buttress
rather than a pillar.

Yet such a stance is more explainable as the imprint of personal considerations rather than as proof of intellectual consistency, for even by her own standards the case for parliamentary democracy is not as weak as she made it out to be. As in
the *polis*, a blend of competition and cooperation is the life of
the party (though Western liberalism values social solidarity
primarily for enhancing the satisfaction of self-interest). The
party system has admittedly resembled Mae West's diamond,
in the sense that goodness has nothing to do with it; but it has
shown a certain durability that Arendt might otherwise have
admired. By contrast the Jeffersonian idea of wards was never
implemented; and the career of the councils has been remark-
ably brief, perhaps because politicization can eventually become irksome, a distraction from other interests and plea-
sures.[29] If the fruits of constant public participation had been
as great as Arendt claimed, the citizens who tasted such de-
lights—whether in the *polis* or in revolutions—might have
struggled harder to prolong the experience. Finally, it is odd
that a champion of novelty could not see what another historian managed to discern: "The full development of the liberal democratic state in the West required . . . the emergence
of legitimate party opposition[,] and . . . a theory of politics
that accepted it was something new in the history of the
world." Amidst the dislocations of industrialization and urbanization, political parties not only stimulated social change
but also helped soften the blow of modernization and helped
meet the needs of some of its victims. The liberal democratic
state has hardly achieved public happiness, but has perhaps involved more citizens in the process of government than the
councils, with their avowed disinterest and noneconomic

focus, were likely to have done. Thus the particular contradiction in Arendt's thought that Canovan stressed is not impossible to resolve. The "ideal of participatory democracy is in principle open to absolutely everybody," Canovan realized, "but . . . only the natural political elite will concern themselves [sic] with politics and run it as they please."[30] Arendt could have assumed that, had the councils maintained themselves in authority, they would have been in good hands.

Arendt insisted that, with the destruction of the revolutionary councils, we have lived in "dark times," in which speech confuses rather than enlightens, in which "the space of appearances" is so shrouded that human beings can no longer disclose "who they are and what they can do." Yet it is one sign of the discontinuity of her thought that Arendt removed her definition of "dark times" from exclusive association with the totalitarian "monstrosities of this century."[31] It is true that the era of Hitler and Stalin has had no monopoly on the denial of political freedom and creativity. Nevertheless the concept of "dark times" was too broad to be useful. By encompassing so much, it explained too little. Indeed by her definition of authentic politics, only a few brief moments in human history have known heroic collective action and eloquence destined for posterity. The implicit inclusion of the other periods in "dark times" not only marked an abandonment of totalitarianism as the central problem of modern politics. It also unduly widened the frame of reference within which her theory of totalitarianism might be understood, and made the burden of our times seem more amorphous than analytically necessary.

Arendt was alarmed that "the space of appearances" had become obscured, for deprivation of the company of others not only makes political action impossible but stifles individuality and self-realization as well. She shared the Greek disdain for the private sphere because those who withdraw from the public realm leave "an almost demonstrable loss. . . . What is lost is the specific and usually irreplaceable in-between which should have formed between this individual and his fellow-man." Arendt was far more worried about the danger of such withdrawal than about the threat that the public realm itself poses to privacy—a term which in her writings almost invari-ably "expresses contempt."[32] Indeed, except for her alienation from the party system, nothing so separated her from the ideals of liberal democracy than her dismissal of privacy, which Louis Brandeis had considered the right most precious to civilized people. "The intensity and complexity of life," he and his law partner had argued, "have rendered necessary some retreat from the world . . . so that solitude and privacy have become more essential to the individual."[33] Without minimizing the virtues of the contemplative life that she so exquisitely embodied, Arendt nevertheless asserted that with-drawal meant the loss of common sense and the deprivation of truth and meaning, qualities which are achieved through discourse with others.[34] For her it was not historically irrele-vant that Germany was "so little imbued with the classic vir-tues of civic behavior. In no other country did private life and private calculations play so great a role." She repeated Martin Luther's warning that those who are alone assume "the worst," and yield most easily to rancor and suspiciousness. Since she believed that liberty is the coefficient of action with others, she had little notion of freedom *from* politics.[35]

Arendt's indifference to the protection of privacy was prob-ably influenced by her study of totalitarianism. For example, she had written that the typical S.S. man's "single-minded de-votion to matters of family and career was the last, and already degenerate, product of the bourgeoisie's belief in the primacy of private interest." In its analysis of Himmler, *The Origins of Totalitarianism* offered a preliminary report on the banal-ity of evil, for "he was not a bohemian like Goebbels, or a sex maniac like Streicher, or a crackpot like Rosenberg, or a fanatic like Hitler, or an adventurer like Goering. He proved his supreme ability for organizing the masses by assuming that most people" were none of these things, "but first and foremost job holders and good family men."[36] The recollections of Rudolf Hoess, the commandant at Auschwitz, and of Franz Stangl, the commandant at Treblinka, constituted self-portraits of the S.S. man as solid bourgeois, willing to perform the onerous duties of mass murderer but still in his own eyes humane, as evidenced by family loyalty and concern.[37] It might be added that one explanation for the Great Purges in the Soviet Union was that, in the absence of democratic alternatives for winning favor and fervor, older cadres were liquidated to make room for reliable young Bolsheviks. Thus power was transferred to grateful jobholders, and public policy could satisfy certain private interests.[38]

Arendt's thesis that the S.S. marked the perversion of the public realm, which had been invaded by the social sphere, was misleading, however. Himmler was obviously and horribly abnormal, as Arendt was well aware. In his desire to exterminate the Jews, he was only slightly less fanatical than Hitler; only in the last phase of the war did he wager that a cessation of genocidal gassing could be used as a bargaining chip with the Allies. The Reichsfuehrer S.S. was no ordinary burgher. In his belief in reincarnation, mesmerism, herbalism and ancient racial mysticism, in his order that the skulls of the "subhuman" type ("the Jewish-Bolshevik commissar") be preserved for study, Himmler was more of a crackpot than Rosenberg. In his absence of cynicism and in his incorruptibility, he was far less comprehensible than Goebbels or Goering. (Responsible for killing millions, Himmler nevertheless condemned animal hunting as "murder" and warned that members of S.S.—whom he initially selected from photographs—would be severely dealt with if caught in petty theft.)[39] Himmler was not really an "organizer" of the masses, who had every reason to fear him, but of a racial elite he made increasingly selective and praetorian, at least until the final phase of the war. Arendt also characterized the elite of the totalitarian movement not in terms of job-seeking and family responsibilities but of their opposite—"true selflessness."[40] The erosion of ideological militancy in Russia after Stalin's death, the decline of "true selflessness" and the prevalence of corruption, not only confirm the chronological parameters of Arendt's general theory, but also undercut her subsidiary argument by indicating that the Soviet Union has emerged from totalitarianism to the extent that the social sphere has reasserted itself. The demands for more consumer goods, for respite from terror, for relief from the constant fear and from the demand for total enthusiasm for politics were all signs of the end of Stalinism. Post-totalitarian Russia has still prohibited freedom of speech; but there has been greater freedom of conversation, which is the dialogue of the social realm itself.[41]

Despite the conceptual difficulties in Arendt's distinction between the public and private spheres, she continued to be drawn to the problem of how politics in the modern world might be separated from other human activities and emotions. Her first book on politics had analyzed the emergence of "radical evil." *On Revolution,* and especially her discussion of Herman Melville's *Billy Budd,* was about radical goodness, which she had come to consider "hardly less dangerous than absolute evil." This statement is unintelligible to anyone even vaguely familiar with what the Third Reich and the Soviet Union wreaked upon human life and how they befouled the spirit of civilization. Equally baffling is her statement that "pity, taken as the spring of virtue, has proved to possess a greater capacity for cruelty than cruelty itself."[42] Yet the torments of the concentration camps and of the annihilation camps were not inflicted out of pity—which Himmler lavished only on animals. Arendt offered no shred of historical evidence to compare the consequences of pity and cruelty. In quantitative terms alone, the total number of victims of the French Revolutionary Reign of Terror—presumably the manifestation of "radical goodness"—equalled only three days of gassing at Auschwitz. She did not mention John Brown, the American who has typified the violence that can erupt from an excess of fraternalism At Pottawatomie, Kansas in 1856, he and his band killed and mutilated five men—a horrid deed, but not much of a case for Arendt's generalization.

Instead Arendt used *Billy Budd*, a work of fiction, to validate her view that absolute goodness, which is "beyond virtue," can corrode institutions, which are made for men not angels. She supported the death sentence Captain Vere imposed on "the handsome sailor" because laws, she feared, can collapse "not only under the onslaught of elemental evil but under the impact of absolute innocence as well. . . . The absolute spells doom to everyone when it is introduced into the political realm." Billy Budd's murder of Claggart signified the danger of radical goodness, which "shares with 'elementary evil' the elementary violence inherent in all strength and is detrimental to all forms of political organization." Billy represented innocence—meant only as the antonym of experience, not of guilt. For he was, in Melville's tale, a murderer and, in Arendt's view, a political threat as well in the boundlessness of his compassion. Arendt argued that Captain Vere, the politically dutiful man, was right to execute the foretopman, the morally beautiful man, because virtue is deadly when limitless.[43] She objected to radical goodness not because it is good but because it is radical.

Ostensibly Arendt wished to keep intact the public realm,

with its fabric of laws and institutions. In fact she seemed anxious to protect only a certain kind of politics; and it is no accident that her interpretation of Melville's story echoes that of Gifford Maxim, the feverish Whittaker Chambers figure in Lionel Trilling's novel, *The Middle of the Journey*. Maxim too deemed the story an invaluable parable of the necessary defeat of goodness.[44] Indeed *On Revolution* might have been titled *Against Revolution*. Several commentators have recognized the conservatism of Arendt's influence and instincts,[45] which became egregious in her critique of *Billy Budd*. She did not explain what particular social purpose was served by capital punishment, which is shown as having a troubling and disturbing effect on the other participants and witnesses. Many readers of Melville's tale are also likely to wonder whether perhaps some unjust error has not been committed, whether the law has not been too inflexibly applied against one whose nature was so benign, whose influence on the rest of the crew was apparently so wholesome. In fact Captain Vere would have had considerably more discretion under the Articles of War than Arendt—in her remorseless disparagement of pity—allowed for. Far from being legally compelled to hang Billy to keep political institutions intact, Vere could have referred the case to a general court martial, given the foretopman a milder punishment, or let him off entirely. In a way that Arendt refused to acknowledge, British law would have permitted Captain Vere to make the distinction between Billy's capacity to make love and a mutineer's unwillingness to make war.[46]

It may well be that "to Melville an absolute was incorporated in the Rights of Man" (which was also the name of the ship from which Billy Budd was taken when he was impressed into the British navy). But Arendt neglected to mention Melville's acknowledgment in the preface to *Billy Budd* that the mutiny in the royal navy—the background to his story—

brought overdue reforms.[47] It may well be ominous to introduce the absolute into politics; but a work of fiction cannot be used to "prove" or carefully identify such a danger, and the radicalism of the French Revolution hardly spelled "doom to everyone." The revolutionaries indeed had a passion for equality, as shown in J. L. Talmon's historical critique of ideological extremism, *The Origins of Totalitarian Democracy* (which the author of *On Revolution,* moving on, did not cite). But equality is one of the characteristics of the *polis,* as is the freedom of public participation; and these revolutionary virtues redeemed—not doomed—those whom the Revolution inadequately freed from the vestiges of feudalism and (in Santo Domingo) from the chains of slavery. The concept of "radical evil" central to the argument in *The Origins of Totalitarianism* was endowed with a historical specificity absent from the discussion of "absolute goodness" in *On Revolution.*

Arendt's insistence on the separation of the public and social realms was therefore neither pertinent nor persuasive. Such a viewpoint cannot be easily or satisfactorily imposed on Melville's text, nor can it be historically vindicated in Arendt's polemic against revolution. And, at least by implication, she herself changed her mind by the end of the decade, abandoned her absolute hostility to the absolute, and accepted the urgency of intense moral claims. The occasion was the war in Vietnam—but not, as we have seen, the civil rights movement; in her ambiguous praise of John F. Kennedy, Arendt did not mention that he had been the first President to recognize the moral claim of the black struggle for dignity. Acts of civil disobedience against military intervention in Indochina posed an important challenge to American justice, and most if not all the protesters would have endorsed Stokely Carmichael's assertion that "there is a higher law than the law of government. That's the law of conscience." Yet, surprisingly,

Arendt saw no threat here to American political institutions. On the contrary, she argued, the law should be bent to permit this political expression of morality; cadres of disobedient protesters should be considered another form of voluntary association, whose freedom of assembly and action deserved Constitutional protection.[48]

Arendt ordinarily regarded conscience as "unpolitical" and sought to keep such private virtues as compassion and love out of the public realm. She argued that political deeds could not be judged by ethical criteria, only in terms of greatness and glory.[49] That did not prevent her from defending conscientious objectors as really political actors, nor from attacking totalitarianism on profoundly moral grounds. Arendt's view of the relationship between politics and morality was not utterly consistent, for the effort to separate them is inherently futile.

It was in her last discussion of totalitarianism, however, that the disunity and even confusion of her thinking became most evident. What provoked her final reflections was the achievement and decline of Bertolt Brecht. His career had transected both forms of totalitarianism; his hostility to Nazism had helped make him the greatest literary figure ever absorbed within the ambit of Stalinism. The poet and playwright once found himself in the New York apartment of Sidney Hook, who was defending the innocence of the old Bolsheviks accused in the Moscow purge trials. Brecht replied with a paradox: "The more innocent they are, the more they deserve to die."[50] Arendt's own interpretation of Brecht's remark went as follows: "The more innocent of what? Of what they were accused, of course. And what had they been accused of? Of conspiring against Stalin. Hence, precisely because they had not conspired against Stalin, and were innocent of the 'crime,' there was some justice in the injustice." She then asked:

"Hadn't it been the plain duty of the 'old guard' to prevent
one man, Stalin, from turning the revolution into one gigantic crime?" But Hook, according to Arendt, "did not catch
on," did not realize that Brecht was criticizing Stalinist tyranny "in his own teasingly cautious way"; and therefore the
philosopher obtusely kicked the poet out of his apartment.[51]
Interpreting Brecht's paradox in its most attractive light,
Arendt thus veered close to acceptance of his objection to
criticism of the purges.

For anyone to instruct Sidney Hook in how to catch the
logical drift of a political argument has its amusing side. More
importantly, Arendt's interpretation was unsatisfactory either
as exegesis or as ethics. Brecht in fact had no pity for those
trapped in the coils of the system that they themselves, as
Bolsheviks, had wrought. He had no interest in salvaging
their lives or their reputations. For one who had in *Die Mass-
nahme* (1930) insisted on the primacy of party discipline and
advised playgoers to "embrace the butcher," such indifference
amounted to a defense of Stalin. Since Brecht was quite consistent in his squalid apologetics, the conclusion is inescapable
that Hook understood perfectly and was correct to regard
Arendt's gloss on Brecht's remarks as "arbitrary and far-
fetched."[52] Arendt, betrayed perhaps by her fondness for
paradox, did not understand, and implied that those who do
not rise up against a tyrant deserve what they get, which in this
case was usually a bullet in the back of the neck. She argued
that "a poet's real sins are avenged by the gods of poetry" and
claimed that Brecht was punished by the atrophy of his artistic
gift—for after he moved to East Berlin in 1949, he wrote precious little until his death seven years later. The critic Erich
Heller tried in vain to persuade Arendt that other explanations for Brecht's poetic decline were possible, such as "aging
or preoccupation with other matters (as, for instance, running

a theatre and training actors)." But she insisted that the explanation "*had* to do with ethics," Heller recalled, "and she was lovable and admirable in her moral resoluteness."[53]

Closer inspection of her essay, however, reveals no moral resoluteness at all, and not even intellectual clarity. Brecht's career touched important bases in the history of the response to totalitarianism; yet Denis Donoghue's claim "if there is a moral circle of reference she [Arendt] is close to its center" could not be easily substantiated by her analysis of "poor B. B." Unlike Martin Esslin's excellent biography, Arendt's study of Brecht was inattentive to his personal failures; for the only penalty she believed he paid was aesthetic not ethical. In developing this, her final argument on the subject of totalitarianism, she managed to come down on all sides, displaying little of the authority and lucidity that marked *The Origins of Totalitarianism*. For example, Arendt asserted that poets should be judged not as citizens but as artists. She added that they should, however, be judged *by* citizens, whose competence to judge poetry she chose not to examine. She thus allowed for civic and personal irresponsibilty, if indulged in by versifiers, for those excesses she made excuses. Whether poets on the average behave worse than other citizens did not pique her curiosity; no moral resoluteness there. She did not wonder whether the *poètes maudits* like Villon and Pound are at all typical. They probably are not; Arendt's own obituary for Auden indicated that it is not impossible for poets to exhibit sanity and good sense.[54]

As for "poor B. B.," she did not at first blame his decline on Stalinist apologetics: "The fact of Brecht's doctrinaire and often ludicrous adherence to the Communist ideology as such need hardly cause serious concern." (This from the author of *The Origins of Totalitarianism*, but let it pass.) Then Arendt rather unexpectedly argued that his Communist ideology led Brecht "to lie" about the Third Reich which, in poems like

"Burial of the Agitator in the Zinc Coffin," implied that the difference between Nazi Germany and capitalist countries was one of degree. "This was a double lie," she countered, "for in capitalist countries opponents were not beaten to death and shipped home in sealed coffins; and Germany was not a capitalist country any longer, as the Messrs. Schacht and Thyssen were to learn, to their sorrow."[55] The differences were of course considerable, but not for the reasons Arendt offered. Concurrent with the decimation of the labor movement in Germany, Harlan County miners and Republic Steel strikers, among others, were murdered in America for their opposition to their employers. And the fact that American businessmen, from Richard Whitney to Louis Wolfson, from gamblers to electric generating equipment price-fixers, have at various times been imprisoned does not prove that the United States government ever became anticapitalist.

Nor did Brecht's lies, if that is what they were, prevent him from writing several excellent poems in the 1930s and 1940s, including some about the Germany he fled. Even Arendt, quite inconsistently, realized this and conceded that Brecht "could sin *and* write good poetry." The overall level of his poems clearly did degenerate however, but neither the character of Brecht's sins nor the nature of his "punishment" was specified in Arendt's essay. Perhaps his sin was less his Stalinism than his presence "in the thick of things—and . . . this is no good place for a poet to be." If so, artists are granted dispensation from what she otherwise exalted: public freedom and action. As for Brecht's punishment, Arendt offered no evidence of any anguish, or any sense of guilt. Since she considered the artistic mediocrity and near-silence of the East Berlin years his "punishment," it follows from her argument that, had Brecht died a natural death in Zurich in 1948, his sins would have been without earthly consequence. But in fact, with his West German copyright to provide a ready source of

Western currency, he died in full knowledge of the esteem
with which his work was held in the West. Some punishment.
In her assessment of Brecht's legacy, Arendt's final plea not
for justice but for mercy was therefore all the more puzzling
and inappropriate.[56]

Brecht's career, which was most creatively pursued under
republican forms of government, cannot be understood without ample reference to the Nazi Germany from which he was
exiled, the Stalinism which he embraced, or the Communist
Germany to which he returned.[57] Whether such associations
indelibly affected his art—its syntax and imagery, its aims and
its audience, its location within a broader cultural tradition—
was left unexplored in her essay. That is unfortunate, for
Brecht was the most political poet of the century, though in
his lifetime he held only one political office—on Augsburg's
brief revolutionary council after World War I. Perhaps in
some small way, that experience endeared him to Arendt. He
was also the most gifted and incorrigible writer ever to be
sucked into the maelstrom of totalitarian politics. Perhaps the
best poem ever written about the Soviet dictator was a sort of
funeral oration, "The Heirs of Stalin," in which Yevgeny Yevtushenko was "appealing to our government,/to double/and
treble/the sentries guarding this tomb."[58] It was a sentiment
Brecht apparently never felt. Arendt's essay was a shard of her
own lapsed interest in the subject of totalitarianism, a dis-
appointing fragment of a conclusion to otherwise brilliant
writing on the insinuation of this phenomenon into modern
history.

Arendt resisted the temptation to make *The Origins of Totalitarianism* the foundation of her entire thought, to permit
that book's preoccupations to control the direction of her
later concerns. The achievement that her 1951 volume represented bestowed upon Arendt the authority to range widely
in political philosophy, even at the risk of seeming to forget

or ignore her own earlier conclusions. Thus, for example, she wrote that the legacy of the camps might be "to invalidate all obsolete political differentiations from right to left and to introduce beside and above them the politically most important yardstick for judging events in our time, namely: whether they serve totalitarian domination or not."[59] Though basically conservative, Arendt was not even mentioned in the comprehensive history of postwar thought, George H. Nash's *The Conservative Intellectual Movement in America* (1976). She was not always easy to locate on a spectrum from right to left, but that difficulty was not due to an obsessive hostility to totalitarianism as she once understood it. Arendt simply refused to grant to her insights of the period 1941–1950 dominion over her later thought, though such openness does not of course have to be seen as a liability. It is at least a change worth noting. Otherwise she would not in 1965 have criticized Marx for having "strengthened more than anybody else the politically most pernicious doctrine of the modern age, namely that life is the highest good, and that the life process of society is the very center of human endeavor." The reader of *The Origins of Totalitarianism* might have thought that "the politically most pernicious doctrine of the modern age" was the ideological organization of death, which haunted and pervaded the Holocaust kingdom. One measure of the distance Arendt established from her most famous book would be to recall Rabbi Fackenheim's injunction to Jews living after the Holocaust: "Why not suicide? Because after the Nazi celebration of death, life has acquired a new dimension of sanctity. Why not flight into madness? Because insanity had ruled the kingdom of darkness, hence sanity, once a gift, has now become a holy commandment. . . ."[60] After the camps, the possibilities of life itself became all the more precious and could never again be taken for granted in civilized society. If it was obtuse to exalt survival at all costs, it was also erroneous to disparage these processes and preconditions that made conceivable the communal action and speculative grandeur that Arendt prized.

Indeed so neglectful did Arendt appear toward the grand themes of the 1951 book that some critics found her thought vulnerable to the dangers of totalitarianism itself, and they accused her of propounding views that were in themselves totalitarian. Her stress on the idea of freedom as collective action and public participation, N. K. O'Sullivan suggested, ignored "the possibility that totalitarianism may . . . be seen as a development—albeit a perverse one—of the ideal that she places at the center of her own political thought." George Kateb's indictment was more detailed, for he noticed how proximate her political ideals were to some of the attributes of the Bolshevik and Nazi leaders, who "did not act out of crass motives. . . . They had no interests, no goals, no love of power for its own sake. They were profoundly anti-utilitarian." He added that "their activity, as conceptualized by Arendt, was in the service of a rebellion against the human condition, an assertion of the unnatural or artificial against the natural or the everyday. But so in her view is political action when rightly done." [61] It was an unsettling indictment aimed at the systematic self-consciousness of the entirety of her work.

Admittedly no political thinker has exceeded Arendt in proclaiming the centrality of politics and the glories of the public realm. Whatever her disdain for parliamentary maneuvering or for the administration of the welfare state, she regarded the achievement of the *polis* and the promise of the revolutionary councils as the supreme human enterprises. Benjamin Schwartz scarcely exaggerated in calling her thought "the religion of politics," for Arendt believed that "public happiness" transcended in value private well-being and personal fulfillment. For her politics was indeed like a vocation. The distinctive force of her viewpoint can be highlighted by contrasting it with the prevalent school of American political science. Far from almost investing politics with an aura of sanctity, or defining the public realm as the arena of heroism immortalized in poetry, some pluralists have had difficulty describing the complex processes of self-government in an attractive light. For example, "instead of assuming that politics is a normal and natural concern of human beings," Robert Dahl preferred to "make the contrary assumption that . . . politics is a remote, alien, and unrewarding activity."[62] (It may require too many meetings.) With its recognition of legitimate private interests and aspirations, as well as its stress upon compromise and civility, the pluralist position is obviously incompatible with totalitarianism. Given the politicization Arendt would regard as ideal, no such assumption attaches itself to her writings, however natural and explicit her hostility toward totalitarianism.

The best defense of Arendt's writings against this bizarre charge was Leroy Cooper's, though presented within a different context. In her philosophy, he argued, four justifications for participation in government could be found: "(1) the disclosure of the self through speech and action; (2) the joy of acting together with our peers and beginning something new; (3) the confirmation of our self-identity and the assurance of the reality of the world; and (4) the display of excellence and greatness." None of these justifications would have made sense within the prison walls of totalitarian societies. Rather than permitting free speech and free action, Nazi Germany and Stalinist Russia aimed to produce automatons and robots, not —in Arendt's ideal—creative and spontaneous individuals who sought to bring something new into the world. To the extent that the terror was ubiquitous, the scope of action was restricted. Even, and perhaps especially, in the entourages of Hitler and Stalin, there was no "joy of acting together with

. . . peers." Indeed Arendt observed that "no ruler before
Stalin and Hitler contested the freedom to say yes—Hitler
excluding Jews and gypsies from the right to consent and
Stalin having been the only dictator who chopped off the
heads of his most enthusiastic supporters, perhaps because he
figured that whoever says yes can also say no."[63] Even for those
invested with special power and privilege, German and Soviet
politics was not the arena of equals, stalwart and self-confident
in their freedom, open in their pursuit of human excellence,
but—for those who had to meet and live with the dictators—
an experience of intrigue, abject fear and terror, submission
and adulation. In the suspiciousness and paranoia that pervaded the world of the dictators, politics did not confirm
reality but negated it instead.[64] With some exceptions the
elites of these two nations—and politically only the elites
mattered—were characterized by dullness and mediocrity, not
by "excellence and greatness." Totalitarianism was in short
the antithesis of "public happiness."

Arendt's exaltation of politics was therefore utterly alien to
the totalitarian universe, which aimed at politicization in
order to maximize domination. Nevertheless, while any suggestion that Arendt's thought bears serious resemblance to
totalitarian thinking must be repudiated, her own fading interest in the phenomenon was not without its ironies. Her
insistence upon the novelty of such regimes did not prevent
her from valuing the founding of new political forms. The
insinuation of radical evil into the world did not lead her to
champion the pursuit of absolute virtue. The contempt that
the leaders of the Third Reich evinced toward utilitarian considerations did not make her into a utilitarian. The indifference to economics that she ascribed to Stalinism and Nazism
failed to heighten her own sensitivity to the importance of
economics to political life. The chilling use these regimes
made of technology did not make her a neoprimitive, any

more than their perversion of language into lies led her to value silence over speech. Though their ideologies violated common sense, she refused to make that the sole touchstone of truth. Nor was it "the burden of our times" alone that drove her to the idealization of antiquity and to adopting a conception of politics derived from Periclean Athens. The totalitarian impulse to make everything an intensely political issue did not cause her, as it did David Riesman, to see the advantages of apathy in combating tyranny. Had her 1951 masterwork not been written, it would have been hard to infer from her later contributions to political theory that she had drawn certain significant lessons from what Karol Wojytla (Pope John Paul II) was to call the worst evil of human history—the totalitarian "age of a new enslavement, the age of the concentration camp and the oven."[65]

Whatever strange and superficial resemblances may be said to exist between her exaltation of politics and the totalitarian imperative can generally be traced to her emphasis upon the authority of the community. Even her theory of consciousness held that the self is known and identity achieved only through the consciousness of others. It is the presence and perception of others that license the reality and meaning of one's life, and it is by action in the public realm that the self is substantiated. Arendt seemed to allow for two exceptions: the poet and, following Cato, the philosopher, who by thinking is never less alone than when by himself.[66] Though she described in exhilarating terms the spontaneous and creative founding of new institutions, she also, paradoxically, valued permanence and stability, which are the achievements finally of storytellers and sages—and they may work best alone. As a diagnostician of human dilemmas, Arendt was typically adept at making trenchant distinctions among the conditions of loneliness, solitude and isolation, drawn partly from Epictetus.[67] Nevertheless her sense of human worth was primarily collective.

This stress upon communal definitions of human dignity
entailed risks of which Arendt was insufficiently aware. It is
instructive that, when one critic in Wilhelmine Germany
complained of the inferior citizenship to which the Poles in
Pozen province were being reduced, Max Weber replied:
"Wir haben die Polen erst zu Menschen gemacht" (it is we
who made the Poles into human beings).[68] Weber could not
have been expected to foresee the logical implications of a
communal standard of what it means to be human. Arendt,
however, should have known that such a standard means that
the community may choose to terminate its recognition and
protection. Her own inordinate preference for the public
virtues, her tendency to associate private interests with selfish
withdrawal and abandonment of common sense, could only
weaken the very ideals which need sustenance against even
less dangerous and implacable forms of political organization.

What one misses in Arendt's thought, for all its subtlety,
originality and immediacy, is a fuller appreciation of liberalism as a force inherently hostile to totalitarianism. For as a
set of political principles, not as an ideology masking particular economic interests, liberalism has been the most effective
historical foe of total domination. Its commitment to representative government under the aegis of law, its cognate philosophical tendencies toward secularism, positivism and skepticism have not rendered their adherents impotent in dark
times. More consistently than any other modern political
tendency, it has aimed to strike a sensible balance between the
rights of the individual and the exigencies of community.
Unlike some other refugee intellectuals (Karl Popper, Karl
Mannheim, Franz Neumann), life in England or America did
not really temper Arendt's fidelity to continental political
thought. The absence in her writings of any reference, say, to
Orwell hints at a certain inability to appraise how much of
value still remained in the primary Anglo-American tradi-

tions of attentiveness to political means and hostility to unjust authority. Arendt's failure to nurture a sufficient appreciation for liberalism suggests a significant discontinuity in her thought, a decline in concern for what sort of politics, viable under modern conditions and verified by modern history, might best resist a recurrence of the plague.

Chapter 6

⚜

THE ORDEAL OF JEWRY

THE philosophic depth and ethical interest of *The Origins of Totalitarianism* naturally open the question of whether there is also a religious dimension to Arendt's thought. Such an interpretation was offered by Philip Rieff, who insisted that the avoidance of "a theological vocabulary" did not mean that Arendt was without "theological assumptions." The case for her classification as a "covertly religious-ethical" writer was based on very limited evidence, however. The preface of her book argued that without the rise of totalitarianism, "we might never have known the truly radical nature of evil." Rieff deemed that passage "incomprehensibly cruel if not recognized as an expression of Miss Arendt's covert theological assumptions. The punishment visited as totalitarianism, like the punishment visited by God throughout history, is at the same time a revelation of the abyss of possibility. The punishment," Rieff concluded, "is . . . an opportunity to repent and to live under a 'new law'. . . . Like men, even the new law must be limited, lest it become demonic."[1] Just as Cotton Mather had claimed that satanic forces verify divine reality, so too—according to Rieff—Arendt implied that the historical experience of hell on earth raises a presumption that heaven too exists.

The case against such an interpretation, however, was overwhelming. The statement in Arendt's preface was one of fact, a prelude to her discussion of such evil as previously known only to medieval fantasies of divine retribution. Arendt did not regard totalitarianism as the penalty imposed for the "demonic will to freedom,"[2] though it is true that in the camps every evil was possible. No such argument bound together her facts and interpretations in *The Origins of Totalitarianism*; nor did her definition of freedom acknowledge the risks of license, the abuse of Eden, the dangers of the demonic. She did not think in terms of balance or polarity, or that it was desirable to curtail freedom (in her sense). Believing instead that public happiness is far more valuable than private virtues, Arendt argued that freedom and happiness are ideally congruent. The symmetrical proofs for heaven and hell would have been foreign to her thinking; the *polis* was for her already the image of an earthly paradise.

It is true that Arendt believed in God, at least according to one of her closest friends.[3] She once described atheists as "fools who pretended to know what no man can know"—though, so baldly put, such a statement is quite as applicable to believers. She also quoted the remarkable precognition of John Adams, who feared the "possibility that the government of nations may fall in the hands of men who teach the most disconsolate of all creeds, that men are but fire flies, and this *all* is without a father. . . ." The result, Adams continued, might be "to make murder itself as indifferent as shooting plover, and the extermination of the Rohilla nation as innocent as the swallowing of mites on a morsel of cheese."[4] Nazi officials of course described the Final Solution as "de-lousing," and Arendt referred to the impersonal and random death in the camps as the equivalent of squashing a gnat. Yet only rarely and ambiguously did she go on record in favor of theism: "I am perfectly sure that this whole totalitarian catastrophe would not have happened if people had still believed in God, or in hell rather—that is, if there still were ultimates. There were no ultimates."[5] This remark was made almost in passing, and was neither defended nor developed. Otherwise she did not directly endorse the wisdom of Adams' position; and she felt no need to propose religion as a viable defense against totalitarianism, as a form of political and social security. She derided affirmations of faith when attached to political motives rather than to purity of religious conviction; and she found "rather funny" the occasional argument that "one can or ought to organize religion as an institution only because one likes to have a culture."[6]

In the dozen books she wrote, Arendt had ample opportunity to tackle the question of faith, and her near-silence suggests that the theological assumptions beneath *The Origins of Totalitarianism* were very deeply buried. To insert her work into an authentic religious tradition would by that very inclusion thin out the tradition. It would be more accurate to recognize Arendt's as a "thoroughly secular philosophy"[7] whose central motif was politics—the vocation in which the full potential and stature of humanity might be achieved. Whatever her private faith, it did not inform her vision of human drama and destiny, nor support her conception of the confrontation with absolute evil, which she analyzed without reference to transcendent meaning or purpose.

Yet to insist on the worldliness of her philosophy does not exhaust the subject, for she was also a Jew who had done advanced graduate work in theology under Rudolf Bultmann. While the primary influence upon her was Hellenic, Arendt's first book was on a Christian saint; and she wrote brilliantly on the goodness of Jesus. (Such interest in the dominant Western faith hardly made her unique among German Jewish intellectuals; Martin Buber's dissertation was largely devoted to Christian mysticism, and the first major publication of the poet Nelly Sachs, who also became an Israeli, had a

"Christological" orientation.) Arendt was actively involved in the Zionist movement and Jewish cultural reconstruction for fifteen years of her life. Her own knowledge of Judaism was apparently slight, however, and not always accurate. Arendt died unconsecrated by a religious ceremony, and the New York *Times* obituary tersely noted that she had "no religious affiliation." Yet she never attempted to disguise her origins; and when she delivered a series of lectures in Cologne less than a decade after the war, she began: "I am a German Jew driven from my homeland by the Nazis."[8] According to Steiner, "the humanism of the European Jew" vibrated throughout her "work and context of reference"; and Lichtheim also regarded Arendt as a representative of Weimar culture.[9] She certainly embodied the most energetic and responsive traditions of German scholarship; and it was due to education, not idiosyncrasy, that she insisted that, to understand modern politics, one must understand Aristotle, Cicero and Augustine as well. In the erudition and incandescence that marked Weimar culture, in its openness to "outsiders" and the breadth of its curiosity, in its brilliance and boldness and above all its premonition of disaster, Arendt's attitudes toward the Jews and toward Germans were nurtured and given sustenance in their final moments of creative interaction.

Her writings on the Jews can be properly analyzed only with reference to her conception of politics and history. The Jews of the Diaspora, Arendt claimed, have not really had a history because they lacked "a world to win," a field of action. Instead of inserting themselves in the world through great deeds, the Jews were mostly subject to the will of others, weightless under the burden of oppression. The chosen people were not a choosing people, not free to act but forced to react; and their historiography, Arendt believed, was for too long an apologetic affair, a ceremony of innocence which hampered inquiry into the Jews' responsibility for their own fate.[10] Theirs was not a history, as Lewis Namier once remarked, but "only a Jewish martyrology." They had never breathed the air of the *polis*. In other words, they were not a political people, which for Arendt was the most important frame of judgment. In accepting the Lessing Prize from the Free City of Hamburg, she mentioned pariah peoples like the Jews, who were able to develop the most acute and adhesive feelings of fraternity. Yet they also paid a price in "so radical a loss of the world, so fearful an atrophy of all the organs with which we respond to it—starting with the common sense with which we orient ourselves in a world common to ourselves and others and going on to the sense of beauty, or taste, with which we love the world—that in extreme cases, in which pariahdom has persisted for centuries, we can speak of a real worldlessness. And worldlessness, alas, is always a form of barbarism."[11]

A mere fourteen years after the Holocaust, telling a German audience about Jewish "barbarism" was not exactly *le mot juste*. But apart from that, Arendt was presenting a rather special slant on the Jewish past. Her vision of politics was essentially heroic, and she considered courage to be "the political virtue par excellence." In reading the *Pirke Abot* (Sayings of the Fathers), Trilling was also struck by one omission: "The Rabbis, in speaking of virtue, never mention the virtue of courage," which is "more remarkable in that they knew that many of their number would die for their faith."[12] Perhaps a philosophy that accepted Achilles as exemplary would have little if any place for Akiba. Nevertheless there is another side to Jewish history besides suffering and destitution, for those whose temperaments are responsive to an enlarged sense of the heroic. Such an interpretation of Jewish history would also notice recalcitrance and resilience, plurality and variety, prevalence over enemies and redemption in Zion, the incomparable drama of continuity across five millennia and five continents. If it provokes too much resistance to refer to Jewish survival as a miracle, then measure all the implausibilities and improbabilities over which a small people triumphed, though at a terrible cost. If a definition of politics invalidates the Jewish response to hatred and exploitation, if it does not embrace more than valorous deeds and noble oratory, or include the subtler arts of diplomacy and the weapons that the weak have used to deflect the strong, then perhaps it is insufficient. Without minimizing the dolorous effects of pariahdom, a cogent interpretation of the Jewish past might nevertheless be open to its grandeur, "pledged to the marvellous."

Arendt herself was part of that history. She spent six years in the Paris office of Youth Aliyah, helping children escape to Palestine. She contributed political journalism to *Aufbau*, appealing for a Jewish army to fight the Axis. She worked with Rabbi Judah L. Magnes, a leader of Palestine's Ichud faction, in the movement that promoted Arab-Jewish reconciliation. She served as research director of the Commission for Jewish Cultural Reconstruction, which tried to salvage what remained of Jewish cultural treasures and artifacts after the Holocaust. She served on the board of directors of the Conference on Jewish Social Studies, for whose journal she had written her early penetrating analyses of anti-Semitism. Its editor, Salo Baron, was with her when she died. Yet her own writings in no way shone with *ahavat yisrael* (love for the people of Israel), a term she seemed unfamiliar with when Gershom Scholem accused her of lacking a special commitment to and feeling for the Jewish people.[13] It was indeed odd that Arendt, who noted in her Lessing Prize address how fully pariah peoples can develop fraternal warmth, lacked such sentiments herself.

Arendt in fact agreed with Scholem's assessment, in the sense that she had "never . . . 'loved' any people or collective.

. . . I cannot love myself or anything which I know is part and parcel of my own person." That was surely an unnatural and superhuman proclamation, which ought to be treated with some skepticism; for neither the responsibility of intellectual detachment nor the right to offer criticism is incompatible with special concern for one's own people. As the philosopher Abraham Kaplan put it, "My own children are undoubtedly in themselves no more lovable than anyone else's, but they are the ones *I* love. Humanist universalism does not obligate me either to deny my feelings or to diffuse them." A character in Isaac Bashevis Singer's latest novel puts it a bit differently: "I love the Jews even though I cannot stand them."[14] Here was one paradox in which Arendt took no delight. She acknowledged that the "wrong done by my own people naturally grieves me more than wrong done by other peoples. This grief, however, . . . is not for display." Some tendentiousness was evident, however, in her attitude toward the Jews, who never seem to have brought her any pride—only grief. Arendt could write about the suffering done *by* her people but showed little overt emotion recounting the suffering done *to* her people. For she believed that "compassion" is politically irrelevant and inconsequential, and that "suffering has never been an argument in politics."[15] The public realm was not supposed to make allowance for the private wrong, for personal outrage, for the claim of mercy.

Here Arendt was even harsher than a revolutionary socialist she eulogized, for whom compassion was suspect if it was localized. "Why do you come with your special Jewish sorrows?" Rosa Luxemburg asked a correspondent in 1917. "I cannot find a special corner in my heart for the ghetto. I feel at home in the entire world." Luxemburg was born in Zamosc, which was also the hometown of the Yiddish writer Isaac Loeb Peretz. The cosmopolitan daughter of Zamosc need not have worried that too much attention might be lavished on the ghetto; a little over two decades after she dismissed those sorrows, no Jews were left alive in Zamosc.[16] A critic of the authoritarian dangers of Leninism, and finally a victim of right-wing German gangsterism, Luxemburg could hardly have been blamed for not foreseeing the horror to come. Nevertheless her disparagement of Jewish vulnerability and anguish, which were so noticeable and proximate, is unsettling in its obtuseness. It is an irony of intellectual history that the meaning of such catastrophes was best explored by an admirer of Luxemburg and a representative German Jewish intellectual. *The Origins of Totalitarianism* in no way neglected or minimized the importance of the Jews in the eyes of Gentiles, and Arendt implicated herself in her people's fate far more than Luxemburg ever did. But both abandoned a religious tradition, which they could no longer find compelling, and rejected an ethnic particularism as well as nationalism for the sake of a wider allocation of concerns. Cynthia Ozick once called such cosmopolitanism simply another form of the Jewish parochialism that Luxemburg and to a large extent Arendt scorned.[17] What is not easy to reconcile is Arendt's account of Jewish destiny and her exaltation of the imperatives of community.

Both the deliberate atrophy of emotional life when applied to politics and a studied avoidance of national sentiments in particular helped account for the opposition to Zionism she developed by the end of the 1940s. Of the four references to Zionism in *The Origins of Totalitarianism*, two were favorable, one unfavorable, and one misleading. Arendt unequivocally praised the Jewish response to the Dreyfus affair, which "gave birth to the Zionist movement—the only political answer Jews have ever found to anti-Semitism and the only ideology in which they have taken seriously a hostility that would place them in the center of world events." Zionism marked the end of "the old Jewish indifference to political

issues." But she deplored the decline of human rights implicit in the establishment of the state of Israel, which meant
that the Jews too saw no protection for the sense of dignity
except within the boundaries of a sovereign nation. And
Arendt also noted, in the context of her analysis of homelessness, that "the Jewish question" was solved at a price—"a new
category of refugees, the Arabs, thereby increasing the number of the stateless and rightless."[18] But the refugee problem
was not primarily created by the Zionists, as the fast or unin-
formed reader might have surmised, but by the Arab states,
who urged the Palestinians to get out of the way of their
rockets and advancing armies and who refused to absorb
hundreds of thousands of the refugees into their own societies.
The Zionists, who alone among the combatants accepted the
United Nations partition plan, asked the Arabs in their midst
not to flee; and those who remained within the new democracy of Israel were neither stateless nor—except when national
security was involved—rightless. Arendt never mentioned another category of refugees in the Middle East—the Jews who
fled Arab lands, often after cruel discrimination. Their numbers were as great as the Arabs who fled Palestine.

She was quite justified in denouncing the terrorism and extremism that unfortunately accompanied the birth of the
third Jewish commonwealth. Along with Hook, Einstein,
Zelig Harris, Seymour Melman and others, she condemned the
American visit in 1948 of Menachem Begin, who "preached
an admixture of ultra-nationalism, religious mysticism, and
racial superiority." In the aftermath of an ugly, isolated incident, the Deir Yassin massacre, Arendt and other signatories
of a letter to the *Times* called Begin's Herut (Freedom) Party
"closely akin in its organization, methods, political philosophy
and social appeal to the Nazi and Fascist parties"[19]—surely a
ludicrous overreaction. Her own sympathies lay with the
"heirs of the universalist spirit" at Hebrew University and on

kibbutzim, but she withheld her admiration for the larger achievements of the state itself. Fearing that the claims of "national sovereignty" constituted "a dangerous event" for Jews and other small peoples, Arendt called for a confederation of Jews and Palestinian Arabs instead of Jewish independence.[20] By 1950, however, the possibility of shared sovereignty was foreclosed.

The complicated emotions involved in identity obviously caused some short-circuiting in Arendt's powers of reasoning. Qualities she exalted could even have been found, if she were seriously looking, where Jewish life prior to the Holocaust was most vital and invulnerable to modernity. Explicating the inner life of Eastern European Jewry, Maurice Samuel once observed that "public service of any kind was touched with the odor of sanctity." Even Samuel's translation of the term for such a servant, *klal tuer,* might have been taken from Arendt's language: "doer of public things."[21] Anti-Zionism does not inexorably flow from her political philosophy. *The Origins of Totalitarianism* had identified the problem that no nation wished to receive refugees from oppression; Israel, however, had welcomed beleaguered Jews and even took them from mental institutions in Europe. Had Trotsky survived assassination attempts another eight years, he would have found refuge under the "Law of Return"—a possibility which the most threatened of all political exiles did not categorically exclude. (Arendt did not publicly blame Arab nations for refusing to absorb Palestinians, an inhospitality for which Israel has often been condemned.) Also integral to the thrust of Arendt's book was her critique of mass society as one in which "human beings . . . are still related to one another but have lost the world once common to all of them."[22] Yet by that definition Israel was not a mass society but a community, seeking to found something new out of the fragments of a lost world. For the first time in two millennia, Jews were acting in

Arendt's sense as political men and women, asserting themselves in the regional and international "public space" and showing a capacity to protect themselves, as European nation-states had been unable or unwilling to do for them.

Nor were the Israelis deficient in physical courage, a quality Arendt had not discovered among Diaspora Jewry. The military valor of the Israelis was so impressive that, immediately after the Six-Day War, Harold Macmillan expressed the hope that future Britons would emulate Israel: "In the time of Elizabeth we were only two million people, in the time of Marlborough only five or six million, in the time of Napoleon only ten million. The other day, while the world debated, Israel's three millions imposed their will on their enemies. They had what any great people need—resolution, courage, determination, pride. These are what count in men and nations."[23] They are what counted in Arendt's admiration for the ancient Greeks as well, but in the Jews she could not find the same qualities that Macmillan had. It is not necessary to endorse all aspects of Israeli life to see how extraordinary its achievements in nation-building have been.

There is a paradox here. Irving Howe has testified to the extent to which *The Origins of Totalitarianism* enhanced the sense of Jewish identity among many New York intellectuals. Arendt's book helped give an analytical framework for the "new rush of feelings, mostly unarticulated" that the Holocaust produced. Her writings exercised a "strong impact," Howe recalled, primarily because they "offered a coherent theory, or at least a coherent picture of the concentration camp universe. We could no longer escape the conviction that, blessing or curse, Jewishness was an integral part of our life." Yet despite the effect of her work upon the ethnic consciousness of some American intellectuals, Arendt herself was an unmoved mover; and the effect of her writing went far beyond the circles Howe was describing. Denis Donoghue, for instance, recalled her early article in *Partisan Review* on the Nazi camps: "The essay was free from hysteria, violence, vituperation; there was only violence within—Wallace Stevens' great phrase—animating the prose."[24] This detached empathy was among her most formidable resources in *The Origins of Totalitarianism*. But it seemed amiss when she chose to write directly about Germans and Jews once again in her most controversial book, *Eichmann in Jerusalem*, originally published in the *New Yorker* in February and March of 1963.

Part of the controversy swirled around the style of the book itself, though it may be assumed that problems of writing generally reflect deeper problems of thinking. Arendt's prose was rarely elegant, but it was more than adequate to bear the heavy freight of her subject. In *Eichmann in Jerusalem*, however, Trevor-Roper regretted that "her style is not as lucid as her argument requires." Jewish readers in particular apparently found the book "curiously unfeeling" and "cold and abstract."[25] That did not mean that a study related to the Holocaust was supposed to be warm and folksy, such critics asserted, but that perhaps Arendt might have displayed the same measure of sympathy for Eichmann's victims that she managed to summon projecting herself into Eichmann's mind and motivation. William Phillips noticed, at times, "an unfortunate tone, that comes either from clumsy writing or from some undercurrent of bias, so that one has the feeling that the Jewish leaders, if not the Jews as a whole, are somehow being criticized for things that Hannah never succeeds in making entirely explicit."[26]

That undercurrent of bias was quite manifestly anti-Zionist.[27] Scholem, who was among those troubled by her "heartless, frequently almost sneering and malicious tone," was offended by one of the most commented-upon passages in the book, a paraphrase of the defendant's recollections under police interrogation. Eichmann's superior in the Sicherheitsdienst (S.D.), Arendt wrote, "required him to read Theodor Herzl's *Der Judenstaat,* the famous Zionist classic, which converted Eichmann promptly and forever to Zionism." Such passages, Scholem wrote her, "amount to a mockery of Zionism; and I am forced to the conclusion that this was, indeed, your intention." Arendt replied: "I never made Eichmann out to be a 'Zionist.' If you missed the irony of the sentence— which was plainly in *oratio obliqua,* reporting Eichmann's own words—I really can't help it." [28] She did not equate emotional detachment with manifest anti-Zionism.

Arendt's explanation of the passage corresponded with defenses offered by Mary McCarthy and, in a rare concession to criticism of one of its articles, the *New Yorker* itself. Dwight Macdonald yielded to irony himself, though with the realization that it is "a dangerous device if the reader, from stupidity or calculation, insists on reading it straight." When one critic of Arendt insisted that no "Zionist" could direct the extermination of European Jewry, Macdonald replied, "Obviously. One might expect even Miss Arendt to see *that.*" It might also be obvious to note that irony is a way of establishing some distance from what is unbearable to contemplate. For Arendt it was "not a mode of heaping contempt upon the victims," Michael Kowal wrote, "but an instrument that the mind forges for dealing with the strains placed upon it by the heart." [29]

Nevertheless the manner of Arendt's approach was not quite satisfactory. If there was so much misreading by scholars and intellectuals, perhaps some of the fault may well have been the author's; the "stupidity and calculation" of readers should not be entirely to blame. One philosopher was puzzled because "in her other writings Miss Arendt exhibits no particular talent for irony or ever indulges in it." For Eichmann to tell his captors that he was forever committed to Zionism after reading Herzl was a grotesque joke. For Arendt to repeat it in the form she adopted, in *oratio obliqua*, could only mean that it was at the expense of Jews whose need for Israel and definition of Zionism were very different from hers. "If this be irony," Marie Syrkin asked, "at whom is it directed?"[30] Arendt's reaction was quite different when the defendant gave a fairly correct definition of the categorical imperative and proclaimed a Kantian sense of duty. When Eichmann thereby tried to make himself into a Kantian, Arendt was quite forthright in repudiating such an association: "This was outrageous, on the face of it."[31] In this instance she insisted upon the rectification of names.

Replying to Scholem, Arendt made no attempt to rebut the accusation of anti-Zionist bias. She complained instead that "those who merely report certain unpleasant facts are accused of lack of soul, lack of heart." This was an evasive defense, though Arendt, in her reply to Eric Voegelin's criticism of *The Origins of Totalitarianism*, had earlier insisted on the right to be passionate when such fundamental issues were at stake.[32] Later scoffed at for the "high pitch" of "ethical revulsion"[33] she brought to the study of Germany and Russia, Arendt found herself defending her right to suppress emotions for the sake of the neutral presentation of unpalatable facts. But heartlessness alone is not what troubled many readers of *Eichmann in Jerusalem*, for those familiar with her earlier works recognized the olympian touch, the intellectually histrionic style in which the largest gestures were made without qualification and without hesitation. What was ultimately in dispute was not *ahavat yisrael*, which can be an elastic and inexact standard, but whether a lack of feeling diminished and even distorted her powers of historical judgment. The issue was not whether the facts were unpleasant, but whether they could be accurately conveyed without coloration.

More so than with any of her other books, questions were raised whether *Eichmann in Jerusalem* indeed presented facts at all. Before the articles appeared in print, the *New Yorker* had assigned the task of checking her information to Bill Honan, who knew German and later became editor of the New York *Times'* "Arts and Leisure" section. Honan spent four months at the YIVO Institute, the major American archive for sifting through the ashes of what was destroyed in the Holocaust. According to one account, Arendt "was shocked and dismayed when her story came back looking as if someone had written a dissertation on it in the margins, and refused to go along with some of the emendations. Some fairly heavy collisions followed"; still, the *New Yorker* later defended her report as "quiet, moral, rational."[34] That judgment has long been challenged. Marie Syrkin called *Eichmann in Jerusalem* "a tract in which the author manipulates the material with a high-handed assurance"; Walter Laqueur was troubled to find more errors than might be expected from so learned an author on so serious a subject.[35] A dissertation was indeed written in the margins on Arendt's articles—*And the Crooked Shall Be Made Straight*, by the attorney Jacob Robinson.

Two particular "facts" might be mentioned to indicate that Arendt was doing something more than conveying—and then getting blamed for—unpleasant information. In the *New Yorker* version and in the hardcover edition, Leo Baeck, the liberal Berlin rabbi who spurned offers to leave Germany and who was sent to Theresienstadt, was regarded among Germans and non-Aryans alike as the "Jewish Fuehrer." Baeck was a recognized leader of German Jewry and a saintly man. Arendt could not have been unaware of the nasty connotation of the German word for "leader." In fact the source of her statement that Baeck was the "Jewish Fuehrer" was not, as she implied, a Jew, but rather an associate of Eichmann's, Hauptsturmfuehrer Dieter Wisliceny.[36] In the paperback revision, Arendt dropped the phrase. Moreover she noted that "the blond beast" Heydrich was considered a "half-Jew" and that, as the engineer of the Final Solution, "he had betrayed his own people." Heydrich's origins were indeed ambiguous, even more so than Arendt indicated; the chief of the political police had to defend himself against "racial slander" because his grandmother, after giving birth to his father, remarried a man named Süss. Nevertheless neither Süss nor her first husband were non-Aryans. Heydrich helped extinguish but did not betray the Jewish people.[37]

It is true that several leading Nazis, including Himmler, had cast doubt on the purity of Heydrich's genealogy—for motives of their own. But Arendt's transmission of their suspicions as fact signified one of the undercurrents of bias running through her book—since the alleged Jewish origin of Heydrich, Lionel Abel observed, had "nothing to do with Eichmann or his problems. But it does have very much to do with one of Miss Arendt's main contentions: namely, that Jews played an important role in the murder of their fellow Jews."[38] As early as 1944, she had not disguised her hostility to the "Jewish plutocracy," whose machinations had been smothered under the rhetoric of religious and ethnic unity against a bigoted world. Here Arendt was decisively influenced by the writings of Bernard Lazare, the Dreyfusard who dismissed Zionism as a form of escapism, a substitute for the confrontation with anti-Semitism on the continent of Europe itself. The French publicist had also urged a struggle within Jewish society itself, for rebellion against bigotry outside had to be matched with opposition to a privileged leadership that claimed to defend minority rights. Arendt took from the pronouncements of Bernard Lazare, whose essays she later edited and published, the sense of obligation to unmask the political ineptitude of those whom she regarded as the antecedents of the *Judenräte*. Her condemnation of Jewish complicity in *Eichmann in Jerusalem* therefore had its sources not only in Raul Hilberg's *The Destruction of the European Jews* (1961), where the historical indictment is more fully stated, but in a French antagonist of Herzl half a century earlier. And as Sharon Muller has convincingly demonstrated, Arendt drew upon *The Origins of Totalitarianism*, and upon her criticism of the bourgeois social realm as a displacement of politics, in her subsequent indictment of the "parvenus" who complied so readily with their Nazi conquerors.[39] This was the source of the "undercurrent of bias" that puzzled William Phillips.

In the book on Eichmann, her description of "the moral collapse of respectable Jewish society" took up only about a dozen pages in a 256-page work, yet it sparked a fire-storm of controversy—and later led to serious research into the question of Jewish complicity. In those dozen pages her own attitudes toward the nature of political responsibility, toward the meaning of community and toward Jewish life crystallized. The pressing psychological urgency of those concerns undercut her claim that *Eichmann in Jerusalem* was simply the report of a trial,[40] in which she had no choice but to record unappealing facts as objectively as possible.

When universalists see fit to refer to their own Jewish origins, it is almost a certain signal that they are about to say something that those who did not stray as far from the Jewish fold are likely to find offensive. Three examples can be cited to suggest the import of some of these personal passages. "As a Jew writing in a Jewish weekly to Jews," Walter Lippmann once told readers of the *American Hebrew*, something would have to be done about the bad taste and ostentatiousness of "the rich and vulgar and pretentious Jews of our big American cities." Such persons, Lippmann feared, exacerbate the problem of anti-Semitism. Two decades later Justice Frankfurter described himself as a member of "the most vilified and persecuted minority in history"—and then dissented from a majority opinion of the Supreme Court upholding the principle of religious freedom. In the aftermath of the Six-Day War, I. F. Stone took the unusual step of announcing that he was writing "as a Jew"—and then proceeded to "report the Arab side" of the struggle against Israel.[41] Just as the brief shift to the first person in the analysis of statelessness infused *The Origins of Totalitarianism* with personal meaning, so too the lone self-reference in *Eichmann in Jerusalem* was revealing. "To a Jew," she wrote, the "role of the Jewish leaders in the destruction of their own people is undoubtedly the darkest chapter of the whole dark story."[42] Arendt did not explain why only on this issue was she writing and judging as a Jew. Surely any humane individual must regard as "the darkest chapter" of the Holocaust the extremism of the Nazis' own depravity and bestiality. What was most painful and abominable was what they did, not how some Jews responded. What was shocking and unbelievable was the ferocity of the desire to commit mass murder, not the inadequacy of terrorized victims in the face of the unprecedented.

"Wherever Jews lived," Arendt wrote, "there were recognized Jewish leaders, and this leadership, almost without exception, cooperated in one way or another, for one reason or another, with the Nazis." Members of the *Judenräte* did comply with Nazi demands, and she mentioned some of their unsavory acts of appeasement. Those who lived outside the camps, like Zionist emissaries, negotiated with the Nazis in a manner she described as "mutually highly satisfactory." Other Jews cooperated with the machinery of death even inside the gates of hell, such as the *Sonderkommando* who picked the corpses clean and had them cremated.[43] Instead, Arendt argued, the leaders should have warned their people of the in-

comparable disaster facing their communities. When the
Final Solution was known, the *Judenräte* should not have
continued to function. Rather than cooperate in the enterprise of mass murder, the *Judenräte* should have done nothing
except invite anarchy, for "the Nazis numbered hundreds of
thousands while millions of Jews would have gone underground."[44]

Arendt was not advocating resistance in the sense of fighting back, and perhaps it is a sign of the ambiguity of her accusation that even so formidable a reader as Steiner got it wrong.
He interpreted *Eichmann in Jerusalem* as an inquiry into the
problem of why the Jews "did not revolt," and then criticized
Arendt for "a failure of imagination." But Steiner's objection
is what logicians call an *ignoratio elenchi*, since her book
pointed out the futility of armed resistance to Nazism and
mentioned the horrible torture and death inflicted upon
Dutch Jews who had attacked police in Amsterdam.[45] Nor was
Arendt accusing the Jewish leaders of being traitors, though
that seems to be the charge from which Lucy Dawidowicz
directly defended them. "For all their weaknesses, failings,
and wrongdoings," Dawidowicz insisted, as though rebutting
Arendt, the Jewish leaders had no "common goals and aspirations with the Germans. . . . The officials of the *Judenräte*
were coerced by German terror to submit and comply. To say
that they 'cooperated' or 'collaborated' with the Germans is
semantic confusion and historical misrepresentation." *Eichmann in Jerusalem* never clearly condemned the Jewish
leadership as Quislings, though Arendt did remark that "the
establishing of Quisling governments in occupied territories
was always accompanied by the organization of a central Jewish office."[46] While Arendt found venality, delusions, fear and
selfishness among the representatives of the Jewish communities, she never mentioned any desire to join the Nazis' New
Order. Nevertheless, for those who chose to read such impli-

cations in her description of complicity, her remarks about
Jewish cooperation "for one reason or another" were wide
open.

The accusations were indeed vague, and not adequately
placed within historical context. Even when some Jews
grasped the full extent of Nazi aims, no one could know how
quickly the war might end, or whether through delay, diplomacy, appeasement, and willingness to provide labor, many
might be spared. It was unclear whether Arendt was condemning the Jewish leaders for their shortsighted folly, or
whether the main point was the disastrous consequences of
their policy, which only became apparent in retrospect.[47] Since
The Origins of Totalitarianism had stressed the unprecedented nature of Nazi aims and methods, her criticism of the
bedeviled victims of genocide was utterly ahistorical. Arendt
never explained how the Jewish leaders might have been expected to advocate alternative policies based upon what
emerged in exhaustive detail and horror after the war, nor
did she clarify whether her own proposal—doing nothing—
should have been universally pursued by the Jewish leaders.
One of her most intelligent defenders, Mary McCarthy, offered the following exegesis of Arendt's position: "Where the
terror ruled—in the camps, prisons and ghettoes—Miss
Arendt . . . does not propose that anyone could have done
anything but obey." But this interpretation only clouded
Arendt's case, because the terror was in fact everywhere.
"Where on earth does Miss McCarthy suppose that the Jewish
Councils functioned?" Syrkin inquired. "Miss Arendt's stric-
tures fall most heavy on the Jewish Councils in the Polish
ghettoes; nor does she exclude the Jewish Council in the concentration camp of Theresienstadt from her list of the culpa-
ble."[48] Arendt never got down to cases to show when and how
it was feasible to do nothing.

Moreover she did not draw a sharp enough distinction between the question of cooperation and, as John Gross pointed out, "a quite separate matter, the personality-change frequently undergone by prisoners in concentration camps, which has been documented by Bruno Bettelheim and others." In noting the "submissive meekness" with which so many Jews went for "resettlement," Arendt cited only the testimony of David Rousset, who was in 1947 recalling a different, chilling phenomenon—the "walking dead" of the other kingdom.[49] This distinction apparently escaped Bettelheim himself, one of the few American reviewers with a Jewish background to endorse without qualification the theses of *Eichmann in Jerusalem*. Distinctions were not easy to maintain; in any event dissolution of identity was the theme of the actor Robert Shaw's *The Man in the Glass Booth*, which derived its title and several of its formulations from Arendt. Its mad protagonist is Goldman, a Jew impersonating in an Israeli courtroom his cousin, an S.S. killer who bore responsibility for atrocities in a camp in which Goldman himself had been an inmate. In the novel from which the play was adapted, Goldman twice mentions Arendt. Of course she never went so far as to make Jews and Nazis interchangeable, but she did insist that totalitarianism blurred the difference between victim and executioner, which was "part of the system and had . . . nothing to do with the Jews."[50] If the system was so powerful and pervasive, however, it is hard to see how the *Judenräte* could be held accountable for their passivity or blamed for their abject compliance. If the leaders were granted a certain margin of responsibility for their choices and actions, then the centrality of terror and unlimited domination to Arendt's 1951 definition of totalitarianism had been —at the very least—overstated.

No dozen pages Arendt ever wrote generated so much controversy, or required such a combination of historical knowledge and moral poise to evaluate. Two decades after the Holocaust, Laqueur still hesitated to pass judgment: "The border-line between passive resistance and the legitimate defense of Jewish interests on the one hand, and activities that helped the Nazis to carry out their policy of mass murder on the other, does not appear always very distinct even now—how much less clear at the time." In retrospect, Isaiah Trunk sug-gested the outlines of such a distinction. Perhaps only when the occupiers demanded compliance not with labor alloca-tion but with "resettlement," Trunk wrote, did the Councils face "a tragic dilemma never before experienced by a com-munity representative organ. Cooperation then reached the morally dangerous borderline of collaboration." Arendt's al-ternative of chaos and flight was based on the fact that the Nazis themselves made Jewish cooperation integral to their policy of extermination. Rather than hunting down the Jews house-by-house or in the forests, the Nazis wanted their prey to identify and separate themselves, to assign themselves to fulfill the quotas, to line up in orderly fashion for transpor-tation and "resettlement," to die as efficiently as possible.[51]

Bettelheim, a survivor of both Buchenwald and Dachau, elaborated on Arendt's hypothesis: "The reaction of the Ger-man people to the crimes committed against the Jews might have been very different if each Jew who was taken had to be dragged down the street, or shot down on the spot. Again and again when German citizens witnessed utter brutality against Jews, there was at least some reaction among the civilian pop-ulation; and the Nazis were extremely sensitive to it."[52] Those not dragged out by their stalkers might have gone into hiding; and while this possibility could not have been realized by an entire people, more might have managed to escape had the *Judenräte* dissolved or refused to cooperate. A small fraction of those hauled off to the labor battalions survived, but vir-tually everyone who remained—trapped and immobile—in the ghettos perished. As a proposition in abstract logic, Macdonald contended, an alternative like Arendt's could hardly have led to a more horrendous fate for European Jewry than what actually happened; and noncooperation could scarcely have made matters worse.[53] Her most heated critics virtually forgot that Arendt's hypothesis was about how to *save* Jewish lives. She wished to subvert the deterministic tendency of historical thought, in the belief that the political and moral choices facing the Jews were wide enough to have permitted somewhat less devastation. This, at any rate, was the case in behalf of Arendt's very concise hypothesis.

But would a different Jewish response have mitigated the tragedy? Would noncompliance have reduced Jewish suffering and death? Would such a policy have managed more successfully—to quote from the Yom Kippur liturgy—to "avert the evil decree"? Historical evidence suggests that the margin of choice was terribly thin. The mass murder of Jews did not depend primarily upon the existence of the councils, however highly the Nazis came to value their services. Where there was no *Judenrat,* as in Greece and Yugoslavia, the local populations were still deported and decimated. Before the Wannsee conference to implement the Final Solution in a systematic manner, the *Einsatzgruppen* had murdered about a million helpless men, women and children without significant utilization of the *Judenräte*. Perhaps a million Jews died of famine and disease. By 1942, Dawidowicz has written, "the Germans managed with amazing facility to deport over a quarter of a million Jews from the Warsaw ghetto . . . precisely because the Jews of Warsaw were [in Arendt's words] 'unorganized and leaderless.' " If the appeasement policy was not in fact essential to the process of extermination, the depiction of "the moral collapse of respectable Jewish society" is robbed of much of its political relevance.[54]

Bettelheim's endorsement of Arendt's thesis did not correspond to his own behavior. Seized in Vienna and taken to Buchenwald in 1938, he did not engage in passive resistance or risk being shot on the spot. Bettelheim did not act as though his heroism might have prevented or diminished the genocide to come. Understandably enough he wanted to survive. (Bettelheim was released shortly before the outbreak of war through the personal intervention of Herbert Lehman and Eleanor Roosevelt, who respected his work on autism.) "When I was released from the camp," the psychiatrist recalled, "I did not tell about it, not as long as I or my mother were still on German soil. All I did tell others was to get out of Germany in a hurry, or they would perish."[55] His comprehensible response to Nazi terror suggested some of the psychological difficulties that would have been involved in noncompliance.

Readers of *Eichmann in Jerusalem* were given no sense of how limited were the opportunities to go underground. Most of the Jews, and therefore most of the victims, were in the East, where vicious anti-Semitism was so prevalent that even the anti-German partisans frequently turned Jews over to the Nazis. (Hungarian peasants surrendered the Palestinian Hannah Senesh to be tortured and killed.) The resistance fighters of the Warsaw ghetto got precious little help from the Polish underground in their struggle against a common enemy. However ominous the ultimate German design to depopulate the East to make room for colonization, the conquerors' genocidal anti-Semitism found welcome support and eager collaborators in the Ukraine, Poland, Croatia, Hungary, Rumania and elsewhere. For those who tried to escape from the villages and ghettos, Nathan Eck concluded, "daily miracles were necessary." Jews needed money over the course of a war that lasted almost six years, and refuge had to be found among Christians who often demanded payment. It was invaluable to have been

born with "Aryan" features. Under such conditions most—
though not all—of those who opted for Arendt's alternative
simply vanished.[56]

It is true, as Macdonald pointed out, that the fate of European Jewry could scarcely have been more gruesome. The
two-thirds of the population that was annihilated included
ninety percent of Polish Jewry, seventy percent of Hungarian
Jewry, and sixty percent of Ukranian Jewry. But such awful
figures could be contemplated only in retrospect, only after it
became known how fully Hitler had kept his explicit promise
to crush European Jewry. What if the Jews had acted according to Arendt's proposal? Ernst Simon, an Israeli professor of
education, wondered what an historian like Arendt might
have concluded on the basis of two relevant facts—"[1] the
flight of the leaders, and [2] its result—chaos, and enormous
numbers of victims. If we assume . . . that the number of victims would indeed have been smaller than five or six million,
then Hannah Arendt would not have known the standard of
comparison and would then have been able to reckon only
with the negative consequences of the escape of the leaders,
their abdication of responsibility in the time of greatest need,
and their having saved their own lives without regard for the
fate of others." Simon's criticism here was epistemological and
did not in itself undermine Arendt's claim that non-coopera-
tion would have been more effective. He added: "We can just
about imagine the severity and the ironic brilliance she would
have devoted to a condemnation of those who escaped." Little
imagination was necessary, however, as attested by her unflat-
tering reference to Pinchas Freudiger, the only witness at the
Jerusalem trial who had been an eminent member of a *Judenrat*. Freudiger was a former Hungarian baron who was bitterly
denounced by spectators in the courtroom, to which he responded that Hungarian Jews had no possibility of refuge
anywhere. Yet Arendt tartly noted that "he himself fled, to

Rumania, because he was rich and Wisliceny helped him."[57]

The most important dependent variable in the equation of the Holocaust was not the response of the Jewish leaders. What mattered most was not their fear or their villainy, their passivity or their selfishness, but rather the intensity of the Nazi desire to kill. That design might be deflected or postponed by the tenacity of indigenous peoples and their governments—heroically in Denmark, somewhat effectively in Bulgaria and Italy, tragically absent virtually everywhere else. Poland was ruled directly by the German occupiers; not even a Quisling government was permitted. Within the context of the disaster, each nation responded somewhat differently to the imposition of the Final Solution; and such responses, more than the political skills of the *Judenräte*, determined the vulnerability of the Jews in their midst.[58] Far from constituting "the darkest chapter of the whole dark story," the cooperation of the Jewish councils, even when most sordid, could occur only within the atmosphere of degradation and deprivation which Nazi rule imposed.

Arendt mentioned—quite properly—the delusions and the corruption of the councils, but she neglected to note the limited but important positive achievements of the Jewish organizations. Someone had to distribute the meager rations that were permitted the famished Jews packed and squeezed into the ghettos. Someone had to provide for sanitation, for medical assistance, for education. "In an attempt to mitigate the terror aroused by the press gangs which seized people at random on the streets," one survivor of the Warsaw ghetto explained, "the *Judenrat* offered to provide labor battalions at specified times and in specified numbers. . . ."[59] Employment saved some lives; but even apart from basic communal tasks, from day-care centers to tenement committees to lending libraries, the organizations helped maintain morale in the face of still unbelievable catastrophe, and struggled to achieve a semblance of normality and even of various forms of resistance to Nazi brutality. The leaders that emerged assumed awesome responsibiilties without being able to exercise corresponding power. Not all their achievements required the establishment of councils, but, through complicity, beleaguered communities might decelerate the process of total collapse.[60]

Arendt, who was ordinarily a champion of communal life and political organization, was also insensitive to the desperate, heroic and rarely successful work of the Zionists. Their efforts, Syrkin pointed out, necessarily meant " 'selection,' since, legally or illegally, only a few could escape." Even the organization which Arendt had helped direct, Youth Aliyah, "the rescue operation which saved thousands of Jewish children by arrangement with the Nazis, meant 'selection.' "[61] Without such organized work, which involved contact with German officials who favored emigration as the "solution" to the "Jewish problem," those children and other Jews would presumably not have been saved at all. Perhaps because Arendt's theory of totalitarianism stressed the pulverization of communal life, she ignored evidence of the resilience of the organized effort to survive and to prevail over the disaster. Though she cherished the values inculcated through communal life, Arendt noticed only the most repugnant features of Jewish Councils under the impact of the Holocaust. She thus promoted a viewpoint which was compatible with the Nazis' own cynical evaluation of the role of the councils.

Yet her harshness toward the terrorized and helpless members of the *Judenräte* was not consistent with her attitude toward other failures that signified the general moral collapse of Europe. The decisive moral distinction between killers and bystanders ought to be kept in mind. Some bystanders nevertheless responded more bravely than others. One of the very few places on the continent where the terror did not rule was the Vatican, whose shabby accommodation to Nazism has been amply documented.[62] Almost half the membership of the S.S. was Catholic, as was forty percent of the population of the Reich. Most of the countries which Germany conquered or was allied with had Catholic majorities. Yet despite Papal claims of spiritual leadership, no public condemnation of the Holocaust came from the Vatican. It was an excommunicable offense to be a duellist, but not to be a mass murderer. Yet Arendt's judgment of the conduct of Pius XII was far less biting than her criticism of the terrorized leaders in the helpless ghettos of Eastern Europe. "No one can say what actually would have happened had the Pope protested in public," she lamely wrote;[63] the confidence and forthrightness that marked her speculation on the policy of the councils somehow failed her here.

One man who did nothing, thus following the retrospective advice Arendt offered to the Jewish leaders, was Karl Jaspers. In exile in Switzerland, Jaspers certainly did not act dishonorably nor lend his prestige to the resurgence of barbarism. On the other hand, he did not assert himself in the public space, did not embody the valor of action, did not reach for the eloquence of political speech, did not engage in the collective enterprises by which individual achievement nicks the memory. "In the years of National Socialism," Arendt's teacher recalled, "I . . . remained internally free and did not yield to any pressure by committing a bad act or saying a false word in public, but I did nothing in the fight against this crime. I omitted to do what my heart told me to do. . . . I am no hero and do not want to be considered one." Yet Arendt did not chide Jaspers for his failure to join the anti-Nazi resistance. With no consistency whatsoever she praised her former teacher for his political isolation, for "the magnificence of this position."[64] Was this "the tradition of German philosophy" from which Arendt claimed she had sprung?

194 *Into the Dark*

The case of one of Arendt's other teachers was even more perplexing. Four months after Hitler had become Chancellor of the Reich, Martin Heidegger's rectoral speech to the students of Freiburg hailed "our great and magnificent awakening." The philosopher told the audience: "You should not allow axioms and ideas to regulate your lives. The Fuehrer, and he alone, is the present and future reality and law of Germany." A year later Heidegger was no longer Rector, and he abandoned political commentary whether for or against the regime. Nevertheless his pro-Nazism caused a break in his friendship with Jaspers that was never healed; and for the same reason Arendt's postwar essay, "What Is Existenz Philosophy?," was somewhat more favorable to Jaspers' thought than to Heidegger's.[65] Yet in a 1971 essay she eulogized Heidegger's thought and career, and nothing better demonstrated the distance Arendt had traveled since *The Origins of Totalitarianism*. The philosopher's record in 1933 indicated a very imperfect opposition to the inhuman, yet Arendt wrote that Heidegger's thought "comes from the primeval, and what it leaves behind is something perfect." She could not avoid the fact that he once chose "to get involved in the world of human affairs," yet Arendt's apology evaded the moral problems that such involvement posed. She essentially offered three defenses: (1) Heidegger had neglected to read *Mein Kampf* (as though resistance to Nazism depended on a fuller bibliography); (2) even Plato succumbed to the lure of tyranny (though bad precedents can always be found); (3) "Heidegger himself corrected his own 'error' more quickly and more radically than many of those who later sat in judgment over him —he took considerably greater risks than were usual in German literary and university life during that period" (although these hypocritical judges were not identified, and evidence of Heidegger's courageous acts was not provided).[66]

However commendable this loyalty to a former mentor,

who at least did not "escape from reality" in 1933,[67] Arendt's paltry set of excuses suggested a commitment worthy of a better cause. That commitment supposedly was founded upon a disinterested judgment that relies upon universalist standards, yet these standards were not consistently applied and upheld. She fully acknowledged that Jewish behavior under the impact of Nazi occupation did not markedly differ from that of other subjugated peoples; Arendt, therefore, had less recourse than, say, Hilberg to cite Jewish traditions of compliance to account for the acceleration of the catastrophe.[68] Nevertheless, the contrast between her gingerly treatment of Heidegger and Pius XII, for example, and her icy disdain for the terrorized Jewish elders could scarcely have been greater. The scales were imbalanced. Yet *Eichmann in Jerusalem* was designed to be a judgment of a judgment, a trial report. The book's "sadly limited subject," Arendt wrote, was to determine whether justice had been done in Jerusalem—not to recount the Holocaust, and not to delineate the nature of totalitarianism.[69] Yet her previous work on the history of the Third Reich, her attitudes toward the Jews and toward Israel, and the stance of intellectual independence she found so natural all were necessarily bound up in formulating that judgment. In evaluating the trial of Adolf Eichmann, Arendt managed to articulate anew her attitudes toward the nation-state, toward the rights of humanity, toward Jew-hatred and other issues that had distinguished her diagnosis of *The Origins of Totalitarianism*.

Despite her own anti-Zionism, Arendt's attitude toward the judicial proceedings against Eichmann cannot be classified as hostile. In some instances she supported the various Israeli legal claims; and while she offered specific criticisms, they were quite sensible and prudent. As such they stood in contrast with the bizarre and grotesque complaints against Israel that the trial provoked. One Unitarian minister, for example, professed "in the ethical sense . . . [to] see little difference between the Jew-pursuing Nazi and the Nazi-pursuing Jew." William Stringfellow, an Episcopalian theologian and lawyer, even managed to compare the trials of Jesus and Eichmann: "The defendant in the earlier case was rather different from the present defendant, but nevertheless, he was accused of subverting the Jewish nation. The authorities, as in Eichmann's case, had apprehended him by trick, and there was a dispute about who had jurisdiction to try him." Stringfellow added that "the difference in the two trials is that Eichmann's condemnation does not save a single man from bondage and service to death, while the condemnation of the other defendant set men free from death and from the power of death in their own sin. In both trials, Israel has been confounded in her longing for righteousness."[70] Such exercises in frivolity, so oblivious to the pain of the Holocaust and so perverse an expression of the Christian spirit, were quite alien to the nature of Arendt's objections to the trial of Eichmann in Jerusalem.

The legal controversy that began in 1960 was divided into several components: the manner of Eichmann's capture, the right of the state of Israel to prosecute and punish him, the nature of the accusations brought against the defendant, the fairness of the proceedings, the verdict that was reached and the sentence that was passed upon him. Arendt specifically blamed Israel for fumbling three issues that had arisen ever since Nuremberg—"the problem of impaired justice in the court of the victors; a valid definition of the 'crime against humanity'; and a clear recognition of the new criminal who commits this crime."[71] These criticisms were presented with much ambivalence in the text itself, for she often repeated arguments that had been advanced in legal circles, only to offer effective rebuttals of the very positions she apparently favored. Arendt's discussion of the legal controversy was the least original part of her book, but it was hardly without interest.

The problem of impaired justice in the victors' court had several dimensions, which Telford Taylor, who had been the chief American prosecutor at Nuremberg, concisely summarized. "As a model for the shaping of international law," Taylor argued, "there is little to be said for trying a man at a place far distant from the scene of his actions, in a land to which he had been brought by clandestine force and which was not yet a nation at the time of the alleged crimes." This argument was more fully developed in a pamphlet by Stanford law professor Yosal Rogat, whose analysis Arendt closely followed. Since Eichmann had been abducted from the territory of another sovereign nation, Argentina, only an illegal Israeli act had made trial in Israel possible at all—which Rogat did not consider an auspicious beginning for a judicial procedure. Rogat also pointed out the problem of retroactivity, since Israel had not been a state at the time Eichmann's crimes were committed. And the fact that those crimes had been committed outside the territorial limits of Israel rendered its jurisdiction—its right to try Eichmann—more dubious. Nevertheless Rogat acknowledged that the trial itself was not "plainly" in violation of international law (perhaps nothing is); but "while the legality of Israel's actions *within* international law is ambiguous, the overall impact of the trial *on* international law is clearly undesirable." [72]

That impact may have been less severe than Rogat feared, so long as it is granted that the International Military Tribunals at Nuremberg constituted a salutary precedent in international law. There, too, a question of jurisdiction had arisen, because, as Arendt observed after the war, the Germans themselves did not revolt against the Nazi regime and its henchmen (as, say, the Italian partisans had done with Il Duce). Since the German resistance was so impotent, there was no alternative to a trial by the victors, that is, by those whose existence Nazi terror and aggression had violated.[73] Those who had not participated in the struggle against the Third Reich did not claim a right to render verdicts on its leaders and did not challenge the right of the victors to do so.[74]

Yet in the decade or so after Nuremberg, only Israel—not the United States, not West Germany, not Argentina—had shown any interest in apprehending Nazi criminals responsible for genocide against Jews. Just as there was no alternative to the International Military Tribunals, except to permit the guilty to escape the force of law, Israel could persuasively claim that the alternative to its seizure of Eichmann was that he remain free. As one writer to the New York *Times* put it, "no other nation, legally constituted body, or duly established authority sought the apprehension of that arch murderer. . . . No other government cared whether this criminal was ever captured. No other nation, legislator, or official cared."[75] Lemkin had urged the International Conference for Unification of Criminal Law to make genocide universally punishable, but his proposal had been rejected. If the ends of justice were to be served, if a mass murderer were to be put on trial, Arendt therefore reasoned, "the realm of legality offered no alternative to kidnapping." That act was in itself illegitimate, and the United Nations Security Council censured Israel. But under international law the methods by which a person is apprehended do not abrogate the power of a court to try him. Eichmann was not an Argentine citizen but himself a fugitive from justice, and Argentina did not respond to the Israeli abduction by requesting extradition.[76] At least some of the fears that Rogat and Taylor expressed for the future of international law were therefore unwarranted.

These were among the most pertinent objections to the Israeli operation, though Arendt did not completely share them. "Once the Jews had a territory of their own," she responded, "they obviously had as much right to sit in judgment on the crimes committed against their people as the Poles had to judge crimes committed in Poland." As Poland had executed Rudolf Hoess, the commandant of Auschwitz, for his crimes against citizens of Poland, as Czechoslovakia tried Nazis for their crimes in Prague and Bratislava, so Israel was later within its rights to try Adolf Eichmann. She found objections to the trial based on the principle of territorial jurisdiction "legalistic in the extreme," since the war against the Jews, like the war against the Allies, obeyed no territorial limits. The Jews whom the Nazis slaughtered were not killed as Hungarians or Poles or Greeks but as Jews, whose claims for national sovereignty could not be established until 1948, when it was too late to save the victims but not too late to punish one of their chief tormenters. Arendt added that "the argument that no Jewish State had existed at the time when the crime was committed is surely so formalistic, so out of tune with reality and with all demands that justice must be done, that we may safely leave it to the learned debates of the experts." That rebuttal was not completely responsive, and one of the legal experts dealt with the issue of retroactivity more persuasively: "No sane legislator *could* have contemplated such crime to be even possible and no tribunal could have been provided for its adjudication in advance." Indeed common law crimes were punished in England and the United States, for example, before their proscription in the statute books. The case for Israeli jurisdiction became even stronger when Arendt contrasted the exceedingly light sentences meted out in German courts to former Nazi criminals, who were hardly being brought to justice in the area where their crimes had been committed.[77]

The question of due process within the courtroom was also

part of the debate as to whether "impaired justice" had been
imposed upon Eichmann. Both Rogat and Arendt expressed
doubt that the former Obersturmbannfuehrer S.S. could be
provided with an adequate defense in the *Beth Hamishpat*.
Following Rogat, she asserted that "the most serious flaw" in
safeguarding the defendant's rights was the court's refusal to
"admit witnesses for the defense," since other Nazi war criminals—those who had been intimately associated with Eichmann during the war—would have been subject to prosecution once they set foot on Israeli soil. Some witnesses whom
the defense proposed were in fact granted immunity but preferred not to come to Israel. Sixteen others were interrogated
by West German, Austrian and Italian courts of law, using
questionnaires approved by the prosecution, defense and the
Jerusalem court itself.[78] Although some American academics
believed that "there was no prospect of a fair trial," Telford
Taylor's rebuttal deserves quotation: "I don't believe he
would have been acquitted anywhere. This idea that a trial is
unfair because the outcome is almost inevitable is a spurious
one." The expectation that a given defendant has a real
chance of acquittal, Taylor added, is in fact a demand of more
than fairness. In Jerusalem Eichmann did enjoy all that was
necessary—"fair opportunity to bring forward anything that
might be unexpectedly exculpatory or mitigating."[79]

Eichmann himself did not deny the factual nature of the
charges against him. He acknowledged his responsibility for
transporting the Jews of Nazi-occupied Europe (except for
Poland and Russia) to the camps. "One question," Harold
Rosenberg insisted, "would have sufficed to complete the formulation of his culpability: 'Weren't you the head of Sec. IV
B4 of R.S.H.A. (*Reichssicherheitshauptamt*) charged with the
extermination of the Jews of Europe, and did you not carry
out the function assigned to you to the best of your ability?' "
It is impossible to conceive any truthful answer to this ques-

tion except an affirmative, for Eichmann's guilt was not really in dispute. The *Beth Hamishpat* was more a court of the victims than of the victors; but it was, in Arendt's term, a "successor" to the Nuremberg trials,[80] which she had favored. She defended Israel in the controversy over jurisdiction; and in praising in several places in her book the fairness with which the Israeli judges conducted the trial,[81] she in effect showed how thin the charge of "impaired justice" actually was.

Without directly criticizing the Israeli seizure or questioning Israel's right to try Eichmann, Arendt discussed other possibilities in the pursuit of justice, though the extent of her endorsement of them was ambiguous. Two sympathetic readers of her book have interpreted it as proposing that Eichmann should have been killed on the spot by his Israeli trackers, who would then have been tried for murder.[82] Arendt cited two precedents: (1) in 1926 in Paris, Shalom Schwartzbard murdered Simon Petlyura, who had led Ukrainian bands that had massacred an estimated one hundred thousand Jews during the Russian Civil War in 1918–1920; and (2) in 1921 in Berlin an Armenian named Sogomon Tehlirian assassinated Talaat Bey, a major figure in the Turkish deportation and massacre of over a million Armenians in 1915. Both of the avengers surrendered themselves to the police and demanded a trial, in which the guilt of their particular victims could be proven. Thus the pogroms and massacres could be documented and laid before the conscience of a world that had previously failed to bring the perpetrators of genocide to justice.

"The advantages of this solution" struck Arendt as obvious: "The trial, it is true, is . . . a 'show' trial . . . but its 'hero,' the one at the center of the play, on whom all eyes are fastened, is now the true hero, while at the same time the trial character of the proceedings is safeguarded." In other words the trial "is not 'a spectacle with prearranged results' but contains that element of 'irreducible risk' which, according to [Otto] Kirch-

heimer, is an indispensable factor in all criminal trials."
Schwartzbard and Tehlirian were both members of ethnic
groups deprived of their own state or legal system, and in the
1920s no international tribunal had been established to try
mass murderers like Simon Petlyura or Talaat Bey. Arendt
nevertheless rejected this alternative to trying Eichmann in
Jerusalem—on Zionist grounds. In 1960 the Jews had a state
(whatever her criticisms of its formation), and therefore the
recourse Schwartzbard felt obliged to take was no longer necessary. Moreover, Arendt insisted, murder by government
agents would have been dishonorable and "altogether unjustifiable."[83] The best alternative was therefore a trial—but not
necessarily by the Israelis.

Instead, she apparently subscribed to Jaspers' suggestion
that Israel hear the factual evidence but not pass sentence because, in Arendt's paraphrase, "the legal nature of the crime
in question was still open to dispute." In the light of the rest
of her analysis, this claim made little sense. An international
tribunal, according to Jaspers, would then properly have been
convened to determine the sentence and execute it. Such a
tribunal, according to Nahum Goldmann, the president of
the World Jewish Congress, should have been established in
Jerusalem, with representatives from each of the nations that
had endured Nazi conquest and occupation serving on the
bench.[84] These proposals all attempted to confront the nature
of the crimes Eichmann had committed, which some legal
theorists defined as crimes against humanity rather than specifically against one people.

Israel justified its prosecution of Eichmann on the basis of
his crimes committed against the Jewish people, which meant,
according to Rogat, that "Israel defined the crime in terms of
the particular group injured, rather than in terms of the nature of the acts committed, and assumed that the victims
rather than the larger community should punish it." Such an

argument was fraught with internal tension, because, as Rogat shrewdly pointed out, "the very act of establishing a unique right to prosecute as a victim puts into question a right to judge." Morton Horwitz of Harvard Law School insisted that "the idea that a crime against Jews is not a crime against humanity is tantamount to asserting that humanity itself has no responsibility in such cases." This broader concern was also the basis of Telford Taylor's suggestion of an international tribunal (under United Nations auspices), though his even stronger and more ingenious preference was for Israel to hold an inquest before turning Eichmann over to West Germany for trial. Prime Minister Ben-Gurion had made no secret of the "educational" purposes of the trial, and Taylor therefore argued that the West Germans had far more to learn from the trial of Adolf Eichmann than the Israelis needed to know.[85]

Though Arendt was uncomfortable with the exclusivity of the Israeli claims, she understood the force of the Zionists' argument that their state, too, could exercise the right to prosecute and punish the murderers of the Jews. For the first time since the year 70, "Jews were able to sit in judgment on crimes committed against their own people" without having "to appeal to others for protection and justice." With this assertion of Israeli rights, the Jews did not have to "fall back upon the compromised phraseology of the rights of man—rights which, as no one knew better than they, were claimed only by people who were too weak . . . to enforce their own laws."[86] On that basis, the case for returning Eichmann to West Germany for sentencing, as Taylor advocated, was not persuasive, especially since capital punishment had been abolished there. Because of the identity of the defendant himself, Israel was especially reluctant "to appeal to others for protection and justice."

For in at least one respect Eichmann differed from the

major Nazi criminals, apart from Streicher, who were sentenced to death at Nuremberg. He was not involved in war crimes as such, in the planning and execution of aggressive war, or in the use of forced labor to perpetuate that war. Eichmann's sole responsibility, when the Final Solution was ordered, was to facilitate the killing of Jews, on which he was the leading "expert" within the S.S. His was a crime against humanity; and by trying him, Israel drew attention to a crime that had not been emphasized, even at Nuremberg. There, in 1946, "witnesses to the great atrocities [in the camps] were used very sparingly," one historian of the International Military Tribunals has noted. "Planning of aggressive war was the big issue for the Americans, and they emphasized only those war crimes that suggested the existence of a conspiratorial plan or could be related to war planning." The charge of conspiracy to wage aggressive war was stressed so heavily at Nuremberg that the *defense*, to prove that the death camps were secret and tangential to the issue of general conspiracy, put the ex-commandant of Auschwitz himself on the stand.[87] This distortion of justice, this suppression of the screams of the victims, the state of Israel intended to rectify.

Since the end of the Second World War, Arendt had consistently argued that genocide is not a war crime, not a series of "inhuman acts" for some familiar though criminal purpose. She propounded the view that "totalitarian domination . . . has broken the continuity of Occidental history," in part because its policies and perpetrators "cannot be judged by traditional moral standards or punished within the legal framework of our civilization." Commenting on the trials in Frankfurt (after Eichmann's execution) of some of the S.S. men stationed in Auschwitz, Arendt emphasized the inadequacy of the 1871 German penal code under which the indictments were drawn: "There was no article that covered organized murder as a government institution, none that dealt with

the extermination of whole peoples as part of demographic
policies. . . ." The Frankfurt defendants had participated in
"administrative massacres" not envisioned in 1871. What occurred in Auschwitz required in some cases a reversal of the
rules, she insisted; it was guilt that had to be presumed, innocence that had to be proved.[88] Arendt insisted that Nazism was
something more than the culmination of millennia of anti-
Semitism, even though racial hatred was the starting point of
her own *Origins of Totalitarianism*—which Rogat considered
"the best analysis we have" of how unbearable was the strain
the Nazis' "absolute evil" placed upon the legal system. The
Jerusalem court, she claimed, had focused so fully on the
crimes against the Jewish people that it failed to understand
the extinction of the six million as an "attack upon human
diversity itself." Tried under Israeli rather than international
law, Eichmann was therefore misconceived as exclusively the
embodiment of Jew-hatred. He had in fact committed "crimes
against humanity"; for "the international order, and mankind
in its entirety, might have been grievously hurt and endangered" had the Allies lost the Second World War.[89]

The gravity of the issue here masked the querulousness of
Arendt's remarks. She was "apparently unaware," Jacob Robinson suspected, "that criminal codes do not define common
law crimes as violation of the law of the national community,
but more exactly as separate punishable acts." The function
of a criminal court is to apply existing law, such as the 1950
Israeli provision for punishment of Nazis and Nazi collaborators. While Eichmann had been assigned the primary responsibility within the R.S.H.A. for the "resettlement" of Jews,
his crimes, according to the judges in Jerusalem, "afflict the
whole of mankind and shock the conscience of nations." Eichmann had committed "grave offenses against the law of nations itself," the judges announced, thereby finding him
"guilty of crimes against the Jewish people, of crimes against

humanity, of war crimes and of membership in criminal associations."[90] It is hard to see what else the judges, whose responsibility was to apply the law, were supposed to do to make clearer the full scope of Eichmann's violation of the human order. Arendt did not explain how an Israeli court acted *against* the interests of humanity in trying and punishing Eichmann for his specific crimes against the Jews. Not only Jewish interests but also broader standards of justice were served when Israel—and Israel alone—found, prosecuted and convicted the former Obersturmbannfuehrer of the S.S.

Though Arendt refuted several criticisms of the trial others presented, her own somewhat equivocal opposition to this expression of Jewish sovereignty fit into a larger pattern. It was apparently one of her beliefs that those commonly deprived of public space cannot be expected to understand their own best interests, whether it be the *enragés* of the earth pursuing economic objectives as a relief from their misery, or American blacks giving the desegregation of public education higher priority than the abrogation of intermarriage laws, or the Jewish State refusing to concede its unsuitability to judge the Third Reich's most lethal "expert" on the Jewish Question. No scholar had been more poignant and convincing than Arendt in demonstrating the hollowness of the language of international human rights in the twentieth century, and it was an achievement of the Jerusalem court to pierce the abstractness of such standards of justice. An international tribunal might have smothered the historical record of deliberate, specific genocide against the Jews. In its attempt to formulate a comprehensive definition of "crimes against humanity," such a court might have issued an opinion equivalent to the Soviet monument at Babi Yar. The plaque there reads only that "citizens of Kiev and prisoners of war" were executed in the vicinity. The visitor has no way of knowing that the approximately 50,000 Soviet citizens murdered there in thirty-six hours in September, 1941, were Jews. At least the Israeli affirmation of the right to judge Adolf Eichmann ensured that the identity of his victims would not be forgotten. By denying in her conception of politics the validity of suffering, Arendt also risked distortion of the anguish of justice. In incorporating the pleas of the victims, Israel was right to assert universal claims in defense of a particular people. In advancing the responsibility to judge Eichmann, the Israeli legal system was restraining the passion for revenge for the sake of general principles. For justice, Michael Walzer has argued in another context, "must be done, for the sake of the victims, on behalf of the victims, though in the name of everyone. It isn't revenge, but it is retribution—and it wouldn't be just if it wasn't."[91]

Arendt's third criticism—that Eichmann represented a new kind of criminal whom the court had failed to understand—was developed with such startling freshness in her book that a separate discussion of her portrait of him is necessary.

Chapter 7

⚑

BANALITY ON TRIAL

ORN into a solidly bourgeois family in the Rhineland
and raised in Austria, Adolf Eichmann had been a salesman before joining the Nazi party and the S.S., in which
he was to be commended for his "comprehensive knowledge
of the methods of organization and ideology of the opponent,
Jewry." When his superiors made the expulsion of Jewry
their policy, Eichmann was actively involved; when their policy was annihilation, he directed "resettlement." In Robert
Jackson's closing address at Nuremberg, Eichmann was described as "the sinister figure who had charge of the extermination program."[1] Shortly before the war was over, Eichmann
had boasted to his associates that he would "jump into his
grave laughing, because the fact that I have the death of five
million Jews [or 'enemies of the Reich'] on my conscience
gives me extraordinary satisfaction."[2]

A decade and a half later, when he reappeared in history
inside a glass booth in an Israeli courtroom, it was that conscience that perhaps most astonished and appalled the report-
er from the *New Yorker*. After studying his career and observing him during the fourteen weeks of the trial, Arendt
concluded that Eichmann was unaware of his own wickedness.
Though she doubted that his judges had understood the novelty of this kind of criminal, she argued that a man like Eich-

mann had committed "his crimes under circumstances that make it well-nigh impossible for him to know or to feel that he is doing wrong." He had personally never killed anyone and had never ordered anyone to be killed. He was "neither perverted nor sadistic," nor was he demonic nor monstrous. He was instead "terribly and terrifyingly normal, and his character constituted the opposite of greatness." Arendt later recalled being "struck by a manifest shallowness in the doer which made it impossible to trace the incontestable evil of his deeds to any deeper level of roots or motives."[3] As the representative product of a totalitarian movement, Eichmann was a mass murderer for whom murder was not fiendish but impersonal and indifferent, a matter of following rules, obeying orders, arranging schedules with utmost meticulousness and dedication. It was having done so with such effectiveness, Arendt suggested, that gave the lieutenant colonel "extraordinary satisfaction."

Arendt resisted the temptation to define Eichmann as the culmination of the forces of bigotry, however coldly and completely the Jews had themselves been defined as "enemies of the Reich." Nazi policy came close to achieving what Proudhon had dreamed of a century earlier: "It is necessary to send this race back to Asia, or exterminate it. What the people of the Middle Ages hated by instinct, I hate by reflection, and irrevocably," for the Jew was "the enemy of human-kind."[4] Without his realizing it, Hitler's first recorded public remarks echoed Proudhon's formulation. Yet Eichmann himself seemed to lack this obsessive wrath formulated into an "idea." He told his Israeli captors that he had felt no hatred for the Jews, and Arendt believed him; he exhibited no "firm ideological convictions or . . . specific evil motives." Though he prided himself on being an "idealist," he really believed in nothing. Though the consequences of his actions were horrible, he lacked any emotional connection to them. Arendt's

book minimized the defendant's commitments, discovered in
him no obsessions, no emotional intensity, no chthonic fury.
Unlike Hitler or Goebbels or Streicher, Eichmann occupied
no firm place in the history of anti-Semitic hysteria. He bore
no resemblance to purely fictional villains like Iago or Mac-
beth because, "except for an extraordinary diligence in looking out for his personal advancement, he had no motives at
all."[5] His own career was all that Eichmann lived for, and
there was no idea what he would have been willing to die for.

Yeats' famous summation of the modern predicament in
"The Second Coming" found no corroboration in Arendt's
portrait, for Eichmann was not "full of passionate intensity."
Even more striking was the break with Jean-Paul Sartre's
classic postwar study of the anti-Semite, a creature dominated
by a "passion," by the "emotions of hate or anger." Sartre's
"man of the crowd" attaching himself to "the tradition of the
mediocre" was extrapolated from the French, whom Nazi
claimants to "scientific" knowledge of the Jewish Question
held in contempt (Proudhon's dream of extermination might
nevertheless be kept in mind). Nor did Arendt's interpretation of Eichmann bear much resemblance to Eric Hoffer's
"true believer," a fanatic whose hatred leads him to an all-
absorbing adherence to mass movements and who revels in
chaos.[6] Adorno's "authoritarian personality" was an ideal type
which no individual could completely embody. Nevertheless,
it is striking that Arendt's description of Eichmann's persona
only partly resembled the high scorers on Adorno's F Scale,
those who exhibited "a mechanical surrender to conventional
values; blind submission to authority together with blind
hatred of all opponents and outsiders; anti-introspectiveness;
rigid stereotyped thinking; a penchant for superstition; vili-
fication, half-moralistic and half-cynical, of human nature;
projectivity." If Arendt was correct, Eichmann was not even
like the police state bureaucrats whom Kennan portrayed as

"brutal, aggressive, unsuccessful natures" who "merge with the born criminal element" and who are quite invisible "in the sunlight of normalcy."[7] Arendt's portrait of Eichmann therefore marked a new phase in the delineation of the totalitarian mind.

As Scholem was perhaps the first to point out, the implications she drew from Eichmann's nature also posed a contrast with the ineluctable theme of "radical evil" in *The Origins of Totalitarianism*. In 1951 she had discerned in the Third Reich and in the Soviet regime the insertion into politics of an absolute that had never previously been experienced. In observing Eichmann, however, Arendt realized that evil could also be banal; and the subtitle of her book was meant to signal her own sense of the particular originality of this aspect of totalitarianism. Behind her phrase, "the banality of evil," she later insisted, "I held no thesis or doctrine, although I was dimly aware that it went counter to our tradition of thought—literary, theological, or philosophical—about the phenomenon of evil." (Melville's Claggart, for example, is gripped by "the mania of an evil nature . . . [which was] born with him and innate, in short 'a depravity according to nature.' ") The tradition of meditation on evil included her own contribution, which her new analysis was intended not to supplement but to displace. For Arendt asserted, after observing Eichmann in Jerusalem, that evil could never be " 'radical' . . . only extreme," because it lacks "depth" as well as "any demonic dimension." Though Scholem himself dismissed "the banality of evil" as a "catchword" rather than "the product of profound analysis," it was arresting enough to become an inescapable part of the language.[8] Over a decade later, the phrase Arendt coined had "attained the status of a Homeric epithet in the world of intellectual journalism," an inhabitant of that world commented, "so that banality and evil are forever yoked together."[9] Her description of Eichmann's wickedness as common in its flatness had itself become something of a commonplace.

Such a concept should not have been too startling in an era in which the pressures of mass society had diminished the ethos of heroism, in which the dictatorial entourage and the loyal followers appeared to be interchangeable. In Nabokov's *Bend Sinister*, the tyrant Paduk is the leader of the Party of the Average Man; and in Padukgrad, "everybody is merely an anagram of everybody else." What struck many observers was that Eichmann's mind was stocked with cliches, inconsistent with one another; his language was that of bureaucracy. He was so little cognizant of what he had done or where he was that Arendt found it difficult to "take him seriously." In defending Arendt's revised interpretation of totalitarianism, Macdonald wondered: "The discrepancy between the personal mediocrity of Stalin and Hitler, the banality of their ideas, and the vastness of the evils they inflicted—is she really the first to notice this?"[10]

The answer is no. There is even a literary antecedent in *Under Western Eyes*, in which the character of Nikita (Necator), Joseph Conrad explained, "is the perfect flower of the terroristic wilderness. What troubled me most in dealing with him was not his monstrosity but his banality. . . . All these people are not the product of the exceptional but of the general. . . ."[11] There are resonances of this theme in the writings of Karl Kraus,[12] and Brecht anticipated Macdonald's awareness of incongruity in commenting about the Nazis: "They are, above all, not great political criminals, but perpetrators of great political crimes, which is something quite different." Konrad Heiden, whose biography of Hitler Arendt admired, depicted him as both "terrible and banal" and described the Fuehrer as "the void . . . disguised . . . as a man." And although Arendt would not have extended this thesis to Hitler himself, Herbert Lüthy also wondered how the historian of

the Third Reich could "make the catastrophic magnitude of
the events tally with the inconceivable commonplaceness of
the individual who set them in motion."[13] In a formulation
that Macdonald and Lüthy echoed, Deutscher's biography of
Stalin had drawn attention to the "baffling disproportion between the magnitude of the second revolution [in the 1930s]
and the stature of its maker, a disproportion which was not
noticeable in the revolution of 1917." For Lenin's supreme
political skills were evident before then to his rivals and enemies, while the enormity of the upheavals of the 1930s managed "to reflect their greatness upon the leader"—whose individual role was in fact even more indispensable than Lenin's
had been in making the Bolshevik revolution of 1917.[14]

Covering the War Crimes Tribunal, Rebecca West had observed only the sinister allure, the sadism of "maniacs"—not
banality. But discernible outlines of Arendt's interpretation
can be found in Trevor-Roper's 1946 description of Himmler,
though Eichmann was without the eccentricity of his superior,
who was a lethal combination of pedant and crank. On the
other hand the trial of Otto Ohlendorf, who had commanded
one of the mobile execution squads (*Einsatzgruppen*), provoked an insightful report by Tania Long. No effort had been
made to recruit sadists or qualified killers as commandos.
Ohlendorf's unit had murdered 90,000 Jews within one year;
but his victims, Long wrote, "seemed to rest easily on his conscience. He talked in a matter-of-fact tone, admitting each
mass killing as if the victims had been cattle or sheep. Yet in
appearance he is not particularly brutal or inhuman, looking
more like a somewhat humorless shoe salesman one might
meet anywhere." His descriptions of the genocidal operations,
which resembled "an ordinary business transaction,"[15] had
the same toneless manner Eichmann later displayed with his
charts of destruction in the *Beth Hamishpat*. As early as January 1945, Arendt had suspected that, when the occupation of

"the mob man" requires him "to murder people[,] he does
not regard himself as a murderer[,] because he has not done
it out of inclination but in his professional capacity. Out of
sheer passion," she added, "he would never do harm to a fly."
In *The Origins of Totalitarianism* itself, the author had refused to predict "what will happen once the authentic mass
man takes over. . . . [But] it may be a fair guess that he will
have more in common with the meticulous, calculated correctness of Himmler than with the hysterical fanaticism of
Hitler, will more resemble the stubborn dullness of Molotov
than the sensual vindictive cruelty of Stalin."[16] At the center
of totalitarianism could be found not only monstrousness but
mediocrity.

By 1963 Arendt therefore concluded, in a striking sentence,
that "evil in the Third Reich had lost the quality by which
most people recognize it—the quality of temptation." *Eichmann in Jerusalem* was not the first book to draw attention to
this phenomenon, but no other work compelled such attention through the emphatic consistency of her portrait of a
special kind of criminal. As a result, Robert Lowell could not
"think of a more terrifying character in either biography or
fiction or one conceived in quite this manner."[17] She was
sufficiently original to be misunderstood. She never said that
banality is itself evil, nor that there is an Eichmann in everyone. Arendt did not claim, as Lawrence L. Langer believed,
that "the evil caused by an Eichmann might be rooted in a
banality of temperament." He became a mass murderer not
because of his temperament but because he was unaware of
his own wickedness in the assumption of duty. What characterized Eichmann was "sheer thoughtlessness—something by
no means identical with stupidity." He *"never realized what
he was doing"*—and that made him banal, though not commonplace. Such human beings are frightening and dangerous,
Arendt claimed, because their thoughtlessness and distance

from reality "can wreak more havoc than all the evil instincts taken together."[18] Here she overstated her case, since Eichmann was made possible by Hitler, whose personality was fiendish as well as empty. The Fuehrer bore the overwhelming responsibility for the Second World War and for the Holocaust, just as Stalin was incontrovertibly responsible for the vast purges of the 1930s. The evil instincts of the dictators themselves were the demiurges of the world of totalitarian crimes, however much the rulers depended upon unthinking, unblinking bureaucrats to execute their criminal plans.

The danger of thoughtlessness was what Arendt had learned in Jerusalem; "but it was a lesson, neither an explanation of the phenomenon nor a theory about it." Oddly enough she claimed no more for the subtitular reference to "the banality of evil" than "the strictly factual level, pointing to a phenomenon which stared one in the face at the trial."[19] But that level was by no means evident to others, including the prosecutor, judges and other observers. It was clearly an interpretation which, however she may have regretted its inflation when used by others, unified the various perceptions offered of the defendant's career and character. As a result, Macdonald concluded, Eichmann became even more fearsome, "precisely *because* he had no special animus against the Jews, *because* he had no sense he was doing wrong, since he was a loyal and conscientious servant of the state." In 1945 Arendt had already understood that. At least after *Kristallnacht*, the Nazis were not updated Black Hundreds, not wrathful Cossacks, not perpetrators of pogroms on an inconceivable scale. The S.S. believed it had gone well beyond the old-fashioned anti-Semitism it encountered in France and Rumania, and Rudolf Hoess vastly preferred the methods he administered in Auschwitz to the "bloodbaths" of the past. Even before Arendt was likely to have heard of Eichmann, he embodied what she had in mind, for "concerted government action . . .

proved infinitely more detrimental than any popular outburst of Jew-hatred had ever been."[20] It might be added that, if her interpretation was correct, killers like Eichmann are all the more dangerous, for they pose not only a threat to Jews but to everyone.

Arendt's portrait led Lowell to conclude that Eichmann's "life is as close to living in hell as I can imagine, and I am able to see it as such because Miss Arendt has refused to simplify the picture with melodrama or blur it with cliches."[21] The poet neglected the less assimilable point that it was Eichmann's *victims* who had been in hell; but Lowell inadvertently confirmed the aphorism of William Blake that salvation would be granted not to those who "have curbed and governed their passions, or have no passions," but to those who "have cultivated their understandings." Arendt's effort to cultivate her own understanding of the defendant was bound to be disorienting, as she once again showed an almost incomparable skill in analyzing the totalitarian mind, in translating thought processes into terms that do not violate the nature of the responsible intelligence. That made her virtually unique. At Nuremberg neither Rebecca West nor the prosecutors could fathom why the Nazi war criminals "had done what they did. . . . No literate person can now pretend that these men were anything but abscesses of cruelty. But we learned nothing about them we did not know before." In Jerusalem Harold Rosenberg expressed his impatience with the indulgence built into the judicial process: "Why should this self-styled nobody who had hurled into silence so many of the subtlest and most humane intellects of Europe have been permitted to elaborate on each trait of his character, his opinions on all sorts of matters?"[22] Arendt was unusual not only in her interpretation of Eichmann but in the intensity of her belief that his character needed to be limned. Having avoided the fate of so many other of the subtlest and most humane intellects, she could do nothing else.

More so than any other observer of the trial, Arendt sought to stretch the moral imagination, so that a new kind of danger to humanity might be recognized. At the end of the nineteenth century, Nietzsche's descent into madness was punctuated by his statement: "I am just having all anti-Semites shot."[23] In the twentieth century, trying to have all the Jews murdered did not affect one's sanity, for within the totalitarian system it was possible to kill without hatred or any other emotion, without guilt or remorse. Eichmann was of course judged legally sane and fully competent to stand trial. This phenomenon especially unsettled Thomas Merton, who was accustomed to equating sanity "with a sense of justice, with humaneness, with prudence, with the capacity to love and understand other people." Yet those who are sane, the monk concluded, "are the most dangerous," for they may not be in their right minds. It may be added in passing that the comedian Lenny Bruce sometimes brought his night club act to an end by reading, in a German accent, Merton's reflections on Eichmann.[24] Similarly it occurred to Elie Wiesel, who also noticed Eichmann's utter banality, that "if he were sane, I should choose madness. It was he or I. . . . We could not inhabit the same universe."[25] It was a natural reaction, but one which the preeminent student of totalitarianism resisted. Instead she chose moral poise and intellectual coherence, in which the shocks that were registered in the courtroom were put into the service of a thesis. Arendt managed to present evidence in such a way that no other version of Eichmann's career and character was available in her account. Everything in it was designed to project the interpretation of a murderer without motive, a bureaucrat for whom wrong consisted of disobeying orders, a Nazi who was not demonic but thoughtless. The criticisms of her thesis often did not take into account the cohesiveness and totality of her interpretation. They sometimes had far less empirical support as well.

Arendt's acceptance of Eichmann's claim that he lacked hatred for the Jews caused some difficulty, including a simple failure to read competently. The reviewer in the New York *Times Book Review*, Justice Michael Musmanno of the Pennsylvania Supreme Court, claimed that Arendt suggested that "Eichmann loved the Jews," thus twisting lack of hatred into love, which are obviously quite different.[26] The issue Musmanno joined was not what Eichmann did, but why he did it; the judge was unable to locate the demonic motives of the S.S. lieutenant-colonel in carrying out the orders for the Final Solution. Musmanno was not alone in preferring generalizations about the Nazi mentality to the complexities of historical evidence, therefore dismissing Arendt's thesis. "Uninteresting though it may be to say so," Norman Podhoretz asserted, "no person could have joined the Nazi party, let alone the S.S., who was not at the very least a *vicious* anti-Semite; to believe otherwise is to learn nothing about the nature of anti-Semitism." Though much still needs to be learned about the mystery of anti-Semitism, Podhoretz was wrong. Some Germans became Nazis despite, not because of, the party's anti-Semitic ideology.[27] Albert Speer joined the N.S.D.A.P. in 1931 and the S.S. the following year, and at Nuremberg told his judges: "If Hitler had had any friends, I would certainly have been one of his close friends." Yet Speer recalled few expressions of anti-Semitism in Hitler's numerous conversations with him; he took the Fuehrer's hatred of the Jews for granted, but apparently did not share those sentiments. Speer, the Minister of Armaments, knew more about the Holocaust than he claimed to remember after leaving Spandau prison, but "in none of my speeches, letters, or actions is there any trace of anti-Semitic feelings or phraseology." The exploitation of slave labor was a terrifying crime, but students of the technocrat's career have failed to discover ideological hatred in his makeup.[28] Speer's dispassion does not of course demonstrate Eichmann's. It does indicate, however, that ideological consistency could not be enforced, even in the upper echelons of the Third Reich.

Even the first commandant of Auschwitz claimed to "have never personally hated the Jews. It is true that I looked upon them as the enemies of our people. . . . [But] the emotion of hatred is foreign to my nature"—though not, if Rudolf Hoess is to be believed, foreign to Eichmann's. Hoess recalled many conversations with him and found him "completely obsessed with the idea of destroying every single Jew that he could lay his hands on. Without pity and in cold blood [Eichmann insisted] we must complete this extermination as rapidly as possible." Eichmann was certain, the former commandant recalled shortly before his own execution, that "if he could succeed in destroying the biological basis of Jewry in the east by complete extermination, then Jewry as a whole would never recover from the blow."[29] The ferocity of this determination to destroy can in fact be corroborated in an episode that Arendt rather disturbingly garbled. The last major community of Jews to be extinguished was in Hungary, though exceptions to the Final Solution were to be made for about seven thousand families. Instead of going to Auschwitz, they would be permitted to leave Hungary, presumably through Rumania. The Reichsfuehrer S.S. was also interested in currying favor with the advancing Allies. "When Himmler's order to stop the evacuation of Hungarian Jews arrived in Budapest," Arendt wrote, "Eichmann threatened . . . 'to seek a new decision from the Fuehrer,'" according to a telegram from an official in the German Foreign Office stationed in Hungary. Since the telegram hardly showed Eichmann to be a subservient bureaucrat who would never question the order of a

superior, the Jerusalem court considered the telegram "more
damning than a hundred witnesses could be."[30]

How did Arendt account for this desire to break the S.S.
chain of command, to appeal to the Fuehrer in the hope that
no Jewish lives be spared? She denied that it was fanaticism
in the form of anti-Semitism—the most plausible explanation,
and thereby unsuited to Arendt's style of thought. Instead,
she argued, Eichmann's desire to countermand Himmler's
order was based upon his inordinate love of the Leader, whose
word was law in the Third Reich, whose unwritten command
to destroy European Jewry was to be unflinchingly obeyed.
The only trouble with this explanation was that Arendt confused the roles of Himmler and Hitler in granting an exception for some Hungarian Jews, for in fact Hitler himself was
very slightly relenting in his otherwise insatiable impulse to
kill. In seeking "a new decision from the Fuehrer," Eichmann
was in fact trying to keep Hitler himself to his promise to
annihilate Jewish life on the continent.[31] Here, in this conflict of conscience, Eichmann revealed the intensity of his will
to pursue the Final Solution when even his superiors—Himmler to some extent and Hitler in one small instance—chose to
abandon the policy after almost six million Jews had already
been slaughtered. What is disconcerting about Arendt's account here is not only the factual error but, more importantly,
its tendentiousness—the manipulation of evidence to further
an interpretation which should have been presented with
greater shading.

For it is not psychologically impossible that Eichmann's
desire to kill the Jews had assumed the status of an obligation,
a duty to be fulfilled at all costs, once the order had come
down. It was the responsibility with which he had been
charged, and it was an order that was never directly contra-
dicted either by Himmler or Hitler. In the absence of clearly
contradictory signals, Eichmann remained bound to his oath

to the Fuehrer as he understood it, as he understood the Fuehrer's will to destroy the enemies of the Reich. For Eichmann was a paradoxical embodiment of totalitarianism in the extremity of his willingness to destroy and his eagerness to submit. Already in *The Origins of Totalitarianism*, Arendt had seen in the coupling of race and bureaucracy the genesis of the mentality Eichmann came to share. "Bureaucracy," she wrote, "is always a government of experts"; the Jewish Question was what made Eichmann an expert within the S.S. Once he was so defined, the functionary within the totalitarian system "entered the maelstrom of an unending process of expansion." A figure like Eichmann could therefore "obey the laws of the process," identifying himself with those forces of history that Hitler's will articulated. Thus the whole process of expansion and extinction could be kept in motion.[32]

The alternative view, which denied Eichmann's bureaucratic orientation and which depicted him instead as a virulent anti-Semite who happened to find himself behind a desk, was based upon very thin evidence, if any. Rebutting Arendt's interpretation, Stephen Miller has speculated that Eichmann "must have been immensely proud of his days as a Nazi." He must therefore have seen himself "as a heroic warrior, a member of the Volk. . . . As a Nazi, Eichmann probably saw himself as an enemy of bureaucratization, a foreign disease that should not be allowed to infect Germany." After all, Miller continued, "the Nazis gained converts by preaching against bureaucratization—preaching against all the soulless 'rational' forces that were destroying what they thought were the ancient virtues of the German race." This speculation was just that, for it was unsupported by any statements Eichmann ever made, any of the data of his biography. By contrast, Arendt's view was at least based on Eichmann's self-image, however distorted it may have been in Jerusalem, and on the historical record. Miller's judgment, which paralleled the prosecutorial

presentation of Eichmann as an acetylene anti-Semite, was
utterly unempirical, seeking to explain the personality of an
individual solely on the basis of a generalization that Nazi
bureaucracy had to be a contradiction in terms, whatever the
historical proof of the importance of the phenomenon.[33]

🥀

In its very repugnance, Eichmann's emotional life was
bound to exert fascination; and the view that the perpetrator
of such incalculable suffering was banal necessarily generated
controversy. While jettisoning the notion of radical evil,
Arendt did not make sweeping claims that all the evil of the
Third Reich was without monstrousness. But she did insist on
the apparent normality of Eichmann himself, whom she
found grotesquely comic in the failure of the consequences of
his acts to register upon his consciousness. His short-circuited
sense of moral responsibility was so unnerving, so staggering
to contemplate, that it was tempting to find refuge in the villainy, presented by the prosecuting attorney, who "knew Eichmann to be a cunning, flinthearted plotter, with a demonic
personality which certainly was completely indifferent to the
suffering he inflicted . . . and which reveled in the exercise of
power." Eichmann, Gideon Hausner added, "was possessed
of a dangerous, perverted personality." This was also the interpretation of an erstwhile colleague of Arendt's on the Committee on Social Thought at the University of Chicago. For
Saul Bellow, speaking (it can be presumed) as Artur Sammler,
the Nazis knew exactly what they were doing, knew what
murder is. "The banality was only camouflage," the fictional
Holocaust survivor Sammler declaimed. "What better way to
get the curse out of murder than to make it look ordinary,
boring or trite?" The banality of evil was therefore the exploitation of "a tragic history to promote the foolish ideas of
Weimar intellectuals."[34] It was merely a reflection from litera-

ture—the medium, of course, in which Bellow/Sammler also discredited the idea.

Several psychologists concurred. The results of the Szondi test, which is designed to locate antisocial impulses in criminals and which Eichmann took ten times, were sent to Szondi himself. Though the identity of the Israelis' prisoner had presumably not been disclosed, Szondi replied: "You have on your hands a most dangerous person." The psychologist claimed to have tested over six thousand criminals in twenty-four years, of whom this particular subject was the most remarkable. Michael Selzer, a political scientist, sent six other psychologists Eichmann's psychological drawings, also made in Israel, as part of the Bender-Gestalt and the House-Person-Tree Tests. The psychologists were told only the subject's sex, age, and the attribute of having been famous. Emphasizing the subject's violent personality, obsessive-compulsive nature and paranoia, five of the psychologists were, according to Selzer, not "particularly surprised to learn that his name was Adolf Eichmann." (The sixth psychologist had figured the subject out to be similar to Adlai Stevenson.)[35]

There may have been a reason why those five psychologists were not "particularly surprised" when the identity of the subject was revealed. As Thomas Litwack, a psychologist at John Jay College pointed out, the diagnosticians could have assumed, since the test was presented to them by a political scientist, that an important political figure was being evaluated. It would also have been a fair assumption that the subject had committed atrocities or had suffered a terrible breakdown, for "why else would he have been subjected to psychological tests?" Litwack would have been more impressed had the psychologists "picked Eichmann's drawings out of a random sample of drawings as being done by someone particularly violent or psychopathic." That diagnostic skill Selzer's psychologists had not been asked to demonstrate.

There is something much too pat about the audacity of the conclusions that Szondi and the other psychologists are reported to have reached. Even if Eichmann's emotional life had been as violent as the evaluations suggested, the tests could in no way establish a link between such aggressiveness and the virulence of the anti-Semitism commonly attributed to him. Even Selzer conceded that Arendt was correct that Eichmann was not "a Nazi ideologue."[36]

Interestingly enough, *The Nuremberg Mind*, which Selzer coauthored with psychologist Florence Miale in 1975, was vulnerable to similar methodological criticism. The two writers had discerned dangerous abnormalities in the personalities of the Nuremberg defendants, as revealed by Rorschach tests. But "even a well-trained clinician can be influenced by what he expects to find," which is why psychologist Molly Harrower insisted that Rorschach tests "must be scored 'blind.' " Selzer and Miale did not do so. Unfortunately Harrower's own methods do not inspire confidence. She sent the tests of eight of the Nuremberg defendants along with those of eight non-Nazis to other psychologists, who were unable to distinguish the two groups. But Harrower's definitions were too crude to be of any value. Two Nazis, Speer and Ribbentrop, were classified as having "disturbed" or "impoverished" personalities. Hess, whose insanity was plain to observers, did better; his personality was, rather primly, called "less than adequate." But the biggest surprise among the Nuremberg defendants was the "normal personality" exhibited by Eichmann, who was not of course on trial there. Neither Harrower nor *Psychology Today*, which published her article, explained how Eichmann had been flushed out of hiding long enough to take a Rorschach test, which the psychologist then used to reinforce her point that "it *can* happen here."[37]

The brutality of the interior life sometimes claimed for Eichmann resembles less that of typical party functionary than

of the especially violent criminal whose multiple murders, as
in Truman Capote's *In Cold Blood*, constitute "virtually an
impersonal act." No hatred, no hard feelings. "I didn't want
to harm . . . [Herbert Clutter]," Perry Smith recalled, as
Capote listened. "I thought he was a very nice gentleman.
Soft-spoken. I thought so right up to the moment I cut his
throat."[38] Between the Clutters' killers and Eichmann, some
resemblance can perhaps be traced in terms of the absence of
any human connection, any emotional bearing to be attached
to their crimes. They were terrifyingly estranged from the
rest of the human race. The differences however may be more
striking—apart from the fact that murderers like Smith and
Dick Hickok wanted only to disguise their own identities and
cover their tracks, whereas totalitarian executioners seek to
obliterate all trace of their victims. Eichmann could not be
regarded as a psychopathic killer writ large; he was not simply
an ordinary criminal who had been given an S.S. colonel's
uniform and some railroad schedules and allowed to gratify
his lust for blood. Arendt argued on the contrary that, under
happier circumstances, Eichmann was very unlikely ever to
have been a defendant in a criminal court. Had the Weimar
Republic lasted longer, those lethal impulses that the psychologists purported to find in the House-Person-Tree Test
would have almost certainly remained suppressed. Unlike
Shakespearean villains, for example, Eichmann "certainly
would never have murdered his superior in order to inherit
his post."[39] In that respect he fit successfully into a totalitarian
universe noteworthy for its immunity from coup d'etats, for
its dutiful police chiefs. Eichmann was peculiarly scary because of his diligence and devotion, which safeguarded him
against the realization of his own wickedness.

Eichmann in Jerusalem must be regarded therefore as a
partial sequel to *The Origins of Totalitarianism*—because
such a character could flourish in the system that Nazism

established. In the Reich, distance could be achieved between
government and the executors of its policies, between the oral
command and the execution of the eleven million civilians,
Jewish and Gentile, who were victims of the Nazis' crimes
against humanity. Hitler never visited a concentration camp,
immunizing himself against the evil he wrought; Eichmann
was a criminal not because he could not restrain his violent
impulses but because he worked within a political system bent
on destruction. His character and his crimes showed how
magnified had become the problem earlier formulated by
Freud: "The state has forbidden to the individual the practice of wrong-doing, not because the state desires to abolish
wrong-doing, but because the state desires to monopolize it."
Yet in an important sense, the Freud of *Civilization and Its
Discontents* did not anticipate the specific danger totalitarianism posed to human order, for his book stressed the irrational aggressiveness pressing so near the fragile membranes
of organized society, the subterranean fury threatening to
burst through the surface of civility. His sisters, like Kafka's,
were sent to the death camps. Yet the Nazi destruction of
Jewry could be so thorough and so effective in part because
its instruments were not rampaging Cossacks but clerks
scrupulous in their obedience to the law. Writing of Hoess, a
West German journalist observed: "It was preponderantly a
credulous normality . . . that stamped the features of this horror. It has shattered the image of man more lastingly than
ever the collective outbreak of base passions could have
done."[40] Though Arendt herself completely resisted psychoanalytic interpretations of totalitarianism, it can be noted how
fully both id and superego were involved. Not only primitive
hatreds were expressed, but devotion to duty and authority
was demanded. Had Eichmann *not* obeyed his Fuehrer, his
conscience would have troubled him.

The "credulous normality" mentioned by Joachim Fest

could hardly be said to be confined to the era of totalitarian power, the Germany and Russia of the 1930s and 1940s. While it would be preposterous to suggest that anyone would be capable of doing what Eichmann did, a willingness to commit abhorrent acts under cover of authority can hardly be said to be confined to the small minority who may be psychopaths. That, at any rate, was the point of the experiments performed under the supervision of Stanley Milgram, in which "scientists" ordered unwitting subjects to administer shocks to ostensible participants in a learning test. Drawn from the ranks of ordinary people, almost two-thirds of the subjects showed an "extreme willingness . . . to go to almost any lengths on the command of an authority," even when the maximum voltage was supposed to be highly painful and very dangerous. A controlled experiment is not an exact simulation of life outside, and a white-coated social scientist can be regarded quite differently from a uniformed S.S. superior. Nevertheless, Milgram felt obliged to "conclude that Arendt's conception of the *banality of evil* comes closer to the truth than one might dare imagine. The ordinary person who shocked the victim did so out of a sense of obligation—a conception of his duties as a subject—and not from any peculiarly aggressive tendencies." Without feeling "any particular hostility," a representative group of Americans might be willing to serve as guards in a concentration camp, might become "agents in a terrible destructive process" under political conditions ripe for totalitarianism.[41] The S.S. men who staffed the camps were there not because they had previously demonstrated their sadism but only because, for one reason or another, they were unfit for military service. The few who tried to avoid camp duty found pretext to do so, and apparently were not penalized. In Milgram's experiment, none of the volunteers walked out of the room, even as the commands were given to increase the voltage—perhaps dangerously—inflicted upon slow "learners"

who were in fact actors screaming in the next room.⁴² Two
decades after Arendt had expressed doubt that social science
techniques could be applied to what was psychologically incomprehensible, a test was ingeniously devised that showed
how readily the mechanisms of totalitarian domination might
be injected into the lives of ordinary citizens in two Connecti-
cut towns.

What was nicknamed the "Eichmann experiment" demonstrated, according to one philosopher, that "men acquire the
capacity for engaging in evil without experiencing it as such.
They learn how to perform evil acts as part of their job description" so long as they recognize the legitimacy of authority. Wickedness, in other words, lost the power of temptation.
While Léon Poliakov disagreed with much of *Eichmann in
Jerusalem*, he acknowledged that, "once sanctioned by public
authority," even an obsessive desire to destroy Jewry "loses a
great deal of its attraction." As proof, the eminent historian of
the Holocaust cited the "psychological character of those responsible for carrying out the genocide."⁴³ The sanction of
authority, which in Eichmann's case was more significant than
the closure of ideology, thus prevented the Nazi bureaucrat
from realizing that his own lack of personal hatred for Jews
was no excuse for his crimes.

In her portrait of Eichmann, Arendt therefore introduced
into her analysis of totalitarianism the psychological nuances
that were virtually omitted from her earlier book. Because
such political systems draw upon the diligence of ordinary
people, their danger might be greater than even Arendt had
feared in 1951. Radicals in particular drew from Arendt's report the lesson that technological power combined with moral
indifference posed an unprecedented threat to the weakest
segments of American society and even to human survival itself. The absence of a critical stance and the eclipse of independent values, according to this argument, facilitated obedi-

ence to an authority that might not shrink from mass destruc-tiveness.[44] Yet Arendt did not forsake the historical specificity that distinguished *The Origins of Totalitarianism*. To the earlier landscapes of hell, she added—but did not completely substitute—a portrait based in large part on our everyday world. *Eichmann in Jerusalem* did not repudiate her earlier view that the absolute had become implicated in modern poli-tics, but she did realize that the executors of the policies of evil were not necessarily themselves inclined to delve into the demonic roots of totalitarianism.

Her description of the banality of evil was apparently so striking that some critics suspected her of stressing the banal-ity at the expense of the evil. Almost two decades after the Holocaust, Eichmann was the picture of drabness, with his nondescript appearance, his spectacles, his charts, his colorless responses and explanations. The man in the glass booth cut so dull a figure that one of the spectators at the trial yelled from the balcony, "But you should have seen him in his colonel's uniform!"[45] Harold Rosenberg, himself an attorney, noted that the judicial process itself promoted an atmosphere of pal-lid factuality that ran the risk of emotional neutrality. Rosen-berg also suspected that the prosecutor Hausner himself sensed the contrast between the vacuity of the defendant and the horror of what the S.S. officer had accomplished and at-tempted to compensate by exaggerating the fiendishness be-neath the bland persona of Eichmann.[46]

Yet it is doubtful that Arendt was seriously misled by the placid indifference of the prisoner, who was the consumma-tion of one totalitarian type, the indifferent killer. Eichmann's personality was in its blandness not unlike Ohlendorf's in 1946. In his moral obtuseness and stupefying alienation from reality, Eichmann was little different from Hoess, with his rec-ollection of the joys of gardening and raising animals at Auschwitz, of the good treatment he insisted that prisoners

who worked in his home received, of the fun his children had
swimming in the neighborhood. Yet sometimes, Hoess recalled, his "thoughts [would] suddenly turn to incidents that
had occurred during the extermination. I then had to go out
[of the house]. . . . The thought would often come to me: how
long will our happiness last? My wife could never understand
these gloomy moods of mine, and ascribed them to some an-
noyance connected with my work." These reflections were
written in 1946.[47] Had Himmler not committed suicide, he
too would undoubtedly have embodied in the courtroom the
banality of evil rather than mephistophelean villainy. Anyone
who, as the war ended, genially greeted a representative of the
World Jewish Congress by offering to "bury the hatchet,"
would have been incapable of recognizing responsibility for
unprecedented and unredeemable atrocities.[48] In Jerusalem in
1961, Eichmann was not different from, only older than, the
man in the colonel's uniform. Like those whom the Allies
captured at the end of the war, it had been his power, not his
personality, that had rendered him a creature of turpitude.

Though in no way an apologia for Eichmann, Arendt's
book was so constructed that, in arguing against the misunderstanding of the prosecution and the judges, she seemed to be
taking the side of the defendant. In order to penetrate the
void of his personality, she seemed to accept in many strategic
points his own interpretation of his conduct and motives, his
own memory or his claims of forgetfulness. So often was Eichmann given the benefit of the doubt that Marie Syrkin complained that "an the end of the script the only one who comes
out better than when he came in is the defendant. The victim
comes out worst."[49] While it is impossible to exaggerate the
crimes committed by the Nazi regime, the prosecution could
conceivably have overstated the foulness of Eichmann's character; and therefore any attempt to rectify the balance in the
interest of truth would necessarily make the defendant look a

little better. But by projecting herself into the circumstances of his life, by trying to insert herself into the vacuum of his soul, Arendt did not in any way excuse his crimes or absolve him from the charge of genocide. Eichmann came out as less diabolical than Hausner portrayed him, but instead—because of the cogency and perceptiveness of Arendt's analysis—the defendant was repulsive in a new way. By aiming to understand his past, she offered a redefinition of the awful, a special warning of the perilousness of the modern situation.

Her willful stance of objectivity, her independence of spirit, took the form of excessive hostility to aspects of Jewish conduct; and the passages in which Arendt appeared to be blaming the victim loomed larger for many readers than her chronicle of Eichmann's career. The errors attributed to the Jews were laid out with such absence of generosity that they were no less striking than the mediocrity attributed to the defendant. The imbalance of tone, coupled with Arendt's tendency to deflect Hausner's accusations only to construct a different indictment of her own, caused many readers to ignore the less surprising passages in her book—and then to criticize Arendt on the basis of arguments she herself advanced.

Eichmann in Jerusalem made points that reviewers used to discredit her own thesis. For example, after resisting Arendt's report on the banality of evil, Poliakov felt "inclined to agree with the defense attorney's contention that in a normal political order, Eichmann—whatever his private opinions—would have led a model existence."[50] In other words, Eichmann was not a monster out to "prove the villain," not an insane anti-Semite—much as she described him. John Gross suggested that "anyone relying solely on Miss Arendt might be forgiven for assuming that for much of the time Eichmann was no more than a glorified station-master." In fact, Gross asserted, no more than a half dozen officials were above him in the chain of command; Eichmann "gave far more orders than he received." Yet this claim hardly constituted a necessary corrective, because Arendt had stated as much already: "Since Eichmann's immediate superior, the head of IV-B, turned out to be a nonentity, his real superior was always Müller. Müller's superior was Heydrich, and later Kaltenbrunner, each of whom was, in his turn, under the command of Himmler, who received his orders from Hitler."[51] Ranks in the S.S. were deliberately kept low so that authority and rank no longer corresponded; such incongruities had been described in *The Origins of Totalitarianism*.[52] Arendt never depicted this particular functionary as "powerless," as Jacob Robinson claimed she did. Arendt ridiculed the defense claims that Eichmann was a small cog in the machinery of destruction, and added that in any event "the whole cog theory is legally pointless. . . . It does not matter at all what order of magnitude is assigned to the 'cog' named Eichmann," since within the courtroom "all the cogs in the machinery . . . are . . . transformed back into perpetrators, that is to say, into human beings."[53] She did not minimize his role. The court—and in her own way Arendt—passed judgment upon him as a human agent who had exercised enormous power.

In insisting that Eichmann was before the court solely for what he had done, Arendt struck a false note, however, that again disclosed an unnecessary coldness. In objecting to a series of prosecution witnesses who described their agony during the Holocaust, she complained that what should have been on trial was Eichmann's deeds, "not the sufferings of the Jews." Legally there is a distinction between act and injury, and both must be proven by the prosecution. But in this case the distinction made no sense, since causing the Jews unparalleled suffering through his organization of transportation was precisely what Eichmann had done.[54] The victims, who had not been sufficiently heard at Nuremberg, could at last cry out in Jerusalem. They made possible a more complete assessment of Eichmann's deeds. The several days of survivors' testimony helped substantiate a dispassionate and nonpartisan judgment not only from the court but also from the observers of the trial. Even though Arendt had discounted the case for compassion as a political argument, it was surely inescapable in assessing the horror of Eichmann's crimes. In a lapidary conclusion, she imagined herself telling Eichmann from the bench: ". . . Just as you supported and carried out a policy of not wanting to share the earth with the Jewish people and the people of a number of other nations . . . we find that no one, that is, no member of the human race, can be expected to want to share the earth with you. This is the reason, and the only reason, you must hang." [55]

In rendering this judgment, Arendt was not relying, as she had in earlier sections on legal issues, on opinions already current among legal writers. In presenting an alternative rationale for the execution of Eichmann, she drew not upon any statutes in the criminal code but upon the articulation of a more general sense of justice. Nevertheless Ernst Simon called her final verdict so "fictitious . . . that no one can possibly take it seriously." Others, like Scholem, disagreed more politely. He claimed that her final sentence—the "only reason" Eichmann was properly executed—was "based on a prodigious *non sequitur*." For Arendt's argument, the Israeli scholar claimed, "would apply equally to those hundreds of thousands, perhaps millions of human beings," unwilling to share the earth with Jews or with other peoples. Even Macdonald, one of her most stalwart advocates, found Arendt's sentence illogical, since "many people still exist who are quite willing to share the earth with an Eichmann: fascists, Nazis, anti-Semitic fanatics like our own George Lincoln Rockwell, and I don't see how they can be deprived of their human status . . . unless by circular reasoning: if you want to share the earth with an Eichmann, you are not human." [56] The impli-

cations give pause. Should the American Nazis who wanted to
march past several thousand Holocaust survivors in Skokie,
Illinois—according to her logic—have been met with stronger
penalties than an injunction? Could it be extrapolated from
Arendt's verdict that the citizens who in the early sixties displayed their "I Like Eich" bumper stickers deserved to die?

Such an inference would be false, for both Scholem and
Macdonald forgot Gide's famous warning about trying to
understand a writer too quickly. Arendt's reason that Eichmann merited hanging was not merely contained in the pen-
ultimate sentence in the paragraph, but in the entire passage
in which she summarized the findings of guilt. She distinguished between the desire to inflict death on an entire people
and the fact of having done so. "There is an abyss between
the actuality of what you did," she imagined herself addressing the defendant, "and the potentiality of what others might
have done. We are concerned here with what you did, and not
with the possible noncriminal nature of your inner life . . . or
with the criminal potentialities of those around you." Even if
others might have been willing to direct the transport of Jews
to the gassing facilities, even if millions of other Germans
might have acted as you did, Arendt insisted, "this would not
have been an excuse for you." [57] Her verdict was therefore not
an example of circular reasoning, not at all a *non sequitur*.

That is not to say that Arendt's conclusion was free of difficulties, though she quickly disposed of one objection to it.
The position of principled opponents of capital punishment
"would have remained valid"; but they apparently sensed,
she drily remarked, that "this was not a very promising case
on which to fight." For a mass murderer the gallows could
seem grossly inadequate, and Scholem compared Eichmann's
execution to a satyr play after an unspeakable tragedy. Without finding capital punishment in any way unjust, the historian of Jewish mysticism feared that his government had

sealed off a life that still needed to be pondered by his erstwhile countrymen and the survivors. Dead, Scholem suspected, Eichmann belonged too fully to the past that neither Jews nor Germans had yet mastered. Yet not to have imposed the death penalty upon so consequential a criminal would have been much worse. No power could have inflicted retribution upon the defendant that would have been commensurate with the suffering Eichmann caused his millions of victims, yet to have granted him life would have been even more disproportionate. Arendt was therefore right to defend the death penalty, but it is difficult to see how her reasoning was superior to the court's, or how she formulated a more effective deterrent against the future "use of instruments beside which Hitler's gassing installations look like an evil child's fumbling toys." [58]

Her claim for the superiority of her own verdict to that of the court was based on the proposition that international law must take into fuller account genocide without malicious motive, performed as an act of state and under color of national law. Yet nowhere in *Eichmann in Jerusalem* did the author suggest appropriate civic responses to governmental decisions to engage in war or peace, defense or appeasement. Eichmann deserved to be hanged because the Nazis had tried to "determine who should and who should not inhabit the world"; [59] yet such determinations are virtually embedded in the nature of statecraft—though few previous wars have been as devastating as the Second World War and the war against the Jews. The contingency plans of every major military power and alliance today involve precisely such decisions as to who shall live or die should a nuclear Armageddon be on the world's agenda. As a clue to the logical difficulties of her conclusion, Arendt's refusal to share the earth with Eichmann bore a dialectical relationship to the German demand for *Lebensraum*, that perversely exaggerated and paranoid warrant for what

other nations and peoples have traditionally sought through
warfare. In ordering atomic warfare against Japan, the American government under Truman signified its unwillingness to
share the earth with the inhabitants of Hiroshima and Naga-
saki. The case for the military necessity of Truman's decision
was and is a weak one, and the relentless pursuit of the policy
of unconditional surrender was not the only choice open to
the President and his advisors—only the worst one in terms of
needless devastation. Yet Arendt presented no suggestion for
punishing those involved in that decision, which she condemned as a war crime according to the definition of the
Hague Convention.[60] The decision of the Jerusalem court
could at least be enforced through the police power of a
nation-state, whereas Jaspers' proposal of an international
criminal court—which Arendt apparently seconded—remains
as low as it ever was on the agenda of the United Nations, a
body whose general capacity to distinguish criminals from
others has not hitherto been noticeable.

Though Arendt's verdict was not demonstrably sounder
than that of the *Beth Hamishpat*, she identified a problem
that tragically eludes solution. Eichmann's defense of "acts of
state" was properly rejected in Jerusalem, but the fact remains
that only as a bureaucrat within the R.H.S.A. was this "average person" able to perpetrate such crimes.[61] One nation-state
chose to punish a Nazi criminal; but other nation-states, most
egregiously Austria, West Germany, and East Germany, have
been insouciant about former war criminals in their midst.
Yet neither the Israeli judges nor Arendt dealt with the
problem of mass murder when confined to the citizens of one's
own state, though that is surely part of the burden modern
despotism has placed upon international law. The Soviet regime's assault on human diversity was earlier, more prolonged
and vaster than the Reich's, which was why the defense attor-
neys at Nuremberg tried to respond to the charge of con-

spiracy to wage aggressive war by reminding the judges of the Hitler-Stalin pact which divided Poland and made the conflict possible.[62]

Such complications were missing from *Eichmann in Jerusalem*, though Stalin was responsible for killing more Soviet citizens than Eichmann was for killing the non-Aryans of Europe. It is one of the many awful ironies of Eichmann's case, though omitted from Arendt's account, that Israel was blamed for its zeal in bringing a mass murderer to justice, whereas the concurrent "de-Stalinization" in the Soviet Union did not include any effort to punish the perpetrators of totalitarian crimes by instituting the rule of law. An exiled Russian writer recently wondered about Stalin's former foreign minister, Molotov, "who in 1939 told the Supreme Soviet and the world that no ideology, whether Nazi or Fascist, should be opposed by force of arms; Molotov, the man who signed his name under Stalin's on Yakir's death warrant; Molotov, the man whose hands can never be washed clean of the blood of millions." Yet this Soviet embodiment of the banality of evil "spends his days walking up and down Gorky Street, visiting the Lenin Library, and at night, we can be sure, he sleeps, because his type does not suffer from insomnia. . . ."[63] Far from having declined, the nation-state in the era of totalitarianism was free to do something about the imprescriptible rights of man—or to do nothing.

Eichmann in Jerusalem, the editors of *Partisan Review* observed, "provoked as much controversy as any other work we can think of in the last decade." The *New Yorker* nevertheless refused to print letters to the editor that fleshed out the dispute. Irving Howe, who had been Arendt's part-time research assistant after the war, complained that the magazine's policy amounted to a denial of free intellectual exchange, since its readers were deprived of refutations of Arendt's serial report. "As far as the *New Yorker* is concerned," Howe added, "Miss Arendt has the first, the last, the only word." According to Marie Syrkin, the magazine had "ignored, with one exception, all communications, many of which expressed not merely disagreement, but cited flagrant and major errors." The anonymous amplifier of "The Talk of the Town" responded by lamenting a "breakdown of communication" in the controversy, which its policy of suppressing letters to the editor was hardly designed to rectify.[64]

One result was that the dispute spilled over into so many organs of opinion, into so many columns and forums, that the readers of the *New Yorker* could hardly have avoided noticing challenges to the authority of Arendt's pronouncements. Contrary to Howe, intellectual exchange was so vigorous that articles were written not only about her book but also about articles about her book; the bibliography her book spawned is quite extensive. Although denied space in the *New Yorker* to demonstrate Arendt's "vast ignorance," Syrkin, who was one of her ablest critics, tracked her prey in the pages of *Partisan Review, Dissent* and *Jewish Frontier*. Those who shared the sentiment of the philosopher Raziel Abelson, that *Eichmann in Jerusalem* was "irresponsible and in the worst of taste,"[65] had ample opportunity to present their views; and generally the critics outnumbered the defenders of the book. While partisans of Israel and those associated with established Jewish organizations were almost uniformly hostile to Arendt's work, no very solid line separating Jewish and Gentile readers otherwise emerged; nor was the division a clean one between scholars and nonspecialists. Among admirers of the book were Bettelheim, Hans J. Morgenthau and theologian Arthur A. Cohen. Perhaps Arendt's only peer as a scholar of totalitarianism, Carl J. Friedrich, carefully praised *Eichmann in Jerusalem* as "the most revealing study of this particular evidence on the workings of the terror." [66] Nevertheless the most conspicuous defenders of the book tended to be non-scholars like McCarthy and Macdonald, who happened to be her close friends as well. Its attackers were also often nonspecialists, and more likely to be of Jewish background.

The critics tended to be more vociferous, and certainly more heated, than the defenders; and the first attack, launched by Musmanno in the *Times Book Review*, also signaled trouble in the sifting of truth and error. Aside from changing Eichmann's lack of hatred for Jews to love of Jews, Musmanno claimed that Arendt directly called Eichmann a Zionist and that she thought "it was a terrible mistake to punish Eichmann at all"—as though she had not written her own version of a death warrant. She was accused of sympathy for the defendant, which led Arendt to reply that it was hardly plausible that the *New Yorker* and the Viking Press would have published a pro-Nazi account written by a refugee from Nazism. Arendt herself regarded Musmanno, who was briefly and unfavorably mentioned in the text itself, as a most unsuitable choice of a reviewer, since he was *pro domo* (in behalf of the house). Musmanno rejoined that he felt compelled to identify the implications of *Eichmann in Jerusalem* out of a sense of *pro bono publico*.[67]

The obtuseness and the antagonism of this first major review of *Eichmann in Jerusalem* may well have led Arendt to shy away from further direct response to later—and more substantial—criticism. It was not her style to hurl herself directly onto the dark and bloody ground of New York polemicists, for she had developed the knack of writing in a tone of intimidating authority, free of both disarming modesty and of prudent tentativeness. Yet her work was so devoid of self-reference, so untainted by the demands of ego, that the impression was created of impersonally rendered, and therefore objective, judgment. Though she much admired Kant's defi-

nition of judgment ("the elevation to a general standpoint
which a person can determine only by putting himself in the
place of others"),[68] utter absence of bias is of course asymp-
totic, more a duty than a possibility. But since Arendt's particular perspective sprang from the formidable "tradition of
German philosophy," since her detachment seemed so free of
personal animus, since her books were so patently serious and
astringent and unrelieved by the grace of wit or sentiment,
many American readers unaccustomed to such intellectual demands might have felt disagreement with her to have been
rather presumptuous. The storm that broke over *Eichmann
in Jerusalem* was therefore something quite novel in her experience as an author, to which she did not respond effectively. There were indeed flaws in her thesis, especially her treatment of the Jewish response to the Holocaust. But Arendt did
not present the most impregnable defense of her book (which
did not mean truculence); and, what is worse, she could rarely
be flushed out to present any defense at all.

Dissent, for example, sponsored a forum on her book in
which she was invited to speak; but she declined, as did Bettelheim. She also temporarily withdrew from such activities
as the Conference on Jewish Social Studies because of the severity of the opposition to her work.[69] It is true that she permitted *Encounter* to publish an exchange of letters with Scholem; but her response to the specific and substantial issues he
raised was evasive, nor was the epistolary form most conducive
to detailed, scholarly debate. Arendt did agree to participate
in a public discussion of her book at the University of Mary-
land in the spring of 1965. The other commentators were
Macdonald and Podhoretz, who remembers being considered
the only one of her critics she deemed a suitable opponent, for
reasons neither she nor he explained. A faithful record of
Arendt's remarks, to a packed hall, may not have been preserved; but Podhoretz later included her among those Ger-

man-Jewish intellectuals, "who, despite everything, could never get over their love of Germany or their compulsion to regard America as somehow inferior to the country of their birth." The editor of *Commentary* even viewed the theory of totalitarianism as a way of exonerating Germany, since Arendt's version of the theory blamed modern conditions rather than the particularities of German history. Podhoretz added the disclaimer that "no one, least of all Hannah Arendt, ever put it in those terms. . . . But it was there, lurking below the theory." [70] Such an interpretation has the advantage, if nothing else, of exempting its proponent from providing evidence from her writings. Arendt's love of Germany did not impede her from criticizing severely the tolerance of Nazi criminals in the *Bundesrepublik*. Nor can that love alone account for her failure to stress the specific forces within German history. Indifference to national peculiarities and traditions is a flaw in *The Origins of Totalitarianism*, for it has already been noted that, in analyzing Stalinism, she neglected Russian history too.

For the paperback edition of *Eichmann in Jerusalem*, Arendt added a postscript acknowledging that her book had become "the center of a controversy and the object of an organized campaign." [71] But while her postscript clarified some of the key points offered in the earlier text, particularly what she meant by "the banality of evil," the postscript was also arbitrary; for she was quite unresponsive to the specific charges of error and misinterpretation that had already been raised. Syrkin's objections were utterly ignored, and only one of Lionel Abel's criticisms was answered—though Macdonald and McCarthy may have already disposed of Abel's "Aesthetics of Evil" to Arendt's satisfaction. Otherwise she had gotten to like the climate on top of Olympus.

Then in 1967, again in the *New Yorker*, she published an "essay . . . caused by the so-called controversy after the publi-

cation of *Eichmann in Jerusalem*." "Truth and Politics" was
an attempt to consider the legitimacy of an absolute adherence to the truth. She had been struck by "the amazing
amount of lies used in the 'controversy'—lies about what I
had written, on the one hand, and about the facts I had reported, on the other." [72] Yet her article did not delve any more
directly into the controversy itself, offering neither examples
of such lies by her unnamed critics nor proof that truth was
more on her side. "Truth and Politics" cited no instances in
which her facts were ignored or misconstrued (though, with
Musmanno's review in particular, she might easily have done
so.) Nor did she acknowledge that the issue had not been her
facts so much as her interpretation of those facts. The strange
modesty of her claim that "the banality of evil" was meant on
a "strictly factual level" did not fool anyone. Whatever the
philosophic richness of "Truth and Politics," it could not be
considered a rebuttal to the criticism of her book. It was instead an outflanking operation which avoided another confrontation with the historical issues aired in *Eichmann in
Jerusalem*.

Such obliqueness also characterized her reaction to Jacob
Robinson's *And the Crooked Shall Be Made Straight*, though
here Arendt partly returned to the strictly factual level. Walter Laqueur found Robinson's exposition of *Eichmann in
Jerusalem* "devastating on matters of detail," for the author
proved "beyond any shadow of doubt that Miss Arendt has
made literally hundreds of mistakes, has used incorrect statis-
tics, and has quoted out of context." (Relying on this *explication de texte*, Lionel Abel had written that Arendt had committed exactly six hundred errors, a statement not without its
charm. Normally the angered reader claims to find errors too
numerous to mention.) Laqueur might properly have concluded that so many gaffes invalidated Arendt's thesis. But such

mistakes, while unjustifiable and very disturbing, were not necessarily debilitating when so forceful and synoptic a thinker as Arendt was at work; and Laqueur observed that "attacking Miss Arendt's book mainly in its details is not wholly effective."[73] For *Eichmann in Jerusalem* was more than a funnel of biases, though it was understandable that many readers regarded her manipulation of evidence as too high a price to pay for the rare pleasure of unexcelled theoretical acumen put to use. The eccentricities, the censorious thunderbolts, even the errors were in the service of a densely serious and reflective approach to modern politics, so that—however badly punctured—the book simply could not be made to disappear.

Laqueur's wise reluctance to impugn the basic integrity of her work was not fully appreciated however, for Arendt chose the communications column of the *New York Review of Books* to demonstrate to Laqueur and others how unimpressed they ought to have been with "the formidable Dr. Robinson." He had served in the Lithuanian parliament, represented Israel in the United Nations and founded and directed the Institute of Jewish Affairs of the World Jewish Congress. As an attorney with considerable knowledge of the Holocaust, he had not only advised Robert Jackson on Jewish affairs at Nuremberg but also served as Hausner's leading assistant in the prosecution of Eichmann. But just as Arendt had questioned the suitability of Justice Musmanno to review her book for the *Times*, she challenged Robinson's credentials as well. Rather large claims had been made on his behalf by Jewish organizations and by his publisher, and Arendt pointed out that his intellectual prominence had hardly—or only recently—been established, at least among readers of the *New York Review of Books* or *Partisan Review*. Arendt accused Robinson of strictly amateur status, of having only recently become an historian.[74] Arendt seemed to have forgotten that

she herself lacked professional training as an historian; she
had established herself in that vocation, like Robinson, simply
by writing history.

She further complained that his objections to *Eichmann in
Jerusalem* were nothing more than a restatement of the case
of the Israeli prosecution, which "was, in fact, his own case." [75]
Arendt thus did not consider it plausible that even an attorney might be able to present devastating criticisms of her
book. Nor did she explain why Robinson's work for the prosecution of Eichmann disqualified him from comment on
Arendt's use of evidence, or on her understanding of the
defendant. The counsel's knowledge of the scope of Eichmann's career ought to have rendered him superbly fit for
such a task, and Arendt's objections were therefore unfounded.
She raised other issues unrelated to the veracity of her book,
such as the specter of mass society in the hostility of Jewish
organizations toward her book. Rather feverishly she described the Anti-Defamation League, the Jewish Center Lecture Bureau and even the Leo Baeck Institute as "mass organizations, using all the means of mass communication," which
were clumsily attributing to her what she did not say. One
extreme example was the headline in a regional Jewish news-
paper: "Self-Hating Jewess Writes Pro-Eichmann Series."
Nevertheless Arendt feared that "the masses" might be led to
believe "what the image-makers had made me say was the
actual historical truth." [76]

A major portion of her communication to the *New York
Review* did for once come to grips with that actual historical
truth, though of course Arendt could not possibly reply to all
the charges Robinson leveled against it in a book that was almost as long as her own. While accusing the prosecutor of
excessive zeal in the presentation of his case rather than the
impartial marshalling of historical evidence, she did not yield
any ground whatsoever. Arendt also accused him of "a truly

dazzling display of sheer inability to read," of which she had some samples. Robinson too had fallen for her use of *oratio obliqua* and caught Arendt in "contradictions" that were in fact a sophisticated refusal to yield to black-and-white simplicities. If Arendt tended to be oversubtle (as in her distinction between what Eichmann did and what the Jews suffered), Robinson's exegetical enterprise was not nuanced enough. She exposed his ignorance in some matters of detail, such as the question of the legality of the order for the Final Solution and the extent of anti-Semitism in European refugee policies prior to the Second World War. Both Arendt and Robinson presented only evidence which supported their own arguments, and neither acknowledged that something might be said for alternative or opposing views. But since it had been Arendt who had exalted the ideal of nonpartisanship and had insisted on the duty of intellectual independence, Robinson's criticisms appeared the more telling; the tendentiousness of Arendt's writing was therefore rendered more disconcerting. After all her aloofness, she showed a streak of petulance. Nor did Arendt enhance her position when she again attacked the Jewish Councils, and added that their behavior had not been adequately exposed in Jerusalem because of the ties between the *Judenräte* and the Israeli establishment.[77]

Not all of her examples of Robinson's "sheer inability to read" turned out to be convincing. Her sentence about "the darkest chapter in the whole dark story," she claimed, was quite intelligible with the qualification, "to a Jew," since only such a person would be pained by the knowledge of the councils' collaboration with the Nazis. Nevertheless it remained true, as Robinson and others pointed out, that to *anyone* of humane sensibility, the darkest chapter was the Nazi terror itself. Arendt also announced that Robinson himself was trapped in a contradiction, having written that the Jewish leaders acted as they did out of great duress, yet also that they served on the councils "as a rule out of a feeling of responsibility," hence not out of duress. Yet Robinson made plain in the rest of the passage, which Arendt did not quote, what he meant by the assumption of responsibility. "No member of the Jewish Councils offered his services to the Nazis," he wrote; but if there was to be any organized community at all, someone had to deal directly with the occupation forces, whatever the danger to the Jewish representatives and their families.[78] By responsibility, he patently meant duty. Arendt's animus against that leadership had affected her capacity to read the context of Robinson's remarks and, more importantly, to convey the historical ambience within which the councils themselves had operated. Arendt had again mishandled her own defense. Necessarily faced with severe restrictions of selectivity in her response to Robinson's book, she squandered space on matters of credentials and "establishment" hostility, and then permitted the substantive debate to be confined to some of the least developed, least convincing and least impressive passages in her book.

On that note effective communication about *Eichmann in Jerusalem*—one phase of the life of dialogue among intellectuals—sputtered and stopped. Laqueur had called for a fuller account of the Jewish response to the catastrophe than Arendt had provided in her dozen pages, and that appeal was soon to be answered. Though Arendt doubted the necessity for such a work, she correctly predicted that Robinson, with his flair for not seeing the *tallis* for the fringes, would be "most unlikely to produce it." In the following decade, the works of Isaiah Trunk and Lucy Dawidowicz went far toward satisfying that scholarly need by making use of the extensive sources in Yiddish, Hebrew and Polish that were inaccessible to Arendt and Raul Hilberg, whose *Destruction of the European Jews* was published after the trial but in enough time for Arendt to utilize its account of Nazi anti-Semitism and Jewish complicity.[79]

While scholarly works like *Judenrat* and *The War Against the Jews* have revised Arendt's evaluation of Jewish cooperation with Nazi authorities, no interpretation of Eichmann himself has yet displaced Arendt's extraordinary portrayal. The prosecution's depiction, which was disseminated in Robinson's book and in Hausner's *Justice in Jerusalem*, has enjoyed the advantage of conventional wisdom. But the picture of Eichmann as a violent and rabid anti-Semite has simply failed to capture the imagination; for no one else who has investigated Eichmann's life has shown the brilliant psychological acuity and flashes of philosophic insight of Arendt. Those who have disputed her portrait, like Robinson and Michael Selzer, have been forced to define their disagreement within the terms that Arendt so resonantly established. Her book may even have affected certain works of American fiction about the Holocaust, such as Leslie Epstein's *King of the Jews* and William Styron's *Sophie's Choice*. That is one measure of Arendt's cultural impact, though not of course of her historical veracity. While Eichmann's depravity is now more fully incorporated into the charged memory of the Holocaust, her interpretation cannot be regarded as definitive. But it has indelibly enlarged the sense of the perilousness lurking within the everyday world, and has heightened our grasp of the recent history that—under altered conditions—may prefigure our fate.

Chapter 8

☙

CONCLUSION

THE intellectual legacy of Hannah Arendt can be formulated in a cascade of paradoxes. She once described herself as "neither a liberal nor a positivist nor a pragmatist";[1] yet she never defined herself more affirmatively and assertively and—like virtually all serious thinkers—was obviously uncomfortable with such classifications. Arendt was called a Romantic,[2] and yet she was irresistibly drawn to the classic ages of Greece and Rome. Her fidelity to the thought of the ancients, her abstractness, and her indifference to the methods and conclusions of social science estranged her from the empiricist tradition of Anglo-American scholarship. Yet in stressing the irreducibility of facts, in acknowledging common sense as both admirable and unarguable, in insisting that totalitarianism had to be treated not as an essence but as an event,[3] Arendt could not be termed an idealist. Her feeling for the classical world we have lost, her reverence for the West's distant—but now depleted—past, breathed an historical dimension into her work not easily deducible from existentialism. But she was not nostalgic, and it was her aim to explicate the portent of life "between past and future." Arendt was fascinated by etymology and often applied the original meaning of a term to the clarification of contemporary problems, but she was not an analytic philosopher. She was not an incandescent stylist either, though the phrases she coined—such as "the right to have rights" and "the banality of evil"—are part of American Constitutional doctrine and general discourse. Arendt was an influential critic of mass society, but was too committed to the values of community to be considered an individualist. In finding repugnant the political demands for equality and for the redistribution of wealth, she cut whatever ties she had with the left. But her eloquent praise of the revolutionary councils found no echo among conservatives, and no contemporary political order won her unqualified allegiance. Though a refugee from the eruption of mass fanaticism, she did not sentimentalize a more comfortable epoch, nor voice the grievances of a Bourbon on the rocks. Arendt exalted the life of action, yet—at least in the United States—was not an activist. Her primary achievement was in political philosophy, yet she believed that what is most valuable in the world only the poets could salvage and sustain. *The Origins of Totalitarianism* was itself a paradox, for what one reviewer said of Trevor-Roper's *The Last Days of Hitler* could also describe her book: "Though it treated of evil men and degraded themes, it vindicated human reason."[4] Arendt personified the intellectual milieu of enlightened German Jewry, while learning very little from Marx and even less from Freud—whose theories Arendt's students prudently learned not to bring up in her presence.[5] And though she drew inspiration mostly from Aristotle, Montesquieu, Kant and her own teachers, almost all the books she composed bore the unmistakable imprint of her own distinctive intelligence.

For all the forcefulness of her mind and the confidence she had in its powers, Arendt was in some ways an ambiguous, elusive writer. Because of her devotion to rational inquiry and to moral seriousness, because of her love of art and distrust of the masses, she belonged to the Weimar culture of Jewish intellectuals—which therefore made her a "good European," whose cosmopolitanism could not be defined within national frontiers. Vladimir Nabokov once referred to himself as "an American writer, born in Russia and educated in England where I studied French literature, before spending fifteen years in Germany."[6] Arendt was born and educated in Germany, and lived in France, where she worked for the nascent state of Israel. But though she became an American citizen who wrote in English, she was not recognizably and indubitably an American writer. Only by finding safety in the United States was she able to live, think and write at all, yet an editor of her essays is surely correct in insisting that "it is because she remained both a Jew and a European that she gained a place in history, and it is as both a Jew and a European that her life and work should be understood."[7] It is true that she wrote relatively little about the country that rescued her, but the reason Arendt cannot easily be classified as an American thinker has more to do with style than subject.

Her highly speculative bent apparently found little nourishment in the patrimony of American political theory, which has been one of the least impressive aspects of our national culture. Coming out of the matrix of ancient and continental philosophy, Arendt could not have been expected to be stimulated by writers such as John Taylor of Caroline (whom Charles Beard considered the last great American political thinker). In this respect the figure to whom she perhaps responded most favorably was John Adams. He too was fascinated by ancient political thought and by later writers like Montesquieu, and he imbued the political realm with greater significance than did other Founders, such as Jefferson or Washington. But Adams was primarily absorbed by the question of how an effective mixed polity might be established, not how revolutionary communes might be encouraged or perpetuated. And far from praising the egalitarianism enjoyed by the participants in the *polis,* he hoped to see institutions that would recognize and regulate the natural inequalities among human beings. In any event Arendt's interest in Adams did not demonstrate the depth of her involvement in the American heritage of self-government, for even he had felt, as he wrote in 1812, that for over half a century this ambivalent democrat had "constantly lived in an enemies [sic] Country."[8] Arendt was in fact far less critical of American political life than Adams turned out to be, and her writing was explicitly free of the alienation that he expressed.

But despite the enormous respect with which many American intellectuals treated her work, Arendt repudiated the very schools of thought that have characterized the national temper—liberalism, pragmatism and positivism. Equally important however in separating her from the dominant American style was her sense of crisis and—at least in the first edition of *The Origins of Totalitarianism*—her pessimism. By contrast, most of her fellow Americans were secular adherents of what this scholar of St. Augustine would have recognized as the Pelagian heresy. Perhaps the gloomiest of American thinkers has been John Adams' own great-grandson. Yet he was not pessimistic enough. The final passage of *The Education of Henry Adams* records the hope that his spirit and the spirits of his closest friends might be permitted to return to earth in the near future. "Perhaps then," he dared to believe, "for the first time since man began his education among the carnivores, they would find a world that sensitive and timid natures could regard without a shudder." The year Henry Adams picked for such a return was 1938.[9] Just as American society has been unscarred by the burden of misery known in Europe, the American mind has rarely been nicked by the sense of tragedy and has commonly been unwilling to acknowledge limitations upon the human condition. One of Andrew Jackson's slaves, asked if his deceased master would get to heaven, replied: "He will if he wants to." Such optimism has, at least since the Enlightenment, been almost compulsively a part of the national character. Yet even in Arendt's most abstract passages, her thought is so charged with the feeling of peril, so tinged with urgency, that the presence of the barricades can almost be sensed. To deny Arendt a niche in the normative traditions of American thought is hardly meant as derogation, but it is a view that does not require too much resourcefulness of argument to sustain.

In yet another way her writing resisted categorization. The effort to calibrate the impact of totalitarianism would be radically diminished without books that happen to have been written by women—by Nadezhda Mandelstam, Evgenia Ginzburg, Heda Kovály, Anne Frank, Margarete Buber-Neumann, the historian Lucy Dawidowicz, the novelist Ilse Aichinger, the poet Nelly Sachs, and the anonymous Polish author of *The Dark Side of the Moon*. The thinker with whom Arendt has most often been compared is Simone Weil, who was born three years later; and there are indeed some intriguing parallels. By the early 1930s Weil had also concluded that terrible similarities between Soviet Communism and the Nazi movement needed to be stressed, and she pressed her own sense of this symmetry upon disbelieving fellow leftists from Trotsky to André Malraux. Though an independent radical activist, she considered even capitalism preferable to the so-called workers' state that had been established in Russia.[10] Far from dismissing the Fuehrer as a barbarian atavism, Weil insisted during the war that "nothing could be less primitive than Hitler, who would be inconceivable without modern technique and the existence of *millions of uprooted men*."[11] Weil and Arendt also shared a profound admiration for Greek political thought and for Rosa Luxemburg.[12]

But differences should also be noted. Weil died, malnourished, in 1943, having transferred food and gifts to prisoners in Vichy concentration camps. She left behind only literary

Conclusion

fragments—notebooks and essays—rather than a legacy of elaborated ideas. Whereas Arendt stressed the break in Occidental history that totalitarianism signified, Weil underscored the resemblances between Nazism and the ancient Romans, whom she detested. Weil, searching deep in the past for the gnarled roots of totalitarianism, even described ancient Israel in such terms.[13] For unlike Arendt, Weil repudiated her own Jewish origins, found Judaism offensive, and opposed all expressions of Jewish national spirit.[14] No one acquainted with Weil's life and thought can miss the intensity of her religious vocation, which took the form of a hunger for martyrdom. When Weil identified affliction as the way of Christ, when she admitted, "Whenever I think of the crucifixion I commit the sin of envy,"[15] she was releasing emotions remote from Arendt's sensibility, which has by contrast enlarged our comprehension of suffering without intending to endorse it.

The fact that Arendt was, like Weil and several other consequential writers, a woman is about as relevant to the full understanding of her intellectual achievement as the fact that Galileo was white. She was not a feminist; and though her second book (written in German) was on Rahel Varnhagen, Arendt's political philosophy took no special notice of the role, suppression or aspirations of women. The essentials of her philosophy were derived from the public realm rather than the private sphere to which women have historically been confined, and Arendt praised glory and valor far more than mercy or love. She indeed wrote about the power of compassion and love to obliterate the distance between human beings; but in a corpus so impressive for its sweep and comprehensiveness, the interest Arendt showed in the range of the most common—yet private—experiences was scant indeed. The criticism John Jay Chapman once levelled at Emerson could therefore also have been directed at Arendt's work: "If an inhabitant of another planet should visit the earth, he would receive, on the whole, a truer notion of human life by attending an Italian opera than he would by reading Emerson's volumes. He would learn from the Italian opera that there were two sexes; and this, after all, is probably the fact with which the education of such a stranger ought to begin."[16]

Arendt's audience did not of course consist of such strangers; and it can be argued in defense of her work that she was inclined not to begin with the obvious but to assault it. If there is such a thing as an original thinker writing in a nontechnical vocabulary in the twentieth century, Arendt would pass muster. Her work was marked by so much "intellectual passion" that Macdonald, after reading *The Origins of Totalitarianism*, half complained that "the mental texture of the book is almost *too* dense, too *rich*. A paragraph, or even a sentence, often presents so novel and at the same time so persuasive a point of view, that one feels compelled actually to think about it."[17] This was the sort of experience few readers were accustomed to bearing. Arendt had a knack for defining problems in unexpected ways, whether by splitting microscopically thin hairs or by serving up generalizations on a grandiose scale. Anyone who could assert that the enterprise of philosophy went astray well over two millennia ago—because Socrates withdrew from the public realm[18]—showed a talent for startling and unconventional judgment. Kateb called her a "shocking" writer. Her aversion to the accepted wisdom, combined with a relentless severity akin to "fanaticism"[19] in the pursuit and development of ideas, resulted in genuinely fresh and unusual illuminations. Yet her urge to say something new also produced the effect of haphazardness and arbitrariness.[20] Arendt's instinct for the provocative sometimes led her into error; and when she found she could not say anything new, she preferred to say something delphic. Yet, as Riesman observed, the "very errors, exaggerations, and over-systemizations" of authors like Arendt "often turn out, in the unpredictable history of ideas, to be liberating and fructifying for thought."[21] Given a choice, Arendt would rather have been original than right. Had she merely been right, she could not have had such an impact, nor could she have teased so many stunning perceptions from the stuff of history.

Yet Arendt was too sober to be dismissed as flashy or capricious; those perceptions were hard-earned. What was reassuring about her audacity was that it did not call attention to itself, and she never sought to highlight the freshness of her insights by cancelling her intellectual debts. Arendt's books came with the weight of scholarship, enough to have sunk the work of less independent expositors. Her sense of pertinence helped save her from pedantry. It is as though she was more concerned with establishing her learning than her originality. If that was indeed her ambition, she did not fully succeed, because the distinctiveness of her voice and the essentially speculative nature of her calling denied to the body of her work the prudence and balance that completely reassures the academy. Judged by the highest standards, perhaps none of her books has remained utterly indispensable for scholars, an essential item of bibliography, with the exception of *The Origins of Totalitarianism*; and that book and the general theory with which it has been associated have been locked in mutual dependence.

Though Arendt taught for over two decades at several prominent universities, her own uneasy relationship to the academy was undoubtedly due to her unwillingness to be only a scholar. As she once wrote of Dilthey, his "tremendous erudition was something more than extensive knowledge."[22] Arendt's work exhibited a forcefulness that could not be confined to the ideals of objectivity and neutrality which are integral to the contemplative life. This emotional energy made her rather suspect among some political scientists, even

when they acknowledged her considerable powers of analysis—that feline capacity for seeing in the dark. But what gave
The Origins of Totalitarianism its coherence was not only a
technical skill in manipulating descriptions of the political
and social forces that burst the seams of civilization. In tracing
the origins and consequences of totalitarianism, Arendt exhibited not only the narrative and analytical gifts required of
an historian; she also showed the mind of a moralist. The
book's "cohesion comes from the passionate subjectivity of the
author," Rieff suggested, and "its power from her vocabulary
of forces—e.g., the mob and capital, the Jews and the nation-
state—pointing everywhere toward a vista of doom." [23]

For some scholars, a book written in response to a "traumat-
ic shuddering" [24] was bound to appear dubious. For example,
Benjamin Barber and Herbert Spiro expressed grave concern
that the primary effect of the theory of totalitarianism "has
been moral, and hence as ideological as the system it purports
to oppose." Works like Arendt's, they complained, "have reduced world politics to a simplistic duel between the forces of
light and the powers of darkness. . . . The world is at least
somewhat less rational, less predictable, more diversified, less
polarized, more varied, less monolithic—in short, less susceptible to simplistic moral analysis—than theories of totalitarianism are inclined to allow." The excessive logicality and
consistency that Arendt attributed to totalitarian regimes,
Robert Burrowes added, was false to the complex reality of
modern politics. In *The Origins of Totalitarianism*, he wrote,
"systematic analysis frequently gives way without warning to
the vocabulary of outrage and condemnation. . . . At the core
of her often strident and emotional critique is a fundamental-
ism which has its normative basis in the Judeo-Christian and
Western political traditions. Reflecting this belief, her conception of totalitarianism has taken on the character of a
demonic construct . . . that can only be described at best as

caricature and at worst as fantasy." Burrowes, an N.Y.U. political scientist, concluded: "It is perhaps ironic that a person who sees totalitarianism as an attempt to translate reality into fiction should herself produce a fictitious theory."[25] The result was what Canovan termed "a social scientist's nightmare," in which a "sometimes polemical aura" obstructed the understanding of the phenomenon.[26]

Arendt conceded that it was impossible to write about totalitarianism with objectivity. Replying to a review by Eric Voegelin, she acknowledged that, since Nazism and Stalinism had erupted within the human community, no analysis of their origins and legacy could be free of value judgment. Her book had therefore not been composed "*sine ira et studio*, [but] still in grief and sorrow"—though "no longer in speechless outrage and impotent horror." She felt no obligation to apologize for grief and anger (and Voegelin himself recognized the effectiveness and depth of these emotions in heightening the intellectual force of her book).[27] Moreover it is hard to fathom why the neutrality favored in political science is always to be preferred to the historical discernment and moral adroitness that Arendt's book demonstrated, or why even ordinary human responsiveness to political cruelty and horror should be so strenuously resisted.

Those who were discomfited by the personal qualities the author revealed may themselves have something to answer for. Not to make plain one's judgments about totalitarianism itself constituted a moral and political position, and to insist upon neutrality on the subject of unprecedented tyranny offered little assurance that genuine understanding would thereby be enhanced. Arendt at least did not disguise her moral revulsion, nor was she trapped in the illusion that anyone in 1951 or later could be devoid of feelings and judgments about Nazism and Communism. In locating Arendt's fundamental stance, Burrowes proposed no alternative to the Judeo-Christian and Western heritage, itself the source not only of certain ethical injunctions that totalitarianism systematically violated but also of the idea of a value-free social science. Her book did not pretend to be *wertfrei*; but it was a work of the imagination, which Arendt elsewhere defined as concern "with the particular darkness of the human heart and the peculiar density which surrounds everything that is real."[28] Such concern was of course the aim of social science as well; but Arendt's self-consciousness, her awareness of her own values rather than her desire to suppress them, made it more possible for her to penetrate and disclose the ideological mentality she found so dangerous.

Those critical of Arendt's emotional excess also objected to her inadvertent imitation of the exaggerated logicality she attributed to the totalitarian states. These regimes tried to make the world consistent, and Arendt supposedly stressed unduly this explanation of Soviet and Nazi policies. She was thus accused both of an excess of sentiment and of an excess of rationality, qualities not ordinarily thought to be compatible. The indictment itself was therefore rendered somewhat suspect, though Arendt did believe that totalitarian regimes tried to alter reality to correspond with their ideologies. She underestimated the extent to which that reality, in the form of military pressure and threat, restricted the dynamism of the totalitarian regimes. Arendt tended to attribute to ideology the ground for totalitarian behavior explicable by other causes. To that extent the "systematic character of her model" led her to neglect the contingency and caprice that are an ineluctable part of history.[29]

But that did not rob *The Origins of Totalitarianism* of complexity, because Arendt's stress on ideology removed Naziism and Stalinism from the fairly simple world of common sense and self-interest and accentuated their terrifying irrationality. In underscoring the ferocity with which the totalitarian regimes pursued the logic of an idea, Arendt was demonstrating that modern politics has been far more bewildering and dense than social science normally allows for. Contrary to Barber and Spiro, Arendt never claimed that the democracies were "forces of light," since the very design of her book showed how totalitarianism had originated within nineteenth century European society. And contrary to Burrowes, her depiction of this phenomenon assumed "the character of a demonic construct" because that was indeed the reality of the Holocaust kingdom and the Gulag archipelago. Both "the radical nature of evil" and "the banality of evil" could be fully discerned with the introduction of totalitarianism in the modern world. The historical evidence that has accumulated and been made available since 1951 has tended to confirm the terrible accuracy of Arendt's book and the unsparing judgments she rendered. Her remorseless cerebration hardly merited denigration but, given the threat that tyranny posed to the free mind, ought to have been recognized as an expression of moral courage.

While rejecting a spurious objectivity in her explanation of Nazism and Stalinism, she constructed the most convincing articulation of the idea of totalitarianism. The parallels she observed and the break with Western tradition she measured formed the basis of a grand conceptual scheme, while her dark flashes of insight were the signature of brilliance. Yet because of Arendt's philosophical orientation, it was tempting to overlook and even to disparage her book's historical value. According to N. K. O'Sullivan, a political scientist at Hull, the abstractness in which Arendt was at home led her to "the brink of essentialism." Thus "she assumes that because we happen to have the word [totalitarianism], we must therefore be able to find a phenomenon corresponding to it." Another critic similarly found Arendt's work to be ahistorical in its attempt at "describing . . . a fixed essence, not a phenomenon

in flux."[30] Yet the theme of her book was not only the characteristics of total rule but its origins in racism, pan-Germanism,
pan-Slavism, imperialism and bureaucracy. Arendt not only
assumed that a phenomenon corresponded to a word; after
having personally experienced totalitarianism, she provided
evidence at some length for the correctness of her assumption.
Arendt's subject was not a fixed essence but "the dynamics
of the decay of Europe's public life,"[31] and her analysis was
therefore rooted in social experience and historical specificity.
In this respect it is useful to contrast the hypotheses of Karl
Popper, who traced totalitarianism all the way back to Plato,
or Norman Cohn, who located it in medieval millennialism,
or Voegelin, who discerned the phenomenon in the Gnostic
heresies of Joachim of Floris, or Bertrand Russell, who considered Hitler the consequence of Rousseau. Here were assertions scarcely subject to verification.

Yet already during the Second World War, Arendt had denied that various thinkers of the past bore any "responsibility
for what is happening in the extermination camps. Ideologically speaking, Nazism begins with no such traditional basis
at all."[32] She objected to the effort "to dress up the horrible
gutter-born phenomenon with the language of the humanities and the history of ideas . . . a realm in which ideas, like
cloud formations, easily and effortlessly pass and blend into
one another."[33] Though Arendt laid bare the mentality that
had motivated and absolved atrocities, she knew that the primary importance of totalitarianism was not as idea but as
event. The most horrifying and mysterious aspect of it was
simply that it happened, and she therefore added to the compilation of the evils on this planet. Arendt's special accomplishment was to help ensure that such torment would not be
forgotten, even though no complete understanding is possible,
no judgment quite satisfactory, no grappling with its meaning more treacherous. For those who survived the German

and Soviet terror, for their descendants, and for those fortunate enough to have eluded its direct impact, a tension persists. The need to make totalitarianism intelligible risks trivialization in our "normal" world; the awareness that such suffering is finally incomprehensible endangers the need to remember. Yet it is a source of solace that the holes of oblivion do not exist.

NOTES

Preface

1. Dwight Macdonald, "A New Theory of Totalitarianism," *New Leader*, 34 (May 14, 1951), 19.

2. Jacob Cohen, "Through Liberal Glasses Darkly," *Jewish Frontier*, 30 (January 1963), 8n; Bernard Crick, *In Defence of Politics* (Chicago: University of Chicago Press, 1972), p. 11, ch. 2; Irving Louis Horowitz, *Genocide: State Power and Mass Murder* (New Brunswick, N.J.: Transaction, 1977), pp. 5, 33; Alfred Kazin, "The Heart of the World," in Eva Fleischner (editor), *Auschwitz: Beginning of a New Era?: Reflections on the Holocaust* (New York: Ktav, 1977), pp. 67–68; Richard King, *The Party of Eros: Radical Social Thought and the Realm of Freedom* (Chapel Hill: University of North Carolina Press, 1972), p. 8; Hanna Fenichel Pitkin, *Wittgenstein and Justice: On the Significance of Ludwig Wittgenstein for Social and Political Thought* (Berkeley: University of California Press, 1972), pp. 158–161, 208–217, 241–243, 285, 329–330; Philip Rieff, *Fellow Teachers* (New York: Harper and Row, 1973), p. 210.

Chapter 1

1. Karl Jaspers, *Man in the Modern Age* (Garden City, N. Y.: Doubleday Anchor, 1957), p. 187; Hannah Arendt, *Between Past and Future: Eight Exercises in Political Thought* (New York: Viking, 1968), p. 61.

2. St. Augustine quoted in Arendt, *Between Past and Future*, p. 66.

3. Robert E. Meyerson, "Hannah Arendt: Romantic in a Totalitarian Age, 1928–1963" (Ph.D. dissertation, University of Minnesota, 1972), pp. 14–16, 86; Salo W. Baron, "Personal Notes: Hannah Arendt (1906–1975)," *Jewish Social Studies*, 38 (Spring 1976), 187.

4. Baron, "Personal Notes"; Hannah Arendt, "A Reply," *Review of Politics*, 15 (January 1953), 78.

5. H. Stuart Hughes, "Historical Sources of Totalitarianism," *Nation*,

172 (March 24, 1951), 280–281; Dwight Macdonald, "A New Theory of Totalitarianism," *New Leader*, 34 (May 14, 1951), 17.

6. Mary McCarthy, *On the Contrary: Articles of Belief, 1946–1961* (New York: Farrar, Straus and Giroux, 1961), p. 156; Alfred Kazin in "Outstanding Books, 1931–1961," *American Scholar*, 30 (Winter 1961), 612.

7. Terence Ball (editor), *Political Theory and Praxis: New Perspectives* (Minneapolis: University of Minnesota Press, 1977); Melvyn A. Hill (editor), *Hannah Arendt: The Recovery of the Public World* (New York: St. Martin's, 1979).

8. Douglas Davis, "A Life of the Mind," *Newsweek*, 86 (December 15, 1975), 84; Norman Podhoretz, *Making It* (New York: Random House, 1967), p. 247; Philip Nobile, *Intellectual Skywriting: Literary Politics and the New York Review of Books* (New York: Charterhouse, 1974), pp. 183–185, 213; Charles Kadushin, "Who Are the Elite Intellectuals?" *Public Interest*, 29 (Fall 1972), 123.

9. Judith Shklar, "Hannah Arendt's Triumph," *New Republic*, 173 (December 27, 1975), 9; Bernard Crick, "On Rereading *The Origins of Totalitarianism*," *Social Research*, 44 (Spring 1977), 126.

10. Margaret Canovan, *The Political Thought of Hannah Arendt* (New York: Harcourt Brace Jovanovich, 1974); Jacob Robinson, *And the Crooked Shall Be Made Straight: The Eichmann Trial, the Jewish Catastrophe, and Hannah Arendt's Narrative* (Philadelphia: Jewish Publication Society, 1965); Scott E. Edwards, "The Political Thought of Hannah Arendt: A Study in Thought and Action" (Ph.D. dissertation, Claremont Graduate School, 1964); Mary Katherine McKeon Klein, "The Concept of Political Freedom in Hannah Arendt" (Ph.D. dissertation, Boston University, 1973); James T. Knauer, "Hannah Arendt and the Reassertion of the Political: Toward a New Democratic Theory" (Ph.D. dissertation, S.U.N.Y. at Binghamton, 1975); George McKenna, "A Critic of Modernity: The Political Thought of Hannah Arendt" (Ph.D. dissertation, Fordham University, 1967); Meyerson, "Romantic in a Totalitarian Age."

11. Stuart Hughes, *The Sea Change: The Migration of Social Thought, 1930–1965* (New York: Harper and Row, 1975), p. 121.

12. Henry James to Arthur Benson, June 29, 1896, in E. F. Benson (editor), *Henry James: Letters to A. C. Benson and Auguste Monod* (New York: Scribner's, 1930), p. 35.

13. George Orwell to Roger Senhouse, May 6, 1948, in Sonia Orwell and Ian Angus (editors), *The Collected Essays, Journalism and Letters*

of George Orwell, Vol. IV (New York: Harcourt Brace Jovanovich, 1968), p. 421.

14. Leonard Schapiro, *Totalitarianism* (New York: Praeger, 1972), pp. 13–14.

15. Hans Kohn, "Communist and Fascist Dictatorship: A Comparative Study," in Guy Stanton Ford (editor), *Dictatorship in the Modern World* (Minneapolis: University of Minnesota Press, 1935), p. 151.

16. Walter Lippmann, *The Good Society* (Boston: Little, Brown, 1937), pp. 4–5; Robert Allen Skotheim, *Totalitarianism and American Social Thought* (New York: Holt, Rinehart and Winston, 1971), pp. 52–59.

17. Walter Lippmann, *The Cold War: A Study in U.S. Foreign Policy* (New York: Harper and Row, 1972), pp. 23–26, 31; Lippmann, *The Public Philosophy* (Boston: Little, Brown, 1955), p. 83; and Lippmann, "The American Idea," in Clinton Rossiter and James Lare (editors), *The Essential Lippmann: A Political Philosophy for Liberal Democracy* (New York: Random House, 1963), p. 5; Skotheim, *Totalitarianism,* pp. 84–87.

18. James Burkhart Gilbert, *Writers and Partisans: A History of Literary Radicalism in America* (New York: John Wiley, 1968), pp. 197–199, 201–203, 205–206, 241–244; Edmund Wilson to Daniel Aaron, 1961, in Elena Wilson (editor), *Edmund Wilson: Letters on Literature and Politics, 1912–1972* (New York: Farrar, Straus and Giroux, 1977), pp. 359 360.

19. Gilbert, *Writers and Partisans,* pp. 164–168, 199–200, 234; Sidney Hook, *Reason, Social Myths and Democracy* (New York: Humanities Press, 1940), pp. 178–180.

20. Hannah Arendt, "He's All Dwight," *New York Review of Books,* 11 (August 1, 1968), 31–33; Stephen J. Whitfield, "Dwight Macdonald's *Politics* Magazine, 1944–1949," *Journalism History,* 3 (Fall 1976), 86–88.

21. Friedrich A. Hayek, *The Road to Serfdom* (Chicago: University of Chicago Press, 1944), pp. ii, 92; George H. Nash, *The Conservative Intellectual Movement in America: Since 1945* (New York: Basic Books, 1979), pp. 5–9, 349–350.

22. Franz Neumann, *Behemoth: The Structure and Practice of National Socialism, 1933–1944* (New York: Harper and Row, 1966), p. 261.

23. Martin Jay, *The Dialectical Imagination: A History of the Frankfurt School and the Institute of Social Research, 1923–1950* (Boston: Little, Brown, 1973), pp. 99–100, 247–248; Stephen J. Whitfield, "The Imagination of Disaster: The Response of American Jewish Intellectuals

to Totalitarianism," *Jewish Social Studies*, 42 (Winter 1980), pp. 4–5.

24. Erik H. Erikson, "Wholeness and Totality—A Psychiatric Contribution," in Carl J. Friedrich (editor), *Totalitarianism* (New York: Grosset and Dunlap, 1964), pp. 159, 170.

25. Stephen J. Whitfield, " 'Totalitarianism' in Eclipse: The Recent Fate of an Idea," in Arthur Edelstein (editor), *Images and Ideas in American Culture: The Functions of Criticism* (Hanover, N.H.: University Press of New England, 1979), pp. 70–89.

26. Sidney Hook, *Political Power and Personal Freedom* (New York: Criterion, 1959), pp. 145–146.

27. Max Eastman, *Reflections on the Failure of Socialism* (New York: Devin-Adair, 1955), pp. 118, 126; Bertram D. Wolfe, *Communist Totalitarianism: Keys to the Soviet System* (Boston: Beacon, 1961), pp. 269, 276.

28. George F. Kennan, "Totalitarianism in the Modern World," in Friedrich (editor), *Totalitarianism*, p. 17.

29. Benjamin R. Barber, "Conceptual Foundations of Totalitarianism," in Carl J. Friedrich, Michael Curtis, and Benjamin R. Barber, *Totalitarianism in Perspective: Three Views* (New York: Praeger, 1969), pp. 38–39; Michael Curtis, "Retreat from Totalitarianism," in Friedrich, Curtis, and Barber, *Totalitarianism*, p. 116.

30. Herbert Spiro, "Totalitarianism," in *International Encyclopedia of the Social Sciences* (New York: Macmillan, 1968), XVI, 112; Karl Dietrich Bracher, "The Role of Hitler: Perspectives of Interpretation," in Walter Laqueur (editor), *Fascism, A Reader's Guide: Analyses, Interpretations, Bibliography* (Berkeley: University of California Press, 1976), p. 212.

31. Daniel Bell, *The End of Ideology: On the Exhaustion of Political Ideas in the Fifties* (New York: Free Press, 1962), pp. 32–33, and *The Coming of Post-Industrial Society: A Venture in Social Forecasting* (New York: Basic Books, 1973), pp. 113–114.

32. Merle Fainsod, *How Russia Is Ruled* (Cambridge: Harvard University Press, 1953), p. 500; Jerry F. Hough and Merle Fainsod, *How the Soviet Union Is Governed* (Cambridge: Harvard University Press, 1979), pp. 520–523; Richard Pipes, "Revisionist Revision," *Commentary*, 68 (October 1979), 88.

33. Kennedy and Johnson quoted in Bruce Kuklick, "Tradition and Diplomatic Talent: The Case of the Cold Warriors," in Leila Zenderland (editor), *Recycling the Past: Popular Uses of American History* (Philadelphia: University of Pennsylvania Press, 1978), p. 122.

34. *Ibid.*, pp. 122, 125, 128–129; Hook quoted in Nash, *Conservative Intellectual Movement*, 323.

35. Diana Trilling, *We Must March My Darlings: A Critical Decade* (New York: Harcourt Brace Jovanovich, 1977), p. 239; George Orwell, "Looking Back on the Spanish War," in Sonia Orwell and Ian Angus (editors), *Collected Essays*, Vol. II (New York: Harcourt Brace Jovanovich, 1968), p. 256; Herbert Marcuse, *Negations: Essays in Critical Theory* (Boston, Beacon, 1968), p. xv.

36. Herbert Marcuse, *One-Dimensional Man: Studies in the Ideology of Advanced Industrial Society* (Boston: Beacon, 1964), p. 52, and *Five Lectures* (Boston: Beacon, 1970), pp. 86, 94; Whitfield, " 'Totalitarianism' in Eclipse," in Edelstein (editor), *Images and Ideas*, pp. 76–79.

37. Mailer in A. Alvarez, *Under Pressure: The Writer in Society, Eastern Europe and the U.S.A.* (Baltimore: Penguin, 1965), pp. 132–134; Whitfield, "Imagination of Disaster," pp. 1–11.

38. Theodore Roszak, *The Making of a Counter Culture: Reflections on the Technocratic Society and Its Youthful Opposition* (Garden City, N.Y.: Doubleday Anchor, 1969), pp. 9–10; Leslie Fiedler, "Toward the Freudian Pill," in Murray A. Sperber (editor), *Arthur Koestler: A Collection of Critical Essays* (Englewood Cliffs, N.J.: Prentice-Hall, 1977), p. 163.

39. Garry Wills, *Nixon Agonistes: The Crisis of the Self-Made Man* (Boston: Houghton Mifflin, 1970), p. 223.

40. Lillian Hellman, *Scoundrel Time* (New York: Bantam, 1977), pp. 38, 44.

41. Bruce Franklin, Introduction to *The Essential Stalin: Major Theoretical Writings, 1905–52* (Garden City, N.Y.: Doubleday Anchor, 1972), p. 1; Michael Parenti, *The Anti-Communist Impulse* (New York: Random House, 1969), pp. 47, 48n; Robert C. Tucker, *The Soviet Political Mind: Studies in Stalinism and Post-Stalin Change* (New York: Praeger, 1963), p. 85n.

Chapter 2

1. George McKenna, "A Critic of Modernity: The Political Thought of Hannah Arendt" (Ph.D. dissertation, Fordham University, 1967), pp. 196, 197n.

2. Alfred Kazin, in "Outstanding Books, 1931–1961," *American Scholar*, 30 (Winter 1961), 612, and *New York Jew* (New York: Knopf, 1978), p. 200; H. Stuart Hughes, "Historical Sources of Totalitarianism," *Na-*

268   *Into the Dark*

tion, 172 (March 24, 1951), 281; Les K. Adler and Thomas G. Paterson, "Red Fascism: The Merger of Nazi Germany and Soviet Russia in the American Image of Totalitarianism, 1930's–1950's," *American Historical Review*, 75 (April 1970), 1049.

3. Hannah Arendt, *The Origins of Totalitarianism* (Cleveland: World, 1958), pp. 443, 445, and rev. ed. (New York: Harcourt, Brace and World, 1966), p. xi [1958 edition cited hereafter unless otherwise noted]; Hughes, "Historical Sources of Totalitarianism," pp. 280–281; Isaac Deutscher, *Stalin: A Political Biography* (New York: Vintage, 1960), pp. 567–568; Robert Burrowes, "Totalitarianism: The Revised Standard Version," *World Politics*, 21 (January 1969), 276–277.

4. David Schoenbaum, *Hitler's Social Revolution: Class and Status in Nazi Germany, 1933–1939* (Garden City: N.Y.: Doubleday, 1966), pp. 39, 44, 71–72; Barrington Moore, Jr., *Injustice: The Social Bases of Obedience and Revolt* (White Plains, N.Y.: M. E. Sharpe, 1978), pp. 406–410; Robert G. L. Waite, *The Psychopathic God: Adolf Hitler* (New York: Basic Books, 1977), pp. 328, 330–332; Alexander J. Groth, "The 'Isms' in Totalitarianism," *American Polititcal Science Review*, 58 (December 1964), 895.

5. Leonard Schapiro, *The Communist Party of the Soviet Union* (New York: Random House, 1960), pp. 234–236, 436–438, 443.

6. Groth, " 'Isms' of Totalitarianism," pp. 890–895, 898–899, 900.

7. Wolfgang Sauer, "National Socialism: Totalitarianism or Fascism?" *American Historical Review*, 73 (December 1967), 418–419; Raymond A. Bauer, *The New Man in Soviet Psychology* (Cambridge: Harvard University Press, 1952), pp. 177–178; Joachim C. Fest, *The Face of the Third Reich: Portraits of the Nazi Leadership* (New York: Pantheon, 1970), p. 71.

8. Carl J. Friedrich and Zbigniew K. Brzezinski, *Totalitarian Dictatorship and Autocracy* (New York: Praeger, 1961), p. 61.

9. Hans Frank quoted in Jeremy Noakes and Geoffrey Pridham (editors), *Documents on Nazism, 1919–1945* (New York: Viking, 1974), p. 254; H. R. Trevor-Roper, *The Last Days of Hitler* (New York: Collier, 1962), p. 63n; Eberhard Jäckel, *Hitler's Weltanschauung: A Blueprint for Power* (Middletown, Conn.: Wesleyan University Press, 1972), p. 82; Leonard Schapiro, *Totalitarianism* (New York: Praeger, 1972), pp. 56–57.

10. William Styron, Introduction to Richard Rubenstein, *The Cunning of History: The Holocaust and the American Future* (New York:

Harper and Row, 1978), pp. x–xi; Rubenstein, in *The Cunning of History*, pp. 60–61; Margarete Buber-Neumann, *Under Two Dictators* (New York: Dodd-Mead, 1949), p. 202.

11. Robert H. Jackson, Closing Argument, July 26, 1946, in *Trials of the Major War Criminals* (Nuremberg: International Military Tribunal, 1948), XIX, 416.

12. Roy A. Medvedev, *Let History Judge: The Origins and Consequences of Stalinism* (New York: Knopf, 1972), p. 280; David J. Dallin and Boris I. Nicolaevsky, *Forced Labor in Soviet Russia* (New Haven: Yale University Press, 1947), p. 218; Aleksandr I. Solzhenitsyn, *The Gulag Archipelago, 1918–1956: An Experiment in Literary Investigation* (New York: Harper and Row, 1974), I, 564.

13. Victor Herman, *Coming Out of the Ice: An Unexpected Life* (New York: Harcourt Brace Jovanovich, 1979), pp. 240–241.

14. Arendt, *Origins*, pp. 409–411; Walter Laqueur, "Nazism and the Nazis," *Encounter*, 22 (April 1964), 41.

15. Robert C. Tucker, "The Dictator and Totalitarianism," *World Politics*, 17 (July 1965), 572–573.

16. Robert Conquest, *The Great Terror: Stalin's Purge of the Thirties* (New York: Macmillan, 1968), p. 302; Lev Kopelev, *To Be Preserved Forever* (Philadelphia: Lippincott, 1977), p. 147; Roy A. Medvedev, "New Pages from the Political Biography of Stalin," in Robert C. Tucker (editor), *Stalinism: Essays in Historical Interpretation* (New York: Norton, 1977), p. 227.

17. Solzhenitsyn, *Gulag Archipelago* (New York: Harper and Row, 1975), II, 98–99, 101–102; Adam B. Ulam, *The New Face of Soviet Totalitarianism* (Cambridge: Harvard University Press, 1963), p. 95.

18. Medvedev, *Let History Judge*, pp. 148, 354, 364, 507–508; Secret Speech of Khrushchev, in *The Anti-Stalin Campaign and International Communism*, edited by Russian Institute of Columbia University (New York: Columbia University Press, 1956), pp. 69–71; Waite, *Psychopathic God*, p. 83; Walter Laqueur, *Russia and Germany: A Century of Conflict* (Boston: Little, Brown, 1965), p. 297.

19. Schapiro, *Totalitarianism*, pp. 56–57, and *Communist Party of the Soviet Union*, pp. 548–549.

20. Arendt, *Origins* (1966), pp. xxii–xxiv; Ulam, *New Face of Soviet Totalitarianism*, pp. 55–56; Norman Cohn, *Warrant for Genocide: The Myth of the Jewish World-Conspiracy and the Protocols of the Elders of Zion* (New York: Harper and Row, 1967), pp. 19, 180–214.

270   *Into the Dark*

21. Lecture by Alexander Nekrich, Brandeis University, November 1977.

22. Wolfgang Leonhard, *The Kremlin since Stalin* (New York: Praeger, 1962), pp. 45–50; Medvedev, *Let History Judge*, pp. 494–495; Solzhenitsyn, *Gulag Archipelago*, I, 92; Tucker, "Dictator and Totalitarianism," pp. 570–571, 580–581.

23. Richard Hofstadter, *The Paranoid Style in American Politics and Other Essays* (New York: Vintage, 1967), pp. 7, 29.

24. Emil Fackenheim, "The Holocaust and the State of Israel: Their Relation," in Eva Fleischner (editor), *Auschwitz: Beginning of a New Era?: Reflections on the Holocaust* (New York: Ktav, 1977), p. 209; Jacob Robinson, *And the Crooked Shall Be Made Straight: The Eichmann Trial, the Jewish Catastrophe, and Hannah Arendt's Narrative* (Philadelphia: Jewish Publication Society, 1965), pp. 97–99.

25. Jäckel, *Hitler's Weltanschauung*, pp. 48, 62–63, 65; Lucy S. Dawidowicz, *The War against the Jews, 1933–1945* (New York: Bantam, 1976), p. 191; Waite, *Psychopathic God*, pp. iv, 362.

26. Hitler's Political Testament, April 29, 1945, quoted in Noakes and Pridham (editors), *Documents on Nazism*, p. 680; George F. Kennan, "Totalitarianism in the Modern World," in Carl J. Friedrich (editor), *Totalitarianism* (New York: Grosset and Dunlap, 1964), pp. 21–22.

27. Hughes, "Historical Sources of Totalitarianism," p. 282; Burrowes, "Revised Standard Version," *World Politics*, p. 276; Margaret Canovan, *The Political Thought of Hannah Arendt* (New York: Harcourt Brace Jovanovich, 1974), p. 38; N. K. O'Sullivan, "Politics, Totalitarianism and Freedom: The Political Thought of Hannah Arendt," *Political Studies*, 21 (June 1973), 192; Robert Booth Fowler, *Believing Skeptics: American Political Intellectuals, 1945–1964* (Westport, Conn.: Greenwood Press, 1978), p. 6.

28. Alan Bullock, *Hitler: A Study in Tyranny* (New York: Bantam, 1961), pp. 361–367, 506–508, 660–662, 676–678.

29. Deutscher, *Stalin*, pp. 493–497; Medvedev, *Let History Judge*, pp. 300–301; Schapiro, *Communist Party of the Soviet Union*, pp. 502–504; Groth, " 'Isms' of Totalitarianism," pp. 893, 898, 899.

30. William Carr, "National Socialism: Foreign Policy and Wehrmacht," in Walter Laqueur (editor), *Fascism, A Reader's Guide: Analyses, Interpretations, Bibliography* (Berkeley: University of California Press, 1976), p. 172.

31. Deutscher, *Stalin*, pp. 490–491; Friedrich and Brzezinski, *Totali-*

tarian Dictatorship, pp. 247–248, 251, 257–258; Groth, " 'Isms' of Totalitarianism," pp. 893, 898, 899.

32. Albert Speer, *Inside the Third Reich: Memoirs* (New York: Macmillan, 1970), pp. 338, 483.

33. *Ibid.*, 220–221; John Kenneth Galbraith, *A Contemporary Guide to Economics, Peace and Laughter* (Boston: Houghton Mifflin, 1971), pp. 298–300; Hughes, "Historical Sources of Totalitarianism," p. 281.

34. Aleksandr I. Solzhenitsyn, *Letter to the Soviet Leaders* (New York: Harper and Row, 1975), p. 38; Rebecca West, *A Train of Powder* (New York: Viking, 1955), p. 154.

35. Hitler quoted in Arendt, *Origins*, p. 309, and in Rudolph Binion, *Hitler among the Germans* (New York: Elsevier, 1976), p. 98.

36. Hans J. Morgenthau, *Truth and Power: Essays of a Decade, 1960–1970* (New York: Praeger, 1970), p. 374; H. Stuart Hughes, *The Sea Change: The Migration of Social Thought, 1930–1965* (New York: Harper and Row, 1975), pp. 120–121; Karl Dietrich Bracher, "Totalitarianism," in *Dictionary of the History of Ideas* (New York: Scribner's, 1973), IV, 407.

37. Ronald Berman, *America in the Sixties: An Intellectual History* (New York: Harper and Row, 1970), p. 126; Gilbert Allardyce, "What Fascism Is Not: Thoughts on the Deflation of a Concept," *American Historical Review*, 84 (April 1979), 382–383; Leon Botstein, Letter to the Editor, *Partisan Review*, 46, no. 2 (1979), 316.

38. Waite, *Psychopathic God*, 80; Arendt, *Origins*, 309n, and *Eichmann in Jerusalem: A Report on the Banality of Evil* (New York: Viking, 1964), p. 176 [this edition cited hereafter unless otherwise noted].

39. Arendt, *Origins*, p. 387; Friedrich and Brzezinski, *Totalitarian Dictatorship*, pp. 131–132, 138.

40. Arendt, *Eichmann*, pp. 179–180; Bracher, "Totalitarianism," *Dictionary of the History of Ideas*, p. 409; John P. Diggins, *Mussolini and Fascism: The View from America* (Princeton: Princeton University Press, 1972), pp. 464–465; Ernst Nolte, *Three Faces of Fascism: Action Française, Italian Fascism, National Socialism* (New York: Holt, Rinehart and Winston, 1966), p. 220; Hans Buchheim, *Totalitarian Rule: Its Nature and Characteristics* (Middletown, Conn.: Wesleyan University Press, 1968), pp. 28–30.

41. Arendt, *Origins*, pp. 416–417; Dallin and Nicolaevsky, *Forced Labor*, p. 140; Conquest, *Great Terror*, p. 533.

42. Robert Conquest, *The Nation Killers: The Soviet Deportation of*

Nationalities (New York: Macmillan, 1970); Medvedev, "New Pages from the Political Biography of Stalin," in Tucker (editor), *Stalinism*, pp. 212, 227.

43. *Oxford English Dictionary* (Oxford: Clarendon Press, 1972), p. 1214; Raphael Lemkin, *Axis Rule in Europe: Laws of Occupation, Analysis of Government, Proposals for Redress* (Washington, D.C.: Carnegie Endowment for International Peace, 1944), pp. xi, 79, 80, 90–92; New York *Times*, August 30, 1959, p. 82.

44. Raul Hilberg, "The *Einsatzgruppen*," *Societas*, 2 (Summer 1972), 242; Robinson, *Crooked Shall Be Made Straight*, pp. 96–97; Arthur Koestler, *The Invisible Writing* (Boston: Beacon, 1955), p. 366.

45. Arendt, *Origins*, pp. 393, 422, 423–424; Dwight Macdonald, *Memoirs of a Revolutionist: Essays in Political Criticism* (Cleveland: World, 1958), p. 50n; Secret Speech of Khrushchev, *Anti-Stalin Campaign*, pp. 17–18; Medvedev, *Let History Judge*, p. 69.

46. Arendt, *Origins*, p. 429; Dallin and Nicolaevsky, *Forced Labor*, pp. 259–260; Solzhenitsyn, *Gulag Archipelago*, I, 11, 71, and II, 297; Medvedev, *Let History Judge*, pp. 284, 348; Evgenia S. Ginzburg, *Into the Whirlwind* (London: Penguin, 1968), pp. 27, 109–110; Joseph Berger, *Shipwreck of a Generation* (London: Harvill, 1971), p. 122.

47. Solzhenitsyn, *Gulag Archipelago*, I, 146, 308; Medvedev, *Let History Judge*, p. 263.

48. Medvedev, *Let History Judge*, p. 233; Solzhenitsyn, *Gulag Archipelago*, I, 293; Nadezhda Mandelstam, *Hope against Hope: A Memoir* (New York: Atheneum, 1970), p. 11; Arendt, *Origins*, p. 433.

49. Arendt, *Origins*, pp. 337–338, 420; Trevor-Roper, *Last Days of Hitler*, pp. 238, 286–288; Carl J. Friedrich, "The Evolving Theory and Practice of Totalitarian Regimes," in Carl J. Friedrich, Michael Curtis, and Benjamin R. Barber, *Totalitarianism in Perspective: Three Views* (New York: Praeger, 1969), p. 143.

50. Solzhenitsyn, *Gulag Archipelago*, II, 10; Arendt, *Origins*, pp. 423, 425–427.

51. Julien Benda, *The Betrayal of the Intellectuals* (Boston: Beacon, 1955), p. 21; Arendt, *Origins*, pp. 464, 468–469, and "Home to Roost: A Bicentennial Address," *New York Review of Books*, 23 (June 26, 1975), 4.

52. Jacques Barzun, *The House of Intellect* (New York: Harper and Row, 1961), p. 60; Leon Lipson quoted in Israel Shenker, *Words and Their Masters* (Garden City, N.Y.: Doubleday, 1974), p. 223; Vladimir Bukovsky, Introduction to Sidney Bloch and Peter Reddaway, *Psychi-*

atric Terror: Hw Soviet Psychiatric Terror Is Used to Suppress Dissent (New York: Basic Books, 1977), p. 14.

53. Arendt, *Origins*, pp. 469–471; John Plamenetz, *Ideology* (New York: Praeger, 1970), p. 124; Lewis S. Feuer, *Ideology and the Ideologists* (New York: Harper and Row, 1975), p. 136; Berger, *Shipwreck of a Generation*, pp. 52–53.

54. Arendt, "The Hole of Oblivion," *Jewish Frontier*, 14 (July 1947), 24, and "The Seeds of a Fascist International," *Jewish Frontier*, 12 (June 1945), 15; Friedrich and Brzezinski, *Totalitarian Dictatorship*, p. 85.

55. Elie Wiesel, *One Generation After* (New York: Avon, 1972), p. 108; Menachem Begin, *White Nights: The Story of a Prisoner in Russia* (London: Macdonald, 1957), pp. 80–82.

56. Arendt, "Fascist International," p. 15.

57. Arendt, *Origins*, pp. 349–350, 385, and *Between Past and Future: Eight Exercises in Political Thought* (New York: Viking, 1968), p. 252; Dallin and Nicolaevsky, *Forced Labor*, p. 207; Bertram D. Wolfe, *Communist Totalitarianism: Keys to the Soviet System* (Boston: Beacon, 1961), pp. 75–80.

58. Arendt, *Origins*, pp. 384–385; Wolfe, *Communist Totalitarianism*, pp. 56–59, 68–75; Medvedev, *Let History Judge*, pp. 12, 524; Wolfgang Leonhard, *Child of the Revolution* (Chicago: Henry Regnery, 1958), p. 55.

59. Medvedev, "New Pages from the Political Biography of Stalin," in Tucker (editor), *Stalinism*, p. 291, Zhores A. Medvedev, *Ten Years after Ivan Denisovich* (New York: Vintage, 1974), p. 103.

60. Fest, *Face of the Third Reich*, pp. 59, 324n; Hugo Bieber (editor), *Heinrich Heine: A Biographical Anthology* (Philadelphia: Jewish Publication Society, 1956), pp. 1, 2.

61. Arendt, *Origins*, pp. 333, 350, 388; Isaiah Berlin, *Four Essays on Liberty* (New York: Oxford University Press, 1969), pp. 23–25; Speer, *Inside the Third Reich*, pp. 289–290.

62. Fest, *Face of the Third Reich*, p. 304; Arendt, *Origins*, pp. 386, 387, and *Eichmann*, p. 43; Friedrich and Brzezinski, *Totalitarian Dictatorship*, p. 75; Schapiro, *Totalitarianism*, p. 102; Speer, *Inside the Third Reich*, p. 22.

63. Schapiro, *Communist Party of the Soviet Union*, pp. 337, 377; Ulam, *New Face of Soviet Totalitarianism*, p. 52.

64. Arendt, *Origins*, p. 363; Noakes and Pridham (editors), *Documents on Nazism*, p. 487; Raul Hilberg, *The Destruction of the European Jews* (Chicago: Quadrangle, 1961), pp. 43–53; Karl A. Schleunes, *The*

Twisted Road to Auschwitz: Nazi Policy toward German Jews, 1933–1939 (Urbana: University of Illinois Press, 1970), pp. 127, 128; Fest, *Face of the Third Reich*, p. 5.

65. Hitler quoted in Binion, *Hitler*, p. 98; Speer, *Inside the Third Reich*, p. 306.

66. Arendt, *Origins*, pp. 385–386; Schapiro, *Communist Party of the Soviet Union*, p. xi; New York *Times*, June 28, 1961, p. 12.

67. Molotov quoted in Jane Degras (editor), *Soviet Documents on Foreign Policy* (London: Oxford University Press, 1953), III, 366, 390; Medvedev, *Let History Judge*, p. 443; Berger, *Shipwreck of a Generation*, p. 177.

68. Arendt, *Origins*, p. 387.

69. *Ibid.*, pp. 405–406.

70. Hitler's Political Testament, in Noakes and Pridham (editors), *Documents on Nazism*, p. 679; Arthur Koestler, *Darkness at Noon* (New York: Modern Library, 1941), p. 253, and *Invisible Writing*, p. 401.

71. Burrowes, "Revised Standard Version," *World Politics*, p. 278; Hans Morgenthau, "Hannah Arendt on Totalitarianism and Democracy," *Social Research*, 44 (Spring 1977), 127.

Chapter 3

1. George Lichtheim, *The Concept of Ideology and Other Essays* (New York: Random House, 1967), p. 119.

2. Hannah Arendt, *The Origins of Totalitarianism* (Cleveland: World, 1958), p. 419, and *Men in Dark Times* (New York: Harcourt, Brace and World, 1968), p. 18.

3. Arendt, *Origins*, pp. 409–410.

4. Arendt, *Origins* (1966), p. vii, and *Eichmann in Jerusalem: A Report on the Banality of Evil* (New York: Viking, 1963; rev. ed. 1964), p. 69.

5. Arendt, *Origins*, pp. 318, 411, and (1966), p. vii.

6. Arendt, *Origins*, pp. 318–320, 419.

7. *Ibid.*, p. 323; Leon Bramson, *The Political Context of Sociology* (Princeton: Princeton University Press, 1961), pp. 35–36.

8. Arendt, *Origins*, pp. 319, 323.

9. *Ibid.*, pp. 318–323; Isaac Deutscher, *Stalin: A Political Biography* (New York: Vintage, 1960), p. xx.

10. Stalin quoted in Richard Lowenthal, "Totalitarianism Reconsidered," *Commentary*, 29 (June 1960), 509.

11. Lowenthal, "Totalitarianism Reconsidered," pp. 505–506, 508–511; Aryeh L. Unger, *The Totalitarian Party: Party and People in Nazi Germany and Soviet Russia* (London: Cambridge University Press, 1974), p. 263.

12. Osip Mandelstam quoted in Nadezhda Mandelstam, *Hope Against Hope: A Memoir* (New York: Atheneum, 1970), p. 13; William Sheridan Allen, *The Nazi Seizure of Power: The Experience of a Single German Town, 1930–1935* (Chicago: Quadrangle, 1965), pp. 213–214, 277; Richard Grunberger, *The Twelve-Year Reich: A Social History of Nazi Germany, 1933–1945* (New York: Holt, Rinehart and Winston, 1971), pp. 108–115.

13. Arendt, *Origins*, p. 320, and (1966), p. ix.

14. Arendt, *Origins*, pp. 482, 504, 508, and *On Revolution* (New York: Viking, 1965), p. 220.

15. Arendt, *Origins* (1966), p. ix.

16. Joseph Berger, *Shipwreck of a Generation* (London: Harvill, 1971), pp. 203, 205–206; Aleksandr Solzhenitsyn, *The Gulag Archipelago 1918–1956: An Experiment in Literary Investigation* (New York: Harper and Row, 1975), II, 132–135.

17. Adam B. Ulam, *The New Face of Soviet Totalitarianism* (Cambridge: Harvard University Press, 1963), pp. 108–112, 116.

18. Elizabeth Hall, "The Freakish Passion: A Conversation with George Steiner," *Psychology Today*, 6 (February 1973), 58.

19. Robert C. Tucker, "The Dictator and Totalitarianism," *World Politics*, 17 (July 1965), 566.

20. Margaret Canovan, *The Political Thought of Hannah Arendt* (New York: Harcourt Brace Jovanovich, 1974), p. 41.

21. Carl J. Friedrich and Zbigniew K. Brzezinski, *Totalitarian Dictatorship and Autocracy* (New York: Praeger, 1961), pp. 300–301; Tucker, "Dictator and Totalitarianism," pp. 569–571, 574; Karl Dietrich Bracher, "Totalitarianism," *Dictionary of the History of Ideas* (New York: Scribner's, 1973), I, 409–410; Leonard Schapiro, *Totalitarianism* (New York: Praeger, 1972), pp. 27–29, 118–119, 125.

22. Tucker, "Dictator and Totalitarianism," p. 564.

23. Hannah Arendt, "The Nature of Totalitarianism: Discussion," in Carl J. Friedrich (editor), *Totalitarianism* (New York: Grosset and Dunlap, 1966), p. 76; Arendt, *Origins*, p. 461; Dwight Macdonald, *Memoirs of a Revolutionist: Essays in Political Criticism* (Cleveland: World, 1958), p. 35.

24. Hannah Arendt, "Understanding and Politics," *Partisan Review*,

20 (July–August 1953), 379, and "A Reply," *Review of Politics*, 15 (January 1953), 80; Harry Eckstein and David E. Apter (editors), *Comparative Politics* (New York: Free Press, 1963), pp. 435–437.

25. Arendt, "Understanding and Politics," pp. 381–382; Hans J. Morgenthau, "Hannah Arendt on Totalitarianism and Democracy," *Social Research*, 44 (Spring 1977), 127.

26. Franz Neumann, *The Democratic and the Authoritarian State: Essays in Political and Legal Theory* (New York: Free Press, 1957), pp. 126, 233; Friedrich and Brzezinski, *Totalitarian Dictatorship*, pp. 9–10; Hannah Arendt, *The Human Condition* (Garden City, N.Y.: Doubleday Anchor, 1959), p. 181.

27. Carlton J. H. Hayes, "The Novelty of Totalitarianism in the History of Western Civilization," in "Symposium on the Totalitarian State," *Proceedings of the American Philosophical Society*, 82 (February 23, 1940), 93, 96, 98, 100; Marquis de Custine, *Journey for Our Time* (New York: Pellegrini and Cudahy, 1951), p. 321.

28. Arendt, "Nature of Totalitarianism," in Friedrich (editor), *Totalitarianism*, p. 77, and *Origins*, pp. 367, 378, 380.

29. Himmler quoted in Arendt, *Origins*, p. 360; Hermann Rauschning, *Hitler Speaks* (London: Thornton Butterworth, 1939), p. 235; Robert G. L. Waite, *The Psychopathic God: Adolf Hitler* (New York: Basic Books, 1977), pp. 118–121.

30. Daniel Bell, *The End of Ideology: On the Exhaustion of Political Ideas in the Fifties* (New York: Free Press, 1962), p. 345.

31. Hitler's Political Testament in Jeremy Noakes and Geoffrey Pridham (editors), *Documents on Nazism, 1919–1945* (New York: Viking, 1974), p. 678; Rudolph Binion, *Hitler among the Germans* (New York: Elsevier, 1976), pp. 30–31, 100.

32. Stalin quoted in Arendt, *Origins* (1966), p. xvii; Robert C. Tucker, "Stalin, Bukharin, and History As Conspiracy," in Tucker and Stephen F. Cohen (editors), *The Great Purge Trial* (New York: Grosset and Dunlap, 1965), p. xvi.

33. Arendt, *Origins*, p. 387.

34. Allen, *Nazi Seizure of Power*, p. 100; Binion, *Hitler*, p. 73; David Schoenbaum, *Hitler's Social Revolution: Class and Status in Nazi Germany, 1933–1939* (Garden City, N.Y.: Doubleday, 1966), p. xiv.

35. Ribbentrop quoted in Alan Bullock, *Hitler: A Study in Tyranny* (New York: Bantam, 1961), p. 474.

36. Hans Mommsen, "National Socialism: Continuity and Change," in Walter Laqueur (editor), *Fascism, A Reader's Guide: Analyses, In-*

terpretations, Bibliography (Berkeley: University of California Press, 1976), pp. 180–181.

37. William Kornhauser, *The Politics of Mass Society* (Glencoe, Illinois: Free Press, 1959), pp. 62, 123; Arendt, *Origins*, pp. 251, 391, 398, 469; Aryeh L. Unger, *The Totalitarian Party: Party and People in Nazi Germany and Soviet Russia* (London: Cambridge University Press, 1974), p. 13; Hitler memorandum, January 7, 1922, in Noakes and Pridham (editors), *Documents on Nazism*, p. 47.

38. Fritz Morstein Marx, "Totalitarian Politics," in "Symposium on the Totalitarian State," p. 36.

39. Arendt, *Origins*, p. 357; Neumann, *Democratic and Authoritarian State*, pp. 245–246, and *Behemoth: The Structure and Practice of National Socialism, 1933–1944* (New York: Harper and Row, 1966), pp. 47–49, 62–65, 75–77; Hans Buchheim, *Totalitarian Rule: Its Nature and Characteristics* (Middletown, Conn.: Wesleyan University Press, 1968), pp. 90, 92–93, 96, 98.

40. Hitler quoted in Noakes and Pridham (editors), *Documents on Nazism*, p. 257; George H. Sabine, *A History of Political Theory* (New York: Henry Holt, 1937), pp. 764–765.

41. Hitler quoted in Arendt, *Origins*, p. 357; Peter Viereck, *Metapolitics: The Roots of the Nazi Mind* (New York: Capricorn, 1961), p. 230; Norman Rich, *Hitler's War Aims: Ideology, the Nazi State, and the Course of Expansion* (New York: Norton, 1973), I, xlii, 11, 13–14; Eberhard Jäckel, *Hitler's Weltanschauung: A Blueprint for Power* (Middletown, Conn.: Wesleyan University Press, 1972), p. 67; Allen, *Nazi Seizure of Power*, p. 195.

42. Neumann, *Behemoth*, pp. 73–74; Mussolini quoted in *ibid.*, p. 75.

43. Stalin quoted in Arendt, *Origins*, pp. 357n–358n.

44. Neumann, *Behemoth*, p. 67; Schapiro, *Communist Party*, pp. 416, 430, 452, 468; Arendt, *Origins*, pp. 411, 416.

45. Daniel Bell, *Marxian Socialism in the United States* (Princeton: Princeton University Press, 1967), p. 147; Arendt, *Origins*, pp. 364, 366, 396n.

46. Arendt, *Origins*, pp. 368, 390, 398; Joachim C. Fest, *The Face of the Third Reich: Portraits of the Nazi Leadership* (New York: Pantheon, 1970), pp. 44, 125.

47. H. R. Trevor-Roper, *The Last Days of Hitler* (New York: Collier, 1962), p. 63; Binion, *Hitler*, p. 76; Noakes and Pridham (editors), *Documents on Nazism*, pp. 9–10; Wolfgang Sauer, "National Socialism: Totalitarianism or Fascism?" *American Historical Review*, 73 (December

1967), 407; Karl A. Schleunes, *The Twisted Road to Auschwitz: Nazi Policy toward German Jews, 1933–1939* (Urbana: University of Illinois Press, 1970), p. 260; Rich, *Hitler's War Aims*, I, 12–13; Gilbert Allardyce, "What Fascism Is Not: Thoughts on the Deflation of a Concept," *American Historical Review*, 84 (April 1979), 370–371.

48. Trevor-Roper, *Last Days of Hitler*, pp. 64–65, 74, 95; Binion, *Hitler*, pp. 75, 76; Noakes and Pridham (editors), *Documents on Nazism*, pp. 10, 248.

49. Arendt, *Origins*, pp. 364, 395–396, and *Eichmann*, p. 152; Albert Speer, *Inside the Third Reich: Memoirs* (New York: Macmillan, 1970), p. 312.

50. Arthur M. Schlesinger, Jr., "The Cold War Revisited," *New York Review of Books*, 26 (October 25, 1979), p. 49.

51. Buchheim, *Totalitarian Rule*, pp. 38–39; Fest, *Face of the Third Reich*, p. 302; Bracher, "Totalitarianism," *Dictionary of the History of Ideas*, pp. 407, 409; Unger, *Totalitarian Party*, p. 269.

52. Thomas Aquinas, *Summa Theologiae* (New York: McGraw-Hill, 1964), XXVIII, 17 [Ia2ae.90.40].

53. Arendt, *Origins*, pp. 365, 394, and *Eichmann*, p. 148; Hitler quoted in Friedrich and Brzezinski, *Totalitarian Dictatorship*, p. 35; Jäckel, *Hitler's Weltanschauung*, p. 75.

54. Rebecca West, *A Train of Powder* (New York: Viking, 1955), p. 50.

55. Harold J. Laski, *Law and Justice in Soviet Russia* (London: Hogarth, 1935), p. 24; Deutscher, *Stalin*, p. 381; Solzhenitsyn, *Gulag Archipelago*, I, 412; Arendt, *Origins*, pp. 394–395, 398.

56. Arendt, *Origins*, pp. 3, 257, 259, 418, and Hannah Arendt, "The Seeds of a Fascist International," *Jewish Frontier*, 12 (June 1945), pp. 14–15.

57. Arendt, *Origins*, p. 416, and "Fascist International," *Jewish Frontier*, pp. 14–15.

58. Whittaker Chambers, *Witness* (Chicago: Henry Regnery, 1952), pp. 204–205; Arthur Koestler, *The Invisible Writing* (Boston: Beacon, 1955), pp. 324–325.

59. Arendt, *Origins*, p. 491, and "The Hole of Oblivion," *Jewish Frontier*, 14 (July 1947), 25; Rich, *Hitler's War Aims*, I, 10; Mommsen, "National Socialism," in Laqueur (editor), *Fascism*, pp. 198–199.

60. Alan Bullock, *Hitler: A Study in Tyranny* (New York: Bantam, 1961), pp. 479, 491; H. R. Trevor-Roper, "A. J. P. Taylor, Hitler and the War," *Encounter*, 17 (July 1961), 95.

61. William Welch, *American Images of Soviet Foreign Policy: An Inquiry into Recent Appraisals from the Academic Community* (New Haven: Yale University Press, 1970), pp. 162–163.

62. New York *Times*, October 12, 1957, p. 18; Binion, *Hitler*, pp. 45–46; Fritz Fischer, *Germany's Aims in the First World War* (New York: Norton, 1967).

63. Arendt, *Origins*, pp. 391, 392; William Ebenstein, "The Study of Totalitarianism," *World Politics*, 10 (January 1958), 278.

64. Welch, *American Images*, pp. 66, 202; Charles Eade (editor), *The War Speeches of Rt. Hon. Winston Churchill* (London: Cassell, 1951), I, 108.

65. Arendt, *Origins*, p. 159; Arendt, "Approaches to the 'German Problem,' " *Partisan Review*, 12 (Winter 1945), 98; and Arendt, *On Revolution*, p. 1; Jäckel, *Hitler's Weltanschauung*, pp. 87–88.

66. Arendt, *Men in Dark Times*, pp. 39–40, 42–43, and *Origins*, pp. 124, 148n; G. L. Arnold [George Lichtheim], "Three Critics of Totalitarianism," *Twentieth Century*, 150 (July 1951), 31.

67. George McKenna, "A Critic of Modernity: The Political Thought of Hannah Arendt," (Ph.D. dissertation, Fordham University, 1967), pp. 190–191; Benjamin I. Schwartz, "The Religion of Politics: Reflections on the Thought of Hannah Arendt," *Dissent*, 17 (March–April 1970), 157.

68. Arendt, *Origins*, p. 159; Hans Kohn, *Pan-Slavism: Its History and Ideology* (New York: Vintage, 1960), pp. 290–301; Milovan Djilas, *Conversations with Stalin* (New York: Harcourt, Brace and World, 1962), pp. 21, 25–26.

69. Arendt, *Origins*, pp. 159, 222, 236.

70. Hans Kohn, "Where Terror Is the Essence," *Saturday Review*, 34 (March 24, 1951), 11, and *Pan-Slavism*, pp. 200–201; Hitler quoted in A. Rossi, *The Russo-German Alliance: August 1939–June 1941* (Boston: Beacon, 1951), p. 77; Friedrich and Brzezinski, *Totalitarian Dictatorship*, pp. 66–67.

71. Barrington Moore, Jr., *Social Origins of Dictatorship and Democracy: Lord and Peasant in the Making of the Modern World* (Boston: Beacon, 1966), pp. 445, 447; Walter Laqueur, *Russia and Germany: A Century of Conflict* (Boston: Little, Brown, 1965), pp. 51–52, 79, 124–125; John J. Stephan, *The Russian Fascists: Tragedy and Farce in Exile, 1925–1945* (New York: Harper and Row, 1978), pp. 310–311, 345–354.

72. Paul Samuelson, "Wages and Interest: A Modern Dissection of

Marxian Economic Models," *American Economic Review*, 47 (December 1957), 911.

73. J. P. Nettl, "Ideas, Intellectuals, and Structures of Dissent," in Philip Rieff (editor), *On Intellectuals: Theoretical Studies, Case Studies* (Garden City, N.Y.: Doubleday Anchor, 1970), p. 121; Gershom Scholem in *"Eichmann in Jerusalem*: An Exchange of Letters," *Encounter*, 22 (January 1964), 51; Robert E. Meyerson, "Hannah Arendt: Romantic in a Totalitarian Age, 1928–1963," (Ph.D. dissertation, University of Minnesota, 1972), pp. 54–56; James Miller, "The Pathos of Novelty: Hannah Arendt's Image of Freedom in the Modern World," in Melvyn A. Hill (editor), *Hannah Arendt: The Recovery of the Public World* (New York: St. Martin's, 1979), p. 178.

74. Arendt in *"Eichmann in Jerusalem,"* *Encounter*, p. 53; Lichtheim, *Concept of Ideology*, p. 170.

75. Elizabeth Young-Bruehl, "From the Pariah's Point of View: Reflections on Hannah Arendt's Life and Work," in Hill (editor), *Hannah Arendt*, pp. 12–13; Arendt, *Human Condition*, pp. 89–92; W. A. Suchting, "Marx and Hannah Arendt's *The Human Condition,*" *Ethics*, 73 (October 1962), 47, 49, 52, 55n.

76. Arendt, *On Revolution*, pp. 1, 56, 58, 264; James T. Knauer, "Hannah Arendt and the Reassertion of the Political: Toward a New Democratic Theory," (Ph.D. dissertation, S.U.N.Y. at Binghamton, 1975), p. 58; George Lichtheim, *Marxism in Modern France* (New York: Columbia University Press, 1966), p. 112.

77. Sidney Hook, *Reason, Social Myths and Democracy* (New York: Humanities Press, 1940), p. 173, and *Political Power and Personal Freedom* (New York: Criterion, 1959), pp. 111–112, 134–135, 332–338; Michael Harrington, *Socialism* (New York: Saturday Review Press, 1972), chs. 3–4; Rosa Luxemburg, *The Russian Revolution and Leninism or Marxism?* (Ann Arbor: University of Michigan Press, 1961), pp. 68–72, 77–79, 107–108; Solzhenitsyn, *Gulag Archipelago*, I, 27–32, 34, 297n, 353, 434–435, and II, 10, 17; Deutscher, *Stalin*, pp. 359–362, 552–554; Roy A. Medvedev, *Let History Judge: The Origins and Consequences of Stalinism* (New York: Vintage, 1974), pp. 31–33, 89, 149–150, 385–386, 423–424, 426–427, and "On Solzhenitsyn's *Gulag Archipelago,*" in Kathryn Feuer (editor), *Solzhenitsyn: A Collection of Critical Essays* (Englewood Cliffs, N.J.: Prentice-Hall, 1976), pp. 104–106; George Lichtheim, *Marxism: An Historical and Critical Study* (New York: Praeger, 1961), pp. 346, 365–366, 371–372, 373.

78. Hannah Arendt, "The Ex-Communists," *Commonweal*, 57 (March

20, 1953), 597, and "Nature of Totalitarianism," in Friedrich (editor), *Totalitarianism*, p. 134.

79. Nicholas Berdyaev, *The Origin of Russian Communism* (New York: Scribner's, 1937), pp. 170–171; Friedrich and Brzezinski, *Totalitarian Dictatorship*, p. 67.

80. George L. Mosse, *The Crisis of German Ideology: Intellectual Origins of the Third Reich* (New York: Grosset and Dunlap, 1964), pp. 26, 33, 290, 292; Kohn, *Pan-Slavism*, pp. xv, 149, 204.

81. New York *Times*, December 31, 1933, VIII, 2.

82. Hanna Fenichel Pitkin, "The Roots of Conservatism: Oakeshott and the Denial of Politics," *Dissent*, 20 (Fall 1973), 513; Richard J. Bernstein, "Hannah Arendt: The Ambiguities of Theory and Practice," in Terence Ball (editor), *Political Theory and Praxis: New Perspectives* (Minneapolis: University of Minnesota Press, 1977), p. 157.

Chapter 4

1. Saul Bellow, *Herzog* (New York: Viking, 1964), p. 49.

2. Daniel Bell, *The End of Ideology: On the Exhaustion of Political Ideas in the Fifties* (New York: Free Press, 1962), pp. 21, 25; Judith N. Shklar, *After Utopia: The Decline of Political Faith* (Princeton: Princeton University Press, 1957), pp. 159–162; Leon Bramson, *The Political Context of Sociology* (Princeton: Princeton University Press, 1961), p. 34.

3. William Kornhauser, *The Politics of Mass Society* (Glencoe, Illinois: Free Press, 1959), p. 16; James Miller, "The Pathos of Novelty: Hannah Arendt's Image of Freedom in the Modern World," in Melvyn A. Hill (editor), *Hannah Arendt: The Recovery of the Public World* (New York: St. Martin's, 1979), p. 200.

4. Hannah Arendt, *The Origins of Totalitarianism* (Cleveland: World, 1958), pp. 311, 314, and "A Reply," *Review of Politics*, 15 (January 1953), 81; Kornhauser, *Politics of Mass Society*, p. 49.

5. Hannah Arendt, *The Human Condition* (Garden City, N.Y.: Doubleday Anchor, 1959), p. 177; Arendt, *Between Past and Future: Eight Exercises in Political Thought* (New York: Viking, 1968), pp. 146, 152–153, 169; Arendt, "Reflections on Little Rock," *Dissent*, 6 (Winter 1959), 51; and Arendt, *Origins*, pp. 352, 475, 477–478; George McKenna, "A Critic of Modernity: The Political Thought of Hannah Arendt," (Ph.D. dissertation, Fordham University, 1967), p. 186.

6. Arendt, *Origins*, pp. 315, 317; Joachim C. Fest, *The Face of the Third Reich: Portraits of the Nazi Leadership* (New York: Pantheon,

1970), pp. 295–296; Fritz Stern, *The Politics of Cultural Despair: A Study in the Rise of the Germanic Ideology* (Berkeley: University of California Press, 1961), pp. xii–xiv, 268, 272, 274–275.

7. Arendt, *Origins*, pp. 108, 155, 316, and "The Archimedean Point," *Ingenor*, 6 (Spring 1969), 5–9, 24–26; Geoffrey Barraclough, "Hitler's Master Builder," *New York Review of Books*, 15 (January 7, 1971), 6.

8. Gustave LeBon, *The Crowd: A Study of the Popular Mind* (New York: Viking, 1960), pp. 32, 57, 67, 69, 73, 118, 136, 153; Robert G. L. Waite, *The Psychopathic God: Adolf Hitler* (New York: Basic Books, 1967), p. 122.

9. LeBon, *The Crowd*, pp. 203–204; Arendt, *Origins*, p. 186.

10. Arendt, *Between Past and Future*, p. 100; Kornhauser, *Politics of Mass Society*, p. 228.

11. Oscar Lewis, *La Vida: A Puerto Rican Family in the Culture of Poverty—San Juan and New York* (New York: Random House, 1966), pp. xlv–xlviii; Carlton J. H. Hayes, "The Novelty of Totalitarianism in the History of Western Civilization," in "Symposium on the Totalitarian State," *Proceedings of the American Philosophical Society*, 82 (February 23, 1940), 94.

12. Marx, "Totalitarian Politics," in "Symposium on the Totalitarian State," p. 37; Gerard DeGré, "Freedom and Social Structure," *American Sociological Review*, 11 (October 1946), 535–536.

13. Alfred Kazin, *New York Jew* (New York: Knopf, 1978), p. 200; Lenore O'Boyle, "The Class Concept in History," *Journal of Modern History*, 24 (December 1952), 391–397; Bramson, *Political Context of Sociology*, p. 36.

14. *Ibid.*

15. Arendt, *Origins*, pp. 55, 280, 316; Alexis de Tocqueville, *Democracy in America*, edited by Phillips Bradley (New York: Vintage, 1945), II, 336–337.

16. Arendt, *Origins*, pp. 221, 250, 261, 318, 319.

17. Kornhauser, *Politics of Mass Society*, pp. 231–232; Simon Wiesenthal, *The Murderers among Us* (New York: McGraw-Hill, 1967), p. 189.

18. Seymour Martin Lipset, *Political Man: The Social Bases of Politics* (Garden City, N.Y.: Doubleday Anchor, 1963), pp. 102–104, 148–152.

19. Aleksandr I. Solzhenitsyn, *The Gulag Archipelago 1918–1956: An Experiment in Literary Investigation* (New York: Harper and Row, 1974–1975), I, 69–70.

20. Montesquieu quoted in Arendt, *Human Condition*, p. 181.

21. Fritz Wiedemann quoted in Rudolph Binion, *Hitler among the Germans* (New York: Elsevier, 1976), p. 2; Max Horkheimer and Theodor Adorno, *Dialectic of Enlightenment* (New York: Herder and Herder, 1972), p. 237; Arendt, "The Jew as Pariah: A Hidden Tradition" (1944), in Ron H. Feldman (editor), *The Jew as Pariah: Jewish Identity and Politics in the Modern Age* (New York: Grove, 1978), p. 81.

22. Arendt, *Origins*, p. 363.

23. *Ibid.*, pp. 350, 352, 477, and "Understanding and Politics," *Partisan Review*, 20 (July–August, 1953), 383, 386, 387; McKenna, "Critic of Modernity," p. 110; Dwight Macdonald, *Memoirs of a Revolutionist: Essays in Political Criticism* (Cleveland: World, 1958), pp. 42–44.

24. Hans Buchheim, *Totalitarian Rule: Its Nature and Characteristics* (Middletown, Conn.: Wesleyan University Press, 1968), p. 97; Hannah Arendt, "The Aftermath of Nazi Rule," *Commentary*, 10 (October 1950), 344.

25. Robert Conquest, *The Great Terror: Stalin's Purge of the Thirties* (New York: Macmillan, 1968), pp. 199, 208; Roy A. Medvedev, *Let History Judge: The Origins and Consequences of Stalinism* (New York: Knopf, 1972), p. 310; Raul Hilberg, *The Destruction of the European Jews* (Chicago: Quadrangle, 1961), p. 682.

26. Margarete Buber-Neumann, *Under Two Dictators* (New York: Dodd-Mead, 1949), pp. 183–184; Solzhenitsyn, *Gulag Archipelago*, I, 94, 145n

27. Leonard Schapiro, *The Communist Party of the Soviet Union* (New York: Random House, 1960), p. 381; Conquest, *Great Terror*, p. 128.

28. Secret Speech of Khrushchev in *The Anti-Stalin Campaign and International Communism*, edited by the Russian Institute of Columbia University (New York: Columbia University Press, 1956), p. 23; Khrushchev quoted in Conquest, *Great Terror*, p. 225.

29. Arendt, "Understanding and Politics," p. 388.

30. Immanuel Kant, *Religion within the Limits of Reason Alone* (New York: Harper and Row, 1960), p. 32; Emil L. Fackenheim, "Kant and Radical Evil," *University of Toronto Quarterly*, 23 (Fall 1954), 346–348; Reinhold Niebuhr, *The Nature and Destiny of Man* (New York: Scribners, 1941), I. 120n.

31. Arendt, *Origins*, pp. viii, ix, 443, 459; O'Sullivan, "Politics, Totalitarianism and Freedom," *Political Studies*, p. 191.

32. Arendt, *Origins*, pp. 443, 459; Rebecca West, *Train of Powder* (New York: Viking, 1955), p. 51.

33. Waite, *Psychopathic God*, p. 121; Susan Sontag, *On Photography* (New York: Farrar Straus and Giroux, 1977), pp. 19–20.

34. Arendt, *Origins*, pp. 301, 302.

35. Thomas Arnold quoted in Lionel Trilling, *Matthew Arnold* (New York: Columbia University Press, 1949), p. 60; T. S. Eliot quoted in Russell Kirk, *Eliot and His Age* (New York: Random House, 1971), pp. 209–210.

36. Arendt, *Origins*, p. 293.

37. Trotsky quoted in Isaac Deutscher, *The Prophet Outcast: Trotsky, 1929–1940* (New York: Vintage, 1965), pp. 340–342.

38. Hannah Arendt, *Eichmann in Jerusalem: A Report on the Banality of Evil* (New York: Viking, 1963; rev. ed. 1964), p. 156; David S. Dallin and Boris I. Nicolaevsky, *Forced Labor in Soviet Russia* (New Haven: Yale University Press, 1947), pp. 292–295.

39. George F. Kennan, *Memoirs, 1925–1950* (Boston: Little, Brown, 1967), p. 139; Jacob Presser, *Ashes in the Wind: The Destruction of Dutch Jewry* (London: Souvenir Press, 1968), p. 286.

40. Judith Shklar, "Hannah Arendt's Triumph," *New Republic*, 173 (December 27, 1975), 9; Arendt, *Origins*, p. 296; Buber-Neumann, *Under Two Dictators*, pp. 12–13, 215.

41. Arendt, *Origins*, p. 281n; Dallin and Nicolaevsky, *Forced Labor*, pp. 282–283, 292–293, 296; William Sloane Coffin, *Once to Every Man: A Memoir* (New York: Atheneum, 1977), pp. 72–78; Victor Nekrasov, "The Shock of a Secret," *Encounter*, 50 (May 1978), 75–80.

42. Yosef Hayim Yerushalmi, "Response to Rosemary Reuther," in Eva Fleischner (editor), *Auschwitz: Beginning of a New Era?: Reflections on the Holocaust* (New York: Ktav, 1977), pp. 98–105.

43. Andrew Field, *Nabokov: His Life in Part* (New York: Penguin, 1978), pp. 87, 226; Arendt, *Origins*, pp. 295, 296.

44. Arendt, *Origins*, pp. 293, 297; Karl A. Schleunes, *The Twisted Road to Auschwitz: Nazi Policy toward German Jews, 1933–1939* (Urbana: University of Illinois Press, 1970), pp. 237–239; Weizmann quoted in Henry L. Feingold, "Roosevelt and the Resettlement Question," in *Rescue Attempts during the Holocaust: Proceedings of the Second Yad Vashem International Conference* (Jerusalem: Yad Vashem, 1977), pp. 179–180; Louise W. Holborn, "The Legal Status of Political Refugees, 1920–1938," *American Journal of International Law*, 32 (October 1938), 682, 692.

45. Jakov Lind, *Soul of Wood and Other Stories* (New York: Fawcett, 1966), p. 9.

46. [Pollak, Stephen J.], "The Expatriation Act of 1954," *Yale Law Journal*, 64 (July 1955), 1166n, 1190, 1198; Pollak to author, December 20, 1977; Irving Louis Horowitz, *Genocide: State Power and Mass Murder* (New Brunswick, N.J.: Transaction Books, 1977), pp. 33–34.

47. *Perez v. Brownell*, 356 U.S. 44 at 64 (1958) (Warren, C. J., dissenting).

48. *Trop v. Dulles*, 356 U.S. 86 at 92, 102 (1958) (Warren, C.J.); *Kennedy v. Mendoza-Martinez*, 372 U.S. 144 at 161 (1963) (Goldberg, J.).

49. Arthur Koestler, *The Yogi and the Commissar and Other Essays* (New York: Macmillan, 1945), pp. 88–89.

50. David Rousset, *The Other Kingdom* (New York: Reynal and Hitchcock, 1947), p. 172; George Steiner, *Language and Silence: Essays on Language, Literature, and the Inhuman* (New York: Atheneum, 1970), p. 121; Hannah Arendt, "Franz Kafka: A Revaluation," *Partisan Review*, 11 (Fall 1944), 412–422; Nathalie Sarraute, *The Age of Suspicion* (New York: George Braziller, 1963), pp. 49–50.

51. Stalin quoted in Boris I. Nicolaevsky, *Power and the Soviet Elite* (Ann Arbor: University of Michigan Press, 1975), p. 111; Rousset, *Other Kingdom*, pp. 30, 101–102.

52. Henry James, *Hawthorne* (London: Macmillan, 1887), p. 99.

53. Richard H. Rovere and Arthur M. Schlesinger, Jr., *The MacArthur Controversy and American Foreign Policy* (New York: Farrar, Straus and Giroux, 1965), p. 148.

54. Dallin and Nicolaevsky, *Forced Labor*, pp. 51–72, 309; Max Eastman, *Reflections on the Failure of Socialism* (New York: Devin-Adair, 1955), p. 119; John P. Diggins, *Up from Communism: Conservative Odysseys in American Intellectual History* (New York: Harper and Row, 1975), pp. 434–435.

55. Aleksandr Solzhenitsyn, *Warning to the West* (New York: Farrar, Straus and Giroux, 1976), p. 10; Solzhenitsyn quoted in Kathryn Feuer (editor), Introduction to *Solzhenitsyn: A Collection of Critical Essays* (Englewood Cliffs, N.J.: Prentice-Hall, 1977), p. 4.

56. Hilberg, *Destruction of the European Jews*, pp. 263, 265–266; Lucy S. Dawidowicz, *The War against the Jews, 1933–1945* (New York: Bantam, 1976), pp. 202, 203–206, 210–211, 212.

57. Hannah Arendt, "Social Science Techniques and the Study of Concentration Camps," *Jewish Social Studies*, 12 (January 1950), 49, 51, 61, 62; Denis Donoghue, "After Reading Hannah Arendt," *Poetry*, 100

(May 1962), 128; Rudolf Hoess, *Commandant of Auschwitz* (London: Weidenfeld and Nicolson, 1959), pp. 91, 176.

58. Bruno Bettelheim, *Surviving and Other Essays* (New York: Knopf, 1979), pp. 15–16.

59. Arendt, *Origins*, p. 446; Rolf Hochhuth, *The Deputy* (New York: Grove, 1964), pp. 246, 247, 248, 283.

60. Arendt, *Origins*, p. 445; George F. Kennan "Between Earth and Hell," *New York Review of Books*, 21 (March 21, 1974), 3; Pyotr Yakir, *A Childhood in Prison* (New York: Coward, McCann and Geoghegan, 1973), p. 130; Alexander Donat, *The Holocaust Kingdom: A Memoir* (New York: Holt, Rinehart and Winston, 1965), p. 253; Victor Herman, *Coming Out of the Ice: An Unexpected Life* (New York: Harcourt Brace Jovanovich, 1979), pp. 247, 256.

61. George Steiner, *In Bluebeard's Castle: Some Notes toward the Redefinition of Culture* (New Haven: Yale University Press, 1971), pp. 53–55; Arendt, *Origins*, p. 447.

62. Arendt, "We Refugees" (1943), in Feldman (editor), *Jew as Pariah*, p. 56; Terrence Des Pres, *The Survivor: An Anatomy of Life in the Death Camps* (New York: Pocket Books, 1977), pp. 94–95, 201–202, 203.

63. Albert Speer, *Inside the Third Reich: Memoirs*, pp. 375–376; Buber-Neumann, *Under Two Dictators*, pp. 261–262; Arendt, *Origins*, p. 439; Solzhenitsyn, *Gulag Archipelago*, I, 468.

64. Arendt, *Origins*, pp. 444–445, and "The Hole of Oblivion," *Jewish Frontier*, 14 (July 1947), 23; Rousset, *Other Kingdom*, p. 41; Solzhenitsyn, *Gulag Archipelago*, I, 468.

65. Jakov Lind, *Counting My Steps: An Autobiography* (New York: Macmillan, 1969), p. 142; Nadezhda Mandelstam, *Hope against Hope: A Memoir* (New York: Atheneum, 1970), pp. 377, 388–389.

66. Arendt, "Hole of Oblivion," p. 23, and *Origins*, pp. 443, 454.

67. Arendt, *Human Condition*, pp. 46, 283, and *Origins*, pp. 443, 445, 451; Solzhenitsyn, *Gulag Archipelago*, I, 504; Rousset, *Other Kingdom*, pp. 29, 74, 81, 86, 107; Barrington Moore, Jr., *Injustice: The Social Bases of Obedience and Revolt* (White Plains, N.Y.: M. E. Sharpe, 1978), pp. 72–73.

68. Arendt, "Hole of Oblivion," *Jewish Frontier*, 23, and "Home to Roost: A Bicentennial Address" *New York Review of Books*, 23 (June 26, 1975), 4.

69. Conquest, *Great Terror*, pp. 48–50; Arendt, *Origins*, pp. 434–435.

70. Arendt, *Origins*, pp. 448–449; Rousset, *Other Kingdom*, pp. 64, 73–74; Dallin and Nicolaevsky, *Forced Labor*, pp. 4, 26; Herman, *Com-*

ing Out of the Ice, pp. 190, 253, 264; Joseph Berger, *Shipwreck of a Generation* (London: Harvill Press, 1971), pp. 96, 245.

71. Berger, *Shipwreck of a Generation,* pp. 159, 229; Solzhenitsyn, *Gulag Archipelago,* I, pp. 93, 98, 102; Medvedev, *Let History Judge,* pp. 297, 303; Evgenia S. Ginzburg, *Into the Whirlwind* (London: Penguin, 1968), pp. 126, 128; Buber-Neumann, *Under Two Dictators,* pp. 190, 192.

72. Des Pres, *Survivor,* pp. 178–182; Eugen Kogon, *The Theory and Practice of Hell* (New York: Berkeley Medallion, 1958), pp. 254–271; Rousset, *Other Kingdom,* pp. 150, 156–157.

73. Alexander Kendrick, *Prime Time: The Life of Edward R. Murrow* (Boston: Little, Brown, 1969), p. 279.

74. Bruno Bettelheim, "Eichmann, the System, the Victims," *New Republic,* 148 (June 15, 1963), 24–25, and *Surviving,* pp. 92–93; Arthur A. Cohen, *Thinking the Tremendum: Some Theological Implications of the Death-Camps* (New York: Leo Baeck Institute, 1974), pp. 14–15.

75. Maurice Samuel, *In Praise of Yiddish* (Chicago: Cowles, 1971), p. 147; Fritz Stern, *Gold and Iron: Bismark, Bleichröder, and the Building of the German Empire* (New York: Knopf, 1977), p. 548.

76. R. Peter Straus, "His Daughter's Father: Otto Frank," *Moment,* 3 (December 1977), 28; Ernst Schnabel, *Anne Frank: A Portrait in Courage* (New York: Harcourt, Brace, 1958), p. 192.

77. Elie Wiesel, "The Holocaust as Literary Inspiration," in Wiesel, Lucy S. Dawidowicz, et al., *Dimensions of the Holocaust: Lectures at Northwestern University* (New York: Anti-Defamation League, 1977), pp. 10–11; Lucy S. Dawidowicz, "The Holocaust as Historical Record," in Wiesel, Dawidowicz, et al., *Dimensions of the Holocaust,* pp. 23–27.

78. Arendt, *Eichmann,* pp. 232–233; Benjamin quoted in Hannah Arendt, *Men in Dark Times* (New York: Harcourt, Brace and World, 1966), p. 170.

79. Heda Kovály and Erazim Kohák, *The Victors and the Vanquished* (New York: Horizon, 1973), p. 143.

80. Arendt, *Origins,* pp. 452–453, 455; Rousset, *Other Kingdom,* pp. 104, 111; Buber-Neumann, *Under Two Dictators,* p. 215; Ginzburg, *Into the Whirlwind,* pp. 270–271.

81. Arendt, "Nature of Totalitarianism," in Carl J. Friedrich (editor), *Totalitarianism* (New York: Grosset and Dunlap, 1966), p. 78; Ginzburg, *Into the Whirlwind,* p. 15; Solzhenitsyn, *Gulag Archipelago,* I, 46, and II, 298; B. I. Rubina quoted in Medvedev, *Let History Judge,* p. 135.

82. Arendt, *Origins*, pp. 455, 476–478, 479; Arendt, *Men in Dark Times*, p. 72; Arendt, *Human Condition*, p. 177; and Arendt, *Between Past and Future*, pp. 146, 152–153, 169.

83. Arendt, *Origins*, pp. viii, 441, 458–459; Fest, *Face of the Third Reich*, pp. 292–293.

84. Alfred Rosenberg quoted in Friedrich and Brzezinski, *Totalitarian Dictatorship*, p. 100; Fest, *Face of the Third Reich*, p. 168.

85. Raymond H. Bauer, *The New Man in Soviet Psychology* (Cambridge: Harvard University Press, 1952), pp. 79, 89, 102, 142–146, 163; Anatoly V. Lunacharsky quoted in Marx, "Totalitarian Politics," in "Symposium on the Totalitarian State," p. 3; Leon Trotsky, *Literature and Revolution* (New York: Russell and Russell, 1957), p. 256.

86. Arendt, *Origins*, pp. 347, 437; Des Pres, *Survivor*, p. 191; William Barrett, *The Illusion of Technique: A Search for Meaning in a Technological Civilization* (Garden City, N. Y.: Doubleday, 1978), pp. 298–299.

87. Arendt, *Origins*, p. 494.

88. Arendt, *Human Condition*, pp. 12–13.

89. Kazin, *New York Jew*, p. 199; Arendt, *Origins*, pp. 298–299.

90. Arendt, "Understanding and Politics," *Partisan Review*, pp. 378–379, and Arendt in Hill (editor), *Hannah Arendt*, pp. 313–314.

91. Hilberg, *Destruction of the European Jews*, pp. 686–689; Richard Rubenstein, *The Cunning of History: The Holocaust and the American Future* (New York: Harper and Row, 1978), p. 88.

92. Arendt, *Origins*, p. 157.

Chapter 5

1. William Barrett, "Reader's Choice," *Atlantic Monthly*, 211 (March 1963), pp. 158–159; Denis Donoghue, "After Reading Hannah Arendt," *Poetry*, 100 (May 1962), 129.

2. Robert E. Meyerson, "Hannah Arendt: Romantic in a Totalitarian Age, 1928–1963," (Ph.D. dissertation, University of Minnesota, 1972), pp. 321, 324; Peter Fuss, "Hannah Arendt's Conception of Political Community," *Idealistic Studies*, 3 (September 1973), 264; Margaret Canovan, "The Contradictions of Hannah Arendt's Political Thought," *Political Theory*, 6 (February 1978), 5–6, 13, 20.

3. Ernst Vollrath, "Hannah Arendt and the Method of Political Thinking," *Social Research*, 44 (Spring 1977), 161; Mary Katherine McKeon Klein, "The Concept of Political Freedom in Hannah Arendt"

(Ph.D. dissertation, Boston University, 1933), p. iv; Benjamin I. Schwartz, "The Religion of Politics: Reflections on the Thought of Hannah Arendt," *Dissent*, 17 (March–April 1970), 144; George Mc-Kenna, "A Critic of Modernity: The Political Thought of Hannah Arendt" (Ph.D. dissertation, Fordham University, 1967), p. viii; Richard J. Bernstein, "Hannah Arendt: The Ambiguities of Theory and Practice," in Terence Ball (editor), *Political Theory and Praxis: New Perspectives* (Minneapolis: University of Minnesota Press, 1977), pp. 145, 149; Leroy A. Cooper, "Hannah Arendt's Political Philosophy: An Interpretation," *Review of Politics*, 38 (April 1976), 170n–171n; Stan Spyros Draenos, "Thinking without a Ground: Hannah Arendt and the Contemporary Situation of Understanding," in Melvyn A. Hill (editor), *Hannah Arendt: The Recovery of the Public World* (New York: St. Martin's, 1979), pp. 209–210, 212, 216; Michael Denneny, "The Privilege of Ourselves: Hannah Arendt on Judgment," in Hill (editor), *Hannah Arendt*, pp. 250, 260, 270.

4. Klein, "Concept of Political Freedom," p. 6.

5. Sheldon S. Wolin, "Hannah Arendt and the Ordinance of Time," *Social Research*, 44 (Spring 1977), 96; Hannah Arendt, *The Human Condition* (Garden City, N.Y.: Doubleday Anchor, 1959), pp. 30–31, 33–34, 38, and *Between Past and Future: Exercises in Political Thought* (New York: Viking, 1968), pp. 154–155; James T. Knauer, "Hannah Arendt and the Reassertion of the Political: Toward a New Democratic Theory" (Ph.D. dissertation, S.U.N.Y. at Binghamton, 1975), p. 306.

6. Arendt, *Origins*, pp. 118, 146; Arendt, *Human Condition*, pp. 30–31; and Arendt, *The Life of the Mind* (New York: Harcourt Brace Jovanovich, 1978), II, 203; Fuss, "Arendt's Conception of Political Community," p. 261; Knauer, "Arendt and the Reassertion of the Political," pp. 92, 93, 123; Benjamin R. Barber, *Superman and Common Men: Freedom, Anarchy and the Revolution* (New York: Praeger, 1971), p. 62.

7. Hannah Arendt, "Franz Kafka: A Revaluation," *Partisan Review*, 11 (Fall 1944), 417, and *Between Past and Future: Eight Exercises in Political Thought* (New York: Viking, 1968), p. 263.

8. McKenna, "Critic of Modernity," pp. 316–317.

9. Walter Benjamin, *Illuminations*, edited by Hannah Arendt (New York: Harcourt, Brace and World, 1968), pp. 257, 268; James Miller, "The Pathos of Novelty: Hannah Arendt's Image of Freedom in the Modern World," in Hill (editor), *Hannah Arendt*, pp. 181–183.

10. H. D. F. Kitto, *The Greeks* (Baltimore: Penguin, 1960), pp. 131–135, 159–160, 162, 165; Alfred Zimmern, *The Greek Commonwealth: Politics and Economics in Fifth-Century Athens* (London: Oxford University Press, 1931), pp. 279–313; Knauer, "Arendt and the Reassertion of the Political," p. 325.

11. Hanna Fenichel Pitkin, "The Roots of Conservatism: Oakeshott and the Denial of Politics," *Dissent*, 20 (Fall 1973), 513; Benjamin, *Illuminations*, p. 258.

12. Judith N. Shklar, "Hannah Arendt's Triumph," *New Republic*, 173 (December 27, 1975), 9; Arendt, *Human Condition*, pp. 25, 172–173, and *Between Past and Future*, pp. 45–46.

13. Hannah Arendt, "Reflections on Little Rock," *Dissent*, 6 (Winter 1959), 46, 48, 53, 55, 56.

14. Hannah Arendt, *On Revolution* (New York: Viking, 1965), p. 242.

15. Melvin Tumin, "Pie in the Sky," *Dissent*, 6 (Winter 1959), 65; Sidney Hook, "Hannah Arendt's Reflections," *Dissent*, 6 (Spring 1959), 203; John Murray Cuddihy, *The Ordeal of Civility: Freud, Marx, Lévi-Strauss, and the Jewish Struggle with Modernity* (New York: Basic Books, 1974), p. 27n.

16. Dante Germino, *Beyond Ideology: The Revival of Political Theory* (New York: Harper and Row, 1967), p. 142n.

17. Arendt quoted in A. Alvarez, *Under Pressure: The Writer in Society, Eastern Europe and the U.S.A.* (Baltimore: Penguin, 1965), p. 104.

18. Arendt in Hill (editor), *Hannah Arendt*, pp. 315–316, 317–318, 319.

19. Ronald W. Clark, *The Life of Bertrand Russell* (New York: Knopf, 1976), pp. 520, 522–530; Sidney Hook, *Political Power and Personal Freedom* (New York: Criterion, 1959), p. 433.

20. Klein, "Concept of Political Freedom," pp. 4, 27, 85, 95, 112–113.

21. Dwight Macdonald, *Memoirs of a Revolutionist: Essays in Political Criticism* (Cleveland: World, 1958), p. 183; Henry Pachter, "On Being an Exile: An Old-Timer's Personal and Political Memoir," *Salmagundi*, 10–11 (Fall 1969–Winter 1970), 18.

22. Koestler, *The Invisible Writing* (Boston: Beacon, 1955), p. 166; Babel quoted in Lionel Trilling, *Beyond Culture: Essays on Literature and Learning* (New York: Viking, 1965), p. 123; Kraus quoted in Erich Heller, "Dark Laughter," *New York Review of Books*, 20 (May 3, 1973), 24.

23. Arendt, *Human Condition*, pp. 10–11, 73, 133, 171, 176, and *Be-*

tween Past and Future, pp. 154–155, 169; Tom Stoppard, *Travesties* (New York: Grove, 1975), p. 62; George Lichtheim, *Marxism in Modern France* (New York: Columbia University Press, 1966), p. 112.

24. Arendt, *The Origins of Totalitarianism* (Cleveland: World, 1958), pp. 494, 498, and *On Revolution*, pp. 252, 253, 259–268; Ignazio Silone, "After Hungary," *New Leader*, 40 (January 21, 1957), 15.

25. Herman Belz, "New Left Reverberations in the Academy," *Review of Politics*, 36 (April 1974), 268–269, 270–271; Thomas R. West, *Nature, Community and Will: A Study in Literary and Social Thought* (Columbia: University of Missouri Press, 1976), p. 104.

26. Miller, "Pathos of Novelty," in Hill (editor), *Hannah Arendt*, p. 181.

27. Arendt, *On Revolution*, pp. 267, 269, 282, and *Origins*, p. 499.

28. Arendt in Hill (editor), *Hannah Arendt*, p. 334; Arendt quoted in Peter Gay, *Weimar Culture: The Outsider as Insider* (New York: Harper and Row, 1968), p. 70; Canovan, "Contradictions," *Political Theory*, p. 21.

29. Michael Walzer, *Obligations: Essays on Disobedience, War, and Citizenship* (Cambridge: Harvard University Press, 1970), pp. 234–238.

30. Richard Hofstadter, *The Idea of a Party System: The Rise of Legitimate Opposition in the United States, 1780–1840* (Berkeley: University of California Press, 1969), p. xii; Canovan, "Contradictions," p. 18.

31. Hannah Arendt, *Men in Dark Times* (New York: Harcourt, Brace and World, 1968), pp. viii, ix.

32. *Ibid.*, pp. 4–5, and *Human Condition*, pp. 212, 293–294; Nathan Glazer, "Hannah Arendt's America," *Commentary*, 60 (September 1975), 66; O'Sullivan, "Politics, Totalitarianism and Freedom," p. 184.

33. *Olmstead* v. *U.S.*, 277 U.S. 438 at 478 (1927) (Brandeis, J., dissenting); Louis D. Brandeis and Samuel D. Warren, "The Right to Privacy," *Harvard Law Review*, 4 (December 1890), 196, 205, 207, 213.

34. Arendt, *Men in Dark Times*, p. 30; Knauer, "Arendt and the Reassertion of the Political," p. 221; George Kateb, "Freedom and Worldliness in the Thought of Hannah Arendt," *Political Theory*, 5 (May 1977), 141.

35. Arendt, "Organized Guilt and Universal Responsibility" (1945), in Ron H. Feldman (editor), *The Jew as Pariah: Jewish Identity and Politics in the Modern Age* (New York: Grove, 1978), p. 233; Martin Luther quoted in Arendt, *Origins*, p. 477; George McKenna, "On Han-

nah Arendt: Politics As It Is, Was, Might Be," *Salmagundi*, 10–11 (Fall 1969–Winter 1970), 116.

36. Arendt, *Origins*, p. 338.

37. Rudolph Hoess, *Commandant of Auschwitz* (London: Weidenfeld and Nicolson, 1959), pp. 62, 63, 156, 172, 180; Lucy S. Dawidowicz, *The Jewish Presence: Essays on Identity and History* (New York: Holt, Rinehart and Winston, 1977), p. 242; William Kornhauser, *The Politics of Mass Society* (Glencoe, Illinois: Free Press, 1959), p. 93.

38. Zbigniew Brzezinski, *Permanent Purge: Politics in Soviet Totalitarianism* (Cambridge: Harvard University Press, 1956), pp. 8, 34–35, 36, 42–43, 48.

39. Trevor-Roper, *The Last Days of Hitler* (New York: Collier, 1962), pp. 83–84; Joachim C. Fest, *The Face of the Third Reich: Portraits of the Nazi Leadership* (New York: Pantheon, 1970), pp. 113, 115, 116, 122, 123; Jeremy Noakes and Geoffrey Pridham (editors), *Documents on Nazism, 1919–1945* (New York: Viking, 1974), p. 493.

40. Arendt, *Origins*, p. 307.

41. Arthur M. Schlesinger, Jr., *The Politics of Hope* (Boston: Houghton Mifflin, 1963), p. 282.

42. Arendt, *On Revolution*, pp. 77, 85.

43. *Ibid.*, pp. 77, 79, 83, 85–86.

44. Lionel Trilling, *The Middle of the Journey* (New York: Avon, 1966), pp. 162–166; Knauer, "Arendt and the Reassertion of the Political," p. 161n.

45. Alfred Kazin, *New York Jew* (New York: Knopf, 1978), p. 191; John P. Diggins, *Up from Communism: Conservative Odysseys in American Intellectual History* (New York: Harper and Row, 1975), p. 430; Isidore Silver, "What Flows from Neo-Conservatism," *Nation*, 225 (July 9, 1977), 49–50.

46. Thomas J. Scorza, *In the Time before Steamships: Billy Budd, the Limits of Politics, and Modernity* (DeKalb: Northern Illinois University Press, 1979), p. 129; Charles A. Reich, "The Tragedy of Justice in *Billy Budd*," *Yale Review*, 56, N.S. (Spring 1967), 386–389.

47. Arendt, *On Revolution*, p. 79; Herman Melville, *Billy Budd and The Piazza Tales* (Garden City, N.Y.: Doubleday Anchor, 1973), p. 11.

48. Stokely Carmichael quoted in Staughton Lynd, *Intellectual Origins of American Radicalism* (New York: Vintage, 1969), p. viii; Hannah Arendt, *Crises of the Republic* (New York: Harcourt Brace Jovanovich, 1972), pp. 96, 99, 101–102.

49. Arendt, *Crises of the Republic*, pp. 60–62; Kateb, "Freedom and

Worldliness," pp. 160–165, 166–174; Melvyn Hill, Introduction to Hill (editor), *Hannah Arendt*, p. x, Young-Bruehl, "Pariah's Point of View," in Hill (editor), *Hannah Arendt*, pp. 15–18.

50. Sidney Hook, "A Recollection of Berthold Brecht," *New Leader*, 43 (October 10, 1960), 23.

51. Arendt, *Men in Dark Times*, p. 227.

52. Brecht quoted in Martin Esslin, *Brecht: The Man and His Work* (Garden City, N.Y.: Doubleday Anchor, 1961), p. 149; Sidney Hook, Letter to the Editor, *Encounter*, 50 (March 1978), 93.

53. Arendt, *Men in Dark Times*, p. 242; Erich Heller, "Hannah Arendt as a Critic of Literature," *Social Research*, 44 (Spring 1977), 154.

54. Denis Donoghue, "After Reading Hannah Arendt," *Poetry*, 100 (May 1962), 129; Arendt, *Men in Dark Times*, pp. 210, 211–212, and "W. H. Auden," *New Yorker*, 50 (January 27, 1975), 45–46.

55. Arendt, *Men in Dark Times*, pp. 209, 243–244.

56. *Ibid.*, pp. 215, 246–247, 248; Esslin, *Brecht*, p. 86.

57. Herbert Luthy, "Of Poor Bert Brecht," *Encounter*, 7 (July 1956), 33–53.

58. Yevgeny Yevtushenko, *Poetry, 1953–1965* (New York: October House, 1965), p. 161.

59. Arendt, *Origins*, p. 442.

60. Arendt, *On Revolution*, p. 58; Emil L. Fackenheim, *The Jewish Return into History: Reflections in the Age of Auschwitz and a New Jerusalem* (New York: Schocken, 1978), p. 96.

61. O'Sullivan, "Politics, Totalitarianism and Freedom: The Political Thought of Hannah Arendt," *Political Studies*, 21 (June 1973), 193, 198; Kateb, "Freedom and Worldliness," *Political Theory*, p. 165.

62. Robert Dahl, *Who Governs?: Democracy and Power in an American City* (New Haven: Yale University Press, 1961), p. 279; Walzer, *Obligations*, pp. 234–238.

63. Leroy A. Cooper, "Hannah Arendt's Political Philosophy: An Interpretation," *Review of Politics*, 38 (April 1976), 148; Arendt, *Crises of the Republic*, p. 221, and *Origins*, p. 451.

64. Albert Speer, *Inside the Third Reich: Memoirs* (New York: Macmillan, 1970), pp. 252–268, 276–277; Trevor-Roper, *The Last Days of Hitler* (New York: Collier, 1962), pp. 74, 99–103, 229; Secret Speech of Khrushchev in *The Anti-Stalin Campaign and International Communism*, edited by the Russian Institute of Columbia University (New York: Columbia University Press, 1956), pp. 40, 82, 84; Milovan Djilas, *Conversations with Stalin* (New York: Harcourt, Brace and World,

1962), pp. 106–107, 152–153, 181; Svetlana Allilueva, *Twenty Letters to a Friend* (New York: Harper and Row, 1967), pp. 61, 81, 137.

65. David Riesman, *Individualism Reconsidered and Other Essays* (Glencoe, Ill.: Free Press, 1954), p. 124; Karol Wojytla, *Sign of Contradiction* (New York: Seabury, 1979), pp. 51, 157.

66. Arendt, *Human Condition*, p. 46, and *Men in Dark Times*, p. 72.

67. Arendt, *Origins*, pp. 474–477.

68. Max Weber quoted in Hans Kohn, *The Mind of Germany: The Education of a Nation* (New York: Scribner's, 1960), p. 283.

Chapter 6

1. Philip Rieff, "The Theology of Politics: Reflections on Totalitarianism As the Burden of Our Time," *Journal of Religion*, 32 (April 1952), 120–121.

2. *Ibid.*, p. 108.

3. Alfred Kazin, *New York Jew* (New York: Knopf, 1978), p. 199.

4. Hannah Arendt, *Men in Dark Times* (New York: Harcourt, Brace and World, 1968), p. 67; John Adams quoted in Hannah Arendt, *On Revolution* (New York: Viking, 1965), p. 192.

5. Hannah Arendt in Melvyn A. Hill (editor), *Hannah Arendt: The Recovery of the Public World* (New York: St. Martin's, 1979), pp. 313–314, and *Between Past and Future: Eight Exercises in Political Thought* (New York: Viking, 1968), pp. 133–135.

6. Arendt, *On Revolution*, p. 192; Arendt, "A Reply," *Review of Politics*, 15 (January 1953), 82; and Arendt in "Religion and the Intellectuals," *Partisan Review*, 17 (February 1950), 115.

7. George McKenna, "A Critic of Modernity: The Political Thought of Hannah Arendt" (Ph.D. dissertation, Fordham University, 1967), p. 3.

8. New York *Times*, December 6, 1975, p. 32; Arendt quoted in Kazin, *New York Jew*, p. 218.

9. George Steiner, *Language and Silence: Essays on Language, Literature, and the Inhuman* (New York: Atheneum, 1970), p. 149; George Lichtheim, "Three Critics of Totalitarianism," *Twentieth Century*, 150 (July 1951), 29.

10. Arendt, *The Origins of Totalitarianism* (Cleveland: World, 1958), p. 8, and "Jewish History, Revised" (1948), in Ron H. Feldman (editor), *The Jew as Pariah: Jewish Identity and Politics in the Modern Age* (New York: Grove, 1978), p. 105; Benjamin I. Schwartz, "The Religion

of Politics: Reflections on the Thought of Hannah Arendt," *Dissent*, 17 (March–April, 1970), 153; Jean-Paul Sartre, *Anti-Semite and Jew* (New York: Grove, 1960), pp. 66–67, 91.

11. Lewis Namier quoted in Leon Wieseltier, "You Don't Have to Be Khazarian," *New York Review of Books*, 23 (October 28, 1976), 33; Arendt, *Men in Dark Times*, p. 13.

12. Hannah Arendt, *The Human Condition* (Garden City, N.Y.: Doubleday Anchor, 1959), pp. 33, 166; Lionel Trilling, *Sincerity and Authenticity* (Cambridge: Harvard University Press, 1972), p. 85.

13. Salo W. Baron, "Personal Notes: Hannah Arendt (1906–1975)," *Jewish Social Studies*, 38 (Spring 1976), 187–189; Gershom Scholem in *"Eichmann in Jerusalem*: An Exchange of Letters," *Encounter*, 22 (January 1964), 51–52.

14. Arendt in *"Eichmann in Jerusalem,"* *Encounter*, 54, 55; Abraham Kaplan, "The Life of Reason and Historical Piety," *Judaism*, 10 (Fall 1961), 316; Isaac Bashevis Singer, *Shosha* (New York: Farrar, Straus and Giroux, 1978), p. 18.

15. Arendt in *"Eichmann in Jerusalem,"* pp. 54, 55; Arendt, *On Revolution*, 81; and Arendt, "The Hole of Oblivion," *Jewish Frontier*, 14 (July 1947), 23.

16. Rosa Luxemburg quoted in J. P. Nettl, *Rosa Luxemburg* (London: Oxford University Press, 1966), p. 860; Milton Himmelfarb, *The Jews of Modernity* (New York: Basic Books, 1973), p. 344.

17. Cynthia Ozick, "All the World Wants the Jews Dead," *Esquire*, 82 (November 1974), 207.

18. Hannah Arendt, *The Origins of Totalitarianism* (Cleveland: World, 1958), pp. 120, 290, 299, 355, and "The Jewish State: Fifty Years After" (1946), in Feldman (editor), *Jew as Pariah*, p. 169.

19. Albert Einstein *et al.*, Letter to the Editor, New York *Times*, December 4, 1948, p. 12.

20. Arendt, "Zionism Reconsidered" (1944) and "Peace or Armistice in the Near East?" (1950), in Feldman (editor), *Jew as Pariah*, pp. 161, 212–214, 221–222.

21. Maurice Samuel, *In Praise of Yiddish* (Chicago: Cowles, 1971), p. 153.

22. Irving Howe, *Leon Trotsky* (New York: Penguin, 1979), p. 177; Arendt, *Between Past and Future*, p. 90.

23. Harold Macmillan quoted in "Age and Power," *Saturday Review*, 51 (January 27, 1968), 26.

24. Irving Howe, *Decline of the New* (New York: Horizon, 1970), pp.

244–245; Denis Donoghue, "After Reading Arendt," *Poetry*, 100 (May 1962), 127.

25. H. R. Trevor-Roper, "How Innocent Was Eichmann?" London *Sunday Times*, October 13, 1963, p. 35; John Gross, "Arendt on Eichmann," *Encounter*, 21 (November 1963), 66; Daniel Bell, "The Alphabet of Justice," *Partisan Review*, 30 (Fall 1963), 418.

26. Norman Podhoretz quoted in *"Eichmann in Jerusalem—Can One Know the 'Whole' Truth?" Newsweek*, 61 (June 17, 1963), 95; William Phillips, *A Sense of the Present: Essays and Stories of Two Decades* (New York: Chilmark, 1967), p. 77.

27. Hannah Arendt, *Eichmann in Jerusalem: A Report on the Banality of Evil* (New York: Viking, 1963; rev. ed. 1964), pp. 7, 13, 41, 59–61, 198, 200.

28. *Ibid.*, p. 40; Scholem and Arendt, *"Eichmann in Jerusalem,"* pp. 53, 54.

29. Mary McCarthy, *The Writing on the Wall and Other Literary Essays* (New York: Harcourt, Brace and World, 1970), pp. 60–61; "The Talk of the Town: Notes and Comment," *New Yorker*, 39 (July 20, 1963), 17; Dwight Macdonald, *Discriminations: Essays and Afterthoughts, 1938–1974* (New York: Grossman, 1974), p. 315; Michael Kowal, "The Liberal Critic," *Judaism*, 13 (Fall 1964), 500.

30. Harold Weisberg in "Arguments: More on Eichmann," *Partisan Review*, 31 (Spring 1964), 258; Marie Syrkin, "Hannah Arendt: The Clothes of the Empress," *Dissent*, 10 (Autumn 1963), 346.

31. Arendt, *Eichmann*, pp. 135–136; Morris U. Schappes, *The Strange World of Hannah Arendt* (New York: Jewish Currents, 1963), p. 12.

32. Arendt, *"Eichmann in Jerusalem,"* p. 54, and "A Reply," pp. 78–79.

33. H. Stuart Hughes, *The Sea Change: The Migration of Social Thought, 1930–1965* (New York: Harper and Row, 1975), p. 121.

34. Judith Adler Hennessee, "Annals of Checking," in Richard Pollak (editor), *Stop the Presses, I Want to Get Off!: Inside Stories of the News Business from the Pages of [MORE]* (New York: Dell, 1975), pp. 318–319; "Talk of the Town," *New Yorker*, p. 17.

35. Syrkin, "Clothes of the Empress," p. 352; Walter Laqueur, "Footnotes to the Holocaust," in Feldman (editor), *Jew as Pariah*, pp. 253–254; Norman Podhoretz, *Doings and Undoings: The Fifties and After in American Writing* (New York: Farrar, Straus, 1964), p. 337.

36. Arendt, *Eichmann* (1963), p. 105; Raul Hilberg, *The Destruction of the European Jews* (Chicago: Quadrangle, 1961), pp. 292, 536;

Scholem, *"Eichmann in Jerusalem,"* p. 52; Jacob Robinson, *And the Crooked Shall Be Made Straight: The Eichmann Trial, the Jewish Catastrophe and Hannah Arendt's Narrative* (Philadelphia: Jewish Publication Society, 1965), p. 173.

37. Arendt, *Eichmann*, pp. 133–134, 178; Robinson, *Crooked Shall Be Made Straight*, pp. 144–146, 322; Joachim C. Fest, *The Face of the Third Reich: Portraits of the Nazi Leadership* (New York: Pantheon, 1970), pp. 100–101, 107, 335n–337n.

38. Lionel Abel in "Arguments," *Partisan Review*, p. 275.

39. Hannah Arendt, "The Jew as Pariah," in Feldman (editor), *Jew as Pariah*, pp. 76–79; Sharon Muller, "The Origins of *Eichmann in Jerusalem*: An Examination of Hannah Arendt's Interpretation of Jewish History" (unpublished paper, Columbia University, 1979), pp. 2, 19, 25, 30, 33–34, 43–44.

40. Arendt, *Eichmann*, pp. 131–132, 280, 284, 285.

41. Walter Lippmann, "Public Opinion and the American Jew," *American Hebrew*, 110 (April 14, 1922), 575; *West Virginia Board of Education v. Barnette*, 319 U.S. 624 at 646 (1943) (Frankfurter, J., dissenting); I. F. Stone, *Polemics and Prophecies, 1967–1970* (New York: Vintage, 1970), p. 429.

42. Arendt, *Eichmann*, p. 117.

43. *Ibid.*, pp. 60, 123–125, 246, and *"Eichmann in Jerusalem,"* p. 55.

44. Arendt, *Eichmann*, 125; Arendt, Letter to the Editor, *Midstream*, 8 (Summer 1962), 86; and Arendt, quoted in *"Eichmann in Jerusalem,"* *Newsweek*, p. 95.

45. Steiner, *Language and Silence*, p. 167; Bernard Crick, "Hannah Arendt," London *Times*, December 12, 1975, p. 18; Raziel Abelson, "Intellectual Elitism," *New Leader*, 61 (May 22, 1978), 19–20; Arendt, *Eichmann*, p. 117, and Letter to the Editor, *Midstream*, p. 86.

46. Lucy S. Dawidowicz, *The War against the Jews, 1933–1945* (New York: Bantam, 1976), pp. 472–473, 586; Dorothy Rabinowitz, "The Holocaust as Living Memory," in Elie Wiesel, Lucy Dawidowicz, *et al.*, *Dimensions of the Holocaust: Lectures at Northwestern University* (New York: Anti-Defamation League, 1977), p. 44; Arendt, *Eichmann*, p. 117.

47. Yisrael Gutman, "Adam Czerniakow: The Man and His Diary," in Gutman and Livia Rothkirchen (editors), *The Catastrophe of European Jewry: Antecedents, History, Reflections* (Jerusalem: Yad Vashem, 1976), pp. 465–466; Bruno Bettelheim, *Surviving and Other Essays* (New York: Knopf, 1979), p. 269.

48. McCarthy, *Writing on the Wall*, p. 71; Marie Syrkin in "Arguments," *Partisan Review*, p. 254; Arendt, Letter to the Editor, *Midstream*, p. 86.

49. Gross, "Arendt on Eichmann," p. 69; Arendt, *Eichmann*, pp. 11–12.

50. Bruno Bettelheim, "Eichmann, the System, the Victims," *New Republic*, 148 (June 15, 1963), 30; Robert Shaw, *The Man in the Glass Booth* (London: Chatto and Windus, 1967), pp. 180, 186; Arendt, *Eichmann*, p. 283.

51. Walter Laqueur, "Footnotes to the Holocaust," in Feldman (editor), *Jew as Pariah*, p. 257; Isaiah Trunk, "The Jewish Councils in Eastern Europe under Nazi Rule (An Attempt at a Synthesis)," *Societas*, 2 (Summer 1972), 235, 237–238; Arendt, *Eichmann*, p. 117; McCarthy, *Writing on the Wall*, p. 60.

52. McCarthy, *Writing on the Wall*, pp. 59–60; Bettelheim, "Eichmann," p. 30, and *Surviving*, p. 270.

53. Trunk, "Jewish Councils," p. 229; Macdonald, *Discriminations*, p. 313.

54. Dawidowicz, *War against the Jews*, p. 578; Lionel Abel, "Aesthetics of Evil: Hannah Arendt on Eichmann and the Jews," *Partisan Review*, 30 (Summer 1963), 212, 214, and in "Arguments," *Partisan Review*, pp. 270–275.

55. Bettelheim, "Eichmann," pp. 26, 30; David Dempsey, "Bruno Bettelheim is Dr. No," New York *Times Magazine*, January 11, 1970, p. 109.

56. Nathan Eck, "Historical Research or Slander?" *Yad Vashem Studies*, 6 (1967), 399; Abel, "Aesthetics of Evil," p. 227.

57. Ernst Simon, "Revisionist History of the Jewish Catastrophe: A Textual Examination," *Judaism*, 12 (Fall 1963), 414–415; Arendt, *Eichmann*, p. 124.

58. Oscar Handlin, "Jewish Resistance to the Nazis," *Commentary*, 34 (November 1962), 400–401; Eck, "Historical Research," pp. 429–430.

59. Bernard Goldstein, *The Stars Bear Witness* (New York: Viking, 1949), p. 35.

60. Marie Syrkin, "Miss Arendt Surveys the Holocaust," *Jewish Frontier*, 30 (May 1963), 11, and "Clothes of the Empress," p. 348; Gross, "Arendt on Eichmann," p. 67; Abel in "Arguments," *Partisan Review*, p. 216; Gideon Hausner, *Justice in Jerusalem* (New York: Harper and

Row, 1966), p. 196; Lucy S. Dawidowicz, "Visualizing the Warsaw Ghetto," *Shoah*, 1, no. 1 (1978), 6; Isaiah Trunk, *Judenrat: The Jewish Councils in Eastern Europe under Nazi Occupation* (New York: Macmillan, 1972), pp. 412–413, 572–573.

61. Syrkin, "Clothes of the Empress," p. 351.

62. Guenter Lewy, *The Catholic Church and Nazi Germany* (New York: McGraw-Hill, 1964), pp. 242–251, 268–308, 331; Saul Friedländer, *Pius XII and the Third Reich: A Documentation* (New York: Knopf, 1966); Léon Poliakov, "Pope Pius XII and the Nazis," in Eric Bentley (editor), *The Storm over* The Deputy (New York: Grove, 1964), pp. 226–234.

63. Henry L. Feingold, "Who Shall Bear Guilt for the Holocaust: The Human Dilemma," *American Jewish History*, 58 (March 1979), 269; Hannah Arendt, *"The Deputy*: Guilt by Silence?" in Bentley (editor), *The Storm over* The Deputy, pp. 88, 94.

64. Jaspers quoted in Walter Kaufmann, *From Shakespeare to Existentialism* (Garden City, N.Y.: Doubleday Anchor, 1960), p. 316; Arendt, *Men in Dark Times*, p. 76.

65. Heidegger quoted in Valentino Gerratana, "Heidegger and Marx," *New Left Review*, 106 (November–December 1977), 52–53; Stanley Rosen, *Nihilism: A Philosophical Essay* (New Haven: Yale University Press, 1969), pp. 119–124; Arendt, "What is Existenz Philosophy?" *Partisan Review*, 13 (Winter 1946), 46–56; George McKenna, "On Hannah Arendt: Politics As It Is, Was, Might Be," *Salmagundi*, 10–11 (Fall 1969–Winter 1970), 112n.

66. Arendt, "Martin Heidegger at Eighty," *New York Review of Books*, 12 (October 21, 1971), 53–54n, and "Existenz Philosophy," p. 46n; Bernard Elevitch, "Arendt and Heidegger: The Illusion of Politics," *Boston University Journal*, 20, no. 182 (1972), 64, 65.

67. Arendt, "Heidegger at Eighty," p. 54n.

68. Arendt, Letter to the Editor, *Midstream*, p. 86; Hilberg, *Destruction of the European Jews*, pp. 14–17, 664–669; Feingold, "Who Shall Bear Guilt," *American Jewish History*, pp. 278–282.

69. Arendt, *Eichmann*, p. 285.

70. Paul E. Killinger and William Stringfellow quoted in Dorothy Rabinowitz, *New Lives: Survivors of the Holocaust Living in America* (New York: Avon, 1977), pp. 190, 191.

71. Arendt, *Eichmann*, p. 274.

72. Telford Taylor, "Large Questions in the Eichmann Case," New

York *Times Magazine*, January 22, 1961, p. 22; Yosal Rogat, *The Eichmann Trial and the Rule of Law* (Santa Barbara, Calif.: Center for the Study of Democratic Institutions, 1961), pp. 23–28.

73. Arendt, "The Aftermath of Nazi Rule," *Commentary*, 10 (October 1950), 348–349; Karl Jaspers, *The Question of German Guilt* (New York: Capricorn, 1961), p. 55; Harold Rosenberg, "The Shadow of the Furies," *New York Review of Books*, 23 (January 20, 1977), 47; Rebecca West, *A Train of Powder* (New York: Viking, 1955), p. 50.

74. Jaspers, *German Guilt*, pp. 42, 56; Robinson, *Crooked Shall Be Made Straight*, p. 76.

75. Arendt, *Eichmann*, pp. 14, 264; Stephen Klaidman, "The Nazi Hunters: Justice, Not Vengeance," *Present Tense*, 4 (Winter 1977), 21–26; Howard Blum, *Wanted!: The Search for Nazis in America* (Chicago: Quadrangle, 1977); William Sumners, Letter to the Editor, New York *Times Magazine*, January 22, 1961, p. 30.

76. Arendt, *Eichmann*, pp. 239–240, 264; Rogat, *Eichmann Trial*, pp. 24, 29n; Helen Silving, "In Re Eichmann: A Dilemma of Law and Morality," *American Journal of International Law*, 55 (April 1961), 335, 338.

77. Arendt, *Eichmann*, pp. 14–16, 259, 260; Silving, "In Re Eichmann," p. 336.

78. Arendt, *Eichmann*, p. 274; Rogat, *Eichmann Trial*, p. 28; Robinson, *Crooked Shall Be Made Straight*, p. 127.

79. Richard A. Falk, Gabriel Kolko and Robert Jay Lifton (editors), *Crimes of War* (New York: Vintage, 1971), p. 137; Alan Dershowitz, "A Conversation with Telford Taylor '32," *Harvard Law School Bulletin*, 30 (Winter 1979), 31.

80. Harold Rosenberg, "The Trial and Eichmann," *Commentary*, 32 (November 1961), 380; Arendt, *Eichmann*, p. 272.

81. Arendt, *Eichmann*, pp. 4, 5, 146, 258, 259.

82. Bettelheim, *Surviving*, p. 273; Crick, "Hannah Arendt," London *Times*, p. 18.

83. Arendt, *Eichmann*, pp. 265–267; Shalom Schwartzbard, "Memoirs of an Assassin," in Lucy S. Dawidowicz (editor), *The Golden Tradition: Jewish Life and Thought in Eastern Europe* (Boston: Beacon, 1968), pp. 448–457.

84. Arendt, *Eichmann*, pp. 269–271.

85. Rogat, *Eichmann Trial*, pp. 37, 41; Morton J. Horwitz, Letter to the Editor, New York *Times Magazine*, January 8, 1961, p. 4; Taylor, "Large Questions," New York *Times Magazine*, pp. 23, 25.

86. Arendt, *Eichmann*, p. 271.

87. Bradley F. Smith, *Reaching Judgment at Nuremberg* (New York: Basic Books, 1977), pp. 88, 89.

88. Arendt, *Eichmann*, pp. 257, 262, 267–268, 272; Arendt, *Between Past and Future*, p. 26; and Arendt, "On Responsibility for Evil," in Falk *et al.*, *Crimes of War*, pp. 494–495, 496, 498.

89. Rogat, *Eichmann Trial*, p. 13; Arendt, *Eichmann*, pp. 268–269, 276.

90. Rogat, *Eichmann Trial*, p. 26n; Robinson, *Crooked Shall Be Made Straight*, pp. 67–68, 70–71; Judgment of District Court quoted in Hausner, *Justice in Jerusalem*, pp. 411–412; Schappes, *Strange World of Hannah Arendt*, p. 18.

91. Michael Walzer, "Marcel Ophuls and the Nuremberg Trials: The Memory of Justice," *New Republic*, 175 (October 9, 1976), 22–23.

Chapter 7

1. Robert Jackson, Closing Address in *Trial of the Major War Criminals* (Nuremberg: International Military Tribunal, 1948), XIX, 405; Hannah Arendt, *Eichmann in Jerusalem: A Report on the Banality of Evil* (New York: Viking, 1963; rev. ed., 1964), pp. 31, 44.

2. Eichmann quoted in Arendt, *Eichmann*, p. 46.

3. *Ibid.*, pp. 215, 276, and *The Life of the Mind* (New York: Harcourt Brace Jovanovich, 1978), I, 3–4.

4. Proudhon quoted in Lewis S. Feuer, *Ideology and the Ideologists* (New York: Harper and Row, 1975), p. 142.

5. Arendt, *Eichmann*, pp. 26, 41–42, 287, and *Life of the Mind*, I, 4; Harry Eckstein and David E. Apter (editors), *Comparative Politics* (New York: Free Press, 1963), p. 434.

6. Jean-Paul Sartre, *Anti-Semite and Jew* (New York: Grove, 1960), pp. 17, 18, 22, 47; Eric Hoffer, *The True Believer: Thoughts on the Nature of Mass Movements* (New York: Harper and Brothers, 1951), pp. 83–84, 90–91, 142.

7. Max Horkheimer quoted in Martin Jay, *The Dialectical Imagination: A History of the Frankfurt School and the Institute of Social Research, 1923–1950* (Boston: Little Brown, 1973), p. 240; Kennan, "Totalitarianism in the Modern World," in Carl J. Friedrich (editor), *Totalitarianism* (New York: Grosset and Dunlap, 1966), p. 23.

8. Herman Melville, *Billy Budd and The Piazza Tales* (Garden City, N.Y.: Doubleday Anchor, 1973), p. 44; Gershom Scholem and Hannah

Arendt, "*Eichmann in Jerusalem*: An Exchange of Letters," *Encounter*, 22 (January 1964), 53, 56; Arendt, *Life of the Mind*, I, 3–4; David Biale, *Gershom Scholem: Kabbalah and Counter-History* (Cambridge: Harvard University Press, 1979), p. 125.

9. Stephen Miller, "Bureaucracy Baiting," *American Scholar*, 47 (Spring 1978), 208.

10. Vladimir Nabokov, Introduction to *Bend Sinister* (New York: Time, Inc., 1964), p. xv; Arendt, *Eichmann*, p. 54; Dwight Macdonald, *Discriminations: Essays and Afterthoughts, 1938–1974* (New York: Grossman, 1974), p. 311.

11. Joseph Conrad, Author's Note to *Under Western Eyes* (New York: Doubleday, Doran, 1938), pp. ix–x; Herman Singer, Letter to the Editor, *Encounter*, 22 (June 1964), 103.

12. Erich Heller, *The Disinherited Mind: Essays in Modern German Literature and Thought* (Cleveland: Meridian, 1959), pp. 248–250.

13. Bertolt Brecht, *Stücke: Aus dem Exil* (Berlin: Suhrkamp Verlag, 1957), IX, 369; Konrad Heiden, *Der Fuehrer: Hitler's Rise to Power* (Boston: Houghton Mifflin, 1944), pp. 33–35, 36; Lüthy quoted in Joachim C. Fest, *The Face of the Third Reich: Portraits of the Nazi Leadership* (New York: Pantheon, 1970), p. 62.

14. Isaac Deutscher, *Stalin: A Political Biography* (New York: Vintage, 1960), p. 295.

15. Rebecca West, *A Train of Powder* (New York: Viking, 1965), p. 69; H. R. Trevor-Roper, *The Last Days of Hitler* (New York: Collier, 1962), pp. 80–81, 83; New York *Times*, January 4, 1946, p. 6.

16. Hannah Arendt, "Organized Guilt and Universal Responsibility," in Ron H. Feldman (editor), *The Jew as Pariah: Jewish Identity and Politics in the Modern Age* (New York: Grove, 1978), p. 234, and *The Origins of Totalitarianism* (Cleveland: World, 1958), p. 327.

17. Arendt, *Eichmann*, p. 150; Robert Lowell, Letter to the Editor, New York Times *Book Review*, June 23, 1963, p. 5.

18. Lawrence L. Langer, *The Holocaust and the Literary Imagination* (New Haven: Yale University Press, 1975), p. 179; Arendt, *Eichmann*, pp. 252, 287–288.

19. Arendt, *Eichmann*, p. 288; Harry Golden, "A Stranger to the Human Race," in Louis L. Snyder and Richard B. Morris (editors), *A Treasury of Great Reporting* (New York: Simon and Schuster, 1962), pp. 774, 777.

20. Dwight Macdonald, Letter to the Editor, New York *Times Book*

Review, June 23, 1963, p. 5; Hannah Arendt, "Zionism Reconsidered," in Feldman (editor), *Jew as Pariah*, p. 160.

21. Lowell, Letter to the Editor, New York *Times Book Review*, p. 5.

22. West, *Train of Powder*, p. 330; Harold Rosenberg, "The Trial and Eichmann," *Commentary*, 32 (November 1961), 380.

23. Nietzsche to Franz Overbeck, January 6, 1889, in Walter Kaufmann (editor), *The Portable Nietzsche* (New York: Viking, 1954), p. 687.

24. Thomas Merton, *Raids on the Unspeakable* (New York: New Directions, 1966), pp. 45–47; Francine duPlessix Gray, "Thomas Merton: Man and Monk," *New Republic*, 180 (May 26, 1979), 26.

25. Elie Wiesel, *One Generation After* (New York: Avon, 1972), p. 11; Gideon Hausner, *Justice in Jerusalem* (New York: Harper and Row, 1966), p. 7.

26. Michael Musmanno, "Man with an Unspotted Conscience," New York *Times Book Review*, May 19, 1963, p. 1; "A Reply from Judge Musmanno," New York *Times Book Review*, June 23, 1963, p. 4; Dwight Macdonald, Letter to the Editor, in New York *Times Book Review*, June 23, 1963, p. 5.

27. Norman Podhoretz, *Doings and Undoings: The Fifties and After in American Writing* (New York: Farrar, Straus, 1964), p. 348; Carl J. Friedrich and Zbigniew Brzezinski, *Totalitarian Dictatorship and Autocracy* (New York: Praeger, 1961), p. 95.

28. Albert Speer, *Inside the Third Reich: Memoirs* (New York: Macmillan, 1970), pp. 17, 19–20, 94, 112, 515; Lucy S. Dawidowicz, *The Jewish Presence: Essays on Identity and History* (New York: Holt, Rinehart and Winston, 1977), pp. 230–235; Erich Goldhagen, "Albert Speer, Himmler, and the Secrecy of the Final Solution," *Midstream*, 17 (October 1971), 43–48.

29. Rudolph Hoess, *Commandant of Auschwitz* (London: Weidenfeld and Nicolson, 1959), pp. 132, 155, 215.

30. Arendt, *Eichmann*, pp. 146–147.

31. *Ibid.*, pp. 148–149; Marie Syrkin, "Hannah Arendt: The Clothes of the Empress," *Dissent*, 10 (Autumn 1963), 347–348; Jacob Robinson, *And the Crooked Shall Be Made Straight: The Eichmann Trial, the Jewish Catastrophe, and Hannah Arendt's Narrative* (Philadelphia: Jewish Publication Society, 1965), pp. 30–32.

32. Arendt, *Eichmann*, p. 292, and *Origins*, pp. 214, 215; Else Frenkel-Brunswik, "Totalitarianism and Intellectual Life," in Carl J. Freidrich

(editor), *Totalitarianism* (New York: Grosset and Dunlap, 1966), p. 275.

33. Miller, "Bureaucracy Baiting," pp. 208–209; Friedrich and Brzezinski, *Totalitarian Dictatorship*, pp. 19, 189–190.

34. Hausner, *Justice in Jerusalem*, pp. 6, 7; Saul Bellow, *Mr. Sammler's Planet* (New York: Viking, 1970), pp. 15, 18–19.

35. Hausner, *Justice in Jerusalem*, pp. 6–7; Michael Selzer, "The Murderous Mind," New York *Times Magazine*, November 27, 1977, pp. 35, 112, 117, 121.

36. Thomas R. Litwack, Letter to the Editor, New York *Times Magazine*, December 18, 1977, p. 110; Selzer, "The Murderous Mind," p. 120.

37. Molly Harrower, "Were Hitler's Henchmen Mad?" *Psychology Today*, 10 (July 1976), 76, 79, 80.

38. Perry Smith quoted in Truman Capote, *In Cold Blood* (New York: Random House, 1966), pp. 244, 245.

39. Arendt, *Eichmann*, pp. 278–279, 287.

40. Sigmund Freud, *Character and Culture* (New York: Collier, 1963), p. 112; Jakov Lind, *Counting My Steps: An Autobiography* (New York: Macmillan, 1969), p. 97; Fest, *Face of the Third Reich*, p. 277.

41. Stanley Milgram, *Obedience to Authority: An Experimental View* (New York: Harper and Row, 1974), pp. xv, 5–6.

42. Arendt, "Responsibility for Evil," in Richard A. Falk, Gabriel Kolko and Robert Jay Lifton (editors), *Crimes of War* (New York: Vintage, 1971), p. 499; Milgram, *Obedience to Authority*, pp. 22–23.

43. Lionel Rubinoff, "Auschwitz and the Pathology of Jew-Hatred," in Fleischner (editor), *Auschwitz: Beginning of a New Era?: Reflections on the Holocaust* (New York: Ktav, 1977), pp. 361–362; Arendt, *Eichmann*, p. 294; Léon Poliakov, "The Eichmann Trial," *Commentary*, 43 (January 1967), 90.

44. Ronald Berman, *America in the Sixties: An Intellectual History* (New York: Harper and Row, 1970), pp. 114–115; Herbert Marcuse, *One-Dimensional Man: Studies in the Ideology of Advanced Industrial Society* (Boston: Beacon, 1964), pp. 79–80; Norman Fruchter, "Arendt's Eichmann and Jewish Identity," in James Weinstein and David Eakins (editors), *For a New America: Essays in History and Politics from "Studies on the Left," 1959–1967* (New York: Vintage, 1970), pp. 429, 437, 454.

45. Lionel Abel, "The Aesthetics of Evil: Hannah Arendt on Eichmann and the Jews," *Partisan Review*, 30 (Summer 1963), 219–220; John Gross, "Arendt on Eichmann," *Encounter*, 21 (November 1963), 72; Walter Laqueur, "Footnotes to the Holocaust," in Feldman (editor),

Jew as Pariah, p. 255; Harold Rosenberg, "The Shadow of the Furies," *New York Review of Books*, 23 (January 20, 1977), 48.

46. Rosenberg, "The Trial and Eichmann," pp. 376, 380.

47. Hoess, *Commandant of Auschwitz*, pp. 155–157; Fest, *Face of the Third Reich*, pp. 279, 302, 380n, 385n.

48. Himmler quoted in Fest, *Fact of the Third Reich*, p. 123.

49. Syrkin, "Clothes of the Empress," p. 347.

50. Poliakov, "Eichmann Trial," p. 90.

51. Gross, "Arendt on Eichmann," p. 70; Marie Syrkin, "Miss Arendt Surveys the Holocaust," *Jewish Frontier*, 30 (May 1963), 9; Arendt, *Eichmann*, p. 70, and "A Statement," New York *Times Book Review*, June 23, 1963, p. 4.

52. David Schoenbaum, *Hitler's Social Revolution: Class and Status in Nazi Germany, 1933–1939* (Garden City, N.Y.: Doubleday, 1966), p. 240; Arendt, *Origins*, pp. 395, 397–398.

53. Robinson, *Crooked Shall Be Made Straight*, p. 1; Arendt, *Eichmann*, pp. 93, 289.

54. Arendt, *Eichmann*, pp. 5, 6; Syrkin, "Miss Arendt Surveys the Holocaust," p. 7; Morris U. Schappes, *The Strange World of Hannah Arendt* (New York: Jewish Currents, 1963), p. 14.

55. Arendt, *Eichmann*, p. 279.

56. Ernst Simon, "Revisionist History of the Jewish Catastrophe: A Textual Examination," *Judaism*, 12 (Fall 1963), 405; Scholem, "*Eichmann in Jerusalem*: An Exchange of Letters," *Encounter*, 22 (January 1964), 53; Dwight Macdonald, *Discriminations: Essays and Afterthoughts, 1938–1974* (New York: Grossman, 1974), p. 314.

57. Arendt, *Eichmann*, p. 278.

58. *Ibid.*, pp. 252, 273; Gershom Scholem, *On Jews and Judaism in Crisis: Selected Essays* (New York: Schocken, 1976), pp. 298–300.

59. Arendt, *Eichmann*, pp. 273, 277, 279.

60. *Ibid.*, p. 256; Gar Alperovitz, *Atomic Diplomacy: Hiroshima and Potsdam* (New York: Vintage, 1965), pp. 14, 106–116, 236–242; Martin J. Sherwin, *A World Destroyed: The Atomic Bomb and the Grand Alliance* (New York: Knopf, 1975), pp. 194–221, 228–237.

61. Arendt, *Eichmann*, p. 93.

62. Bradley F. Smith, *Reaching Judgment at Nuremberg* (New York: Basic Books, 1977), pp. 104–105; Otto Kirchheimer, *Political Justice: The Use of Legal Procedure for Political Ends* (Princeton: Princeton University Press), pp. 337–338.

63. Victor Nekrasov, "The Shock of a Secret," *Encounter*, 50 (May 1978), 78.

64. "Editors' Note: On Eichmann and the Jews," *Partisan Review*, 30 (Summer 1963), 210; Irving Howe, " 'The New Yorker' and Hannah Arendt," *Commentary*, 36 (October 1963), 318–319; Estelle Gilson, "The Shaping of a Free Man: Irving Howe Profiled," *Present Tense*, 6 (Spring 1979), 26; Syrkin, "Clothes of the Empress," p. 344; "The Talk of the Town: Notes and Comment," *New Yorker*, 39 (July 20, 1963), 17.

65. Syrkin, "Miss Arendt Surveys the Holocaust," p. 14; Raziel Abelson, Letter to the Editor, *Commentary*, 37 (February 1964), 8.

66. Fruchter, "Arendt's Eichmann and Jewish Identity," in Weinstein and Eakins (editors), *For a New America*, pp. 427–428; Gerd Korman, "The Holocaust in American Historical Writing," *Societas*, 2 (Summer 1972), 269; Arthur A. Cohen, *Thinking the Tremendum: Some Theological Implications of the Death-Camps* (New York: Leo Baeck Institute, 1974), p. 23; Carl J. Friedrich, "Evolving Theory and Practice," in Carl J. Friedrich *et al.* (editors), *Totalitarianism in Perspective*, p. 160n.

67. Musmanno, "Unspotted Conscience," pp. 1, 41, and "Reply," *ibid.*, 4–5; Arendt, "Statement," p. 4.

68. Immanuel Kant, *Critique of Judgment* (New York: Macmillan, 1892), p. 172.

69. Irving Howe in "Arguments: More on Eichmann," *Partisan Review*, 31 (Spring 1964), 260; Salo W. Baron, "Personal Notes: Hannah Arendt (1906–1975)," *Jewish Social Studies*, 38 (Spring 1976), 188.

70. Norman Podhoretz, *Breaking Ranks: A Political Memoir* (New York: Harper and Row, 1979), p. 161.

71. Arendt, *Eichmann*, pp. 282–285, 295.

72. Hannah Arendt, *Between Past and Future: Eight Exercises in Political Thought* (New York: Viking, 1968), p. 227.

73. Laqueur, "Footnotes to the Holocaust," in Feldman (editor), *Jew as Pariah*, p. 254; Lionel Abel, Letter to the Editor, *New Republic*, 150 (April 4, 1964), 30; Fruchter, "Arendt's Eichmann and Jewish Identity," in Weinstein and Eakins (editors), *For a New America*, pp. 430, 439; Poliakov, "Eichmann Trial," p. 88.

74. Arendt, " 'The Formidable Dr. Robinson': A Reply" (1966), in Feldman (editor), *Jew as Pariah*, pp. 263–264; New York *Times*, October 28, 1977, II, 3.

75. Arendt, *Jew as Pariah*, p. 263.

76. *Ibid.*, pp. 274–276; *Intermountain Jewish News*, April 12, 1963, quoted in Macdonald, *Discriminations*, p. 308.

77. Arendt, *Jew as Pariah*, pp. 264–271.
78. *Ibid.*, pp. 269–270; Robinson, *Crooked Shall Be Made Straight*, pp. 159, 223–225.
79. Arendt, *Jew as Pariah*, p. 276; and *Eichmann*, p. 282; Joshua Rothenberg, "The Destruction of European Jewry," *Jewish Frontier*, 30 (March 1963), 26–30; Richard Rubenstein, *The Cunning of History: The Holocaust and the American Future* (New York: Harper and Row, 1978), pp. 70–73, 74–75, 110n.

Chapter 8

1. Hannah Arendt, "A Reply," *Review of Politics*, 15 (January 1953), 80.
2. Robert E. Meyerson, "Hannah Arendt: Romantic in a Totalitarian Age, 1928–1963" (Ph.D. dissertation, University of Minnesota, 1972), p. 7; Judith N. Shklar, *After Utopia: The Decline of Political Faith* (Princeton: Princeton University Press, 1957), pp. 107, 122–123, 128, 159.
3. Arendt, "A Reply," *Review of Politics*, p. 80.
4. A. J. P. Taylor quoted in Ved Mehta, *Fly and the Fly-Bottle: Encounters with British Intellectuals* (Boston: Little, Brown, 1962), p. 177.
5. Peter Stern and Jean Yarbrough, "Hannah Arendt," *American Scholar*, 47 (Summer 1978), 377.
6. Nabokov quoted in Andrew Field, *Nabokov: His Life in Art* (Boston: Little, Brown, 1967), p. 64.
7. Ron H. Feldman, Introduction to Feldman (editor), *The Jew as Pariah: Jewish Identity and Politics in the Modern Age* (New York: Grove, 1978), p. 48.
8. Gordon S. Wood, *The Creation of the American Republic, 1776–1787* (Chapel Hill: University of North Carolina Press, 1969), pp. 568, 575, 579, 583, 592.
9. Henry Adams, *The Education of Henry Adams* (Boston: Houghton Mifflin, 1961), p. 505.
10. Simone Pétrement, *Simone Weil: A Life* (New York: Pantheon, 1976), pp. 156, 158, 184–185, 188–190, 293, 343.
11. Weil quoted in *ibid.*, p. 511.
12. *Ibid.*, p. 184.
13. *Ibid.*, pp. 350, 356–360, 363; Hans Meyerhoff, "Contra Simone Weil: 'The Voices of Demons for the Silence of God,'" in Arthur A. Cohen (editor), *Arguments and Doctrines: A Reader of Jewish Think-*

308 *Into the Dark*

ing in the Aftermath of the Holocaust (New York: Harper and Row, 1970), p. 79.

14. *Ibid.*, p. 75; Pétrement, *Simone Weil*, pp. 342, 390–392, 443–444; Simone Weil, "What Is A Jew?," in Georgie A. Panichas (editor), *The Simone Weil Reader* (New York: David McKay, 1977), pp. 79–81.

15. Weil quoted in Richard Rees, *Simone Weil: A Sketch for a Portrait* (Carbondale: Southern Illinois University Press, 1966), p. 168.

16. Hannah Arendt, *The Human Condition* (Garden City, N.Y.: Doubleday Anchor, 1959), pp. 47, 68, 217–218, and *On Revolution* (New York: Viking, 1965), p. 81; Jacques Barzun (editor), *The Selected Writings of John Jay Chapman* (New York: Minerva Press, 1968), p. 190.

17. Dwight Macdonald, "A New Theory of Totalitarianism," *New Leader*, 34 (May 14, 1951), 19.

18. Arendt, *On Revolution*, p. 318; Dante Germino, *Beyond Ideology: The Revival of Political Theory* (New York: Harper and Row, 1967), p. 142.

19. George Kateb, "Freedom and Worldliness in the Thought of Hannah Arendt," *Political Theory*, 5 (May 1977), 141, 142, 143, 160; David Riesman, "The Path to Total Terror," *Commentary*, 11 (April 1951), 392.

20. George Lichtheim, "Three Critics of Totalitarianism," *Twentieth Century*, 150 (July 1951), 31; Philip Rieff, "The Theology of Politics: Reflections on Totalitarianism As the Burden of Our Time," *Journal of Religion*, 32 (April 1952), 123, 124; Benjamin I. Schwartz, "The Religion of Politics: Reflections on the Thought of Hannah Arendt," *Dissent*, 17 (March–April, 1970), 154–155.

21. Riesman, "Total Terror," p. 393.

22. Arendt, "Dilthey As Philosopher and Historian," *Partisan Review*, 12 (Summer 1945), 406.

23. Rieff, "Theology of Politics," p. 120; Kohn, "Where Terror Is the Essence," *Saturday Review*, 34 (March 24, 1951), 10.

24. Eric Voegelin, "The Origins of Totalitarianism," *Review of Politics*, 15 (January 1953), 76.

25. Benjamin R. Barber and Herbert J. Spiro, "Counter-Ideological Uses of 'Totalitarianism,' " *Politics and Society*, 1 (November 1970), 18–19; Robert Burrowes, "Totalitarianism: The Revised Standard Version," *World Politics*, 21 (January 1969), 280.

26. Margaret Canovan, *The Political Thought of Hannah Arendt* (New York: Harcourt Brace Jovanovich, 1974), p. 43; Barber, "Conceptual Foundations of Totalitarianism," in Friedrich *et al.*, *Totalitarian-*

ism in Perspective, p. 4; Henry S. Kariel, *In Search of Authority: Twentieth-Century Political Thought* (Glencoe, Ill.: Free Press, 1964), p. 248.

27. Arendt, "A Reply," pp. 78–79, and *The Origins of Totalitarianism* (New York: Harcourt, Brace and World, 1966), p. vii; Voegelin, "Origins of Totalitarianism," p. 71.

28. Hannah Arendt, "Understanding and Politics," *Partisan Review*, 20 (July–August 1953), 392.

29. Canovan, *Political Thought of Hannah Arendt*, pp. 39, 40, 46–47; H. Stuart Hughes, *The Sea Change: The Migration of Social Thought, 1930–1965* (New York: Harper and Row, 1975), p. 125; Joachim C. Fest, *The Face of the Third Reich: Portraits of the Nazi Leadership* (New York: Pantheon, 1970), p. 343.

30. N. K. O'Sullivan, "Politics, Totalitarianism and Freedom: The Political Thought of Hannah Arendt," *Political Studies*, 21 (June 1973), 192; Norman Podhoretz, *Doings and Undoings: The Fifties and After in American Writing* (New York: Farrar, Straus, 1964), p. 349.

31. Judith N. Shklar, "Hannah Arendt's Triumph," *New Republic*, 173 (December 27, 1975), 9.

32. Hannah Arendt, "Approaches to the 'German Problem,' " *Partisan Review*, 12 (Winter 1945), 95.

33. Hannah Arendt, "Martin Heidegger at Eighty," *New York Review of Books*, 17 (October 21, 1971), 54n.

BIBLIOGRAPHY

Abel, Lionel. "Aesthetics of Evil: Hannah Arendt on Eichmann and the Jews." *Partisan Review*, 30 (Summer 1963), 211–230.

Abelson, Raziel. "Intellectual Elitism." *New Leader*, 61 (May 22, 1978), 19–21.

Adams, Henry. *The Education of Henry Adams*. Boston: Houghton Mifflin, 1961.

Adler, Les K. and Thomas G. Paterson. "Red Fascism: The Merger of Nazi Germany and Soviet Russia in the American Image of Totalitarianism, 1930's–1950's." *American Historical Review*, 75 (April 1970), 1046 1064.

"Age and Power." *Saturday Review*, 51 (January 27, 1968), 26.

Allardyce, Gilbert. "What Fascism Is Not: Thoughts on the Deflation of a Concept." *American Historical Review*, 84 (April 1979), 367–388.

Allen, William Sheridan. *The Nazi Seizure of Power: The Experience of a Single German Town, 1930–1935*. Chicago: Quadrangle, 1965.

Allilueva, Svetlana. *Twenty Letters to a Friend*. New York: Harper and Row, 1967.

Alperovitz, Gar. *Atomic Diplomacy: Hiroshima and Potsdam*. New York: Vintage, 1965.

Alvarez, A. *Under Pressure: The Writer in Society, Eastern Europe and the U.S.A.* Baltimore: Penguin, 1965.

The Anti-Stalin Campaign and International Communism. Edited by the Russian Institute of Columbia University. New York: Columbia University Press, 1956.

Aquinas, Thomas. *Summa Theologiae*, XXVIII. New York: McGraw Hill, 1964.

Arendt, Hannah. "The Aftermath of Nazi Rule." *Commentary*, 10 (October 1950), 342–352.

———. "Approaches to the 'German Problem.'" *Partisan Review*, 12 (Winter 1945), 93–106.

[311]

———. "The Archimedean Point." *Ingenor*, 6 (Spring 1969), 5–9, 24–26.

———. *Between Past and Future: Eight Exercises in Political Thought.* New York: Viking, 1968.

———. *Crises of the Republic.* New York: Harcourt Brace Jovanovich, 1972.

———. "*The Deputy*: Guilt by Silence?" In Eric Bentley (editor), *The Storm over The Deputy.* New York: Grove, 1964.

———. "Dilthey as Philosopher and Historian." *Partisan Review*, 12 (Summer 1945), 404–406.

———. *Eichmann in Jerusalem: A Report on the Banality of Evil.* New York: Viking, 1963; rev. ed. 1964.

———. "The Ex-Communists." *Commonweal*, 57 (March 20, 1953), 595–599.

———. "Franz Kafka: A Revaluation." *Partisan Review*, 11 (Fall 1944), 412–422.

———. "He's All Dwight." *New York Review of Books*, 11 (August 1, 1968), 31–33.

———. "The Hole of Oblivion." *Jewish Frontier*, 14 (July 1947), 23–26.

———. "Home to Roost: A Bicentennial Address." *New York Review of Books*, 23 (June 26, 1975), 3–6.

———. *The Human Condition.* Garden City, New York: Doubleday Anchor, 1959.

———. *The Jew as Pariah: Jewish Identity and Politics in the Modern Age*, edited by Ron H. Feldman. New York: Grove, 1978.

———. Letter to the Editor. *Midstream*, 8 (Summer 1962), 85–87.

———. *The Life of the Mind.* New York: Harcourt Brace Jovanovich, 1978.

———. "Martin Heidegger at Eighty." *New York Review of Books*, 17 (October 21, 1971), 50–54.

———. *Men in Dark Times.* New York: Harcourt, Brace and World, 1968.

———. *On Revolution.* New York: Viking, 1965.

———. *The Origins of Totalitarianism.* Cleveland: World, 1958, and New York: Harcourt, Brace and World, 1966.

———. "Reflections on Little Rock." *Dissent*, 6 (Winter 1959), 45–56.

———. "Religion and the Intellectuals." *Partisan Review*, 17 (February 1950), 113–116.

———. "A Reply." *Review of Politics*, 15 (January 1953), 76–84.

———. "The Seeds of a Fascist International." *Jewish Frontier*, 12 (June 1945), 12–16.

———. "Social Science Techniques and the Study of Concentration Camps." *Jewish Social Studies*, 12 (January 1950), 49–64.

———. "A Statement." *New York Times Book Review*, June 23, 1963, 4.

———. "Understanding and Politics." *Partisan Review*, 20 (July–August 1953), 377–392.

———. "W. H. Auden." *New Yorker*, 50 (January 20, 1975), 39–46.

———. "What Is Existenz Philosophy?" *Partisan Review*, 13 (Winter 1946), 34–56.

——— and Gershom Scholem. "*Eichmann in Jerusalem*: An Exchange of Letters." *Encounter*, 22 (January 1964), 51–56.

"Arguments: More on Eichmann." *Partisan Review*, 31 (Spring 1964), 251–283.

Barber, Benjamin R. *Superman and Common Men: Freedom, Anarchy, and the Revolution.* New York: Praeger, 1971.

——— and Herbert J. Spiro. "Counter-Ideological Uses of 'Totalitarianism.' " *Politics and Society*, 1 (November 1970), 3–22.

Baron, Salo W. "Personal Notes: Hannah Arendt (1906–1975)." *Jewish Social Studies*, 38 (Spring 1976), 187–189.

Barraclough, Geoffrey. "Farewell to Hitler." *New York Review of Books*, 22 (April 3, 1975), 11–16.

———. "Hitler's Master Builder." *New York Review of Books*, 15 (January 7, 1971), 6–15.

Barrett, William. *The Illusion of Technique: A Search for Meaning in a Technological Civilization.* Garden City, N.Y.: Doubleday, 1978.

———. "Reader's Choice." *Atlantic Monthly*, 211 (March 1963), 157–159.

Barzun, Jacques. *The House of Intellect.* New York: Harper and Row, 1961.

——— (editor). *The Selected Writings of John Jay Chapman.* New York: Minerva Press, 1968.

Bauer, Raymond A. *The New Man in Soviet Psychology.* Cambridge: Harvard University Press, 1952.

Begin, Menachem. *White Nights: The Story of a Prisoner in Russia.* London: Macdonald, 1957.

Bell, Daniel. "The Alphabet of Justice." *Partisan Review*, 30 (Fall 1963), 417–429.

314 *Into the Dark*

———. *The Coming of Post-Industrial Society: A Venture in Social Forecasting.* New York: Basic Books, 1973.

———. *The End of Ideology: On the Exhaustion of Political Ideas in the Fifties.* New York: Free Press, 1962.

———. *Marxian Socialism in the United States.* Princeton: Princeton University Press, 1967.

Bellow, Saul. *Herzog.* New York: Viking, 1964.

———. *Mr. Sammler's Planet.* New York: Viking, 1970.

Belz, Herman. "New Left Reverberations in the Academy." *Review of Politics*, 36 (April 1974), 265–283.

Benda, Julien. *The Betrayal of the Intellectuals.* Boston: Beacon, 1955.

Benjamin, Walter. *Illuminations.* New York: Harcourt, Brace and World, 1968.

Benson, E. F. (editor). *Henry James: Letters to A. C. Benson and Auguste Monod.* New York: Scribner's, 1930.

Berdyaev, Nicholas. *The Origin of Russian Communism.* New York: Scribner's, 1937.

Berger, Joseph. *Shipwreck of a Generation.* London: Harvill Press, 1971.

Berlin, Isaiah. *Four Essays on Liberty.* New York: Oxford University Press, 1969.

Berman, Ronald. *America in the Sixties: An Intellectual History.* New York: Harper and Row, 1970.

Bernstein, Richard J. "Hannah Arendt: The Ambiguities of Theory and Practice." In Terence Ball (editor), *Political Theory and Praxis: New Perspectives.* Minneapolis: University of Minnesota Press, 1977.

Bettelheim, Bruno. "Eichmann, the System, the Victims." *New Republic*, 148 (June 15, 1963), 23–33.

———. *Surviving and Other Essays.* New York: Knopf, 1979.

Biale, David. *Gershom Scholem: Kabbalah and Counter-History.* Cambridge: Harvard University Press, 1979.

Bieber, Hugo (editor). *Heinrich Heine: A Biographical Anthology.* Philadelphia: Jewish Publication Society, 1956.

Binion, Rudolph. *Hitler Among the Germans.* New York: Elsevier, 1976.

Bloch, Sidney, and Peter Reddaway. *Psychiatric Terror: How Soviet Psychiatric Terror Is Used to Suppress Dissent.* New York: Basic Books, 1977.

Blum, Howard. *Wanted!: The Search for Nazis in America.* Chicago: Quadrangle, 1977.

Bracher, Karl Dietrich. "Totalitarianism." *Dictionary of the History of Ideas*, IV. New York: Scribner's, 1973.

Bramson, Leon. *The Political Context of Sociology.* Princeton: Princeton University Press, 1961.

Brandeis, Louis D., and Samuel D. Warren. "The Right to Privacy." *Harvard Law Review*, 4 (December 1890), 193–220.

Brecht, Bertolt. *Stücke: Aus dem Exil*, IX. Berlin: Suhrkamp Verlag, 1957.

Brzezinski, Zbigniew K. *Permanent Purge: Politics in Soviet Totalitarianism.* Cambridge: Harvard University Press, 1956.

Buber-Neumann, Margarete. *Under Two Dictators.* New York: Dodd-Mead, 1949.

Buchheim, Hans. *Totalitarian Rule: Its Nature and Characteristics.* Middletown, Conn.: Wesleyan University Press, 1968.

Bullock, Alan. *Hitler: A Study in Tyranny.* New York: Bantam, 1961.

Burrowes, Robert. "Totalitarianism: The Revised Standard Version." *World Politics*, 21 (January 1969), 272–294.

Canovan, Margaret. "The Contradictions of Hannah Arendt's Political Thought." *Political Theory*, 6 (February 1978), 5–26.

———. *The Political Thought of Hannah Arendt.* New York: Harcourt Brace Jovanovich, 1974.

Capote, Truman. *In Cold Blood.* New York: Random House, 1966.

Chambers, Whittaker. *Witness.* Chicago: Henry Regnery, 1952.

Clark, Ronald W. *The Life of Bertrand Russell.* New York: Knopf, 1976.

Coffin, William Sloane. *Once to Every Man: A Memoir.* New York: Atheneum, 1977.

Cohen, Arthur A. *Thinking the Tremendum: Some Theological Implications of the Death-Camps.* New York: Leo Baeck Institute, 1974.

Cohen, Jacob. "Through Liberal Glasses, Darkly." *Jewish Frontier*, 30 (January 1963), 7–10.

Cohn, Norman. *Warrant for Genocide: The Myth of the Jewish World-Conspiracy and the Protocols of the Elders of Zion.* New York: Harper and Row, 1967.

Conquest, Robert. *The Great Terror: Stalin's Purge of the Thirties.* New York: Macmillan, 1968.

———. *The Nation Killers: The Soviet Deportation of Nationalities.* New York: Macmillan, 1970.

Conrad, Joseph. *Under Western Eyes.* New York: Doubleday, Doran, 1938.

Cooper, Leroy A. "Hannah Arendt's Political Philosophy: An Interpretation." *Review of Politics*, 38 (April 1976), 145–176.

Crick, Bernard. "Hannah Arendt." *Times* (London), December 12, 1975, 18.

———. *In Defence of Politics*. Chicago: University of Chicago Press, 1972.

———. "On Rereading *The Origins of Totalitarianism*." *Social Research*, 44 (Spring 1977), 106–126.

Cuddihy, John Murray. *The Ordeal of Civility: Freud, Marx, Lévi-Strauss, and the Jewish Struggle with Modernity*. New York: Basic Books, 1974.

Custine, Marquis de. *Journey for Our Time*. New York: Pellegrini and Cudahy, 1951.

Dahl, Robert. *Who Governs?: Democracy and Power in an American City*. New Haven: Yale University Press, 1961.

Dallin, David J., and Boris I. Nicolaevsky. *Forced Labor in Soviet Russia*. New Haven: Yale University Press, 1947.

Davis, Douglas. "A Life of the Mind." *Newsweek*, 86 (December 15, 1975), 84.

Dawidowicz, Lucy S. (editor). *The Golden Tradition: Jewish Life and Thought in Eastern Europe*. Boston: Beacon, 1968.

———. *The Jewish Presence: Essays on Identity and History*. New York: Holt, Rinehart and Winston, 1977.

———. "Visualizing the Warsaw Ghetto." *Shoah*, 1, no. 1 (1978), 5–6.

———. *The War Against the Jews, 1933–1945*. New York: Bantam, 1976.

Degras, Jane (editor). *Soviet Documents on Foreign Policy*, III. London: Oxford University Press, 1953.

DeGré, Gerard. "Freedom and Social Structure." *American Sociological Review*, 11 (October 1946), 529–536.

Dempsey, David. "Bruno Bettelheim is Dr. No." *New York Times Magazine*, January 11, 1970, 22–23.

Dershowitz, Alan. "A Conversation with Telford Taylor '32." *Harvard Law School Bulletin*, 30 (Winter 1979), 29–31, 52.

Des Pres, Terrence. *The Survivor: An Anatomy of Life in the Death Camps*. New York: Pocket Books, 1977.

Deutscher, Isaac. *The Prophet Outcast: Trotsky, 1929–1940*. New York: Vintage, 1965.

———. *Stalin: A Political Biography*. New York: Vintage, 1960.

Diggins, John P. *Mussolini and Fascism: The View from America*. Princeton: Princeton University Press, 1972.

————. *Up from Communism: Conservative Odysseys in American Intel-lectual History.* New York: Harper and Row, 1975.

Djilas, Milovan. *Conversations with Stalin.* New York: Harcourt, Brace and World, 1962.

Donat, Alexander. *The Holocaust Kingdom: A Memoir.* New York: Holt, Rinehart and Winston, 1965.

Donoghue, Denis. "After Reading Hannah Arendt." *Poetry,* 100 (May 1962), 127–130.

Eade, Charles (editor). *The War Speeches of the Rt. Hon. Winston Churchill,* I. London: Cassell, 1951.

Eastman, Max. *Reflections on the Failure of Socialism.* New York: Devin-Adair, 1955.

Ebenstein, William. "The Study of Totalitarianism." *World Politics,* 10 (January 1958), 274–288.

Eck, Nathan. "Historical Research or Slander?" *Yad Vashem Studies,* 6 (1967), 385–430.

Eckstein, Harry, and David E. Apter (editors). *Comparatve Politics.* New York: Free Press, 1963.

Edwards, Scott E. "The Political Thought of Hannah Arendt: A Study in Thought and Action." Ph.D. dissertation, Claremont Graduate School, 1964.

"*Eichmann in Jerusalem*—Can One Know the 'Whole' Truth?" *Newsweek,* 61 (June 17, 1963), 94–95.

Elevitch, Bernard. "Arendt and Heidegger: The Illusion of Politics." *Boston University Journal,* 20, No. 182 (1972), 62–65.

Esslin, Martin. *Brecht: The Man and His Work.* Garden City, N.Y.: Doubleday Anchor, 1961.

Fackenheim, Emil L. *The Jewish Return into History: Reflections in the Age of Auschwitz and a New Jerusalem.* New York: Schocken, 1978.

————. "Kant and Radical Evil." *University of Toronto Quarterly,* 23 (Fall 1954), 339–353.

Fainsod, Merle. *How Russia Is Ruled.* Cambridge: Harvard University Press, 1953.

Falk, Richard A., Gabriel Kolko and Robert Jay Lifton (editors). *Crimes of War.* New York: Vintage, 1971.

Feingold, Henry L. "Roosevelt and the Resettlement Question," in *Rescue Attempts during the Holocaust: Proceedings of the Second Yad Vashem International Historical Conference.* Jerusalem: Yad Vashem, 1977.

————. "Who Shall Bear Guilt for the Holocaust: The Human Dilemma." *American Jewish History*, 58 (March 1979), 261–282.

Fest, Joachim C. *The Face of the Third Reich: Portraits of the Nazi Leadership.* New York: Pantheon, 1970.

Feuer, Kathryn (editor). *Solzhenitsyn: A Collection of Critical Essays.* Englewood Cliffs, N.J.: Prentice-Hall, 1976.

Feuer, Lewis S. *Ideology and the Ideologists.* New York: Harper and Row, 1975.

Fiedler, Leslie. "Toward the Freudian Pill." In Murray A. Sperber (editor), *Arthur Koestler: A Collection of Critical Essays.* Englewood Cliffs, N.J.: Prentice-Hall, 1977.

Field, Andrew. *Nabokov: His Life in Art.* Boston: Little, Brown, 1967.

————. *Nabokov: His Life in Part.* New York: Penguin, 1978.

Fischer, Fritz. *Germany's Aims in the First World War.* New York: Norton, 1967.

Fleischner, Eva (editor). *Auschwitz: Beginning of a New Era?: Reflections on the Holocaust.* New York: Ktav, 1977.

Fowler, Robert Booth. *Believing Skeptics: American Political Intellectuals, 1945–1964.* Westport, Conn.: Greenwood Press, 1978.

Franklin, Bruce (editor). *The Essential Stalin: Major Theoretical Writings, 1905–52.* Garden City, N.Y.: Doubleday Anchor, 1972.

Freud, Sigmund. *Character and Culture.* New York: Collier, 1963.

Friedländer, Saul. *Pius XII and the Third Reich: A Documentation.* New York: Knopf, 1966.

Friedrich, Carl J. (editor). *Totalitarianism.* New York: Grosset and Dunlap, 1966.

———— and Zbigniew K. Brzezinski. *Totalitarian Dictatorship and Autocracy.* New York: Praeger, 1961.

————, Michael Curtis and Benjamin R. Barber. *Totalitarianism in Perspective: Three Views.* New York: Praeger, 1969.

Fruchter, Norman. "Arendt's Eichmann and Jewish Identity." In James Weinstein and David W. Eakins (editors), *For a New America: Essays in History and Politics from "Studies on the Left," 1959–1967.* New York: Vintage, 1970.

Fuss, Peter. "Hannah Arendt's Conception of Political Community." *Idealistic Studies*, 3 (September 1973), 252–265.

Galbraith, John Kenneth. *A Contemporary Guide to Economics, Peace and Laughter.* Boston: Houghton Mifflin, 1971.

Gay, Peter. *Weimar Culture: The Outsider as Insider.* New York: Harper and Row, 1968.

Germino, Dante. *Beyond Ideology: The Revival of Political Theory.* New York: Harper and Row, 1967.

Gerratana, Valentino. "Heidegger and Marx." *New Left Review,* 106 (November–December 1977), 51–58.

Gilbert, James Burkhart. *Writers and Partisans: A History of Literary Radicalism in America.* New York: John Wiley, 1968.

Gilson, Estelle. "The Shaping of a Free Man: Irving Howe Profiled." *Present Tense,* 6 (Spring 1979), 25–29.

Ginzburg, Evgenia S. *Into the Whirlwind.* London: Penguin, 1968.

Glazer, Nathan. "Hannah Arendt's America." *Commentary,* 60 (September 1975), 61–67.

Golden, Harry. "A Stranger to the Human Race." In Louis L. Snyder and Richard B. Morris (editors), *A Treasury of Great Reporting.* New York: Simon and Schuster, 1962.

Goldhagen, Erich. "Albert Speer, Himmler, and the Secrecy of the Final Solution." *Midstream,* 17 (October 1971), 43–50.

Goldstein, Bernard. *The Stars Bear Witness.* New York: Viking, 1949.

Gray, Francine du Plessix. "Thomas Merton: Man and Monk." *New Republic,* 180 (May 26, 1979), 23–30.

Gross, John. "Arendt on Eichmann." *Encounter,* 21 (November 1963), 65–74.

Groth, Alexander J. "The 'Isms' in Totalitarianism." *American Political Science Review,* 58 (December 1964), 888–901.

Grunberger, Richard. *The Twelve-Year Reich: A Social History of Nazi Germany, 1933–1945.* New York: Holt, Rinehart and Winston, 1971.

Gutman, Yisrael. "Adam Czerniakow: The Man and His Diary." In Yisrael Gutman and Livia Rothkirchen (editors), *The Catastrophe of European Jewry: Antecedents, History, Reflections.* Jerusalem: Yad Vashem, 1976.

Hall, Elizabeth. "The Freakish Passion: A Conversation with George Steiner." *Psychology Today,* 6 (February 1973), 57–69.

Handlin, Oscar. "Jewish Resistance to the Nazis." *Commentary,* 34 (November 1962), 398–405.

Harrington, Michael. *Socialism.* New York: Saturday Review Press, 1972.

Harrower, Molly. "Were Hitler's Henchmen Mad?" *Psychology Today,* 10 (July 1976), 76–80.

Hausner, Gideon. *Justice in Jerusalem.* New York: Harper and Row, 1966.

Hayek, Friedrich A. *The Road to Serfdom.* Chicago: University of Chicago Press, 1944.

Heiden, Konrad. *Der Fuehrer: Hitler's Rise to Power.* Boston: Houghton Mifflin, 1944.

Heller, Erich. "Dark Laughter." *New York Review of Books,* 20 (May 3, 1973), 21–25.

———. *The Disinherited Mind: Essays in Modern German Literature and Thought.* Cleveland: Meridian, 1959.

———. "Hannah Arendt as a Critic of Literature." *Social Research,* 44 (Spring 1977), 147–159.

Hellman, Lillian. *Scoundrel Time.* New York: Bantam, 1977.

Hennessee, Judith Adler. "Annals of Checking." In Richard Pollak (editor), *Stop the Presses, I Want to Get Off!: Inside Stories of the News Business from the Pages of [MORE].* New York: Dell, 1975.

Herman, Victor. *Coming Out of the Ice: An Unexpected Life.* New York: Harcourt Brace Jovanovich, 1979.

Hilberg, Raul. *The Destruction of the European Jews.* Chicago: Quadrangle, 1961.

———. "The *Einsatzgruppen.*" *Societas,* 2 (Summer 1972), 241–249.

Hill, Melvyn A. (editor). *Hannah Arendt: The Recovery of the Public World.* New York: St. Martin's, 1979.

Himmelfarb, Milton. *The Jews of Modernity.* New York: Basic Books, 1973.

Hochhuth, Rolf. *The Deputy.* New York: Grove, 1964.

Hoess, Rudolf. *Commandant of Auschwitz.* London: Weidenfeld and Nicolson, 1959.

Hoffer, Eric. *The True Believer: Thoughts on the Nature of Mass Movements.* New York: Harper and Brothers, 1951.

Hofstadter, Richard. *The Idea of a Party System: The Rise of Legitimate Opposition in the United States, 1780–1840.* Berkeley: University of California Press, 1969.

———. *The Paranoid Style in American Politics and Other Essays.* New York: Vintage, 1967.

Holborn, Louise W. "The Legal Status of Political Refugees, 1920–1938." *American Journal of International Law,* 32 (October 1938), 680–703.

Hook, Sidney. "Hannah Arendt's Reflections." *Dissent,* 6 (Spring 1959), 203.

———. Letter to the Editor. *Encounter,* 50 (March 1978), 93.

————. *Political Power and Personal Freedom*. New York: Criterion, 1959.

————. *Reason, Social Myths and Democracy*. New York: Humanities Press, 1940.

————. "A Recollection of Berthold Brecht." *New Leader*, 43 (October 10, 1960), 22–23.

Horkheimer, Max, and Theodor W. Adorno. *Dialectic of Enlightenment*. New York: Herder and Herder, 1972.

Horowitz, Irving Louis. *Genocide: State Power and Mass Murder*. New Brunswick, N.J.: Transaction Books, 1977.

Hough, Jerry F. and Merle Fainsod. *How the Soviet Union Is Governed*. Cambridge: Harvard University Press, 1979.

Howe, Irving. *Decline of the New*. New York: Horizon, 1970.

————. *Leon Trotsky*. New York: Penguin, 1979.

————. " 'The New Yorker' and Hannah Arendt." *Commentary*, 36 (October 1963), 318–319.

Hughes, H. Stuart. "Historical Sources of Totalitarianism." *Nation*, 172 (March 24, 1951), 280–281.

————. *The Sea Change: The Migration of Social Thought, 1930–1965*. New York: Harper and Row, 1975.

Jäckel, Eberhard. *Hitler's Weltanschauung: A Blueprint for Power*. Middletown, Conn.: Wesleyan University Press, 1972.

James, Henry. *Hawthorne*. London: Macmillan, 1887.

Jaspers, Karl. *Man in the Modern Age*. Garden City, N.Y.: Doubleday Anchor, 1957.

————. *The Question of German Guilt*. New York: Capricorn, 1961.

Jay, Martin. *The Dialectical Imagination: A History of the Frankfurt School and the Institute of Social Research, 1923–1950*. Boston: Little, Brown, 1973.

Kadushin, Charles. "Who Are the Elite Intellectuals?" *Public Interest*, 29 (Fall 1972), 109–125.

Kant, Immanuel. *Critique of Judgment*. New York: Macmillan, 1892.

————. *Religion within the Limits of Reason Alone*. New York: Harper and Row, 1960.

Kaplan, Abraham. "The Life of Reason and Historical Piety." *Judaism*, 10 (Fall 1961), 314–317.

Kariel, Henry S. *In Search of Authority: Twentieth-Century Political Thought*. Glencoe, Ill.: Free Press, 1964.

Kateb, George. "Freedom and Worldliness in the Thought of Hannah Arendt." *Political Theory*, 5 (May 1977), 141–181.

Kaufmann, Walter. *From Shakespeare to Existentialism*. Garden City, N.Y.: Doubleday Anchor, 1960.

——(editor). *The Portable Nietzsche*. New York: Viking, 1954.

Kazin, Alfred. *New York Jew*. New York: Knopf, 1978.

——. "Outstanding Books, 1931–1961." *American Scholar*, 30 (Winter 1961), 612.

Kendrick, Alexander. *Prime Time: The Life of Edward R. Murrow*. Boston: Little, Brown, 1969.

Kennan, George F. "Between Earth and Hell." *New York Review of Books*, 21 (March 21, 1974), 3–6.

——. *Memoirs, 1925–1950*. Boston: Little, Brown, 1967.

Kennedy v. *Mendoza-Martinez*. 372 U.S. 144 (1963).

King, Richard. *The Party of Eros: Radical Social Thought and the Realm of Freedom*. Chapel Hill: University of North Carolina Press, 1972.

Kirchheimer, Otto. *Political Justice: The Use of Legal Procedure for Political Ends*. Princeton: Princeton University Press, 1961.

Kirk, Russell. *Eliot and His Age*. New York: Random House, 1971.

Kitto, H. D. F. *The Greeks*. Baltimore: Penguin, 1960.

Klaidman, Stephen. "The Nazi Hunters: Justice, Not Vengeance." *Present Tense*, 4 (Winter 1977), 21–26.

Klein, Mary Katherine McKeon. "The Concept of Political Freedom in Hannah Arendt." Ph.D. dissertation, Boston University, 1973.

Knauer, James T. "Hannah Arendt and the Reassertion of the Political: Toward a New Democratic Theory." Ph.D. dissertation, State University of New York at Binghamton, 1975.

Koestler, Arthur. *Darkness at Noon*. New York: Modern Library, 1941.

——. *The Invisible Writing*. Boston: Beacon, 1955.

——. *The Yogi and the Commissar and Other Essays*. New York: Macmillan, 1945.

Kogon, Eugen. *The Theory and Practice of Hell*. New York: Berkeley Medallion, 1958.

Kohn, Hans. "Communist and Fascist Dictatorship: A Comparative Study." In Guy Stanton Ford (editor), *Dictatorship in the Modern World*. Minneapolis: University of Minnesota Press, 1935.

——. *The Mind of Germany: The Education of a Nation*. New York: Scribner's, 1960.

——. *Pan-Slavism: Its History and Ideology*. New York: Vintage, 1960.

——. "Where Terror is the Essence." *Saturday Review*, 34 (March 24, 1951), 10–11.

Kopelev, Lev. *To Be Preserved Forever*. Philadelphia: Lippincott, 1977.

Korman, Gerd. "The Holocaust in American Historical Writing." *Societas*, 2 (Summer 1972), 251–270.

Kornhauser, William. *The Politics of Mass Society*. Glencoe, Ill.: Free Press, 1959.

Kovály, Heda and Erazim Kohák. *The Victors and the Vanquished* New York: Horizon, 1973.

Kowal, Michael. "The Liberal Critic." *Judaism*, 13 (Fall 1964), 496–501.

Kuklick, Bruce. "Tradition and Diplomatic Talent: The Case of the Cold Warriors." In Leila Zenderland (editor), *Recycling the Past: Popular Uses of American History*. Philadelphia: University of Pennsylvania Press, 1978.

Langer, Lawrence L. *The Holocaust and the Literary Imagination*. New Haven: Yale University Press, 1975.

Laqueur, Walter (editor). *Fascism, A Reader's Guide: Analyses, Interpretations, Bibliography*. Berkeley: University of California Press, 1976.

———. "Nazism and the Nazis." *Encounter*, 22 (April 1964), 39–46.

———. *Russia and Germany: A Century of Conflict*. Boston: Little, Brown, 1965.

Laski, Harold J. *Law and Justice in Soviet Russia*. London: Hogarth, 1935.

LeBon, Gustave. *The Crowd: A Study of the Popular Mind*. New York: Viking, 1960.

Lemkin, Raphael. *Axis Rule in Europe: Laws of Occupation, Analysis of Government, Proposals for Redress*. Washington, D.C.: Carnegie Endowment for International Peace, 1944.

Leonhard, Wolfgang. *Child of the Revolution*. Chicago: Henry Regnery, 1958.

———. *The Kremlin since Stalin*. New York: Praeger, 1962.

Lewis, Oscar. *La Vida: A Puerto Rican Family in the Culture of Poverty—San Juan and New York*. New York: Random House, 1966.

Lewy, Guenter. *The Catholic Church and Nazi Germany*. New York: McGraw-Hill, 1964.

Lichtheim, George. *The Concept of Ideology and Other Essays*. New York: Random House, 1967.

———. *Marxism: An Historical and Critical Study*. New York: Praeger, 1961.

———. *Marxism in Modern France*. New York: Columbia University Press, 1966.

———— ["G. L. Arnold"]. "Three Critics of Totalitarianism." *Twentieth Century*, 150 (July 1951), 23–34.

Lind, Jakov. *Counting My Steps: An Autobiography*. New York: Macmillan, 1969.

————. *Soul of Wood and Other Stories*. New York: Fawcett, 1966.

Lippmann, Walter. "The American Idea." In Clinton Rossiter and James Lare (editors), *The Essential Lippmann: A Political Philosophy for Liberal Democracy*. New York: Random House, 1963.

————. *The Cold War: A Study in U.S. Foreign Policy*. New York: Harper and Row, 1972.

————. *The Good Society*. Boston: Little, Brown, 1937.

————. "Public Opinion and the American Jew." *American Hebrew*, 110 (April 14, 1922), 575.

————. *The Public Philosophy*. Boston: Little, Brown, 1955.

Lipset, Seymour Martin. *Political Man: The Social Bases of Politics*. Garden City, N.Y.: Doubleday Anchor, 1963.

Lowenthal, Richard. "Totalitarianism Reconsidered." *Commentary*, 29 (June 1960), 504–512.

Luthy, Herbert. "Of Poor Bert Brecht." *Encounter*, 7 (July 1956), 33–53.

Luxemburg, Rosa. *The Russian Revolution and Leninism or Marxism?* Ann Arbor: University of Michigan Press, 1961.

Lynd, Staughton. *Intellectual Origins of American Radicalism*. New York: Vintage, 1969.

Macdonald, Dwight. *Discriminations: Essays and Afterthoughts, 1938–1974*. New York: Grossman, 1974.

————. *Memoirs of a Revolutionist: Essays in Political Criticism*. Cleveland: World, 1958.

————. "A New Theory of Totalitarianism." *New Leader*, 34 (May 14, 1951), 17–19.

Mandelstam, Nadezhda. *Hope Against Hope: A Memoir*. New York: Atheneum, 1970.

Marcuse, Herbert. *Five Lectures*. Boston: Beacon, 1970.

————. *Negations: Essays in Critical Theory*. Boston: Beacon, 1968.

————. *One-Dimensional Man: Studies in the Ideology of Advanced Industrial Society*. Boston: Beacon, 1964.

McCarthy, Mary. *On the Contrary: Articles of Belief, 1946–1961*. New York: Farrar, Straus and Giroux, 1961.

————. *The Writing on the Wall and Other Literary Essays*. New York: Harcourt, Brace and World, 1970.

McKenna, George. "A Critic of Modernity: The Political Thought of Hannah Arendt." Ph.D. dissertation, Fordham University, 1967.

———. "On Hannah Arendt: Politics As It Is, Was, Might Be." *Salmagundi*, 10–11 (Fall 1969–Winter 1970), 104–122.

Medvedev, Roy A. *Let History Judge: The Origins and Consequences of Stalinism*. New York: Knopf, 1972.

Medvedev, Zhores A. *Ten Years after Ivan Denisovich*. New York: Vintage, 1974.

Mehta, Ved. *Fly and the Fly-Bottle: Encounters with British Intellectuals*. Boston: Little, Brown, 1962.

Melville, Herman. *Billy Budd and The Piazza Tales*. Garden City, N.Y.: Doubleday Anchor, 1973.

Merton, Thomas. *Raids on the Unspeakable*. New York: New Directions, 1966.

Meyerhoff, Hans. "Contra Simone Weil: 'The Voices of Demons for the Silence of God,'" in Arthur A. Cohen (editor). *Arguments and Doctrines: A Reader of Jewish Thinking in the Aftermath of the Holocaust*. New York: Harper and Row, 1970.

Meyerson, Robert E. "Hannah Arendt: Romantic in a Totalitarian Age, 1928–1963." Ph.D. dissertation, University of Minnesota, 1972.

Milgram, Stanley. *Obedience to Authority: An Experimental View*. New York: Harper and Row, 1974.

Miller, Stephen. "Bureaucracy Baiting." *American Scholar*, 47 (Spring 1978), 205–222.

Mills, C. Wright. *The Power Elite*. New York: Oxford University Press, 1956.

Moore, Barrington, Jr., *Injustice: The Social Bases of Obedience and Revolt*. White Plains, N.Y.: M. E. Sharpe, 1978.

———. *Social Origins of Dictatorship and Democracy: Lord and Peasant in the Making of the Modern World*. Boston: Beacon, 1966.

Morgenthau, Hans J. "Hannah Arendt on Totalitarianism and Democracy." *Social Research*, 44 (Spring 1977), 127–131.

———. *Truth and Power: Essays of a Decade, 1960–70*. New York: Praeger, 1970.

Mosse, George L. *The Crisis of German Ideology: Intellectual Origins of the Third Reich*. New York: Grosset and Dunlap, 1964.

Muller, Sharon. "The Origins of *Eichmann in Jerusalem*: An Examination of Hannah Arendt's Interpretation of Jewish History." Unpublished paper, Columbia University, 1979.

Musmanno, Michael A. "Man wth an Unspotted Conscience." *New York Times Book Review*, May 19, 1963, 1, 40–41.

———. "A Reply." *New York Times Book Review*, June 23, 1963, pp. 4–5.

Nabokov, Vladimir. *Bend Sinister*. New York: Time, Inc., 1964.

Nash, George H. *The Conservative Intellectual Movement in America: Since 1945*. New York: Basic Books, 1979.

Nekrasov, Victor. "The Shock of a Secret." *Encounter*, 50 (May 1978), 75–80.

Nettl, J. P. *Rosa Luxemburg*. London: Oxford University Press, 1966.

Neumann, Franz. *Behemoth: The Structure and Practice of National Socialism, 1933–1944*. New York: Harper and Row, 1966.

———. *The Democratic and the Authoritarian State: Essays in Political and Legal Theory*. New York: Free Press, 1957.

Nicolaevsky, Boris I. *Power and the Soviet Elite*. Ann Arbor: University of Michigan Press, 1975.

Niebuhr, Reinhold. *The Nature and Destiny of Man*. New York: Scribner's, 1941.

Noakes, Jeremy, and Geoffrey Pridham (editors). *Documents on Nazism, 1919–1945*. New York: Viking, 1974.

Nobile, Philip. *Intellectual Skywriting: Literary Politics and the New York Review of Books*. New York: Charterhouse, 1974.

Nolte, Ernst. *Three Faces of Fascism: Action Française, Italian Fascism, National Socialism*. New York: Holt, Rinehart and Winston, 1966.

O'Boyle, Lenore. "The Class Concept in History." *Journal of Modern History*, 24 (December 1952), 391–397.

Olmstead v. *United States*. 277 U.S. 438 (1927).

Orwell, Sonia, and Ian Angus (editors). *The Collected Essays, Journalism and Letters of George Orwell*, II and IV. New York: Harcourt Brace Jovanovich, 1968.

O'Sullivan, N. K. "Politics, Totalitarianism and Freedom: The Political Thought of Hannah Arendt." *Political Studies*, 21 (June 1973), 183–198.

Ozick, Cynthia. "All the World Wants the Jews Dead." *Esquire*, 82 (November 1974), 103–107.

Pachter, Henry. "On Being an Exile: An Old-Timer's Personal and Political Memoir." *Salmagundi*, 10–11 (Fall 1969–Winter 1970), 12–51.

Parenti, Michael. *The Anti-Communist Impulse*. New York: Random House, 1969.

Perez v. *Brownell*, 356 U.S. 44 (1958).

Pétrement, Simone. *Simone Weil: A Life.* New York: Pantheon, 1976.

Phillips, William. *A Sense of the Present: Essays and Stories of Two Decades.* New York: Chilmark, 1967.

Pipes, Richard. "Revisionist Revision." *Commentary,* 68 (October 1979), 86–88.

Pitkin, Hanna Fenichel. "The Roots of Conservatism: Oakeshott and the Denial of Politics." *Dissent,* 20 (Fall 1973), 496–525.

———. *Wittgenstein and Justice: On the Significance of Ludwig Wittgenstein for Social and Political Thought.* Berkeley: University of California Press, 1972.

Plamenetz, John. *Ideology.* New York: Praeger, 1970.

Podhoretz, Norman. *Breaking Ranks: A Political Memoir.* New York: Harper and Row, 1979.

———. *Doings and Undoings: The Fifties and After in American Writing.* New York: Farrar, Straus, 1964.

———. *Making It.* New York: Random House, 1967.

Poliakov, Léon. "The Eichmann Trial." *Commentary,* 43 (January 1967), 86–90.

———. "Pope Pius XII and the Nazis." In Eric Bentley (editor), *The Storm over The Deputy.* New York: Grove, 1964.

[Pollak, Stephen J.] "The Expatriation Act of 1954." *Yale Law Journal,* 64 (July 1955), 1164–1200.

Presser, Jacob. *Ashes in the Wind: The Destruction of Dutch Jewry.* London: Souvenir Press, 1968.

Rabinowitz, Dorothy. *New Lives: Survivors of the Holocaust Living in America.* New York: Avon, 1977.

Rauschning, Hermann. *Hitler Speaks.* London: Thornton Butterworth, 1939.

Rees, Richard. *Simone Weil: A Sketch for a Portrait.* Carbondale: Southern Illinois University Press, 1966.

Reich, Charles A. "The Tragedy of Justice in *Billy Budd.*" *Yale Review,* 56, New Series (Spring 1967), 368–389.

Rich, Norman. *Hitler's War Aims: Ideology, the Nazi State, and the Course of Expansion,* I. New York: Norton, 1973.

Rieff, Philip. *Fellow Teachers.* New York: Harper and Row, 1973.

——— (editor). *On Intellectuals: Theoretical Studies, Case Studies.* Garden City, N.Y.: Doubleday Anchor, 1970.

———. "The Theology of Politics: Reflections on Totalitarianism As the Burden of Our Time." *Journal of Religion,* 32 (April 1952), 119–126.

Riesman, David. *Individualism Reconsidered and Other Essays.* Glencoe, Ill.: Free Press, 1954.

———. "The Path to Total Terror." *Commentary,* 11 (April 1951), 392–398.

Robinson, Jacob. *And the Crooked Shall Be Made Straight: The Eichmann Trial, the Jewish Catastrophe, and Hannah Arendt's Narrative.* Philadelphia: Jewish Publication Society, 1965.

Rogat, Yosal. *The Eichmann Trial and the Rule of Law.* Santa Barbara, Cal.: Center for the Study of Democratic Institutions, 1961.

Rosen, Stanley. *Nihilism: A Philosophical Essay.* New Haven: Yale University Press, 1969.

Rosenberg, Harold. "The Shadow of the Furies." *New York Review of Books,* 23 (January 20, 1977), 47–49.

———. "The Trial and Eichmann." *Commentary,* 32 (November 1961), 369–381.

Rossi, A. *The Russo-German Alliance: August 1939–June 1941.* Boston: Beacon, 1951.

Roszak, Theodore. *The Making of a Counter Culture: Reflections on the Technocratic Society and Its Youthful Opposition.* Garden City, N.Y.: Doubleday Anchor, 1969.

Rothenberg, Joshua. "The Destruction of European Jewry." *Jewish Frontier,* 30 (March 1963), 25–30.

Rousset, David. *The Other Kingdom.* New York: Reynal and Hitchcock, 1947.

Rovere, Richard H., and Arthur Schlesinger, Jr. *The MacArthur Controversy and American Foreign Policy.* New York: Farrar, Straus and Giroux, 1965.

Rubenstein, Richard. *The Cunning of History: The Holocaust and the American Future.* New York: Harper and Row, 1978.

Sabine, George H. *A History of Political Theory.* New York: Henry Holt, 1937.

Samuel, Maurice. *In Praise of Yiddish.* Chicago: Cowles, 1971.

Samuelson, Paul. "Wages and Interest: A Modern Dissection of Marxian Economic Models." *American Economic Review,* 47 (December 1957), 884–912.

Sarraute, Nathalie. *The Age of Suspicion.* New York: George Braziller, 1963.

Sartre, Jean-Paul. *Anti-Semite and Jew.* New York: Grove, 1960.

Sauer, Wolfgang. "National Socialism: Totalitarianism or Fascism?" *American Historical Review,* 73 (December 1967), 404–424.

Schapiro, Leonard. *The Communist Party of the Soviet Union.* New York: Random House, 1960.

———. *Totalitarianism.* New York: Praeger, 1972.

Schappes, Morris U. *The Strange World of Hannah Arendt.* New York: Jewish Currents, 1963.

Schlesinger, Arthur M., Jr. "The Cold War Revisited." *New York Review of Books,* 26 (October 25, 1979), 46–52.

———. *The Politics of Hope.* Boston: Houghton Mifflin, 1963.

Schleunes, Karl A. *The Twisted Road to Auschwitz: Nazi Policy Toward German Jews, 1933–1939.* Urbana: University of Illinois Press, 1970.

Schnabel, Ernst. *Anne Frank: A Portrait in Courage.* New York: Harcourt, Brace, 1958.

Schoenbaum, David. *Hitler's Social Revolution: Class and Status in Nazi Germany, 1933–1939.* Garden City, N.Y.: Doubleday, 1966.

Scholem, Gershom. *On Jews and Judaism in Crisis: Selected Essays.* New York: Schocken, 1976.

Schwartz, Benjamin I. "The Religion of Politics: Reflections on the Thought of Hannah Arendt." *Dissent,* 17 (March–April 1970), 144–161.

Scorza, Thomas J. *In the Time Before Steamships: Billy Budd, the Limits of Politics, and Modernity.* DeKalb: Northern Illinois University Press, 1979.

Selzer, Michael. "The Murderous Mind." *New York Times Magazine,* November 27, 1977, 35–37+.

Shaw, Robert. *The Man in the Glass Booth.* London: Chatto and Windus, 1967.

Shenker, Israel. *Words and Their Masters.* Garden City, N.Y.: Doubleday, 1974.

Sherwin, Martin J. *A World Destroyed: The Atomic Bomb and the Grand Alliance.* New York: Knopf, 1975.

Shklar, Judith N. *After Utopia: The Decline of Political Faith.* Princeton: Princeton University Press, 1957.

———. "Hannah Arendt's Triumph." *New Republic,* 173 (December 27, 1975), 8–10.

Silone, Ignazio. "After Hungary." *New Leader,* 40 (January 21, 1957), 15–18.

Silver, Isidore. "What Flows from Neo-Conservatism." *Nation,* 225 (July 9, 1977), 44–51.

Silving, Helen. "In Re Eichmann: A Dilemma of Law and Morality." *American Journal of International Law,* 55 (April 1961), 307–358.

330 *Into the Dark*

Simon, Ernst, "Revisionist History of the Jewish Catastrophe: A Textual Examination." *Judaism*, 12 (Fall 1963), 387–415.

Singer, Isaac Bashevis. *Shosha*. New York: Farrar, Straus and Giroux, 1978.

Skotheim, Robert Allen. *Totalitarianism and American Social Thought*. New York: Holt, Rinehart and Winston, 1971.

Smith, Bradley F. *Reaching Judgment at Nuremberg*. New York: Basic Books, 1977.

Solzhenitsyn, Aleksandr I. *The Gulag Archipelago, 1918–1956: An Experiment in Literary Investigation*, I–II. New York: Harper and Row, 1974–1975.

———. *Letter to the Soviet Leaders*. New York: Harper and Row, 1975.

———. *Warning to the West*. New York: Farrar, Straus and Giroux, 1976.

Sontag, Susan. *On Photography*. New York: Farrar, Straus and Giroux, 1977.

Speer, Albert. *Inside the Third Reich: Memoirs*. New York: Macmillan, 1970.

Spiro, Herbert J. "Totalitarianism," in *International Encyclopedia of the Social Sciences*, XVI. New York: Macmillan, 1968.

Steiner, George. *In Bluebeard's Castle: Some Notes toward the Redefinition of Culture*. New Haven: Yale University Press, 1971.

———. *Language and Silence: Essays on Language, Literature, and the Inhuman*. New York: Atheneum, 1970.

Stephan, John J. *The Russian Fascists: Tragedy and Farce in Exile, 1925–1945*. New York: Harper and Row, 1978.

Stern, Fritz. *Gold and Iron: Bismarck, Bleichröder, and the Building of the German Empire*. New York: Knopf, 1977.

———. *The Politics of Cultural Despair: A Study in the Rise of the Germanic Ideology*. Berkeley: University of California Press, 1961.

Stern, Peter, and Jean Yarbrough. "Hannah Arendt." *American Scholar*, 47 (Summer 1978), 371–381.

Stone, I. F. *Polemics and Prophecies, 1967–1970*. New York: Vintage, 1970.

Stoppard, Tom. *Travesties*. New York: Grove, 1975.

Straus, R. Peter. "His Daughter's Father: Otto Frank." *Moment*, 3 (December 1977), 27–30.

Suchting, W. A. "Marx and Hannah Arendt's *The Human Condition*." *Ethics*, 73 (October 1962), 47–55.

"Symposium on the Totalitarian State." *Proceedings of the American Philosophical Society*, 82 (February 23, 1940), 1–102.

Syrkin, Marie. "Hannah Arendt: The Clothes of the Empress." *Dissent*, 10 (Autumn 1963), 344–352.

———. "Miss Arendt Surveys the Holocaust." *Jewish Frontier*, 30 (May 1963), 7–14.

"The Talk of the Town: Notes and Comment." *New Yorker*, 39 (July 20, 1963), 17.

Taylor, Telford. "Large Questions in the Eichmann Case." *New York Times Magazine*, January 22, 1961, 22–25.

Tocqueville, Alexis de. *Democracy in America*, edited by Phillips Bradley. New York: Vintage, 1945.

Trevor-Roper, H. R. "A. J. P. Taylor, Hitler, and the War." *Encounter*, 17 (July 1961), 88–96.

———. "How Innocent Was Eichmann?" *Sunday Times* (London), October 13, 1963, p. 35.

———. *The Last Days of Hitler*. New York: Collier, 1962.

Trial of the Major War Criminals. Nuremberg: International Military Tribunal, 1948.

Trilling, Diana. *We Must March My Darlings: A Critical Decade*. New York: Harcourt Brace Jovanovich, 1977.

Trilling, Lionel. *Beyond Culture: Essays on Literature and Learning*. New York: Viking, 1965.

———. *Matthew Arnold*. New York: Columbia University Press, 1949.

———. *The Middle of the Journey*. New York: Avon, 1966.

———. *Sincerity and Authenticity*. Cambridge: Harvard University Press, 1972.

Trop v. Dulles. 356 U.S. 86 (1958).

Trotsky, Leon. *Literature and Revolution*. New York: Russell and Russell, 1957.

Trunk, Isaiah. "The Jewish Councils in Eastern Europe under Nazi Rule (An Attempt at a Synthesis)." *Societas*, 2 (Summer 1972), 221–239.

———. *Judenrat: The Jewish Councils in Eastern Europe under Nazi Occupation*. New York: Macmillan, 1972.

Tucker, Robert C. "The Dictator and Totalitarianism." *World Politics*, 17 (July 1965), 555–583.

———. *The Soviet Political Mind: Studies in Stalinism and Post-Stalin Change*. New York: Praeger, 1963.

—— (editor). *Stalinism: Essays in Historical Interpretation.* New York: Norton, 1977.

——, and Stephen F. Cohen (editors). *The Great Purge Trial.* New York: Grosset and Dunlap, 1965.

Tumin, Melvin. "Pie in the Sky." *Dissent,* 6 (Winter 1959), 65–71.

Ulam, Adam B. *The New Face of Soviet Totalitarianism.* Cambridge: Harvard University Press, 1963.

Unger, Aryeh L. *The Totalitarian Party: Party and People in Nazi Germany and Soviet Russia.* London: Cambridge University Press, 1974.

Viereck, Peter. *Metapolitics: The Roots of the Nazi Mind.* New York: Capricorn, 1961.

Voegelin, Eric. "The Origins of Totalitarianism." *Review of Politics,* 15 (January 1953), 68–76.

Vollrath, Ernst. "Hannah Arendt and the Method of Political Thinking." *Social Research,* 44 (Spring 1977), 160–182.

Waite, Robert G. L. *The Psychopathic God: Adolf Hitler.* New York: Basic Books, 1977.

Walzer, Michael. "Marcel Ophuls and the Nuremberg Trials: The Memory of Justice." *New Republic,* 175 (October 9, 1976), 19–23.

——. *Obligations: Essays on Disobedience, War, and Citizenship.* Cambridge: Harvard University Press, 1970.

Weil, Simone. "What Is a Jew?" In George A. Panichas (editor), *The Simone Weil Reader.* New York: David McKay, 1977.

Welch, William. *American Images of Soviet Foreign Policy: An Inquiry into Recent Appraisals from the Academic Community.* New Haven: Yale University Press, 1970.

West, Rebecca. *A Train of Powder.* New York: Viking, 1955.

West, Thomas R. *Nature, Community and Will: A Study in Literary and Social Thought.* Columbia: University of Missouri Press, 1976.

West Virginia Board of Education v. *Barnette.* 319 U.S. 624 (1943).

Whitfield, Stephen J. "Dwight Macdonald's *Politics* Magazine, 1944–1949." *Journalism History,* 3 (Fall 1976), 86–89.

——. "The Imagination of Disaster: The Response of American Jewish Intellectuals to Totalitarianism." *Jewish Social Studies,* 42 (Winter 1980), 1–20.

——. " 'Totalitarianism' in Eclipse: The Recent Fate of an Idea," in Arthur Edelstein (editor), *Images and Ideas in American Culture: The Functions of Criticism.* Hanover, N.H.: University Press of New England, 1979.

Wiesel, Elie. *One Generation After.* New York: Avon, 1972.
———, Lucy S. Dawidowicz *et al. Dimensions of the Holocaust: Lectures at Northwestern University.* New York: Anti-Defamation League, 1977.
Wieseltier, Leon. "You Don't Have to Be Khazarian." *New York Review of Books,* 23 (October 28, 1976), 33–36.
Wiesenthal, Simon. *The Murderers among Us.* New York: McGraw-Hill, 1967.
Wills, Garry. *Nixon Agonistes: The Crisis of the Self-Made Man.* Boston: Houghton Mifflin, 1970.
Wilson, Edmund. *Letters on Literature and Politics, 1912–1972.* Edited by Elena Wilson. New York: Farrar, Straus and Giroux, 1977.
Wojytla, Karol. *Sign of Contradiction.* New York: Seabury, 1979.
Wolfe, Bertram D. *Communist Totalitarianism: Keys to the Soviet System.* Boston: Beacon, 1961.
Wolin, Sheldon S. "Hannah Arendt and the Ordinance of Time." *Social Research,* 44 (Spring 1977), 91–105.
Wood, Gordon S. *The Creation of the American Republic, 1776–1787.* Chapel Hill: University of North Carolina Press, 1969.
Yakir, Pyotr. *A Childhood in Prison.* New York: Coward, McCann and Geoghegan, 1973.
Yevtushenko, Yevgeny. *Poetry, 1953–1965.* New York: October House, 1965.
Zimmern, Alfred. *The Greek Commonwealth: Politics and Economics in Fifth-Century Athens.* London: Oxford University Press, 1931.

INDEX

Medvedev, Roy, 42, 84, 125
Merton, Thomas, 217
Milgram, Stanley, 227–228
Miller, Stephen, 221
Molotov, Vyacheslav, 49–50, 214, 237
Montesquieu, Charles, Baron de, 63, 127
Morgenthau, Hans J., 37, 62, 238
Morstein Marx, Fritz, 66, 94
Muller, Sharon, 182
Murrow, Edward R., 121, 122
Musmanno, Michael, 218, 239, 242
Mussolini, Benito, 8, 38, 39. *See also* Fascism

Nabokov, Vladimir, 108, 212, 250
National Socialist German Workers Party (Nazi party), 27, 64, 66, 67, 68, 69, 98, 218. *See also* Hitler, Adolf
Neumann, Franz, 12–13, 164
New Yorker, 180, 237–238, 239
Nuremberg International Military Tribunals, 39, 40, 130–131, 196–198, 201, 204, 216, 224, 232, 236–237

Ohlendorf, Otto, 213, 229
Orwell, George, 7–8, 21, 26, 113, 142
O'Sullivan, N. K., 160, 259–260

Pan-Germanism, 78, 79–80, 87
Pan-Slavism, 78, 79–82, 86, 87, 97
Parenti, Michael, 23–24
Partisan Review, 10–11, 237
Phillips, William, 10, 11, 177, 182
Pitkin, Hanna F., 88
Podhoretz, Norman, 6, 218, 240–241
Poliakov, Léon, 228, 230
Polis, 134–137, 140, 141–142, 143–144, 146, 160, 167
Pollak, Stephen J., 110, 111
Popper, Karl, 164, 260

Rieff, Philip, 166, 256
Riesman, David, 98, 163, 254–255
Robinson, Jacob, 180, 205, 232, 242–246, 247

Rogat, Yosal, 197, 198, 200, 202–203, 205
Rosenberg, Alfred, 30, 36, 103, 127–128
Rosenberg, Harold, 200, 216, 229
Rousset, David, 7–8, 119, 120, 186
Rubenstein, Richard, 131
Russell, Bertrand, 6, 141, 260

Samuel, Maurice, 123, 175
Scholem, Gershom, 171, 177–178, 211, 233, 234–235, 240
Secret police, 42–44, 50, 98–99, 100, 101
Selzer, Michael, 223–224, 247
Shklar, Judith, 6
Simon, Ernst, 190, 233
Solzhenitsyn, Aleksandr I., 24, 31, 37, 47, 84, 115, 125; on Gulag archipelago, 30, 42, 43, 118–119, 120
Sontag, Susan, 103–104
Speer, Albert, 30, 36, 118, 218–219
Spiro, Herbert, 18, 256, 259
Stalin, Joseph, 23, 32, 36, 75, 121, 214; role and power of, 29, 31–32, 43, 54–55, 56, 60–61, 215
Steiner, George, 59, 113, 169, 184
Supreme Court of the United States, 111–112, 138–139, 183
Syrkin, Marie, 179, 180, 103, 192, 230, 238

Taylor, Telford, 197, 198, 200, 203
Tocqueville, Alexis de, 96–97
Totalitarian Dictatorship and Autocracy (Friedrich and Brzezinski), 19, 61, 63
Totalitarianism: historical use of concept of, 8, 13–15, 16–17, 18, 20, 23, 24, 26, 52, 62, 241; human nature under, 127–131; human rights under, 104, 107–108, 109–110, 130–131, 164, 206–207; language under, 142–143, 212; law under, 72–73, 103, 198, 199, 204–205, 237; martyrdom under, 99, 120–121, 122–125; nation-state under, 67–69, 73–78, 79–80; religion and, 35, 129,